CAMBRIDGE IBERIAN AND
LATIN AMERICAN STUDIES

GENERAL EDITOR

P. E. RUSSELL, F.B.A.

PROFESSOR OF SPANISH STUDIES, UNIVERSITY OF OXFORD

Curia and cortes in León and Castile
1072–1295

Alfonso X surrounded by mitred bishops and others.
Add. MS. 20787, fol. 1.

Curia and Cortes in León and Castile 1072–1295

EVELYN S. PROCTER

FORMERLY HONORARY FELLOW OF
ST HUGH'S COLLEGE, OXFORD

CAMBRIDGE UNIVERSITY PRESS

CAMBRIDGE

LONDON   NEW YORK   NEW ROCHELLE
MELBOURNE   SYDNEY

CAMBRIDGE UNIVERSITY PRESS
Cambridge, New York, Melbourne, Madrid, Cape Town, Singapore,
São Paulo, Delhi, Dubai, Tokyo

Cambridge University Press
The Edinburgh Building, Cambridge CB2 8RU, UK

Published in the United States of America by Cambridge University Press, New York

www.cambridge.org
Information on this title: www.cambridge.org/9780521135320

First published 1980
This digitally printed version 2010

A catalogue record for this publication is available from the British Library

Library of Congress Cataloguing in Publication data
Procter, Evelyn Stefanos, 1897–
Curia and Cortes in León and Castile, 1072–1295.

(Cambridge Iberian and Latin American studies)
Bibliography: p.
Includes indexes.
1. Leon (Kingdom). Cortes. 2. Castile. Cortes.
3. Representative government and representation – Spain
– History. I. Title. II. Series.
JN8140.C7P76   328.46'2'09021   79–51750

ISBN 978-0-521-22639-4 Hardback
ISBN 978-0-521-13532-0 Paperback

Contents

Foreword

The Cambridge Iberian and Latin American Studies series exists to provide opportunities for publishing, in English, important original scholarly or critical books and monographs in the Hispanic or Luso-Brazilian fields within the period A.D. 711 to the present day. The Syndics are interested in considering for inclusion in the series work by established or by younger scholars. While most of the titles so far accepted or provisionally accepted are concerned with aspects of Hispanic and Luso-Brazilian history (including the history of ideas and institutions) and literature, it is not the intention that the series should confine itself to these fields. Books in other arts subjects and in linguistic subjects (provided these latter are broad in scope) may be accepted. The imperial history of Spain and Portugal in Europe and overseas, as well as strictly Peninsular history, is included within the scope of the series, though authors of works concerned with most aspects of the history of Latin America will usually find the Cambridge Latin American Studies series a more appropriate outlet.

The Press is particularly concerned to ensure that a substantial proportion of the books to be published in the series are planned so as to be accessible to English-speaking readers who are not themselves Hispanic or Luso-Brazilian specialists. It is also planned to include in the series translations of important studies in the Hispanic and Luso-Brazilian fields originally published in languages other than English.

Oxford
March 1979

P. E. RUSSELL
GENERAL EDITOR
CAMBRIDGE IBERIAN AND LATIN AMERICAN STUDIES

Preface

My interest in the history of medieval Spain began more than fifty years ago when, as Mary Somerville Research Fellow of Somerville College, I was enabled to visit Spain for the first time and work in some of the archives and libraries there. My original intention had been to study the reign of Alfonso X of Castile. I soon learned that the Spanish scholar Antonio Ballesteros was working on this subject and I therefore decided to limit my researches to some aspects of the reign which could be treated separately in articles. During my tenure of the fellowship I gained valuable knowledge of some of the unpublished material available, also of the diplomatic of royal Castilian documents and of the organisation of Alfonso X's chancery. After my return to Oxford as Fellow and Tutor of St Hugh's College I made use in articles of some of the material I had collected.

It was some years later – about the middle 1930s – when my interests had shifted from political to constitutional history, that I first considered the possibility of working on the Castilian cortes. This work was interrupted and set aside for various reasons. The Spanish Civil War of 1936 to 1939 and the World War of 1939 to 1945 made work in Spain itself impossible for nine years. In 1946 my election to the Principalship of St Hugh's College involved me in administration, but throughout my professional career I retained my interest in, and worked intermittently on, Spanish medieval history. It was not, however, until some years after my retirement that I definitely decided to take up again my abandoned project of a book on the Castilian cortes, although on a somewhat different scale and plan. The actual writing of this book – apart from a final revision — was carried out between 1970 and 1976.

I should like to take this opportunity to acknowledge the help and courtesy which I have received from the officials of the various archives and libraries in Spain and Portugal, as well as in the Bodleian and the

British Library, in which I have worked at different times over a long period. I owe a great deal to the two Oxford Colleges with which I am connected and, in the preparation of the present book, to the interest and encouragement of many friends and former colleagues. In particular I am indebted to Professor Derek Lomax who provided me with some transcripts of documents, one of which is included in the appendix of documents, and to Dr Richard Fletcher who kindly checked for me the reference numbers of some documents in the Archivo Histórico Nacional in Madrid where reclassification has been in progress, and also for help on some questions relating to the twelfth century. Finally I cannot adequately express my gratitude to Professor Peter Russell for his help and advice unstintedly given during the final revision of the manuscript and its preparation for the press.

Eynsham, Oxford   E. S. PROCTER
December 1978

PUBLISHER'S NOTE

Sadly, Evelyn Procter died during the final stages of proof correction in March 1980.

Abbreviations

AC	Archivo de la catedral de...
ACA	Archivo de la Corona de Aragón, Barcelona
AFUF	*Archiv für Urkundenforschung*
AGN	Archivo General de Navarra, Pamplona
AHDE	*Anuario de Historia del Derecho Español*
AHN	Archivo Histórico Nacional, Madrid
AHR	*American Historical Review*
AM	Archivo Municipal
ANTT	Arquivo Nacional da Torre do Tombo, Lisbon
BAE	Biblioteca de Autores Españoles
BL	British Library (formerly British Museum)
BN	Biblioteca Nacional, Madrid
BRAH	*Boletín de la Real Academia de la Historia*
CAI	*Chronica Adefonsi Imperatoris*
CDC Oviedo	*Colección de documentos de la catedral de Oviedo*
CD Cuéllar	*Colección diplomática de Cuéllar*
CDIACA	*Colección de documentos inéditos del Archivo de la Corona de Aragón*
CD Jaime I	*Colección diplomática de Jaime I*
CD Murcia	*Colección de documentos para la historia del reino de Murcia*
CD Oña	*Colección diplomática de San Salvador de Oña*
CD Sepúlveda	*Colección diplomática de Sepúlveda*
CHE	*Cuadernos de Historia de España*
Cortes	*Cortes de los antiguos reinos de León y de Castilla*
DA Madrid	*Documentos del Archivo General de la Villa de Madrid*
DHILC	*Documentos para la historia de las instituciones de León y de Castilla*
EHR	*English Historical Review*

xi

ES	*España sagrada*
HC	*Historia Compostelana*
MHE	*Memorial histórico español*
MLR	*Modern Language Review*
Part.	*Partida*
PCG	*Primera crónica general*
PMH	*Portugaliae monumenta historica*
RABM	*Revista de Archivos, Bibliotecas y Museos*
RAH	Real Academia de la Historia
RC Cluny	*Recueil des chartes de l'Abbaye de Cluny*
RC Silos	*Recueil des chartes de l'Abbaye de Silos*

Glossary

abadengo: land held by the church free from temporal services to the king.

adelantado del rey: a court official who acted as deputy for the king in suits before the king's court; *adelantado mayor*: governor of one of the provinces of the kingdom of Castile. He exercised executive, judicial and military authority on behalf of the king.

alcalde: judge in a local court, such as the court of a municipality; *alcalde del rey*: judge of the king's court.

aleve, alevosía: treachery or breach of faith.

alférez: standard-bearer and commander of the army in the king's absence.

alfoz: district surrounding a city or town subject to the jurisdiction of its court.

alguacil: a town official with executive functions; *alguacil del rey*: an official of the king's court with executive and judicial functions.

almojarife mayor: the king's treasurer.

almotacén: a town official whose duties included the inspection of weights and measures and the oversight of trade.

alzada: an appeal from a lower court to the king's court.

assertor: advocate appointed to present a litigant's case.

ayuntamiento: an assembly.

behetría: territory in certain parts of Castile whose inhabitants, although performing the duties of serfs, had the right to change their lord at will; *behetría de linaje*: community with the right to choose a lord from the members of a certain family.

caballero: knight; *caballero de la villa*: knight of the town who owned a war horse and armour and had received from the king some of the privileges enjoyed by a noble knight; *caballero de linaje, caballero hidalgo*: knight of noble lineage.

carta abierta: letter patent; *carta de personería*: mandate given by a town to its representative in the cortes or in a suit before the king's court; *carta rodada*: a royal diploma authenticated by the king's *rueda* (q.v.); after 1260 called *privilegio rodado*.

concejo: the governing body of an autonomous city or town.

conducho: provision for a journey.

corte: vernacular term used in the thirteenth century for the *curia regis*.

cortes: an assembly including representatives of towns on royal demesne; parliament.

coto: land surrounding a cathedral or monastery subject to the jurisdiction of the bishop or abbot.

cuaderno: a document containing laws promulgated and collective petitions granted in the cortes.

Extremaduras: The reconquered lands to the south of the river Duero. In thirteenth-century Castile this term was gradually extended to include the 'kingdom' of Toledo up to the Sierra Morena, but in the fourteenth century these two regions were again distinguished from each other. There was also a Leonese Extremadura.

facendaria: labour services on the construction or repair of roads and bridges.

fazañas: sentences given in law suits which were recognised as precedents in Castile, thus forming a body of case law.

fonsada: military service.

fonsadera: money payment in commutation of military service.

Forum judicum: a Visigothic code of law in use in the kingdom of León; *Fuero juzgo*: a thirteenth-century vernacular translation of the *Forum judicum*.

fuero: local law administered in a particular court such as the court of a municipality.

hermandad: a confederation of cities and towns or, in some cases, of bishops and abbots.

hidalgo: a member of the lesser nobility.

hombres buenos: 'good men', used of persons of any rank or class; *hombres buenos de las villas*: used in the thirteenth century for representatives of the towns in the cortes.

infanzón: a member of the lesser nobility.

infante: title given to the legitimate sons of the king.

mandatio: administrative district in the kingdom of León.

maravedï: a gold coin first minted *c.* 1172 in Castile in imitation of the 'dinar' of the Almorávide emir of Murcia.

martiniega: a customary due payable at Martinmas.

mayordomo: steward, chief officer of the royal household.

merino: a local official appointed by the king; *merino mayor*: in certain provinces of Castile equivalent of the *adelantado mayor* (q.v.); *merino menor*: royal official subordinate to the *merinos mayores*.

moneda: (1) coinage; (2) a tax granted to the king by the cortes in exchange for an undertaking not to issue a new coinage for a period of years; later a customary septennial tax taken without renewed consent and called *moneda forera*; *moneda de la guerra*: a debased coinage issued by Alfonso X during the war with Granada (1264–1266).

montazgo: a toll for the use of the *montes* (q.v.) by migratory flocks.

montes: tracts of uncultivated, mountainous country which afforded rough grazing for the flocks of the inhabitants of neighbouring towns.

Mozárabes: Christians living under Moslem rule.

Mudéjares: Moslems who remained in reconquered lands under Christian rule.

ordenamiento: legislation usually promulgated in the cortes.

pechero: a tax payer.

pecho: any customary payment or tax.

personero: representative, the term usually used for the representative of a town in a suit before the king's court.

pesquisa: inquest, inquiry.

pesquisidor: one commissioned by the king to hold an inquiry.

petitio, petitum: an imposition first levied by Alfonso VII *c.* 1136. It originally required the consent of those paying it, but it soon became a customary payment.

portazgo: a toll on transit for the use of roads and bridges.

postura: a decree of general application.

privilegio rodado: see *carta rodada*.

realengo: royal demesne land.

reto: duel on horseback between nobles or knights in cases involving the personal honour of one of the combatants.

rico hombre: magnate; a member of the highest rank of the nobility.

rueda: a device in the form of two or three concentric circles, derived from the *rota* of the papal chancery, used in León and Castile to authenticate royal privileges.

sello de la poridad: the equivalent of the privy seal in England and of the secret seal in France and Aragon.

servicio: subsidy voted by the cortes.

signifer: standard-bearer and commander of the army in the absence of the king; used in the separate kingdom of León; the equivalent of the *alférez* (q.v.) in Castile.

tenente: the governor of a district called a *tenencia* over which the *tenente* exercised administrative, judicial and military functions.

tercia: the third part of the ecclesiastical tithe used for the repair of churches; *tercia real*: the third part of the ecclesiastical *tercia*, first granted by Pope Innocent IV to Fernando III of Castile for three years; later taken by the king and his successors without a renewed grant.

término: another name for the *alfoz* (q.v.).

vecino: householder in a city or town who enjoyed full rights of citizenship and took part in town government.

yantar: a lord's right to hospitality at the expense of his tenants or a money payment in lieu thereof; taken by the king, the queen, the heir to the throne, certain royal officials acting for the king and by lords of *behetrías*.

Introduction

During the later Middle Ages representative assemblies were in being in most kingdoms of Western Europe: Parliament in England, the States General in France and the Cortes[1] in the various Christian kingdoms of the Iberian Peninsula. All these assemblies exhibited striking similarities, but also specific differences, and all evolved – mainly during the thirteenth century and by much the same process – from the curia. In the eleventh and twelfth centuries the work of government was carried on by the monarch with the aid of an assembly to which various names were given, but which in the twelfth century was generally called the *curia regis*. Differences were due to the varying social structures or local institutions, or to political considerations. England, France, Aragon and Catalonia were more feudalised than were León, Castile and Portugal, and this affected the composition of the curia. In no country, however, was feudalism so complete that tenure became the sole basis for membership of the curia; the feudal vassal owed suit at his lord's court, but this was an obligation rather than a right; if summoned by the king, the vassal must attend, but the king was not bound to summon all who held from him in chief, nor was he unable to summon those who were not his immediate vassals, if he had need of them. In its largest form the curia consisted of members of the royal family, the officials of the king's household and the lay and ecclesiastical magnates of the kingdom. A great assembly of magnates was cumbersome and, for practical reasons, could be summoned only at infrequent intervals. The business of government, however, required daily attention and this routine business was transacted by a much smaller body composed of officials and *familiares* together with those bishops and nobles who might be with the king. These two sorts of assembly were not separate institutions, but two forms of the same

[1] *Cortes* in Castile, León and Aragon; *Cortes* in Portugal; and *Corts* in Catalonia.

institution. It was from the curia in its largest form that the representative assemblies evolved.

The representative assemblies, in their turn, also show differences in the different kingdoms. There is no exact parallel on the Continent to the English shire system and so the knights of the shire, elected in the shire court to represent the community of the shire and who joined with the burgesses to form the 'commons', have no exact counterpart elsewhere. The towns of León–Castile – particularly those of the Extremaduras – were unlike the towns of Northern France or England, although they bore some resemblance to the great towns of Southern France, such as Nîmes, Carcassonne or Toulouse, which dominated the surrounding countryside and controlled less powerful towns. The class of *caballeros de las villas* – knights of the towns of non-noble lineage – which grew up in León, Castile and Portugal during the reconquest, and which gave so military a character to town society and government in those kingdoms, is not found in other countries.

The purpose of this book is, firstly, to collect and examine the ascertainable facts concerning the composition, forms and functions of the *curia regis* in León–Castile during the period under review; secondly, to trace the early appearances of the town representatives in the curia in its largest form and to establish, as far as is possible from the available evidence, at which great assemblies they were present; and, thirdly, to analyse the composition of the cortes – as these representative assemblies were called from the mid-thirteenth century – and their functions in questions of policy, taxation and legislation, with particular reference to the part played therein by the representatives.

The primary sources for the study of institutions are documentary but, as is well known, the royal archives of León–Castile have not survived for the medieval period. There is nothing, therefore, comparable to the English *curia regis* rolls for the twelfth-century curia and, although chancery registers were certainly kept in Castile in the thirteenth century, they have disappeared, so that there is nothing to compare with the chancery registers of the kingdom of Aragon–Catalonia which begin from the mid-thirteenth century and are available in the Archivo de la Corona de Aragón in Barcelona. As far as Castile is concerned we have, therefore, to rely on royal charters kept by their recipients, in most cases cathedrals and monasteries which had better facilities for storing records than had the laity. Many documents from religious houses suppressed in the early nineteenth century and from the archives of the Spanish military Orders of Santiago and Calatrava are now housed in the Archivo Histórico Nacional in Madrid. Most of these documents are grants of lands, rights and privileges, but some information on the activities of the curia can be culled from them and the witness lists appended to twelfth-century solemn diplomas give information on composition. Of special importance are sentences in suits heard before the curia, which remained the highest court of justice for the kingdom until the fourteenth century. Many of these royal documents have been published, notably those of the kings of León and of Castile during the period of the separation of the two kingdoms from 1157 to 1230.[2] Others are printed in various collections, or are scattered in books, including some in eighteenth-century works, not always easily obtainable.

For the history of the cortes the main sources are the *cuadernos* – documents containing both legislative acts promulgated in the cortes and answers to petitions, copies of which were given to the representatives and other participants, generally towards the end of the session, but which were sometimes sent out after the cortes had dispersed. The publication of the *cuadernos* of the medieval kingdom of León–Castile was undertaken by the Real Academia de la Historia in the nineteenth century and resulted in the collection known as *Cortes de los antiguos reinos de León y de Castilla*. The first volume, which reaches to 1349, and was published in 1861, includes the *cuadernos* for the cortes of 1258, 1268, 1286, 1288 and 1293, but not those of 1250, 1252–3, 1261 or 1264. These latter have been published separately at various dates, but in some cases their editors, and those who have made use of them, have not recognised that the documents in question were *cuadernos* of the cortes, but have treated them as privileges granted to individual towns. At many meetings of the cortes there was no legislation, and in such cases we have only chance references in documents to guide us. Alfonso X, for instance, held at least fifteen cortes during his reign of thirty-two years, but for only five of these are *cuadernos* known to exist. Narrative sources are of far less importance for institutional history, and for some periods there are no contemporary chronicles of any length. Those that have proved of use are dealt with in their appropriate place.

The most recent work devoted to the medieval Castilian–Leonese curia is the monograph by the Argentine scholar Nilda Guglielmi:

[2] Gonzalez, *Regesta de Fernando II*; *Alfonso IX*; *El reino de Castilla en la época de Alfonso VIII*.

'La curia regia en León y Castilla'.[3] As this was written shortly before Julio González had published the royal documents for the separate kingdom of Castile, it is based more on Leonese than Castilian sources.

In spite of the publication of the *cuadernos* over a century ago, surprisingly little has been written on the thirteenth-century cortes. Manuel Colmeiro made use of the *cuadernos* in his lengthy *Introducción* to the collection, but his views are out of date and need revision on questions of fact, as well as on interpretation.[4] In 1897 a Russian scholar, Wladimir Piskorski, wrote a monograph on the cortes of Castile from 1188 to 1520 in Russian. The book was thus inaccessible to most Western European historians until 1930, when it was translated into Spanish by Claudio Sánchez-Albornoz. It has since remained the standard work on the subject and has recently been reissued.[5] Piskorski's book does not deal with the period before 1188 and it is mostly based on the sources for the fourteenth and fifteenth centuries, with only rare references to the thirteenth century. Mention should also be made of the monumental study of Alfonso X's reign by Antonio Ballesteros, as this author gives considerable space to meetings of the cortes and quotes at length from the *cuadernos* of 1252/3, 1258 and 1268, though he makes no use of those of 1261 and 1264. This book must, however, be used critically. It was published many years after the author's death, without revision, and without the collection of documents which Ballesteros intended should accompany it. There are few references to the sources used, and none at all for the last two chapters, although in some cases the sources of the author's statements can be found in his earlier books and articles. The work is based on a mass of published and unpublished material, often uncritically handled. It is in its citations of, and quotations from, unpublished documents, many of them conserved in municipal archives, that its chief value for our subject lies. The footnotes to Chapters 6 and 7 of the present work show the use I have made of such citations.[6] There are also two recent and valuable articles on the early cortes by Professor Joseph O'Callaghan.[7] Although I have not been convinced by some of the latter's more conjectural conclusions, these two articles constitute an important contribution to our knowledge of the thirteenth-century cortes.

[3] *CHE* xxiii–xxiv, 116–26; xxviii, 43–101.
[4] Colmeiro, *Cortes de los antiguos reinos de León y de Castilla. Introducción.*
[5] *Cortes de Castilla.*
[6] Ballesteros, *Alfonso X el Sabio.*
[7] 'The beginnings of the cortes of León–Castile', *AHR*, lxxiv, 1503–37; 'The cortes and royal taxation during the reign of Alfonso X', *Traditio*, xxvii, 379–98.

I can make no claim that this book is a definitive study of the subject. Much remains to be done on some aspects of it. Many questions remain unanswered. One such question is, 'Which towns actually sent representatives to the thirteenth-century cortes?' The available evidence is insufficient for any definite conclusion and for this reason I have not attempted to answer it. What is urgently needed is a thorough search among medieval documents in Spanish municipal archives, many of which are uncatalogued and sometimes difficult to gain access to. Such searches might uncover hitherto unknown *cuadernos*, or other types of records, such as accounts noting payments to representatives, or mandates issued to them or royal writs of summons. This, however, is work which can best be carried out by Spanish scholars.

Finally, it is hoped that this book may be of use not only to Hispanists but also to those with a general interest in medieval and constitutional studies, or in comparative institutions, especially to those working on the English medieval parliament.

I

The *curia regis* in the kingdom of León–Castile under Alfonso VI, Urraca and Alfonso VII

Organisation

During the two centuries between the recognition of Alfonso VI as king of Castile as well as of León in 1072, and the death of Sancho IV in 1295, the *curia regis*[1] under that name or, towards the end of the period, under the vernacular substitute *corte*, was the main governmental institution. Its activities are not always easy to trace, especially during the twelfth century, when sources are comparatively meagre. But institutions are not static and the Leonese–Castilian *curia regis* changed and developed throughout the two centuries. Thus, if we collect together evidence from the whole period, our resulting analysis will give a composite picture which will not be true for any given reign, although it will approximate more to conditions in the thirteenth than in the twelfth century, while, on the other hand, the evidence available for some of the earlier reigns is too meagre to provide more than bare outlines. The two centuries can, however, be conveniently subdivided into three shorter periods: from 1072 to 1157, during which time the two kingdoms of León and Castile were united and there was one curia for both kingdoms; the period of the separation of the kingdoms from 1157 to 1230, during which some divergence in their institutions was apparent, and when the representatives of the towns first began to attend great assemblies; and, finally, the period after 1230, when the two kingdoms were again united and when the differentiation of the cortes from the *corte* became definitive and a distinct judicial tribunal within the *corte* also appeared for a short time. Yet even within these periods it is necessary to pay considerable attention to chronology. There is also some overlapping, as the cortes, which will be our main concern during the last period, had its origins in the second period,

---

[1] Modern Spanish historians usually use the term *curia regia*, but in medieval documents *curia regis* is used.

7

while the *corte* continued to exercise most of the functions of the curia up to the end of the thirteenth century, and was not superseded by the cortes. However, this division of the two centuries, although it inevitably necessitates repetitions, gives a clearer view of the development of the curia than would an analytical account of its membership and functions based on evidence from the two centuries as a whole.

The main sources for the first period can be briefly enumerated. Royal documents form the most important of our sources and many are available in print. Strictly contemporary narrative sources are few and often meagre. The most important are the *Historia compostelana* and the *Chronica Adefonsi Imperatoris*. The *Historia*, which deals mainly with the see of Compostela under Diego Gelmírez (bishop from 1100, archbishop from 1120) until his death in 1140, is a combination of a narrative with a register of documents. It was compiled by three, possibly four, authors, two of whom were undoubtedly French, at various dates during the first half of the twelfth century.[2] The *Chronica*, if, as has been suggested by its editor, its author was Bishop Arnoldo of Astorga, must have been written between 1144 and 1152.[3] Other chronicles have little importance for our subject. The *Crónica* of Bishop Don Pelayo and the *Historia silense*, both written in the first quarter of the twelfth century, each give a few pages only on Alfonso VI.[4]

The *curia regis* was not a new institution at the end of the eleventh century, although it acquired a new name. During the tenth century the kings of León, like their predecessors the kings of Asturias, were aided in the work of government by a number of persons, lay and ecclesiastical, who formed their immediate entourage and who subscribed their diplomas. The variations in these lists of witnesses show that we are not dealing with a body of fixed composition, but the use of such terms as *aula regia*, *toga palatii*, *conventus* and *concilium* in the royal documents of the tenth century suggests that they represented something more than a chance collection of individuals. In the eleventh century the terms used included *magnati palatii*, *primates palatii*, *optimates regis* and *schola regis*, terms which suggest an integrated

---

[2] On this chronicle, see Galindo Romeo, *La diplomática en la 'Historia compostelana'*; Biggs, *Diego Gelmírez*, xiii–xl; and Reilly, 'The *Historia Compostelana*; the genesis and composition of a twelfth-century Spanish *gesta*', *Speculum*, XLIV, 75–85.

[3] See pp. ix–xxi of Sánchez Belda's edition on authorship.

[4] On the above chronicles, see Sánchez Alonso, *Historiografía española*, I, 113–17, 122–4, 152–4.

body based on service in the king's household, and also the generic *concilium*. To these, also in the course of the eleventh century, was added the term *curia regis*, a name which was to supersede the earlier names and to remain in use until the vernacular took the place of Latin as the official language of Castile–León in the middle of the thirteenth century. It is generally held that the word *curia* was introduced from north of the Pyrenees in the reign of Fernando I (1035–65), the first king of the Navarrese dynasty to rule over León and Castile.[5] This is possible, but definite evidence of its use under Fernando I is lacking.[6] Although the word does occur in documents of the last quarter of the eleventh century,[7] it was still only used sparingly in the time of his son, Alfonso VI, and it is not found with any frequency until well into the twelfth century. French influence was strong under Alfonso VI, so that its introduction from France may have occurred during his reign, and not during that of his father. In the narrative sources, *curia* made a tardy and uncertain appearance. It was not used in Bishop Pelayo's *Crónica*, nor in the *Historia silense*. The *Chronica Adefonsi Imperatoris* used it only of the court of the Almorávide king Ali, in the sense of the place where he resided.[8] The chronicle in which it was used most frequently is the *Historia compostelana*, where its appearance reflects French influence.[9] During this period the older terms continued in use alongside *curia*. *Magnati palatii* and *de aula regis* were used in documents of the first two decades of Alfonso VI's reign, but died out thereafter.[10] *Schola regis* also continued in use during the reign of Alfonso VI.[11] The conservative author of the *Chronica Adefonsi Imperatoris* used both *magnati palitii* and *schola regis*.[12] *Concilium* continued to be used at times for judicial sessions and also for some of the great assemblies to which all the ecclesiastical and lay magnates were summoned, such as the assembly in 1135, at which Alfonso VII was crowned as

[5] Cf. G[arcía] de Valdeavellano, *Historia de España*, I, 573; Guglielmi, 'La curia regia en León y Castilla', *CHE*, XXIII–XXIV, 117–18.
[6] *ES*, XXXVIII, ap. XVII (?1056), which uses *curia*, is suspect.
[7] E.g. Menéndez Pidal, *España del Cid*, II, 850 (26 March 1075); *Cartulario de S. Millán*, no. 234 (1077); *ES*, XVI, ap. XXI (25 May 1087), etc.
[8] *CAI*, § 104, 105 (p. 82).
[9] *HC*, 126, 127, 156, 349, 434, 452, 456, etc.
[10] Escalona, *Sahagún*, ap. III, *escs.* CVII (1073), CXVIII (25 Nov. 1085), CXIX (14 May 1087); García Villada, *Paleografía española*, I: *Texto*, 247 (1080); Menéndez Pidal, *España del Cid*, II, 849 (26 March 1075); *ES*, XXXVIII, ap. XX (13 Aug. 1083); XVI, ap. XXI (25 April 1087).
[11] *DHILC*, no. XXV (31 March 1091); *CD Oña*, I, nos. 116 (23 March 1103), 121 (12 Dec. 1105); Serrano, *Obispado de Burgos*, III, no. 62 (22 Sept. 1105).
[12] *CAI*, § 91 (p.70), § 187 (p. 147).

Emperor, and that held at Palencia in 1156.[13] In spite of this use of *concilium* for some extraordinary assemblies, the documents of Alfonso VI's reign show that *curia regis* was equated both with the *magnati palatii* and also with specially summoned assemblies. In a document of 26 March 1075 the phrases 'in presentia regis et magnatorum palatii' and 'in presentia regis et omnium nobilium ejus curie' are both used, as are 'omnes magnati nostri palatii' and 'omnes magnati curie regis' in one of 25 April 1087.[14] On the other hand, in a document of 24 September 1089 sentence is said to have been given 'per iudicium et consilium comitum, baronum suorem et maiorum de sua escola et meliorum de sua terra, cunctis uocatis ad suam curiam'.[15] In the first two instances the 'magnati curie regis' are clearly the equivalent of the *magnati palatii* but, in the third example, the 'curia' embraces not only the king's immediate entourage but also others, specially summoned to attend.

The lists of *confirmantes* which appear at the foot of documents of Alfonso VI, Urraca and Alfonso VII give us some information about the composition of the curia. The numbers vary greatly. In the documents of Alfonso VI the number of those confirming varies from five to over fifty, although numbers smaller than fifteen or larger than thirty are rare. Under Queen Urraca the numbers, generally speaking, are smaller than in the preceding reign, and are often under ten and rarely over twenty. This may be partly accounted for by the political conditions of the reign, when many of the nobles were disaffected. The numbers increase again during the reign of her son Alfonso VII, but there are fewer instances of numbers over thirty than under Alfonso VI.[16] An examination of these lists of *confirmantes* shows that while some names occur often, others appear much less frequently. The core of the court was formed by members of the royal family, a handful of great officials and the king's immediate retinue, who accompanied him on his endless journeyings through his dominions. To these would be added a fluctuating number of prelates and nobles who might, for some reason or other, have business with the king, or through whose dioceses or magistracies the king might be passing. These together made up the

---

[13] *Cartulario de S. Vicente*, no. 79 (1078); *ES*, XL, *ap.* xxviii (28 Feb. 1078); López Ferreiro, *Iglesia de Santiago*, IV, *ap.* v (13 Nov. 1127); *CAI*, § 71 (pp. 54–6) (1135); *ES*, xviii, *ap.* xxiii (9 Nov. 1156).

[14] Menéndez Pidal, *España del Cid*, II, 847–51; *ES*, xvi, *ap.* xxi.

[15] Sánchez-Albornoz, *Estudios*, 307–8, no. vi.

[16] For the numbers of *confirmantes* under Alfonso VII, see Rassow, 'Die Urkunden Kaisers Alfons VII, von Spanien', *AFUF*, x, 392, 402–3, 411.

normal personnel of the court. But from time to time much larger numbers were assembled, including all or most of the bishops and the most powerful of the nobles.

Among the royal *confirmantes* in Alfonso VI's documents were included his successive queens: Inés, Constancia, Berta, Isabel and Beatriz; his sisters Urraca and Elvira; his only son the Infante Don Sancho, who was killed at the battle of Uclés in 1108; his eldest daughter and ultimate successor Doña Urraca and her husband Raymond of Burgundy, Count of Galicia, as well as his illegitimate daughter Doña Teresa and her husband Henry of Burgundy, Count of Portugal. In Queen Urraca's documents her sisters Elvira and Sancha, her son Alfonso, who from 1116 ruled jointly with his mother, and her daughter Sancha all appear as *confirmantes*. Under Alfonso VII his sons Sancho and Fernando confirm from 1139 and 1144 respectively, his two wives Berenguela and Rica are noted in the Emperor's superscription but rarely appear among the *confirmantes*; his sister Sancha and some of his younger children confirm from time to time. How far the women of the royal family took an active part in the proceedings of the curia it is impossible to say, but their inclusion among the *confirmantes* was not a mere formality. Alfonso VI's sister Urraca, on whose advice the king largely relied, intervened, for example, in the law suit between him and the *infanzones* of Valle de Langreo.[17] The author of the *Chronica Adefonsi Imperatoris* thought highly of the prudence and wisdom of Alfonso VII's first wife Queen Berenguela, and of his sister Doña Sancha,[18] while his second wife Rica was named, together with his sister, among the counsellors who advised him on the grant of revised *fueros* to Sahagún.[19]

The principal officials of the court were the *armiger*, the *maiordomus* and, from the twelfth century, the chancellor, the heads respectively of the army, the household and the chancery. The offices of *armiger* and *maiordomus* both date from the tenth century.[20] The *armiger* who, besides leading the army in the absence of the king, carried the royal standard in battle, was also called *signifer*. After 1133 these titles gave place to that of *alférez*. The title *dispensator regis* appears to be merely an alternative for that *maiordomus*, as Pelayo Vellídez was entitled *dispensator regis*, *maiordomus in palatium regis* and *maior in domum*

[17] *DHILC*, no. xix (27 March 1075).
[18] *CAI*, § 12 (p. 14), § 45 (p. 38).
[19] Escalona, *Sahagún, ap.* iii, *esc.* clxviii (18 Dec. 1152).
[20] *Barrau-Dihigo*, 'Chartes royales léonaises', *Revue Hispanique*, x, nos. xi, xiv, xv, xx, xxiv, xli; *ES*, xvi, *ap.* vii; xxxiv, *ap.* xxiv; xxxvii, *ap.* v.

regis during the decade 1075 to 1085.[21] On the other hand, the office of *economus* – steward – seems to have been a separate office as both the *maiordomus* and the *economus* sometimes confirm the same document. It is possible, however, that we are here dealing with different names for the same office in León and Castile respectively, and some evidence in support of this is provided by the fact that Ermigild Rodríguez, who held the title *economus* between 1087 and 1093, on two occasions was placed among a group of *confirmantes* under the heading *De legione provincia.*[22] The office of *economus* continued to appear under Urraca and Alfonso VII.[23] Other officials who are found for short periods include a *prepositus regis* in the early years of Alfonso VI, and a *dapifer regine* or *curie* under Urraca.[24] The *maiorinus* (*merino*) was a local official who figured among the *confirmantes* in all three reigns. Under Alfonso VI the *merinos* in Castile, Nájera, Calahorra, Burgos, León, Campos, Carrión and Astorga appeared from time to time; under Alfonso VII the *merinos* in Carrión, Burgos, Saldaña, León and the Asturias were those most frequently at court.[25] The *merino* was normally engaged in the administration of his locality, but from time to time his business would take him to the king's court, or the itinerant court would pass through his district and, on such occasions, he would take part in discussions in the curia and confirm royal documents.

Unlike the offices of *alférez* and *maiordomus*, that of chancellor did not appear until the twelfth century and the use of the title was occasional only until 1127. It was twice used by the notary Martín Peláez in 1112, and again in 1119 when he appeared as *regis cancellarius* in a document of Alfonso VII, issued in the lifetime of the king's mother; but the title generally used under Urraca by the official who

[21] *ES*, xxvi, ap. viii (1 May 1075); Escalona, *Sahagún, ap.* iii, *esc.* cxiii (10 May 1079); Serrano, *Obispado de Burgos*, iii, no. 25 (22 Feb. 1085).

[22] Escalona, *Sahagún, ap.* iii, *escs.* cxix (14 May 1087), cxxvii (23 Nov. 1093); *ES*, xxxvi, *ap.* xxviii (12 Nov. 1073); Sánchez-Albornoz, *Estudios*, 308 (24 Sept. 1089); *DHILC*, no. xxv (31 March 1091).

[23] E.g. Colmenares, *Historia de Segovia*, i, 230–1 (11 Nov. 1123); *CDC Oviedo*, no. 154 (15 May 1143).

[24] *Cartulario de S. Millán*, no. 266 (21 July 1087); *CD Oña*, i, no. 99 (1 May 1092); *ES*, xxxviii, *ap.* xxxiii (2 Dec. 1118); *Cartulario de Arlanza*, no. xc (22 Feb. 1119); *RC Cluny*, v, no. 3947 (21 August 1120).

[25] Escalona, *Sahagún, ap.* iii, *escs.* cxiii (10 May 1079), cxix (14 May 1087), cxxvii (23 Nov. 1093), clvii (8 March 1132); Serrano, *Obispado de Burgos*, iii, no. 25 (22 Feb. 1085); Rassow, *AFUF*, xi, nos. 9, 11, 25, 27, 28, 29 (various dates from 1137 to 1149); *RC Silos*, no. 47 (2 June 1137); *RC Cluny*, v, nos. 4072 (29 July 1142), 4076 (29 Oct. 1143); *Cartulario de Vega*, nos. 9 (10 Nov. 1145), 11 (28 Feb. 1147), etc.

took the queen's orders and instructed the scribe was *notarius*.[26] In 1127 Alfonso VII granted the offices of royal chaplain and chancellor to Diego Gelmírez, archbishop of Santiago de Compostela.[27] This concession was renewed in 1140 to Archbishop Berengar and his successors in perpetuity.[28] The duties of the chancellor were not performed by the archbishops in person, but by deputies appointed by them who consistently used the title *cancellarius regis*. Of Alfonso's five chancellors, the most important was Master Hugo, who held office from 1135 to 1152, with the notary Giraldus under him until 1149. During Alfonso VII's reign many reforms and innovations were introduced in the chancery. Mandates or writs were being used from at least as early as 1128 for the transmission of administrative orders and the earliest known diplomas sealed with the pendant wax seal belong to 1146. The formulas of the diplomas also become more regular and Carolingian minuscule becomes the rule.[29] By the end of Alfonso VII's reign the differentiation of the chancery from the curia may be considered complete. The *almojarife* – treasurer – never appears among the *confirmantes* in this period, possibly because the position was usually held by a Jew, and little is known of the office or its holders.

The number of bishoprics in Alfonso VI's dominions in 1072 was twelve: Braga, León, Lugo, Mondoñedo, Nájera, Oca (later moved to Burgos, Oporto, Orense, Oviedo, Palencia, Santiago de Compostela and Túy. Before the death of Alfonso VII eight more sees had been added. The archbishopric of Toledo was revived in 1085 and the sees of Avila, Coimbra, Osma, Salamanca, Segovia, Sigüenza and Zamora were restored or created between 1080 and 1121. Coria was created in 1142. On the other hand, after the accession of Afonso Henriques as Count of Portugal, the archbishops of Braga and the bishops of Coimbra and Oporto and of other Portuguese sees created later did not attend the curia of Alfonso VII, and, instead, confirmed the documents of Afonso Henriques.[30] The numbers of bishops who confirmed individual

[26] Sánchez Belda, 'La cancillería castellana durante el reinado de Doña Urraca', *Estudios dedicados a Menéndez Pidal*, IV, 587–99. The two diplomas of 1112 are copies, but are accepted as genuine by Sánchez Belda. Two of the three are published by López Ferreiro, *Iglesia de Santiago*, III, *aps.* nos. XXVII, XXXVI.

[27] *HC*, 461–2.

[28] Pub. Millares Carlo, 'La cancillería real en León y Castilla hasta fines del reinado de Fernando III', *AHDE*, III, 257–8 (12 Aug. 1140).

[29] Millares Carlo, *AHDE*, III, 254–6; Rassow, *AFUF*, X, 345–8, 386–7; Fletcher, 'Diplomatic and the Cid revisited: the seals and mandates of Alfonso VII', *Journal of Medieval History*, II, 305–32.

[30] *Chancelarias medievais portuguesas*, I, nos. 5 (27 May 1128), 14 (18 March 1129), 22 (15 Jan. 1130), 23 (April 1130), etc.

charters varied considerably. Documents without any ecclesiastical *confirmantes* were by no means rare, especially in the early years of Alfonso VII's reign.[31] When only one bishop confirmed it is probable that he was the bishop of the diocese in which the king was then residing, but as the place of issue was rarely noted before 1135, this cannot always be proved.[32] The number of prelates who confirmed was usually small and in most documents was three, four or five. Such numbers can be accounted for by casual attendance, but when numbers such as twelve, fourteen or nineteen occur some sort of special summons must be postulated.[33] Abbots appeared frequently among the *confirmantes* of Alfonso VI's documents, but much less often in those of Doña Urraca.[34] Under Alfonso VII it became rare for abbots to confirm, but they appear from time to time and they were certainly present at such extraordinary assemblies as the Council of León in 1135 and the assembly held at Salamanca in January 1154.[35] The *clerici* who appeared in some of Alfonso VI's charters were probably attached to his chapel, or were in attendance on one of the bishops. This group does not confirm in documents of later reigns.[36]

In most documents of this period some of the laymen who confirmed were *comites*. Aa a rule the number of counts was small – five or less. The title dates from the tenth century, when the count exercised military, judicial and administrative power over the *comitatus* as a subdivision of the kingdom, but, by the end of the eleventh century, *comes* had become a title of honour, and the *comitatus* was no longer the normal subdivision of the kingdom. The title was bestowed by the king; it was not hereditary, although most of those who bore it belonged to a limited number of families.[37] Alfonso VI created the counties of

---

[31] Rassow, *AFUF*, xi, nos. 3 (1 May 1127), 4 (6 March 1128), 5 (1 May 1129), etc.

[32] *Ibid.* no. 1 (12 Dec. 1126): Diego, bishop of León, confirms. *Cartulario de S. Vicente*, no. 173 (29 May 1131); *Cartulario de Vega*, no. 6 (1 March 1133); *CDC Oviedo*, no. 149 (18 Aug. 1132): all confirmed by Alfonso, bishop of Oviedo; Rassow, *AFUF*, xi, no. 40 (Palencia, 21 Dec. 1152): Raimundo, bishop of Palencia, confirms; nos. 48, 49 (Toledo, 4 Nov. 1154): confirmed by Juan, archbishop of Toledo.

[33] E.g. *ES*, xvi, *ap.* xxix (6 Jan. 1154): twelve bishops confirmed; Colmenares, *Historia de Segovia*, i, 277–8 (28 Jan. 1155): fourteen bishops; Rassow, *AFUF*, xi, no. 53 (4 Feb. 1155): nineteen bishops.

[34] E.g. *Fuentes de Castilla*, iii, no. lxxxvi (8 Dec. 1072); *RC Silos*, no. 18 (16 Jan. 1073); *ES*, xxxviii, *ap.* xxi (14 March 1075); López Ferreiro, *Iglesia de Santiago*, iii, no. xxxii (3 Jan. 1115); iv, no. ii (18 May 1123).

[35] Rassow, *AFUF*, xi, nos. 1 (12 Dec. 1126), 9 (Feb. 1137), 44 (8 Oct. 1153); *CAI*, § 69 (p. 54); *CDC Oviedo*, no. 162.

[36] *ES* xxxvi, *ap.* xxvi (17 Nov. 1072); xxxviii, *ap.* xxi (14 March 1075), etc.

[37] *CAI*, § 4 (pp. 7–8), § 7 (pp. 10–11); Escalona, *Sahagún*, *ap.* iii, *esc.* xliv (2 April 1127).

Galicia and Portugal for his two Burgundian sons-in-law, Raymond and Henry, who confirmed as 'Reimundus totius Gallecie comes regisque gener' and 'Henricus Portugalensis provincie comes regisque gener' in a number of documents.[38] In these counties they exercised the power of vice-regents, and both counties became hereditary. Galicia was reunited to the crown when Alfonso, son of Raymond and Urraca, became king of Castile and León, and Portugal developed into a separate kingdom under Afonso Henriques, the son of Henry and Teresa. These were, however, exceptional cases. A new division, the *tenencia*, was taking the place of the *comitatus*. The *tenencia* was an extensive territorial jurisdiction over which the *tenente*, appointed by the king, exercised judicial, military and financial functions. It may first have appeared under Fernando I, although it was not until the reign of Alfonso VII that the formula *N. tenens M.* became frequent in documents. The *tenencia* might be held by a count, or by a noble without that title, and a count might either hold land or be *comes sine terrae*.[39]

A title which was becoming obsolete by the end of the eleventh century but which still occurs occasionally in Alfonso VII's documents is that of *potestas*. It is also found in the *Chronica Adefonsi Imperatoris* and in such phrases as *comites et potestates* to denote the greater nobles collectively.[40] Other titles of dignity, such as *princeps* or *dux*, are found in documents or in narrative sources, and the nobles collectively are also referred to as *consules, proceres* or *optimates*.[41] All these titles refer to the greater nobles, those who later were known as *ricos hombres*. Of the attendance of the lesser nobles or *infanzones* we have less evidence.[42] They were very numerous and most of them had no direct connection with the king, although some held land of him, or were his vassals, or held posts at court, and these would form part of the curia. The Cid, Rodrigo Díaz, an *infanzón* of Castile, confirmed some of

---

[38] *Cartulario de S. Millán*, no. 288 (7 April 1098); Serrano, *Obispado de Burgos*, III, nos. 47 (2 Feb. 1099) 62 (22 Sept. 1105); *RC Cluny*, v, no. 3735 (25 Jan. 1100); *ES* XXXVIII, *ap.* xxx (19 March 1106).

[39] G[arcía] de Valdeavellano, *Instituciones españolas*, 506.

[40] Rassow, *AFUF*, XI, nos. 15 (3 Nov. 1139), 16 (15 Nov. 1139), 22 (June 1144), 24 (4 Dec. 1144), 31 (23 April 1149); *CD Oña*, I, nos. 191 (19 Dec. 1144), 201 (12 Sept. 1147); *CAI*, § 92–3 (pp. 70–1).

[41] *RC Silos*, nos. 29 bis (1088), 52 (1150); *ES*, XXXVI, *ap.* XLIII (22 July 1109); *CAI*, § 7 (p. 10), § 75 (p. 59), § 81 (p. 63), § 85, 86 (p. 66), § 91 (p. 69); *HC*, 95, 115, 126, 225, etc.

[42] *DHILC*, no. XXVII (2 Dec. 1093): 'inter milites non infimis parentibus ortos sed nobiles genere, necnon et potestate, qui vulgari lingua infanzones dicuntur'.

Alfonso VI's documents.[43] The king also had his household knights, men of noble birth who depended on him, lived at court and served under him in war.[44] A small and distinct group was formed by the foreign *vassali* of Alfonso VII. García Ramírez and his successor Sancho, kings of Navarre, Ramón Berenguer IV, count of Barcelona, and Alphonso, count of Toulouse, all did homage to Alfonso VII and became his vassals. From time to time these foreign rulers visited Alfonso's court and on such occasions their names were included among the *confirmantes*.[45]

How far did these lists of *confirmantes* correspond to the members of the court actually present? The wide variations in numbers suggest that they did, but there are other factors which have to be taken into consideration. In all three reigns up to 1150, certain persons appear as *testes* alongside the *confirmantes*. The *testes* were usually a small group, four or five in number, and, except during the years 1135 to 1150, or in certain documents where there were no *confirmantes*, the *testes* were not men of standing and their names were given without patronymics: Citi, Petrus, Dominicus, etc. Their names were frequently, but not always, introduced by the phrase 'Qui presentes fuerunt'.[46] The different functions of the *testes* and the *confirmantes* have been discussed in detail for the reign of Alfonso VII by Peter Rassow, who does not reach a completely satisfactory solution; however, his suggestion that the *confirmantes* were members of the curia present with the king who, even if their advice and consent were neither asked nor required, were at least cognisant of the king's act, while the *testes* were present at the actual writing of the document, is a possible one.[47] If this is so, then the disappearance of the *testes* after 1150 may be consequent on the adoption of the seal as a sign of authentication.

Occasionally the *confirmantes* included persons other than members of the curia, who had an interest in a specific donation. Some of the monks of Sahagún confirmed the *fueros* granted to the town on 26 November 1085, and members of the chapter of Santiago de Com-

---

[43] Menéndez Pidal, *España del Cid*, II, 833–4.
[44] *CAI*, § 46 (p. 38); 'cum militibus regis'.
[45] Rassow, *AFUF*, XI, no. 30 (26 March 1149): 'Rex Garsias Navarre qui tunc in curia imperatoris erat cf.'; *Cartulario de S. Millán*, no. 311 (26 July 1150): 'Garsia rex Navarre'; *RC Silos* no. 57 (28 Oct. 1155): 'Comes Barchilonie et Santus rex Navarre, eo temporis Vassalli imperatoris confirmant.'
[46] Escalona, *Sahagún*, *ap.* III, *esc.* CXXV (25 Oct. 1093); *Cartulario de S. Vicente* no. 137 (26 Dec. 1110); *Cartulario de Vega*, no. 6 (1 March 1133).
[47] Rassow, *AFUF*, X, 392, 402.

postela a donation to the cathedral in May 1107.[48] The inclusion of such persons tended to die out as the redaction of documents became increasingly regular under Alfonso VII. In some cases the names of additional *confirmantes* were added later. One way by which donations were confirmed by later kings was by the addition of their names and *signa* to the original grant, and other names might be added at the same time.[49] On the other hand, there were cases when the names of all present were not given, but phrases such as 'Alii multi boni et nobiles confirmant' were added.[50] Then again, there are sometimes discrepancies between references in the text to those present and the *confirmantes*. A judicial sentence of 1075 stated that the suit was heard 'in presencia...multorum nobilium bonorum hominium Episcoporum, Clericorum, Monacorum, Laycorum', but the twenty-two *confirmantes* were all laymen, and a donation of 26 September 1119 stated that it was made by Alfonso VII 'in presentia multorum terre nobilium' but was confirmed by only twelve *confirmantes*.[51] Chancery usage has also to be allowed for; it was probably this which accounts for the virtual disappearance of the abbots from the lists of *confirmantes* of Alfonso VII's reign and also for the small number of officials who were included. By and large, however, at this period the lists of *confirmantes* indicated those present in the curia on any given occasion.

The composition of the curia was very fluid. At one extreme was a small restricted group of those individuals who were habitually with the king; at the other an essembly to which all lay and ecclesiastical magnates were summoned. Between these two extremes there was room for many variations. Some assemblies included a number of, but not all, the bishops and great nobles as, for example, the curia at Sahagún consulted by Doña Urraca before her reconciliation with her son Alfonso in 1116. Again, meetings for a province of the kingdom only might be summoned, as in 1109 when 'omnes Gallaetiae nobiles, Consules, et Principes' at León recognised the young Alfonso as heir to his dead father's county of Galicia or, two years later, when Queen Urraca 'Proceres Gallaetiae suamque Curiam universaliter convocavit'

---

[48] Escalona, *Sahagún ap.* III, *esc.* CXVIII; López Ferreiro, *Iglesia de Santiago*, III, *ap.* XXIII.

[49] See Sánchez Belda, 'Notas de diplomática', *RABM*, LIX, 92–4; Tomás Marín, 'Confirmación real en documentos castellano–leoneses', *Estudios dedicados a Menéndez Pidal*, II, 583–93.

[50] *RC Cluny*, v, no. 3988 (7 March 1122); *Cartulario de S. Vicente*, no. 156 (1122).

[51] *ES*, XXXVIII, *ap.* XIX (26 March 1075); López Ferreiro, *Iglesia de Santiago*, III, *ap.* XXXVI. These twelve include the archbishop of Santiago and four bishops.

to assemble at Easter at Compostela.[52] It is probable that the curia in its largest form met comparatively seldom, but that meetings to which some additional members were summoned were more frequent.[53] The small curia was drawn from both León and Castile, although its composition probably varied somewhat according to the locality in which the king was residing. There are some donations to the Leonese monastery of La Vega which were confirmed exclusively by Leonese bishops and nobles, but, as a rule, those confirming diplomas included persons from both kingdoms, whatever the purpose of the document. The meetings of the small curia were informal and required no special summons. In the case of the extraordinary curia, whether for a province or for the whole kingdom, or the curia augmented by some bishops and nobles from more distant parts of the kingdom, some sort of special summons, either verbal or by writ, was necessary. No such writs of summons have survived for this period and summons may well have been verbal.

Functions of the curia

The curia was essentially a consultative body, whose advice the king might seek on any matter, and it intervened in all branches of government: in questions affecting the crown, in matters of external and internal policy, in administration and in legislation. It was also the highest judicial tribunal of the kingdom. The monarchy in Asturias and León during the first two centuries of its existence had been elective within the royal family, but by the end of the tenth century it had become hereditary. The accession of the Navarrese dynasty with Fernando I made no change for, although he had conquered León, he could also claim it in right of his wife Sancha of León. Sometimes the curia was consulted. Fernando's division of his kingdom between his three sons which gave Castile to his eldest son Sancho II, León to Alfonso VI and Galicia to the youngest, García, was carried out with the agreement of an extraordinary assembly of magnates.[54] It led to civil war between the brothers. After the assassination of Sancho II, Alfonso VI, on his return from exile at Toledo, was accepted by the Castilian nobles, however reluctantly, as the nearest male heir of the dead king.

The assembly of the Galician nobles, summoned by Alfonso VI to

[52] HC, 225, 94–6, 126–8.
[53] Guglielmi, CHE, xxviii, 64–6.   [54] Historia silense, 87.

meet at León after the death of his son-in-law Raymond of Galicia, was concerned not with the succession to the kingdom but to the county.[55] Its purpose was to safeguard the rights of Raymond's and Urraca's son Alfonso Ramírez to his father's county, should his mother remarry. With the death of the Infante Don Sancho at the battle of Uclés on 30 May 1108, Urraca, as the eldest daughter of the king, became heir to the throne.[56] It was probably the threat from the Almorávide armies which led Alfonso VI to declare Urraca his heir, before the nobles mustered at Toledo for the campaign against the Almorávides.[57] The circumstances of Urraca's marriage to Alfonso I of Aragon, whether it took place before or after Alfonso VI's death in June 1109, and whether it was the work of Alfonso VI or the decision of Urraca herself under pressure from the magnates, are uncertain but are immaterial to the fact that Urraca succeeded by hereditary right. The scanty documentary sources give some support to the view that the marriage took place before Alfonso's death.[58]

The agreement concluded between Alfonso I of Aragon and Urraca in December 1109 which recognised their co-sovereignty over their joint dominions, seriously affected the rights of Alfonso Ramírez. By this treaty a son born to Alfonso I and Urraca was recognised as heir to both kingdoms; if there was no child of the marriage, then the survivor governed them, and thus it was only after his step-father's death that the rights of Alfonso Ramírez to succeed to his mother's kingdom could be recognised. There is no reference in the text to any consultation or consent, but as the treaty provided that Alfonso I's vassals should do homage to Urraca and her vassals should swear allegiance to the Aragonese king, the curia in both kingdoms must have been consulted.[59] The immediate result of the treaty of 1109 was the revolt of the Galician nobles in support of the rights of Alfonso Ramírez. The breakdown and dissolution of the marriage nullified the treaty and in 1116, after Urraca had taken counsel with an assembly of bishops and magnates specially summoned to Sahagún, an accord was reached between the queen and her son by which the latter was associated with his mother in the government of the kingdom.[60] Thus, the curia in one form or another played some part in these obscure events.

---

[55] HC, 95.
[56] On the Infante Don Sancho, see Lévi-Provençal, *Islam d'Occident*, 144–6.
[57] HC, 115.
[58] On the question of Urraca's marriage and her succession to the throne, see Ramos y Loscertales, 'La sucesión del Rey Alfonso VI', *AHDE*, XIII, 36–99.
[59] See *ibid.* 67–9, for the text of the treaty.   [60] HC, 224–6.

The division of Alfonso VII's dominions between his sons Sancho and Fernando was decided on by the Emperor long before his death and, so far as we know, without any consultation with the curia. This decision of Alfonso VII to grant the kingdom of Castile to his eldest son Sancho, and that of León to his second son Fernando, had already been taken in 1143.[61] Six years later Sancho, then aged fourteen, was granted by his father the *regnum Naiare* – that is, the region of La Rioja of which Nájera was the chief town. Increasingly, during the rest of the reign, Sancho acted as vice-regent in Castile, and in 1151 was described as 'reigning in Castile' under the Emperor.[62] He made various donations to the cathedrals and monasteries of Castile from such Castilian towns as Carrión, Almazán, Soria, Segovia, Nájera and Calahorra. During these years he had his own household and officials, including a *maiordomus*, an *alférez* or *armiger* and a *capellanus* who confirmed his documents, and a chancery organised under a chancellor with a *notarius* or a *scriptor*.[63] Of the activities of Fernando during his father's lifetime we have less knowledge, but in a document of 1155 he used the title 'Dei gratia Legionis et Galletiae rex',[64] and he frequently resided in the kingdom of León, where he had passed his childhood in the household of Count Fernando Pérez. The author of the *Crónica latina* written during the first half of the thirteenth century, stated that this division was made on the advice of Fernando Pérez, and this may well be so.[65] What appears clear is that in this unwise and retrograde decision, which was to split Alfonso's dominions after more than eighty years of union, the curia had no part.

Questions of policy such as war, peace and the making of treaties with foreign rulers were matters which might be discussed in the curia. More information about such matters is to be found in narrative sources than in documents. Both the *Historia compostelana* and the *Chronica Adefonsi Imperatoris* give numerous references to consultation during the reigns of Urraca and Alfonso VII: during rebellions and civil wars, wars against other Iberian kingdoms or campaigns against the Moors. In view of the king's reliance on his magnates in military matters, we should expect such counsels of war to be normal,

61 AHN, Clero, *carp.* 526/11 (1 March 1143). I am indebted to Dr Richard Fletcher for this reference.
62 González, *Reino de Castilla*, ii, nos. 3 (27 Feb. 1149), 4 (8 Aug. 1151).
63 *Ibid.* ii, nos. 3–29, of various dates from 1149 to 1157.
64 González, *Regesta*, 345. For the activities of the two *infantes* during their father's lifetime, see González, *Reino de Castilla*, i, 139–44, and *Regesta*, 17–19.
65 *Crónica latina*, 23.

although we have not always evidence of them. The *Historia compostelana* recorded that Queen Urraca took counsel with Bishop Diego Gelmírez and the nobles of Galicia before attacking the traitor Arias Pérez in 1110; that in 1115 the reconciliation between the queen and the bishop took place in the presence of the Galician nobles; and that in the next year, after further discord, a second reconciliation was effected on the advice of the magnates of the whole kingdom.[66] Again Urraca took counsel with Diego Gelmírez and the Galician nobles before launching a punitive attack on the rebel burgesses of Compostela.[67] In 1134 Alfonso VII, 'sicut jam consilio suorum Baronum disposuerat', began a campaign against the Moors with a large army of horse and foot.[68] Similar references to consultations are to be found in the *Chronica Adefonsi Imperatoris* before the king's first campaign in Andalusia in 1133, before the siege of Oreja in 1139 and during the siege of Coria in 1142.[69] Before concluding the Peace of Támara with his step-father, Alfonso I of Aragon, the young Alfonso VII asked for, and accepted against his own inclination, the advice of his nobles to conclude peace.[70] Actual treaties were generally ratified in the presence of the concluding parties and a small number of named bishops and nobles from either side who may have negotiated the agreement, with or without the presence of other persons. The Treaty of Carrión of 1141, between Alfonso VII and Ramón Berenguer III, count of Barcelona, was concluded in the presence of Berengar, bishop of Salamanca, Bernardo, bishop of Sagunto, Pedro, bishop elect of Burgos, seventeen lay magnates from both Castile and Catalonia and 'aliorum nobilium in curia domini imperatoris existencium'.[71]

The curia and the church councils

The period from 1072 to 1157 saw the gradual differentiation of the institutions of church and state under the impetus provided by the reformed papacy. The chief instruments of the popes were *legati a latere* sent on special missions to lay rulers and frequent ecclesiastical councils held under their presidency to deal with specifically ecclesiastical matters. Such legatine missions and church councils were

---

[66] *HC*, 126–8, 194–6, 205–27.
[67] *Ibid.* 227 (1117).
[68] *Ibid.* 555 (1134).
[69] *CAI*, § 33 (p. 30), § 145 (p. 113), § 160 (p. 124).
[70] *Ibid.* § 10, 11 (p. 13).
[71] *Liber feudorum maior*, I, 37–8, no. 28 (21 Feb. 1141).

numerous in León–Castile from 1080 to 1157. The king and the lay magnates usually, but not always, attended church councils and approved their decisions.[72] The bishops and abbots attended the extra-ordinary meetings of the curia, although rather as great landowners than as spiritual advisers. Thus, the composition of the two types of assembly was often the same. One distinction between them was, however, clear. The curia was presided over by the king; the church councils were presided over by a papal legate, who might be either a *legatus a latere*, as in the case of the Council of León in 1090 over which Cardinal Renier (later Pope Pascal II), presided, and that of Carrión in 1130, under Cardinal Humbert; or else they might meet under the presidency of the archbishop of Toledo as *legatus natus*, as, for example, the Councils of Palencia in 1113 and León in 1114.

The business transacted at these councils was mainly concerned with the organisation and administration of the church. At Burgos, probably in 1080, the Roman Liturgy was substituted for the Mozarabic Rite. Bishops were deposed at Husillos (1088), León, Carrión and Valladolid (1155); elections of bishops took place at Palencia and Carrión and diocesan boundaries were fixed at Husillos and Carrión.[73] Surviving decrees dealt mainly with ecclesiastical discipline. By those promulgated at León in 1114, the laity were forbidden to do violence to the church or its possessions, or to appropriate the ecclesiastical tithes; simony was prohibited; those who married within the prohibited degrees of con-sanguinity were to be separated; clergy were not to have women in their houses except as laid down in canon law; monks and clergy who relinquished their vows were to be excommunicated; monks were to be subject to their abbots and were not to hold property or public offices. One clause laid down that merchants, pilgrims and labourers were to go about their avocations securely and in peace.[74]

The king certainly exercised great influence in such councils. The deposition of Diego I of Compostela in 1088 was instigated by Alfonso VI, who had long held him in prison; the deposition was

---

[72] There were no laity at the ecclesiastical council of Compostela in 1124, at which the *Pax Dei* was proclaimed. *HC*, 417–19; López Ferreiro, *Iglesia de Santiago*, IV, *ap.* IV.

[73] *Crónica del Obispo Don Pelayo*, 80 (Burgos); *HC*, 16–17 (Husillos), 17–18 (León, 1090), 182–3 (Palencia, 1113), 190–2 (León, 1114), 497–500 (Carrión). On the first three of these, see Maldonado, 'Las relaciones entre el derecho canónico y el derecho secular en los consilios españoles del siglo XI', *AHDE*, XIV, 250–60.

[74] *HC*, 190–2. Decrees of León, confirmed at a provincial council at Compostela, presided over by Diego Gelmírez.

subsequently quashed by the Pope. In 1136 Alfonso VII asked for a legate to be sent to determine the boundaries of the dioceses of Sigüenza, Osma and Tarragona, and his request resulted in the Council of Burgos, held by the legate Cardinal Guy.

A council which was summoned by Alfonso VII, but which was presided over by the archbishop of Toledo as legate, and which exhibited the characteristics of an ecclesiastical assembly, howbeit with some anomalies, was held at Palencia in 1129. As its decrees were included in the *Cortes de los antiguos reinos de León y de Castilla*, it is necessary to examine them to determine whether they can be considered as secular legislation promulgated with the consent of the curia.[75] Our knowledge of this assembly comes exclusively from the *Historia compostelana*, which gives both a narrative account of events and the text of the decrees. The initiative came from Alfonso VII who, because of the disturbed state of his kingdom, determined to summon all the bishops, abbots, counts, princes and great men to Palencia. When once, however, Archbishop Diego Gelmírez had arrived, the king consigned the business into his hands and he, together with Archbishop Raimundo of Toledo and the bishops, drew up the decrees which were afterwards promulgated with the approbation of the king.[76] The *Historia compostelana* here exaggerated the importance of the role of Diego Gelmírez. The preamble of the decrees showed clearly that it was the archbishop of Toledo who presided, in the role of papal legate: 'ego Raymundus Toletane sedis archiepiscopus et primas ac S.R.E. legatus, una cum pontificibus quorum inferius nomina scripta esse videntur'. The part of the king was to approve: 'et imperatore nostro A. presente atque favente'. The plural 'statuimus' was used throughout the decrees.[77] The majority of them dealt with ecclesiastical discipline: concubines of the clergy were to be put away; wandering monks were to be compelled to return to their monasteries; adulterers and the incestuous were to be parted; lay investiture was forbidden; and the clergy were not to bear arms. All these were subjects proper to a church council. On the other hand, there were a number of decrees which dealt with secular matters, particularly with questions of law and order: the princes of the land were not to punish those subject to them without just judgment; *portaticum* (toll) was to be taken as and where customary in the reign of Alfonso VI; cattle were not to be seized or

---

[75] *Cortes*, I, no. VI.
[76] *HC*, 482–6. The text in *Cortes* is taken from that in *HC*.
[77] The decrees are headed 'Decreta Pontificum'; this title is omitted in *Cortes*.

distrained; all men were to obey the king. Some were both secular and ecclesiastical as, for example, the first clause which forbade any man to harbour or protect not only traitors, robbers and thieves but also perjurers and the excommunicated. Sanctions were both ecclesiastical and secular, and false coiners were subject to the double penalty of excommunication and blinding at the king's order. The proportion of secular legislation is high and shows the confusion – perhaps interdependence would be the better word – of church and state. But the presidency of the archbishop of Toledo, and the attribution of the decrees to the bishops, mark this as a church council rather than a meeting of the enlarged curia.

At times the king transacted secular business during a church council, and bishops and abbots used the opportunity afforded to gain confirmations of existing grants of land and privileges, or grants of new ones. Thus, Alfonso VII confirmed his mother's grants to the church of Astorga at the Council of Burgos.[78] At the Council of Valladolid in February 1155 he granted a three weeks' fair to Sahagún, confirmed to the monastery of Celanova all the lands which it had lost during the civil wars of Urraca's reign and granted lands to the church of Santiago de Compostela.[79]

The role of the curia in day-to-day administration

The part of the curia in the day-to-day administration is not easy to determine. The majority of the surviving royal charters of this period are grants of royal lands and rents to churches and monasteries. Such donations were matters for the king and his immediate family, whose names follow the royal superscription: 'Ego Adefonsus Hispaniae Rex et Imperator una cum filiis meis Sancio et Fernando'. As we have seen, these solemn diplomas were confirmed by a number of lay and ecclesiastical persons who were present at the time with the king and made up his curia. This did not, however, imply that they had been specifically asked either their advice or their consent. What was confirmed was that the document set forth the royal act. From time to time, however, there was a reference which showed that some sort of consultation had taken place, but such donations are a small proportion only of those which survive. The enumeration of such instances gives a

---

[78] ES, xvi, ap. xxvi (pp. 451–3) (2 Oct. 1136): 'Guidone Sanctae Romanae Ecclesiae Cardinali et Legato, eo tempore in Burgis concilium celebrante'.
[79] Escalona, Sahagún, ap. iii, esc. clxx; Rassow, AFUF, xi, no. 53 (4 Feb. 1155); López Ferreiro, Iglesia de Santiago, iv, ap. xxv.

false impression, unless it is remembered that the number of documents in which there is no reference to advice or consent is far greater than the number in which such a reference occurs. The general impression gained from an examination of published documents of this period is that the curia played a passive rather than an active part. Nor can it be said that advice and consent were asked for and recorded even where the donation in question was particularly important or of some special kind. Most of these donations were grants of land or confirmations of earlier grants (*cartae donationis, cartae confirmationis*); in the majority of such cases there is no reference to consultation. Occasionally, however, some such reference is made as, for example, in a grant of 15 February 1149, where the charter was read before and confirmed by the whole curia.[80] Again, when Alfonso VII restored to the abbey of Sahagún its dependent house of San Salvador de Nogal, which he had expropriated earlier in his reign, he did so *seniori consilio*,[81] but when, in 1155, he restored to the monastery of Celanova lands which it had lost during the civil wars of Urraca's reign, there was no reference to consultation.[82] Many of these charters were grants of immunities to cathedrals and monasteries and defined the *coto* or district under the lordship of the bishop or abbot in which he exercised special rights. Here again, there were references to advice or consent in some cases but not in others. There was no reference to any participation by the curia in Alfonso VI's diploma granting the *mandatio* of Langreo to the see of Oviedo, although it was made on the occasion of a ceremonial visit with a great company to see the relics kept at Oviedo; nor was there any reference to consultation in Alfonso VII's confirmation of the *coto* of the monastery of Santo Domingo de Silos in 1155, nor in his confirmation of the possessions and immunities of the cathedral of Orense in 1157.[83] On the other hand, Alfonso VII confirmed his mother's grant of the *coto* of Santiago de Compostela after he had heard it read 'coram omni concilio nobilium meorum uirorum'.[84]

All alienation of royal lands and regalian rights affected the economic position of the crown but the economic implication of some acts was more direct and obvious. In the autumn of 1072 Alfonso VI

---

[80] *Fuentes de Castilla*, I, no. XIII (pp. 58–60): 'hanc cartam fieri iussi et coram testibus legere audivi, propriis manibus roboravi'. 'Et tota curia imperatoris cum episcopis qui ibi aderant et proceribus suis visores, auditores et confirmatores'.
[81] Escalona, *Sahagún, ap.* III, *esc.* CLIV (2 April 1127).
[82] Rassow, *AFUF*, XI, no. 53 (4 Feb. 1155).
[83] *ES*, XXXVIII, *ap.* XXI (14 March 1075); *RC Silos*, no. 58 (28 Oct. 1155); *ES*, XVII, *ap.* IV (1157).
[84] López Ferreiro, *Iglesia de Santiago*, IV, *ap.* V (13 Nov. 1127).

abolished the *portaticum* (toll) collected at the castle of Santa María de Autares at the point where the pilgrim road to Santiago de Compostela entered Galicia. The principal gainers were the pilgrims who followed this route to the shrine of the Apostle, and they included not only Spaniards but Italians, French and Germans, as was mentioned in the document. This was an act of piety on the part of the king and the curia's consent was not specified.[85] Sometimes the curia played a more active part. In 1077 Alfonso VI agreed to double the *censum* or annual gift of 1,000 *mancales* which had been paid by Fernando I to the abbey of Cluny, and this promise was renewed in 1090 at the Easter festival in the presence of Abbot Hugh of Cluny. The documents concerned with the promise of 1077 had no reference to consultation or consent, but the renewed undertaking of 1090 was made with the advice and consent of the lay and ecclesiastical magnates: 'communicato etiam cum uxore mea regina consilo, et primum Toletano archiepiscopo et ceteris episcopis meis et primoribus regni mei, fidelibus mcis volentibus, consentientibus, laudantibus astipulantibus, constituo de prefato censu duplicato', as the king's *carta* stated.[86]

Coinage was a regalian right, as it was in all Western European kingdoms: a matter for the king alone. In the earlier centuries of the reconquest the kings of Christian Spain had relied on the coinage of the Frankish and Hispano-Arabic rulers. The first Spanish king to coin money was Sancho the Great of Navarre and the practice was continued by his son García IV and his grandson Sancho IV of Navarre. Fernando I of Castile, possibly, and Alfonso VI, certainly, coined money and under the latter there were royal mints at Lugo, León, Toledo and Compostela.[87] This right was jealously guarded, but from time to time the kings granted the whole or part of the profits of a mint to a bishop or monastery.[88] Thus, Alfonso VI granted the mint at Compostela to Diego Gelmírez and the story of the concession as told in the *Historia compostelana* shows with what reluctance it was made.[89] Under the stress of war, Urraca granted to the monastery of Sahagún, in 1116, the right to have a mint 'quia ex guerra que est inter me et regem

---

[85] *ES*, xxxvi, ap. xxvi (17 Nov. 1072).
[86] *RC Cluny*, iv, nos. 3441, 3509, 3638. On the question of the *censum* and the date of the first promise to double it, see David, *Etudes historiques sur la Galice et le Portugal*, 402–3.
[87] Sánchez-Albornoz, *Estudios*, 452–3. No coins of Fernando I have survived, but Sánchez-Albornoz thinks he coined money, as his brother and nephew did in Navarre. Mateu y Llopis disagrees, *Moneda española*, 128–9.
[88] Mateu y Llopis, *Moneda española*, 131–5.
[89] *HC*, 68; Sánchez-Albornoz, *Estudios*, 462–5.

aragonensem non nulla nobis oritur necessitas', with the proviso that the coinage was to be shared between the queen, the abbot and the monks. Three years later her son Alfonso VII made a similar grant for much the same reason – 'quia propter instantem undique guerram non nulla nobis oritur necessitas' – but with the modification that the coinage was to be divided between himself and the abbot, eliminating the share of the monks.[90] Indeed, under Alfonso VII such concessions were frequent. They included the grant of a tenth part of all royal rights in Burgos, including the coinage, to the bishop; 'decimam de moneta qui fit in civitate Legionis' and other royal rights to the bishop of León; a quarter of the money minted in Segovia to its cathedral; a tenth of that minted in Toledo to the canons; and a third of that minted in Salamanca to its bishop and chapter.[91] At some time Alfonso VII also confirmed the concession made by Alfonso VI to the archbishops of Santiago de Compostela, but retained for himself the coinage minted there, in return for a promise that the money of Santiago only should circulate in Galicia.[92] In none of these transactions was the advice of the curia asked.

The Almorávide invasion of 1086 and the subsequent extinction of the petty Muslim states of Southern Spain had a disastrous effect on the financial resources of the Leonese–Castilian monarchy, for they brought to an end the system of *parias* (tribute) paid by the Muslim kingdoms, which had enriched the treasuries of Fernando I and of Alfonso VI.[93] The monarchy was left with only its customary resources with which to organise resistance to the Almorávide armies threatening its southern frontiers. As a result, Alfonso VI adopted the temporary expedient of obtaining an extraordinary tax from some of his subjects. On 31 March 1091 the chancery passed an important document addressed to Pedro, bishop of León, Count Martín Laínez and all the inhabitants, both great and small, 'in tota terra de Legione', in which he modified the procedure to be followed in suits between Jews and Christians, in return for a capitation tax for the prosecution of the war

[90] Escalona, *Sahagún*, ap. III, escs. CXLVI, CXLIX (15 Oct. 1116, 8 Oct. 1119).
[91] Serrano, *Obispado de Burgos*, III, no. 89 (8 July 1128); Guallart and Laguzzi, 'Algunos documentos reales leoneses', *CHE*, I–II, no. 1 (p. 364) (11 June 1135); Colmenares, *Historia de Segovia*, I, 238, 243–5 (9 April 1136); Rassow, *AFUF*, XI, 76–7, no. 10 (12 May 1137); Marcos Rodríguez, *Catálogo del archivo catedralicio de Salamanca*, no. 11 (p. 11) (20 Oct. 1137).
[92] López Ferreiro, *Iglesia de Santiago*, IV, ap. XLVI: Privilege of Fernando II (11 March 1171).
[93] Sánchez-Albornoz, *Estudios*, 484; Grassotti, 'Para la historia del botín y las parias en León y Castilla', *CHE*, XXXIX–XL, 51–9.

against the Almorávides. What concerns us here is the second part of
the document. The rules on procedure end with the statement: 'Omnia
que superius scripta sunt vobis confirmo, ut firmiter maneant roborata
evo perenni et secula cuncta.' Then follows immediately: 'Hoc autem
feci cum consensu vestre voluntatis, sicut vobis bene complacuit, ut
reddatis mihi de unaquaque corte populata tam de infanzones quam
etiam de villanos duos solidos in isto anno una vice, et amplius non
demandent eos vobis altera vice.'[94]

Thus, the king, at the request of the inhabitants 'in tota terra de
Legione', modified the judicial procedure in cases between Jews and
Christians in favour of the latter, and in return was granted an extraordinary tax of a specific amount, to be taken once only, from every
occupied holding, whether belonging to an *infanzón* or to a *pechero*.
The document was confirmed, as was customary, by bishops and nobles
from all parts of Alfonso's dominions, but there is nothing to indicate
that they were consulted or that their assent was given – those who
assented and who were to pay the tax were the inhabitants 'in tota
terra de Legione'. This raises the question, what was denoted by this
phrase? Was it simply the *tierra* or *término* surrounding the city of
León and subject to the jurisdiction of its court, or was it the ancient
kingdom of León as inherited by Alfonso VI in 1065, but probably
exclusive of Asturias and also of the lands to the south of the Duero,
then in process of colonisation? The phrase is often used to refer to the
kingdom, and this interpretation is supported by the reference in the
procedural rules to the bishop of Astorga and the abbot of Sahagún as
well as to the bishop of León. In either case the tax was far from being
a general tax imposed on all Alfonso's subjects; there is no evidence
that it was imposed on any other part of his dominions, or that the king
had further recourse to such an expedient. Its importance should not
be overstressed.

The financial straits of Queen Urraca arose from war with Aragon
and from civil war and rebellion, but both she and Alfonso VII, during
the earlier years of his reign, relied largely on gifts extorted from the
church and on the sale of lands and rights to churches in return for
treasure. There are numerous references in the *Historia compostelana*
to sums obtained by both monarchs from the church of Santiago de
Compostela.[95] In 1112 Urraca received great sums of gold and silver
from the treasury of the cathedral of Oviedo, in return for the cession

[94] *DHILC*, no. xxv; also publ. *ES*, xxxv, *ap.* 1.
[95] E.g. *HC*, 126, 448–54, 494, etc.

of the town and castle of Oviedo and other lands to the bishop, and a confirmation of all lands that had been held by the church, without contradiction, for the past thirty years.[96] In 1120 she received precious vessels of gold and silver from the cathedral of Astorga, in return for lands contiguous to the church and for the restoration of property lost in the reign of Fernando I.[97] Early in his reign Alfonso VII seized lands and goods from the monasteries of San Salvador de Nogal and Sahagún, as appears from the acts of restoration of 2 April 1127 and 4 August 1129.[98]

Claudio Sánchez-Albornoz has shown that about 1136 a new imposition, known as *petitio*, began to appear. It was not mentioned in a series of donations made between 1123 and 1135 to the cathedrals of Toledo, Sigüenza, Burgos and León, which enumerated the royal rents, in certain places, granted in whole or in part to these churches. Nor was it included in exemptions from royal tributes granted to the abbey of Sahagún in 1126 and to the cathedral of Astorga in 1130. It was, however, included in a grant to the church of Osma of a tenth of the royal rents in San Esteban de Gormaz in 1136 and, in 1141, the canons of León cathedral were exempted from contributing to any *petitio* or *pecta* taken from the citizens of León, either by consent or by force. In 1154 the Infante Don Sancho confirmed his father's grant to the church of Osma.[99] The name *petitio* indicates that this new imposition was asked for and required consent. How was such consent obtained? How often was *petitio* taken? And was it a general tax or imposed on certain places only? Sancho's confirmation in 1154 related to a number of places, but it was only in Osma and San Esteban de Gormaz that it was included among the royal rents named. This seems to show that *petitio* was taken in certain places only. It appears, therefore, that the king was able to increase his revenues by means of extraordinary demands for money, but that such impositions were in theory free gifts, which required consent. We have no evidence how such consent was obtained, but it was most probably negotiated locally by royal officials. For the first half of the twelfth century there is no evidence that the consent of the curia was required.

From time to time the curia intervened in the enactment of

---

[96] *CDC Oviedo*, no. 131; also in *ES*, xxxviii, *ap.* xxxii, under the incorrect date 1114.

[97] *ES*, xvi, *ap.* xxiv. Cf. Sánchez-Albornoz, *Estudios*, 486–8, for other examples.

[98] Escalona, *Sahagún*, *ap.* iii, *escs.* cliv, clv.

[99] Sánchez-Albornoz, *Estudios*, 496–502; the document of 1154 is published by González, *Reino de Castilla*, ii, no. 12.

legislation. In León in this period, the Visigothic code, known as the *Forum judicum*, was recognised as the law of the land. It is referred to in the decrees of the Council of Coyanza in 1050,[100] and it is cited in a number of law suits and donations during the tenth and eleventh centuries.[101] It was confirmed to the Mozárabes of Toledo by Alfonso VI, after his conquest of the city in 1085. In Castile, on the other hand, law was customary and was supplemented by *fazañas*, which were sentences in judicial suits recognised as precedents, and which constituted a body of case law. Written legislation during this period falls under four headings: local law, that is, *fueros* or charters granted to particular cities and towns; *placita* or judicial decisions given general application and modifications of judicial procedure; royal edicts; and, finally, general laws applicable to a province or to the whole kingdom. Local law increased under Alfonso VI and Alfonso VII. Town *fueros* applied not only to those who dwelt within the walls of the town to which they were granted but also to all those who inhabited the *alfoz* or surrounding district, which also came under the jurisdiction of the town court. In the case of the larger towns, this district covered a wide expanse of country and included hamlets, villages and small towns. Thus, the town *fueros* helped to spread a network of enacted law over the kingdom. *Fueros* could be given or approved by any *dominus terrae*, be he bishop or abbot, king or count or other lay lord. Those granted by the kings were generally granted without any reference to the curia: for example, Alfonso VI's grant of *fueros* to Sahagún in 1085 at the request of the abbot; the *fuero* granted to Logroño in 1095; the confirmation of the *fueros* of León by Queen Urraca in 1109; Alfonso VII's confirmation of the *fueros* of Lara in 1135 and of San Zoil de Carrión in 1142; and his grant of the *fueros* of Mansella to the men of Villa Celama in 1153.[102] On the other hand, Alfonso VI took counsel with his chief men in 1076 to restore and revise the ancient customs of the city of Nájera, and affirmed them 'presentibus meis obtimatibus', while the *fuero* given to Vallunquera in 1102 was granted 'Coram magno exercitu militum' on the eve of war with the Moors.[108] The

---

[100] *Cortes*, I, no. III, cl. 9.

[101] Barrau-Dihigo, *Revue Hispanique*, x, nos. XXIV, XXXV (8 Aug. 994); *ES*, XXXVI, *ap.* IV (13 July 1000); XVI, *ap.* XVII (28 June 1046); XXXVIII, *aps.* XIX (26 March 1075), XX (13 Aug. 1083).

[102] Escalona, *Sahagún*, *ap.* III, *esc.* CXVIII (26 Nov. 1085); D. Hergueta, 'El fuero de Logroño', *BRAH*, L (1907), 325–36; *ES*, XXXV, *ap.* II; *Cartulario de Arlanza*, no. XCV (3 May 1135); Rassow, *AFUF*, XI, no. 20 (7 Sept. 1142); González 'Aportación de fueros leoneses', *AHDE*, XIV, 561–3.

[108] *Cartulario de S. Millán*, no. 226; González, *AHDE*, XVI, 629–31.

granting of revised *fueros* to the townsmen of Sahagún in 1152, in which the lordship over the town was confirmed to the abbot of Sahagún, although the condition of the burgesses was much ameliorated, was made by Alfonso VII after consultation with his second wife the Empress Rica, his sister Doña Sancha, the bishops of León, Palencia and Oviedo, Counts Fernando Pérez of Galicia, Gutierre Fernández and Pons de Minerva, 'et aliis mei imperii melioribus', together with Abbot Domingo and the monks who were partners with the king in the transaction.[104]

The curia and legislation

Legislation, which arose out of the judicial functions of the curia – as, for example, when a sentence was generalised to have the force of law – naturally entailed the participation of the curia. An example of this occurred in the reign of Alfonso VI. In 1089, as the result of a land suit between the Infanta Doña Urraca and Bishop Pedro of León, the king 'per iudicium et consilium comitum, baronum suorum et maiorum de sua escola et meliorum de sua terra, cunctis uocatis ad sua curiam' promulgated a decree to the effect that lands held by the king, the *infantes*, the church, the nobles or held *in benefactoria* should not pass into the possession of persons of a different status, and made this applicable to his whole kingdom – 'affirmauit in toto suo regno'.[105] Redress of abuses of the law at this period appear to have been a matter for the king alone. Thus, in 1072, Alfonso VI forbade the abuse by which, when a homicide could not be traced to its perpetrator, the royal officials exacted a collective fine from the neighbouring villages, and instead laid down that, if the villagers were able to purge themselves, either by oath or by the ordeal of boiling water, no fine was to be exacted from them, 'sed sint salvi et liberati quos Deus salvare et liberare voluerit'.[106] This decree was issued on the occasion of the king's visit to Oviedo, when he also abolished the *portaticum* taken at Santa María de Autares.

Of general legislation nothing has survived. The editors of the *Cortes de los antiguos reinos de León y de Castilla* included two sets of decrees for the first half of the twelfth century – those issued at the Council of Oviedo in 1115 and those of the Council of Palencia in

---

[104] Escalona, *Sahagún*, ap. III, *esc.* CLXVIII (18 Dec. 1152); cf. Puyol y Alonso, *Abadengo de Sahagún*, 82–90.
[105] Publ. Sánchez-Albornoz, *Estudios*, 307–8, no. VI (24 Sept. 1089).
[106] *ES*, XXXVI, ap. XXVI (19 Nov. 1072).

1129. With the latter we have already dealt. The former have even less claim to be considered as secular legislation, promulgated in the curia. In 1115 the country was torn by civil war between Queen Urraca and her husband Alfonso I of Aragon. The decrees of Oviedo originated in an assembly of the nobles and people of Asturias, summoned by Bishop Pelayo of Oviedo, and held in the cathedral of Oviedo. They were later accepted throughout the whole kingdom: 'haec institutio subscripta, que per totam Hispaniam habetur, habuit initium in Ovetensi Ecclesia tempore Pelagii Ovetensis Episcopi, et subscriptis omnibus hominibus', according to the preamble, which also gives the date: 'Era MCLIII apud Ovetum in Ecclesia Sancti Salvatoris congregatis principibus et plebe totius praedictae regionis in die sancto Pentecostes'. The constitution there agreed on consisted of three clauses each beginning with the plural 'statuimus' and taking the form of undertakings on oath not to seize cattle as pledges, not to commit theft and not to commit a breach of sanctuary which was carefully defined. The sanctions were ecclesiastical: excommunication, penance, compulsory tonsuring, etc. The whole is closely related to the Peace of God. The text, in the form in which it has survived, is followed by the *confirmantes* who fall into a number of groups: the queen Doña Urraca, her children and dependants, her sisters Elvira and Teresa with their children and dependants, all of whom are given in the third person: 'Regina autem Domina Urraca...hanc constitutionem praescriptum confirmavit et iuravit.' The laity (283 names in all) are grouped under localities: 'ex terra Tinegiae', 'ex territoriis Legionis et Astoricae', etc. The 'subscriptiones episcoporum' include the names of the three archbishops – Bernardo of Toledo, Diego Gelmírez of Santiago de Compostela and Pelayo of Braga – and of twelve bishops – Muño of Mondoñedo, Diego of Orense, Pelayo of Astorga, Gonsalvo of Coimbra, Diego of León, Pedro of Palencia, Pedro of Segovia, Bernardo of Sigüenza, Paschal of Burgos, Sancho of Avila, Muño of Salamanca and Bernardo of Zamora. Finally, there are a number of individual confirmations added under different dates: the confirmation of Alfonso VII 'sub era MCLXII' (A.D. 1124) – in error for era 1164 (A.D. 1126), the year in which he became sole ruler on his mother's death; that of the Infante Don Afonso Henriques of Portugal 'sub era MCLVIII' (A.D. 1120); and those of Alfonso I of Aragon and his brother Ramiro the monk *in diebus illis*. In each case these signatories undertook to enforce the constitutions in their dominions.[107]

---

[107] *Cortes*, I, no. v, taken from Risco's edition of the decrees in *ES*, xxxviii, *ap.* II.

Even apart from this last group of later signatories, these *confirmantes* cannot be those of the original assembly. There is no evidence that Queen Urraca, or any member of the royal family, was present at Oviedo. The laity do not come from the northern provinces but from all parts of Urraca's dominions, and thus do not correspond to the princes and people of the Asturias, who alone are mentioned as present at Oviedo in the preamble of the decrees. The bishops are the majority of the bishops of León, Castile and Portugal and again there is no evidence that they attended the assembly. Among those omitted is, surprisingly, Pelayo of Oviedo, at whose instance and in whose cathedral church the assembly was said to be held. Nor do these episcopal *confirmantes* correspond to the year 1115. As Risco pointed out, when he published the text, Santiago de Compostela did not become an archbishopric until 1120, Sancho was not bishop of Avila until 1121, nor Muño bishop of Salamanca until 1124.[108] The first known reference to Bernardo as bishop of Zamora belongs to 1121.[109] Nor could all these bishops have confirmed at any one date. Pelayo of Astorgo died before 22 November 1121,[110] but Muño did not become bishop of Salamanca until 1124.

Legislation of some sort was promulgated on the occasion of the coronation of Alfonso VII as Emperor at León on Whit Sunday 1135. Our knowledge of this occasion is derived solely from the *Chronica Adefonsi Imperatoris* which, however, gives a sufficiently detailed account. According to it, Alfonso VII held a council 'cum archiepiscopis, episcopis et abbatibus, comitibus et principibus, ducibus et iudicibus, qui in illius regno erant'. Besides these great men who constituted the curia, there were also present a great crowd of monks, clerks and ordinary people 'ad videndum sive ad audiendum vel ad loquendum verbum divinum' – a crowd of spectators, who had no official part in the proceedings, but who were present throughout and probably acclaimed the decisions arrived at. The assembly lasted three days. On the first the meeting was held in the cathedral and treated of matters pertaining to the salvation of the souls of the faithful. The second day was given over to the actual coronation, followed by feasting. On the third day the council met in the royal palace and treated of

[108] *ES*, xxxviii, 259–60.
[109] Fita, 'Bernardo de Perigord', *BRAH*, xiv, 456–60.
[110] BN, MS. 4357, nos. 504, 505: two private documents of 22 Nov. and 28 Dec. 1121 which include the phrase 'eo anno quo migravit episcopus Pelagius in Astorica'. I owe this reference to Dr Richard Fletcher.

matters 'quae pertinent ad salutem regni totius Hispaniae'.[111] This threefold division clearly recalls the decree of the Council of León in 1017 which laid down that ecclesiastical causes should first be tried, then royal and lastly those of the people.[112] On the last day the Emperor gave customs and laws to his whole kingdom, as they had been in the time of Alfonso VI; he commanded that all persons and families lost to the church were to be restored; all towns and lands destroyed in time of war were to be recolonised; and all vines and trees replanted. Judges were instructed to root out crime by means of such punishments as death and mutilation. No actual decrees have survived. Contemporary documents add nothing to the account of the *Chronica*, except to correct the date from 3 June to 26 May which was the date of Whit Sunday that year.[113] The Council of León was an altogether exceptional assembly, largely ceremonial but in which, although there was no clear-cut distinction between ecclesiastical council and secular curia, the sessions dealing with matters pertaining to the church and those pertaining to the state were separated by the solemn coronation and were held, the former in the cathedral, and the latter in the royal palace.

The legists of the fourteenth century who drew up the *Ordenamiento de Alcalá* (1348) and the unofficial *Fuero viejo* (1356) made use of a collection of laws, now lost, which they believed to have been promulgated by Alfonso VII at Nájera, and some modern historians have, therefore, postulated a curia or cortes of Nájera in 1137 when Alfonso VII visited that town. The view most generally held now is that this lost *Ordenamiento de Nájera* was an unofficial compilation, put together some time in the thirteenth century; that some of its contents derived from the twelfth century is probable, but whether such elements were based on customary or written law, we do not know, and there is no contemporary evidence that Alfonso VII issued laws at Nájera, although he may have done so.[114]

Judicial functions of the curia

We know most about the curia as a judicial tribunal. This is not

[111] *CAI*, § 69–71 (pp. 54–7).
[112] *Cortes*, I, no. II, cls. I, VI (under date 1020); also publ. Vázquez de Parga, *Fuero de León*, 24–5, cls. I, VI, VII.
[113] *Cartulario de Arlanza*, no. XCVII; *RC Silos*, no. 44.
[114] Sánchez, 'Para la historia de la redacción del antiguo derecho territorial castellano', *AHDE*, VI, 307–11; García Gallo, 'Textos de derecho territorial castellano'; *AHDE*, XIII, 313–17; Sánchez-Albornoz, 'Dudas sobre el Ordenamiento de Nájera', *CHE*, XXXV–XXXVI, 315–36.

necessarily because its judicial functions were its most important ones but, to some extent, because the parties to a suit required written evidence of the sentence and a number of such sentences have survived, while discussion and deliberation did not necessarily require a written record. Yet, even allowing for this, it is patent that the judicial sessions exhibited a formality and a degree of clarity which were lacking from some manifestations of the curia's activities. Most of the suits of which we have a record concerned the kingdom of León, but the king's court was formed of persons from both León and Castile, and there was no division of the court to match the provenance of the cases heard. As Menéndez Pidal pointed out, the Cid, Rodrigo Díaz, a lesser noble of Castile, was appointed as an *ad hoc* judge in a suit in which the litigants belonged to the Asturias, and in which judgment was given according to the *Forum judicum*.[115]

The king himself was at times a suitor, as in 1075, in the case between Alfonso VI and the *infanzones* of Valle de Langreo, as to whether the lands held by the *infanzones* were, as they claimed, alodial, or, as the king claimed, belonged to royal demesne;[116] or, in a suit in 1126 between Archbishop Diego Gelmírez of Santiago de Compostela and Alfonso VII as defendant, concerning the castle of Cira, which the archbishop claimed by donation of Queen Urraca, but which the king had granted as a fief to Juan Díaz.[117] The *curia regis* was the sole court for pleas of the nobles[118] and so suits in which counts and other lay magnates were involved were numerous. In most of the cases an ecclesiastic or an ecclesiastical corporation was implicated. At this date cases between ecclesiastics might either be heard in the king's court, or in an ecclesiastical court, such as that of the archbishop of Toledo, or they might be resolved by the papacy or by papal judges delegate. Thus, in 1090 a suit between Bishop Arias of Oviedo and Abbot Ramiro of San Vicente de Oviedo was heard before Alfonso VI,[119] and in 1140 one between the bishops of Calahorra and Burgos was judged in the court of Alfonso VII.[120] On the other hand, a suit between the bishops of Burgos and Oviedo during the first decade of the twelfth century came before Archbishop Bernardo of Toledo,[121] and the

---

[115] Menéndez Pidal, *España del Cid*, I, 218.
[116] *DHILC*, no. XIX; also in *ES*, XXXVIII, *ap.* XXII.
[117] *HC*, 439–40. Cf. Guglielmi, *CHE*, XXVIII, 73–4.
[118] G[arcía] de Valdeavellano, *Instituciones españolas*, 557.
[119] *CDC Oviedo*, no. 98 (23 March 1090).
[120] Llorente, *Provincias vascongadas*, IV, no. 117 (pp. 74–5), (3 Nov. 1140).
[121] *CDC Oviedo*, no. 121 (*c.* 1101–9).

long-drawn-out dispute as to whether the archpresbiterate of Bezonces, Trasancos and Seaya belonged to the diocese of Santiago or to that of Mondoñedo, which dragged on from 1102 to 1122, was resolved by the papacy.[122]

As examples of suits between ecclesiastical and lay litigants, one in 1078 between the bishop of Lugo and Counts Vela, Ovela and Rodrigo Ovéquez and one in 1093 between Bishop Pedro of León and the *infanzones* of Valle de Vernisga can be cited.[123] In some cases a group of *infanzones* from a particular locality were impleaded collectively. This was so in the suit with the bishop of León just cited; in that between Alfonso VI and the *infanzones* of Langreo and in an earlier case between the abbot of Cardeña and the *infanzones* of Valle de Orbaneja.[124] Towns rarely appeared in the king's court in this period, but in 1149 the men of Castrotorafe were the defendants in a suit with the chapter of Santiago de Compostela.[125] Free tenants of the monasteries, or those who claimed to be free tenants, were from time to time impleaded either as individuals or as groups. In 1077 the abbot and monks of San Millán complained that two tenants refused to do services for their holdings 'quia dicunt illi genuos vel absolutos ab omni servitio debemus esse'.[126] In 1091 the men of Villavicencio refused to recognise the lordship of the abbot of Sahagún, and the consequential suit was heard in the king's court; it was ended by the submission of the villagers.[127]

Most of these suits were either land suits or suits concerning ecclesiastical patronage which was treated as a matter of real property. In times of strong government the church used the king's court to regain lands lost during periods of disorder. So, in 1078, Bishop Vistruario of Lugo sued Counts Vela, Ovela and Rodrigo Ovéquez for possessions held by the church of Lugo at the death of Fernando I, but lost during the civil wars between his sons.[128] In 1093 Bishop Pedro of León claimed lands which had once belonged to the see, but which were then held by a number of *infanzones* whose fathers and grandfathers had held them, and who refused to surrender them 'nisi iudicio

[122] *HC*, 74–84, 374–8.
[123] *ES*, xl, *ap.* xxviii (28 Feb. 1078); xxxvi, *ap.* xxxvii (2 Dec. 1098); also in *DHILC*, no. xxvii.
[124] *Fuentes de Castilla*, iii, no. xiv (17 April 1073).
[125] López Ferreiro, *Iglesia de Santiago*, iv, *ap.* xviii (8 March 1149).
[126] *Cartulario de S. Millán*, no. 232.
[127] *DHILC*, no. xxvi (5 Aug. 1091).
[128] *ES*, xl, *ap.* xxviii (28 Feb. 1078).

et imperio Regis'.[129] Patronage cases included one in 1078 between the monastery of San Vicente de Oviedo and Count Muño González, in which both parties claimed the church of San Pedro in Valle de Pravia by gift of its founder.[130] Although in cases between the church and a layman, the sentence was usually in favour of the church, this was not always so, and in 1118 a certain Muño made good his claim to half the church of San Mamed de Touros, against Abbot Pedro of Santa María de Ribeira.[131] Other suits concerned pasturage rights, as that between the abbot of Cardeña and the *infanzones* of Valle de Orbaneja,[132] or questions of lordship and service, as in that between the abbot of Sahagún and the men of Villavicencio.[133]

The procedure followed by the king's court was that laid down in the *Forum judicum*, although its rules were probably not rigorously applied, and suits were begun by simple petition and answer. Hearings were public, oral and formalistic as in all Germanic judicial systems. Under the *Forum judicum* advocates (*assertores*) could be appointed to present a litigant's case. In the two cases in which Bishop Arias of Oviedo claimed the monastery of San Salvador de Tol from lay ex-propriators, *assertores* appeared for both parties.[134] In the suit between Abbot Diego and the monks of Sahagún against the men of Villavicen-cio, Count Martín Laínez appeared as *assertor* for the latter – 'in voce de homines iam supradictos'.[135] This practice did not extend to Castile, but *assertores* were sometimes appointed in cases involving Castilian litigants as, for example, in 1073 when the Cid, Rodrigo Díaz, and Don Cipriano, *merino* of Burgos, appeared as *assertores* for Abbot Sisebut of Cardeña – 'qui tenebant voce de abbate domno Sisebuto de Karadigna'.[136] Bishops and magnates usually attended in person; when a monastery was involved, it was generally the abbot who came to court.

But what of collective litigants, such as groups of *infanzones*? Did all attend, or a selected number? What of communities such as cathedral chapters or towns? How did they appear before the king's

[129] *DHILC*, no. xxvii (2 Dec. 1093); also publ. *ES*, xxxvi, *ap*. xxxvii.
[130] *Cartulario de S. Vicente*, no. 79 (p. 86).
[131] Sáez, 'El monasterio de Santa María de Ribeira', *Hispania*, iv, no. 7 (pp. 188–9) (5 July 1118).
[132] *Fuentes de Castilla*, iii, no. xiv (17 April 1073).
[133] *DHILC*, no. xxvi (5 Aug. 1091).
[134] *ES*, xxxviii, *aps*. xix (26 March 1075), xx (13 Aug. 1083). The procedure was the same in both cases.
[135] *DHILC*, no. xxvi (5 Aug. 1091).
[136] *Fuentes de Castilla*, iii, no. xiv (17 April 1073).

court? The available evidence is scanty. In the three suits in which the *infanzones* of a certain district were impleaded, the names of a number of them were given: thirteen from Valle de Orbaneja, twenty-three from Valle de Langreo and nine from Valle de Vernisga, and, in the first case, it is definitely stated of those named that 'tenebant voce de homines de Valle de Orbanelia',[187] but at this period there seems to be no clear distinction between an advocate and a representative. It was not until the revived study of Roman law in the twelfth century had permeated through Western Europe that the legal theory of the corporate body reached its maturity, but before this the community had a real existence, even if it had not acquired a full legal personality. Some of the records from the later part of the period, towards the mid-twelfth century, provide evidence of a rudimentary form of representation. In the case in 1147 between Archbishop Pedro and the chapter of Santiago de Compostela and Abbot Roberto and the monks of Antealtares, the abbot was accompanied by one of his monks and the *cantor*; in 1149 one of the canons of Santiago was present with Archbishop Pedro and four men of Castrotorafe, of whom one 'erat uozeyrus de consilio', also attended.[188] We do not know how such persons were selected but, in the case of a cathedral or monastery, presumably in chapter and, in the case of a town, in the *concejo* or town council. Nor do we know what instructions or powers they may have reeived from those they 'represented'.

After each litigant had presented his case, *ad hoc* judges were appointed by the king in the presence of, and from among, the members of the curia.[139] It was the function of these judges to give judgment of proof. At times the whole curia was joined with the judges in the judgment.[140] There are also records of cases in which there were no references to *ad hoc* judges, and the judgment was given by the curia or by the king with the advice of the curia, while in some records phrases such as 'iudicauit rex' or 'iudicauit dominus Imperator' were used, as though judgment was given by the sovereign alone.[141]

---

[187] *Ibid.* III, no. xiv (17 April 1073); *DHILC*, no. xix (27 March 1075), xxvii (2 Dec. 1093).

[188] López Ferreiro, *Iglesia de Santiago*, iv, *ap*. xviii.

[139] *ES*, xxxviii, *aps*. xix (26 March 1075), xx (13 Aug. 1083).

[140] *Cartulario de S. Millán*, no. 234 (1077): 'sicut iudicatum fuerat a iudicibus et a nostra curia'.

[141] Llorente, *Provincias vascongadas*, iv, no. 117 (pp. 74–5) (3 Nov. 1140); *DHILC*, no. xxvi (pp. 39–40) (5 Aug. 1091); *Cartulario de S. Millán*, no. 289 (1099); López Ferreiro, *Iglesia de Santiago*, iv, *ap*. xviii (1 March 1149). Cf. Guglielmi, *CHE*, xxiii–xxiv, 257.

Two cases, determined on consecutive days before an enlarged curia on 26 and 27 March 1075, on the occasion of Alfonso VI's visit to Oviedo, together provide references to nearly all the types of proof used in the king's court. On 26 March in the suit between Arias, bishop of Oviedo, and Counts Vela and Bermudo Ovéquez for the possession of the monastery of San Salvador de Tol, both parties produced their title-deeds; those put forward by the counts were pronounced by the judges to be false – 'non esse autenticas'; those produced by the bishop were then examined, and reference was made 'ad Librum judicum' on the question of the donor's right to make the grant, and on the church's right to hold in perpetuity land which it had held unchallenged for thirty years. Judgment was then given that two clerks of the cathedral of Oviedo should swear to the authenticity of the documents produced by the bishop. At this point the counts decided to compromise and reach agreement with the bishop, so as to avoid being liable for the pecuniary penalties laid down in the bishop's charters, should their authenticity be upheld.[142] In the suit on the following day King Alfonso himself was one of the parties. On 14 March he had granted the *mandatio* of Valle de Langreo to the church of Oviedo, but the *infanzones* who lived in the district pleaded that their lands were alodial and that their grandfathers and fathers had held them 'sine ullo tributo regali vel servitio fiscali' and that they, therefore, owed no services to the church. The king, Alfonso VI, asserted that the lands in question had been royal demesne of the kings of León from the time of Alfonso V. The king offered proof by battle, between a knight and any one of the *infanzones*, or trial *per Librum judicum*, but the *infanzones* sought and obtained, through the good offices of the Infanta Doña Urraca and the members of the curia, proof 'per veridicos exquisitores', a method which in the event went against them and vindicated the king.[143]

Thus, in these two suits we have references to documentary proof, judgment *per Librum judicum*, oath, trial by battle, inquisition and compromise between parties. Documentary proof in this period was rarely accepted by itself, but was generally combined with oath or inquisition. Oaths were also exacted in cases where no documents were produced, as in the land suit between Bishop Pedro of León and the *infanzones* of Valle de Vernisga, when the judgment was that the

---

[142] *ES*, xxxviii, *ap.* no. xix; also Menéndez Pidal, *España del Cid*, ii, 847–51; for comment, see *ibid.* i, 215–16.
[143] *DHILC*, no. xix (pp. 30–1); also *ES*, xxxviii, *ap.* xxii; for comment, see *ibid.* 85–6, and Menéndez Pidal, *España del Cid*, i, 216–17.

bishop should prove his case by the oaths of three clerks of the church of León.[144] Judgment *per Librum judicum* or *juicio del Libro* was judgment, as we have seen, according to the precepts laid down in the Visigothic *Liber judicum*, a manuscript of which was kept in the eleventh century in the church of San Isidoro in León, in the charge of one of the canons of the church, who judged by it. It was used only in cases in which the litigants were Leonese.

Trial by battle was the only form of ordeal used in the royal court, and was probably exceptional. Alfonso VI's revised rules of procedure in cases between Christians and Jews permitted, as one method, trial by combat with shields and staves, either between the litigants themselves, or between champions who fought in their stead. The regulations favoured the Christian, who had the right to decide whether champions should be employed or not. If the Jew were defeated, the pecuniary penalty appropriate to the case was divided between the Christian suitor and the king, but if the Christian were defeated, the whole sum went to the king, whose chattels the Jews were.[145] Cases between Christians and Jews were probably decided in local courts, but the procedure in the king's court would be the same. It was sometimes used in boundary suits: thus, the boundaries between Segovia and Avila were settled *post litem* under Alfonso VII.[146] Combat on horseback took place in the procedure known as *reto*, which was used in suits between nobles concerned with questions of personal honour, such as accusations of breach of faith or treachery.

Inquisition, later to be known in the vernacular as *pesquisa*, was a form of inquiry by which specially appointed *inquisitores* took sworn evidence on questions of fact locally, and it is analogous to the English inquest. It was used, for example, in cases of ecclesiastical patronage, and in land and boundary suits. The records of this period do not give much detail about the procedure, but the inquisitors, who were men of position and substance, were either appointed by the litigants, as in the suit between Alfonso VI and the *infanzones* of Valle de Langreo, when the king appointed Count Muño Gonsálvez and the *infanzones* appointed Juan Ordóñez, a member of the curia, or else they were appointed by the king as president of the court, as in the suit between the canons of Santiago de Compostela and the men of Castrotorafe in 1149, when Alfonso VII appointed as inquisitors Bishop Bernardo of Zamora and

---

[144] *DHILC*, no. xxvii (pp. 40–3) (2 Dec. 1093); *ES*, xxxvi, *ap.* xxxvii.
[145] *DHILC*, no. xxv (pp. 36–7) (31 March 1091); *ES*, xxxv, *ap.* i (pp. 411–14).
[146] González, *Reino de Castilla*, ii, no. 169: confirmation of Alfonso VIII.

two justices of Zamora. Evidence was taken locally from among the older and wiser inhabitants.[147] In the case between Alfonso VI and the *infanzones* of Valle de Langreo, the procedure was extremely rapid. The king's grant to the church of Oviedo was dated 14 March and the final sentence was pronounced on 27 March. But the case was exceptional: the king was a party to the suit; he and his court were in the vicinity, and the inquiry was carried out on the spot. Many, perhaps most, suits were terminated by agreement, after judgment of proof had been given, but before the proof had been carried out, when one litigant feared that the proof would go against him and thought it politic to come to terms.[148]

As in all legal systems largely based on Germanic custom, there was no clear distinction between civil and criminal cases, and all suits were initiated by private accusation. There are no records of what we should call criminal cases, but there are many references to *calumniae*, actions which were punishable by fines (*caloñas*) to the king, as well as involving compensation to the injured party. These *calumniae* were reserved for the hearing of royal judges ('pertinent ad voz regie') and correspond to crown pleas in England. They included homicide, rape, violence and theft. In many royal grants of immunities to churches, these crown pleas are enumerated either because they were reserved to the crown, or else because they were specifically granted away, in which case no royal *merino* or other official might enter the *coto*: 'nec pro furto, nec pro rauso, nec pro homicidio, nec pro forcia, nec pro calupnia aliqua', as Alfonso VII's confirmation of the *coto* of the cathedral of Túy has it.[149]

These different functions were in most cases exercised by the curia in all its forms – restricted, provincial, augmented or extraordinary – but some distinction, according to function, can be discerned between the small and the great curia. Consent to donations was normally a function of the small curia, but some of the donations to which consent was asked were granted in an augmented or extraordinary curia. In such cases the reason was probably convenience; bishops, abbots and lay magnates specially summoned to attend a curia used the opportunity to ask for new privileges or the confirmation of existing ones. Thus, Alfonso VII confirmed the *coto* of Santiago de Compostela in 1127,

[147] *DHILC*, no. xix; López Ferreiro, *Iglesia de Santiago*, iv, *ap.* xviii.
[148] E.g. *DHILC*, nos. xxvi (5 Aug. 1091), xxvii (2 Dec. 1093).
[149] *ES*, xxii, *ap.* x (Aug. 1142); see also *ES*, xvi, *ap.* xx: grant by Alfonso VI to the church of Astorga (18 Feb. 1085); *ES*, xxxvi, *ap.* xliii: grant by Urraca to church of León (22 July 1109).

after his mother's grant had been read 'coram omni concilio nobilium meorum uirorum' and in 1149 a donation was made: 'et tota curia imperatoris cum episcopis qui ibi aderant et proceribus suis, visores, auditores et confirmatores'.[150] The renewal of Alfonso VI's promise to double the *censum* paid to Cluny was clearly the direct result of the visit of Abbot Hugh of Cluny to Alfonso VI, then holding a great curia in Burgos.[151] Justice was generally administered in the restricted curia, but some cases were heard in great assemblies. Here the status of the suitors might be a decisive factor. Suits in which the king or other members of the royal family were involved were heard before the extraordinary curia as, for example, the suits between Alfonso VI and the *infanzones* of Langreo in 1075, that between the Infanta Doña Urraca and Bishop Pedro of León in 1089 and that between Alfonso VII and Archbishop Diego Gelmírez of Santiago de Compostela in 1126, all of which were heard before the curia in its largest forms.[152] Other suits heard in the great curia included the two brought by Bishop Arias of Oviedo over the possession of the monastery of San Salvador de Tol.[153] The final settlement of the dispute between Bishop Martín of Oviedo and Bishop Juan of Lugo was made possible by the royal grant of Castello de Suaron to the church of Oviedo in an assembly on 2 January 1154, comprising most of the lay and ecclesiastical magnates of the kingdom; the actual agreement between the two bishops was made on 19 January before Alfonso VII and all the bishops of the kingdom.[154] Not all suits in which bishops were involved were heard before the great curia; the suit brought by Bishop Pedro of León against the *infanzones* of Valle de Vernisga seems to have been heard in the small curia and the charter recording the agreement made between the two parties was confirmed by only eleven persons.[155] Matters of policy and questions of peace and war were usually debated in specially summoned assemblies or with the magnates present with the army, before or during a campaign. Urraca was recognised as Alfonso VI's heir by all the magnates assembled in the host at Toledo;[156] as queen, she took counsel with a specially summoned assembly of bishops

---

[150] López Ferreiro, *Iglesia de Santiago*, IV, *ap.* V; *Fuentes de Castilla*, I, no. XIII (pp. 58–60) (15 Feb. 1149).
[151] *RC Cluny*, IV, no. 3638: 'cum…ceteris episcopis meis et primoribus regni mei'.
[152] *DHILC*, no. XIX (pp. 29–31); Sánchez-Albornoz, *Estudios*, no. VI (p. 307); *HC*, 435–9.
[153] *ES*, XXXVIII, *aps.* XIX, XX.
[154] *CDC Oviedo*, nos. 162, 163.
[155] *DHILC*, no. XXVII (pp. 40–3).
[156] *HC*, 115.

and magnates at Sahagún before her reconciliation with her son in 1116.[157] Alfonso VII, in 1133, 'convocavit omnes comites suos et maiores regni sui et duces' and consulted them on his intention to invade Andalusia.[158] On some occasions, however, the wording suggests a small body of selected advisers. Thus, Alfonso VII pardoned the rebel Gonzalo Pérez and granted him Luna, after consulting Queen Berenguela, the Infanta Doña Sancha and other counsellors whom he knew to be prudent in such matters.[159] In 1139 he ordered the siege of Oreja 'consilio accepto cum propriis consiliaribus'.[160] General legislation, which applied to all the king's dominions, such as that promulgated on the occasion of Alfonso VII's coronation as Emperor, was announced in the great curia. Taken as a whole the evidence shows that the more important matters of policy were generally dealt with in the great curia, but that in some cases the division of business between the different forms of the curia was a simple question of convenience.

[157] *Ibid.* 225.
[158] *CAI*, § 33 (p. 30).
[159] *Ibid.* § 45 (pp. 37–8).
[160] *Ibid.* § 145 (p. 113).

2

The *curia regis* in the separate kingdom of León
(1157–1230)

With the death of Alfonso VII and the division of his dominions between his two sons, it becomes necessary to consider the curia in the two kingdoms of León and Castile separately in order to trace the developments which took place in each and to determine the differences between them. In both countries, the general characteristics of the curia remained the same as they had been in the preceding period, but various alterations and developments can be discerned, and they are not identical for the two kingdoms.

León is badly served by narrative sources. There are no contemporary chronicles of any length for the second half of the twelfth century and of those written in the first half of the thirteenth century, the *Crónica latina de los reyes de Castilla*, as its modern name implies, treats of Castile, and refers to León only incidentally; the *De rebus Hispaniae* of Rodrigo of Toledo is also very definitely centred on Castile, leaving only the *Chronicon mundi* of Lucas of Túy written from a Leonese point of view. On the other hand, documentary records are more numerous than for the earlier period. There is also a considerable body of legislative enactments.

Under Fernando II (1157–88) the term *concilium* continued to be used in the dating clause of various documents passed at the time of the assembly held at Salamanca in September 1178,[1] although the agreement between the Orders of the Temple, the Hospital and Santiago, made in the Council, used the term *curia*.[2] *Concilium* was also used to describe the assembly held at Benavente in 1181.[3] Under Alfonso IX

---

[1] González, *Regesta*, 459–60: 'Facta carta apud Salamancam, in celebratione generalis concilii, mense Septembris, sub era MCCXVI'.

[2] García Larragueta, 'La Orden de San Juan en la crisis del Imperio hispánico del siglo XII', *Hispania*, XII, no. 20 (pp. 516–17): 'era MCCXVI, mense Septembris, quando rex Fernandus habuit curiam suam in Salmantica'.

[3] González, *Regesta*, no. 41: 'a tempore illo quando concilium meum cum meis baronibus feci apud Beneuentum'.

the term *curia* was used indifferently for all meetings, whatever their composition. Thus, it was used for extraordinary assemblies in 1188, 1208 and 1217[4] as well as on frequent occasions for the ordinary sessions of the small curia. We do not find in León, as we do in Aragon and Catalonia, during the first half of the thirteenth century, the use of the attributive adjectives *solemnis* or *generalis* with *curia* to distinguish the great from the small assemblies.[5] It is possible, however, that such phrases as 'de rogatu nobilium totius curie' or 'cum tota curia mea' denoted an extraordinary assembly, but we have too little evidence of composition on the occasions when they were used to be certain of this.[6] Modern Spanish historians use the description *curias plenas* when referring to the meetings of the extraordinary curia. This is convenient, provided it is realised that it does not conform to medieval usage. *Plena* is used with *curia* only in the ablative in the phrase 'in plena curia', and it appears but rarely in León. It was used in the decrees issued at Benavente in 1202: 'Hec acta sunt...apud Benaventum in plena curia.' This was certainly an extraordinary assembly, and one at which citizens were present; its business was largely judicial.[7] It was not used, however, for the assemblies in 1188 and 1208, at both of which the towns were represented, nor at those of 1194 and 1217, which were extraordinary meetings but without the participation of the towns.[8] A few other documents contain the phrase 'in plena curia'. In a record of a land suit heard before the king at Oviedo in 1200, reference was made to the sale of lands 'coram rege Adelfonso in plena curia'.[9] A document of Alfonso IX conceded that vassals of the bishop of León should pay *yantar* with the bishop and not with the *concejo* of León, 'sicut iam alia uice in plena curia mea mandaui et concessi'. This appears to refer back to a former judicial decision.[10] An attestation of 1221 that Gil Manrique did homage for the castle of Villalobos was dated 'Facta carta apud Cemoram et confirmata in plena curia domini regis et in concilio'.[11] This act of homage does appear to have taken

[4] González, *Alfonso IX*, II, nos. 11, 223, 342.
[5] For Aragon, see Miret i Sans, *Itinerari de Jaume I*, 25; *CD Jaime I*, nos. CLIII, CLIV. For Catalonia, see Procter, 'The development of the Catalan *Corts* in the thirteenth century', *Homenatge a Rubió i Lluch*, III, 534–7, and references given there.
[6] González, *Regesta*, 471 (1 Aug. 1180); *Alfonso IX*, II, nos. 38 (23 Nov. 1190), 419 (7 March 1222), 625 (n.d.).
[7] González, *Alfonso IX*, II, no. 167 (11 March 1202).
[8] *Ibid.* II, nos. 11, 84, 223, 342.
[9] *CDC Oviedo*, no. 215.
[10] González, *Alfonso IX*, II, no. 413 (20 Oct. 1221).
[11] *Ibid.* II, no. 415 (14 Nov. 1221).

place in a great assembly, although nothing else is known about it, but
the other two examples hardly appear to be sufficiently important to
have taken place in great assemblies. What, then, does 'in plena curia'
mean? It is possible that it denotes a public or open session at which
suits might be heard and homage done, although it is clearly used but
rarely, and the great curia was not entitled *curia plena*.[12]

The most striking addition to the composition of the curia during
this period was the attendance on at least three occasions of citizens
and townsmen. Their presence was attested in the preambles of
ordinances promulgated by Alfonso IX in 1188, 1202 and 1208. This
is by far the most important development in the history of the curia,
but we shall reserve discussion of it for a later chapter.[13] Otherwise,
there were not many differences in the composition of either the
restricted or the enlarged curia from the earlier period. The number of
confirmantes in solemn documents under both Fernando II and Alfonso
IX (1188–1230) varied from ten to twenty-five with few exceptions
and they consisted almost exclusively of prelates and *tenentes*.

From the beginning of the reign of Fernando II a new form of
document – the *carta rodada* – appeared. It took its name from the
rueda, a circular device modelled on the papal *rota* which became one
of the main signs of authenticity. The *rueda* consisted of a lion enclosed
in two concentric circles, between which was the legend: 'Signum
Fernandi regis Legionis' (or, after 1162, 'regis Hispaniorum'), or,
under Alfonso IX, 'Signum Adefonsi regis Legionis'. Under the latter
king, the *rueda* was not used on all solemn privileges. Frequently the
signum – the lion – was depicted without the enclosing circles. There
were also solemn documents without either *rueda* or *signum*, but simply
with the *confirmantes*; this type of document increased in number
towards the end of Alfonso's reign.[14] The formulas of the solemn
privileges of the independent Leonese kings did not differ materially
from those used under Alfonso VII, but the layout of the documents
becomes increasingly stereotyped. The *rueda* or *signum* was drawn at
the foot of the document in the centre; above was the subscription of
the king, below, the names of the chancery officials. The *confirmantes*
were ranged in columns to either side of the *rueda*, the bishops in the
first column and the lay magnates in the second. Individual documents

---

[12] I have not found 'in Plena curia' used in documents of the first half of the
twelfth century, but *HC*, 437–40, uses 'coram plenaria curia' when referring to
the suit between Alfonso VII and Archbishop Diego Gelmírez in 1126.
[13] Chapter 5, below.
[14] Millares Carlo, *Paleografía española*, 205–7.

show variations, but the above was the usual pattern. Far simpler were the letters patent (*cartas abiertas*) and the mandates (*mandatos*) – the latter without *confirmantes* – comparatively few of which have survived from this period.[15] Members of the royal family were included in the royal superscription and subscription, but not normally among the *confirmantes*. The archbishop of Santiago and eleven bishops – those of Orense, Lugo, Mondoñedo, Astorga, Coria, León, Oviedo, Túy, Salamanca, Zamora and, from *circa* 1165, Ciudad Rodrigo – owed allegiance to the kings of León. For a short period in 1162 and 1163, when Fernando II occupied a large part of the kingdom of Castile, the archbishop of Toledo and some of the Castilian bishops also confirmed.[16] From 1179 the chancery began to note episcopal vacancies in the list of *confirmantes* in such phrases as 'vacat Cauriensis' or 'sede Cauriensi vacante'.[17] Very occasionally an abbot appeared among the *confirmantes*, sometimes seemingly because the document in question concerned his abbey,[18] but there were cases which cannot be accounted for thus.[19] We know, however, that abbots attended extraordinary meetings of the curia as, for example, the Council of Salamanca in 1178.[20]

Only two of the great officials appeared regularly – the *mayordomo* and the *alférez* (who during both reigns was called *signifer*). From 1206 to 1210 no *mayordomo* confirmed. Under Alfonso IX, a *submaiordomus* appeared from time to time and, between 1198 and 1204, during Alfonso's marriage to Berenguela of Castile, a *maiordomus reginae*. The separation of the kingdoms involved alterations in the titular chancellorship of the archbishops of Santiago de Compostela, and in 1158 Fernando II confirmed Archbishop Martín as chancellor of the kingdom of León, but the work continued to be carried out by a deputy.[21] Under Alfonso IX *merinos* of León, Galicia and Extremadura appeared from time to time, but there were also periods during which these provincial officials were not mentioned.[22] In Fernando II's documents a number of magnates bore the title *comes*, but in the following

---

[15] For a detailed account of the diplomatic of the documents of the Leonese kings, see González, *Regesta*, 161–237; *Alfonso IX*, i, 479–564.
[16] González, *Regesta*, nos. 8, 9.
[17] *Ibid.* nos. 37, 41; *Alfonso IX*, ii, nos. 112, 113, 115, 121; for references to other vacancies, nos. 208, 209, 280, 282, 283, 593, 594, 598.
[18] *Alfonso IX*, ii, nos. 233, 355, 357.
[19] *Ibid.* ii, no. 137.
[20] *ES*, xviii, *ap.* xxv.
[21] Millares Carlo, *AHDE*, iii, 261–3.
[22] For Alfonso's lay officials, see González, *Alfonso IX*, i, 322–7.

reign this title appeared less and less frequently until by the end of the reign it had virtually died out. The majority of the lay magnates held *tenencias*, although in the early years of Fernando II's reign the *tenencia* was rarely noted; after 1167 the formulas used were 'N. dominans in M.', or 'N. tenens M.', or simply 'N. in M.'. Both *mayordomo* and *signifer* could hold *tenencias* and several were often held by one person, especially in the later years of Alfonso IX's reign.[23] Besides the *tenentes*, other magnates appeared who were qualified as *vassali*. Most of these were Castilian or Portuguese exiles, who had found a refuge at the court of León. Occasionally the title *judex* was appended to a name, and evidence of the presence of professional judges and legists at court is to be found in documents containing judicial sentences. Under Fernando II the masters of the Temple in León and of the Order of Santiago (founded 1170) and the prior of the Order of St John sometimes confirmed, but not frequently. They rarely appeared in Alfonso IX's documents.[24]

As in the earlier period, the question arises, how far is it safe to assume that the inclusion of the name of a bishop or *tenente* among the *confirmantes* is proof of his actual presence at court? In some cases, mainly, but not exclusively, in texts of treaties, the lists are headed with some such phrase as 'Isti sunt qui presentes fuerunt.'[25] But what are we to conclude when no such indication is given? The marked variations in numbers still seem proof of presence, but there are also arguments on the other side. We have already noted that episcopal vacancies were recorded from 1179. From 1191 the names of the *confirmantes* were no longer given in the nominative, but in the ablative, with or without *existente*, and thus 'Petro Compostellano archiepiscope existente' takes the place of 'Petrus Compostellanus archiepiscopus conf.', etc. This may be significant for our purpose, or it may be a mere change in chancery usage. Towards the end of Alfonso IX's reign, the number of occasions on which the archbishop and all the eleven bishops were named were very numerous. Again, the names of the archbishop of Santiago de Compostela and the bishops of Oviedo, León, Salamanca, Ciudad Rodrigo, Astorga and Orense all appeared in a document of

---

[23] For a list of *tenencias* and *tenentes* under Alfonso IX, see *ibid.* I, 347–61.

[24] E.g. González, *Regesta*, nos. 40, 41, 52; also pp. 458, 468, 475, 479, 495, 507 (various dates between 1178 and 1186).

[25] *CDC Oviedo*, nos. 173 (March 1161), 178 (6 July 1164): grants to the bishop of Oviedo; González, *Alfonso IX*, II, nos. 135 (8 Dec. 1199), 205(26 March 1206), 251 (27 June 1209): treaties between León and Castile.

17 October 1215,[26] but we know that they attended the Fourth Lateran Council which opened on 11 November,[27] and this allows a very short time to get from Castell Rodrigo on the Portuguese frontier to Rome. The most we can say is that, while for the reign of Fernando II it seems probable that the *confirmantes* were present, it might be rash to assume that this continued to be so after the accession of Alfonso IX.

For the meetings of the extraordinary curia all or most of the lay and ecclesiastical magnates were summoned, as is shown by the use in documents of such phrases as 'cum consilio et deliberatione episco-porum, comitum et baronum nostrorum', or 'cum aliquantis Episcopis et abbatibus, convocatis hinc inde Comitibus Regni et Baronibus et ceteris rectoribus Provinciarum', or 'cum prelatorum et judicum consilio et deliberatione atque omnium principum nostrorum con-sensu'.[28]

Because of the dearth of narrative sources for León, little is known of the political activities of the curia, but it appears to have continued and, perhaps, to have increased its intervention during this period. It was only at the time of Alfonso IX's death in 1230 that any serious question arose about the succession. When Alfonso VII died on 21 August 1157, recrossing the Sierra Morena after a campaign in Andalusia, his second son, Fernando, left the army hastily with his magnates and returned to León to make sure of his kingdom.[29] On his death in 1188, his son, Alfonso, was accepted as king of León in spite of the hostility and intrigues of his Castilian stepmother, Urraca López.[30] The succession question in 1230 was far more complicated. Alfonso IX was twice married – to Teresa, daughter of Sancho I of Portugal, and to Berenguela, daughter of Alfonso VIII of Castile. Both marriages were within the prohibited degrees of consanguinity and both were dissolved at the behest of the papacy. The marriage with Teresa took place in 1191 and was dissolved in 1194; of her three children – Sancha, Fernando and Dulce – the two younger returned to Portugal with their mother.[31] The marriage to Berenguela took place in

---

[26] González, *Alfonso IX*, II, no. 329.
[27] Rivera, 'Personajes hispanos asistentes en 1215 al IV Concilio de Letrán', *Hispania Sacra*, IV, 335-55.
[28] González, *Regesta*, 395 (15 July 1167); *ES*, XVIII, *ap.* XXV (10 Sept. 1178); González, *Alfonso IX*, II, no. 85 (undated, but refers to decrees issued at León in 1194).
[29] Rodrigo, *De rebus Hispaniae*, lib. VII, *cap.* XI.
[30] González, *Alfonso IX*, I, 37-8, 43-5.
[31] *Ibid.* I, 60-3, 66.

1197, as a means of restoring peace with Castile. It was denounced by Innocent III who, in 1199, declared any children of the marriage to be illegitimate.[32] It was presumably this which led Alfonso VIII of Castile to insist that his grandson, Fernando, born to Berenguela early in August 1201, should be recognised as Alfonso IX's heir and that the whole kingdom of León should swear to this.[33] We do not know how or when this oath was taken. The marriage was dissolved in 1204 and Berenguela returned to Castile, but retained the title Queen of León. By the Treaty of Cabreros in 1206 between Alfonso VIII and Alfonso IX, her son Fernando was again acknowledged as heir to his father, who undertook that homage should be done to him.[34] Again, we do not know when or by whom this homage was done. The death of Teresa's son, another Fernando, in 1214 removed a possible future claimant to the throne of León, but the accession of Berenguela's son, Fernando III to the throne of Castile in 1217 complicated matters, as the union of the two kingdoms of León and Castile in his person would inevitably mean the absorption of the older but smaller kingdom by the more powerful Castile. In an attempt to save the independent identity of León and out of hostility to Castile, Alfonso IX left his kingdom by will to his two daughters, that is to say, Sancha and Dulce, his surviving children by his first wife. Fernando's claims were, however, supported by the towns of León and he was duly proclaimed king in November 1230. Rodrigo of Toledo adds to his account the statement that it was because of the oath taken to Fernando at Alfonso VIII of Castile's insistence that his half-sisters failed to obtain the kingdom.[35] We cannot determine the extent of the intervention of the curia in these various marriage negotiations but we know that it was with the advice of his *familiares*, a word which suggests a small inner circle of counsellors, that Alfonso IX sought Berenguela's hand in marriage,[36] and in 1217 he had certainly endowed his daughters, Sancha and Dulce, with a number of towns and castles 'una cum consensu curie mee'.[37]

We have seen in the preceding chapter that during the first half of the twelfth century the curia in the kingdom of León–Castile, generally in its augmented form, was consulted on the making of war, peace and

---

[32] *Documentación pontificia hasta Inocencio III*, no. 196 (p. 214).
[33] *Ibid.* nos. 276 (5 June 1203): Innocent III to Alfonso VIII; 305 (20 June 1204): Innocent III to the archbishops of Toledo and Compostela, etc.
[34] González, *Alfonso IX*, II, no. 205 (26 March 1206).
[35] *Crónica latina*, 104–5; Rodrigo, *De rebus Hispaniae, lib.* VII, *cap.* XXV.
[36] Rodrigo, *De rebus Hispaniae, lib.* VII, *cap.* XXXI.
[37] González, *Alfonso IX*, II, no. 342 (6 Jan. 1217).

treaties. For the reigns of Fernando II and Alfonso IX of León evidence of consultation is scanty. In the short war between León and Castile in 1158 Fernando II consulted his magnates before meeting Sancho III at Sahagún.[38] As in the past, the texts of treaties of peace were normally witnessed by a number of bishops and magnates from both the contracting kingdoms, some of whom had probably carried out the preliminary negotiations leading up to the treaty. The text of the Treaty of Fresno–Lavandera between Fernando II and Alfonso VIII in 1183 gives considerable information about such negotiations. A small commission consisting, for Castile, of the archbishop of Toledo, the bishop of Avila and the prior of the Hospital, and, for León, of the archbishop of Santiago de Compostela, the bishop of Ciudad Rodrigo and the master of the Temple, was appointed to discuss terms of peace, and held a preliminary meeting at Paradinas, where a tentative agreement was drawn up. Finally, the two kings met between Fresno and Lavandera, and the text of the treaty was agreed and ratified in the presence of the members of the commission, together with the bishops of Lugo, Burgos, Segovia, Osma and Albarracín 'et multi de utroque regno, principes et nobiles et alii plurimi'.[39]

Alfonso IX, in the decrees which were promulgated at the first curia of his reign at León, in 1188, at which citizens (*cives*) as well as bishops and nobles were present, promised 'quod non faciam guerram vel pacem vel placitum, nisi cum consilio episcoporum, nobilium et bonorum hominum per quorum consilium debeo regi'.[40] The *boni homines* of this clause have been taken to be good men of the towns, and the clause has been interpreted as meaning that Alfonso undertook that, in the future, he would not make war, peace or a treaty without the advice of the bishops, lay magnates and representatives of the towns – that is, an assembly which would later be called *cortes*. It has been further assumed that Alfonso IX did, in fact, consult such assemblies before his various wars, although there is no evidence whatever that he did so.[41] But were the *boni homines* of this decree the good men of the towns? The term *boni homines* was not exclusively applied to townsmen at this period.[42] It is, in fact, used in three others of the decrees of

[38] Rodrigo, *De rebus Hispaniae, lib.* VII, *cap.* XIII.
[39] González, *Regesta*, no. 46; also in González, *Reino de Castilla*, II, no. 407.
[40] González, *Alfonso IX*, II, no. 11; also in *Cortes*, I, no. VII, cl. 3.
[41] Colmeiro, *Introducción*, 12, 143; G[arcía] de Valdeavellano, *Historia de España* 1045, and *Instituciones españolas*, 416; Piskorski, *Cortes*, 188; Guglielmi, *CHE*, XXVIII, 86.
[42] Carlé, 'Boni homines y hombres buenos', *CHE*, XXXIX–XL, 133–68, discusses the

1188, in none of which were the *boni homines* referred to in fact townsmen. In the preamble and the conclusion of the document quoted above, the representatives were called *cives*. If Alfonso IX had intended to associate representatives of cities and towns with questions of foreign policy, why not use *cives* instead of the ambiguous *boni homines*? Who then were the *boni homines* of this decree? The most probable solution is that they were members of the curia who were neither bishops nor magnates. This was indeed a common use of the term during the thirteenth century, when such phrases as 'avido conseio... con los obispos y con los ricos omes y con otros omes buenos de nuestra corte' occur again and again in documents.[43] Thus, the undertaking given by the king in 1188 did not constitute a new limitation on the king's power, but was simply a pledge to observe the custom followed under earlier sovereigns.

In the earlier years of Fernando II's reign, references in donations to the advice or consent of the curia were few, although they occasionally occurred, as, for example, in 1167 when the king extended the *coto* of the cathedral of Lugo with the advice of his bishops, counts and barons.[44] After 1176, however, the curia took a quite unaccustomed part in grants of lands, privileges and immunities, and phrases such as 'de consilio curie mee', or 'de rogatu curie', or the like, occur in numerous instances.[45] These donations were made to churches, monasteries and the military orders. Some of them were made in great assemblies, as, for example, a grant to the monastery of San Pelayo de Oviedo dated 'in celebratione generalis concilii' at Salamanca in 1178.[46] This active participation of the curia was apparently due to the prodigality of the king, which seriously weakened the financial position of the crown. In 1181 an act of resumption was agreed on at the great curia at Benavente and a further resumption was decreed by Alfonso IX, in accord with the decision of the Curia of León in 1188.[47]

During Alfonso IX's reign specific references to the participation of

different meanings of *boni homines* but assumes (p. 153, n. 82) that in this decree they were representatives of the towns.

[43] See Procter, 'The interpretation of clause 3 of the decrees of León (1188)', *EHR*, LXXXV, 45–53, for a detailed consideration of this question.

[44] González, *Regesta*, 395 (15 July 1167).

[45] E.g. *ibid.* nos. 37, 38, 42, 49, 54; see also pp. 444, 449, 450, 451, 456, 467, 468, 471, 472, 486, 493, 494, 495, for documents of various dates from 1176 to 1184.

[46] Cited in González, *Regesta*, 459.

[47] *Ibid.* no. 41 (30 March 1181); González, *Alfonso IX*, II, no. 662 (n.d.); see also no. 5 (4 May 1188) for a reference to the excessive liberality of Fernando II.

the curia in donations occur from time to time, as, for example, in 1190 when the lordship of the bishop of Orense over the city was confirmed by the king 'inspiratione diuina et meorum fidelium inductis consiliis', and when various privileges were granted to the church of León 'de consilio tocius curie mee'.[48] In 1208 the canons of León were exempted from *portazgo* throughout the kingdom in the great curia 'cum assensu domini Petri, Compostellani archiepiscopi, ceterumque episcoporum, et principum optimatum et militum Regni mei'.[49] In 1211, after a dispute between the bishop and *concejo* of Túy, new *fueros* were granted by Alfonso IX 'habito consilio et deliberatione cum magnatibus et uassallis nostris qui presentes erant'.[50] There was, however, nothing under Alfonso IX that corresponded to the constant intervention of the curia in the latter years of his father's reign. This decrease in the curia's participation in the granting of donations may be due to the greater care which Alfonso IX exercised over the royal fisc, and partly, also, to a decline in the relative power of the nobles.[51]

The division of Alfonso VII's dominions into the separate kingdoms of León and Castile adversely affected the royal fisc in León, where much of the land was in the hands of the church and the nobles. Under Fernando II, from 1167 onwards, an impost called *petitum*, which was the *petitio* of Alfonso VII under another name, was frequently mentioned in documents. In grants of proportions of the royal rents of specific lands to monasteries and churches, *petitum* was generally included or, when towns were granted to churches, *petitum* was among the dues from which the inhabitants were exempted.[52] There is no evidence of how these levies were negotiated, nor how consent was obtained, nor is it possible to say how long the original conception of *petitum* as an occasional free gift lasted, and it may have survived until the last decade of the century. But *petitum* was increasingly associated in documents with *pecho*, *fonsadera* and *facendaria*, all of which were customary fiscal charges levied on the *pecheros*.[53] Nobles and their *solariegos* (serfs on the demesne land of a lord) were exempt from it, but the clergy and their tenants only if specially exempted until, in the

---

[48] González, *Alfonso IX*, II, nos. 37 (28 Sept. 1190), 38 (23 Nov. 1190).
[49] *Ibid.* II, no. 223 (Feb. 1208).
[50] *Ibid.* II, no. 275 (May 1211).
[51] *Ibid.* I, 226.
[52] Sánchez-Albornoz, *Estudios*, 503–5, and documents cited in n. 51 and published in González, *Regesta*, and *Alfonso IX*, II.
[53] Sánchez-Albornoz, *Estudios*, 510–16.

decrees of León of 1208, freedom for cathedral clergy from *petitum* was included in the privileges granted to the church in the Leonese kingdom.

About the time that *petitum* became a customary payment, a new tax – *moneda* – appeared. Among some judicial sentences pronounced by elected judges at Benavente in 1202 was one defining the regalian right of coinage. It was laid down that if the king wished to alter the value of his coinage, then all his subjects must receive it, but if either the king or his subjects wished for a sale of the coinage, that is, an undertaking by the king not to alter the coinage for a given period of years, in exchange for a capitation tax, then the consent of both parties was required, and, if agreed, only the canons of cathedral churches, and knights and their immediate households, were excused from the payment of this *moneda*. On this occasion Alfonso IX sold the coinage for seven years for a capitation tax of 1 *maravedí* from every non-exempt person.[54]

There is no definite evidence that the coinage was sold at any earlier meeting of the great curia. It is possible that there was such a transaction at Alfonso's first curia in 1188, which took place fourteen years before the curia of 1202. The beginning of a reign would be a natural time for an alteration of the coinage, but this is pure conjecture, nor is there any evidence that the great curia met seven years later in 1195. There are, however, some documents belonging to the decade before 1202, which may refer to this tax. One difficulty is that *moneda* means both the coinage and the tax in lieu of an alteration of the coinage, and it is not always certain which is the intended meaning. In November 1194 Alfonso IX granted to the Order of Santiago 'totam decimam mee monete de terra Legionis, Zamore, Villefrance et mearum Asturiarum', and a few weeks later 'decimam partem tallii totius monete regni mei'.[55] Then, again, in April 1195, he granted to Bishop Martín of Zamora and to the canons of the cathedral 'decimam partem mearum monetarum et portatici ac fructuum singulis annis mei cellarii de Cemora' as had formerly been granted to Bishop Bernardo by Alfonso VII and Fernando II.[56] Some years later, in 1199, Alfonso IX confirmed earlier concessions excusing twenty-five workmen, employed in building the cathedral of Salamanca, from the payment of certain dues in such a manner that nothing should be exacted from

[54] González, *Alfonso IX*, II, no. 167; also in *Cortes*, I, no. VIII, cl. 6.
[55] González, *Alfonso IX*, II, no. 89 (29 Nov. 1194), 90 (28 Dec. 1194).
[56] *Ibid.* no. 91 (5 April 1195).

them 'pro aliqua fazendaria seu pecto uel petito aut fossato, licet moneda mittatur in Salamanca uel in suo termino'.[57] What does *moneda* signify in these documents? Is it coinage or a tax? It has been given both interpretations.[58]

Grants of coinage which had been conceded by earlier kings as a rule took the form of grants of a proportion – a half, a quarter or a tenth, as the case might be – of the coinage of a particular mint, and such grants were generally made to the bishop or cathedral clergy of the city in which the mint was situated. Thus, Alfonso VII granted 'decimam totius monete, que in Toleto fuerit fabricata' to the cathedral of Toledo, and made a number of other similar grants.[59] Some of Alfonso VII's concessions were confirmed and extended by Fernando II who, in 1167, confirmed his father's grant to the bishop of Salamanca of a third of the money coined in the city and also granted him the right to appoint custodians, as the king did, for the two-thirds of the coinage which he retained.[60] Nineteen years later the right to one-third of the gold coinage of Salamanca was granted to Bishop Vidal.[61] Similar concessions were made to the archbishops of Santiago de Compostela. In 1171 the half of the coinage retained by Alfonso VII for the king was remitted to the archbishop, and in 1182 it was also conceded that, even if the king depreciated the coinage, that minted in Santiago de Compostela might retain its value, did the archbishop so wish. Finally, in 1193 Alfonso IX granted to the archbishop the right to coin gold *maravedíes*.[62] All such grants refer to specific mints and are completely unambiguous. The grants made to the Order of Santiago and to the bishop of Zamora appear to be grants of this sort, although the second grant to the Order has a wider implication and extends to the whole kingdom.[63] That of 1199, however, differs. It is a grant of exemption to a number of persons from the payment of dues to which they would

[57] *Ibid.* no. 130 (31 July 1199).
[58] Sánchez-Albornoz, *Estudios*, 475, assumes that the grant of 29 Nov. 1194, which he incorrectly dates 1197, refers to the tax. Lomax, *Orden de Santiago*, 166, assumes that the grants to the Order of Santiago refer to the coinage. O'Callaghan, 'The beginnings of the cortes of León–Castile', *AHR*, LXXIV, 1519, n. 69, thinks it probable that the grants of 1194 and 1195 refer to the coinage.
[59] Rassow, *AFUF*, XI, 10.
[60] Gonzáles, *Regesta*, no. 14 (Oct. 1167).
[61] *Ibid.* no. 58 (27 Oct. 1186). Alfonso VIII of Castile first coined gold *maravedíes* in 1172; Fernando II of León began to mint gold coins at a later date, cf. Mateu y Llopis, *Moneda española*, 163–4.
[62] López Ferreiro, *Iglesia de Santiago*, IV, aps. XLVI (11 March 1171), LVII (1182); V, *ap.* IV (17 June 1193).
[63] González, *Alfonso IX*, II, no. 74 (1194), refers to gold coinage but the document is so deteriorated that it is impossible to say what was granted.

normally be subjected. *Moneda* which is excluded from this exemption is clearly a tax.

There is no evidence of a renewal in curia of the *moneda* at the end of the seven-year period from 1202, nor at any time during the rest of Alfonso's reign. Nor is there any evidence of a series of septennial curias at which such renewals could have been agreed. On the contrary, none of the known great assemblies of Alfonso IX's reign fits in with such a series, based on 1202, except that of 1188. On the other hand, *moneda* continued to be imposed. In 1207 Alfonso IX conceded to his ex-Queen Berenguela the royal rents in a number of places 'preter monetam'.[64] In 1209 he granted certain rents, except *moneda*, to the cathedral of Santiago de Compostela.[65] Similarly, grants of lands in which *moneda* was reserved to the crown were made to the cathedral of Astorga in 1224, to the monastery of Meira in 1225 and to the monastery of Montederramo in 1229.[66] When, in the same year, Alfonso IX exchanged Villafáfila for Cáceres with the Order of Santiago, he reserved to the crown *moneda* in Villafáfila.[67] When exemption from royal dues was granted to the vassals of the Order of Alcántara in Vecilla, *moneda* was retained.[68] In these grants the word was associated with pecuniary rights and dues payable to the crown. In a few cases individuals were exempted from payment of *moneda*; the canons and clergy of the cathedral of Zamora were thus exempted in 1223, although the canons were covered by the general exemption granted to the canons of cathedrals in 1202, and an undated writ addressed to the royal collectors of *moneda* instructed them not to demand the tax from the household servants of the canons of Santiago.[69] Later documents also refer back to *moneda* under Alfonso IX. In Fernando III's sentence in favour of the bishop of Túy in his suit against the *concejo* of Túy in 1250, the king laid down that the bishop was to do him homage for the city and 'darme Moneda et conducho como lo dieron en tiempo de mio Padre'.[70] In 1254 Alfonso X confirmed to the canons of León their exemption from *moneda* which they had enjoyed under his grandfather and his father.[71] We shall have to return later to this question of *moneda*.

One marked characteristic of this period in León was the great increase

---

[64] *Ibid.* no. 219 (7 Sept. 1207).   [65] *Ibid.* no. 239 (Feb. 1209).
[66] *Ibid.* nos. 445 (30 Nov. 1224), 451 (9 April 1225), 603 (19 Aug. 1229).
[67] *Ibid.* no. 597 (May 1229).   [68] *Ibid.* no. 516 (4 Dec. 1227).
[69] *Ibid.* nos. 431 (22 June 1223), 665.   [70] *ES*, xxii, *ap.* xviii (4 July 1250).
[71] Ballesteros, *Itinerario*, 55, n. 1 (4 April 1254).

in general legislation, much of which was undoubtedly promulgated in, and with the consent of, the great curia. We have little exact knowledge of legislation under Fernando II, as no decrees have survived, but laws were promulgated at the Councils of Salamanca in 1178 and of Benavente in 1181. The object of the first of these two assemblies was 'ad tollendum pravas consuetudines et informandam morum rectitudinem' and, more specifically, the recovery of royal and ecclesiastical lands.[72] The text of an agreement made between the Orders of the Temple, of the Hospital and of Santiago at Salamanca also stated that at this assembly the king 'instituciones terre sue per decreta sua firmiter ordinavit'.[73] The assembly was attended by bishops, abbots, counts, barons and other rulers of provinces, and among documents passed there were royal privileges restoring lost and alienated lands to the sees of Mondoñedo and Oviedo.[74] We do not know what evil customs were annulled, nor how usages were reformed, nor what royal decrees were promulgated, but the assembly apears to have been more successful in checking the alienation of church lands than of royal lands, and three years later Fernando II revoked grants of royal lands at the Council of Benavente 'ubi statum mei regni melioraui et omnes incartaciones mihi accepi'.[75] We have no further information about the steps taken to ameliorate the condition of the kingdom.

For the reign of Alfonso IX we are much better informed as the texts of a series of decrees promulgated in 1188, 1194, 1202, 1204, 1208 and 1228 as well as a number of single edicts have survived. Most of these were issued in great curias with the common consent of those present. The decrees of 1188, 1202 and 1208 were all issued in assemblies at which not only lay and ecclesiastical magnates but also citizens and townsmen attended. The earliest set of decrees is undated; but it clearly belongs to the beginning of the reign, and can be assigned to 1188. As well as these decrees, an act of resumption was promulgated and the donations of Fernando II were revoked.[76] As new donations confirming some of these date from April 1188, the curia must have been held in the first months of the year.[77] The decrees of 1188 were a comprehensive undertaking of good government, and in the first of

[72] ES, xviii, ap. xxv (10 Sept. 1178).
[73] García Larragueta, Hispania, xii, no. 20 (pp. 516–17).
[74] ES, xviii, ap. xxv; CD Oviedo, no. 193.
[75] González, Regesta, no. 41 (30 March 1181).
[76] González, Alfonso IX, ii, nos. 11, 662 (n.d.). The decrees of 1188 are also published in Cortes, i, no. vii.
[77] González, Alfonso IX, i, 46.

them Alfonso IX swore to observe the good customs (*mores bonos*) of his ancestors to all men of his kingdom, both clergy and laity, an undertaking which recalls that made by Alfonso VII on the occasion of his coronation as Emperor in 1135. We have already noted the king's promise not to make war, peace or a treaty without consulting his curia. Most of the remaining decrees dealt with the suppression of crimes of violence, with justice and with judicial procedure. No action was to be taken against a man accused to the king, until his case had been heard in the king's court and the accusation proved; false accusers were to be punished. Property was protected, trees and vines were not to be cut down and no one was to seize with violence the possessions, moveable or immoveable, of another nor take sureties from another, except through the justices and *alcaldes* appointed for this purpose. Unlawful distraint was to be punished as trespass with violence and the plough-oxen of the *rusticus*, the animals he had with him in the field and his person were protected from distraint. If an accused person denied that he was guilty of violence, the truth of his denial was to be proved by inquisition. Fines were to be imposed on judges who failed to do justice, on those who impeded the course of justice and on those who were guilty of contempt of court. The inviolability of a man's house was guaranteed against violent entry, and if the master or mistress of a house was killed as a result of such entry, then the housebreaker was *alevosus et traditor*. If a man changed his residence from one town or district to another, the justices of the place to which he had moved must hear any accusation arising in his place of origin, which was legally brought against him. The passing of land into mortmain was forbidden. Causes which ought to be heard before local courts were not to be heard in the king's court, or before the judges of León, except as permitted by the local *fueros*. The procedure to be followed in most of these circumstances was defined, and was probably in most cases a reassertion of existing procedure. How far the decrees were successfully put into effect it is difficult to say, but the fact that some of the decrees of 1188 dealing with unlawful distraint were re-enacted in 1194, and again in 1204, suggests that the king's attempt to extirpate violence was only partially successful.

Closely connected with these first decrees were some others, dated July 1188, which dealt with thieves and malefactors and which, as the preamble stated, were drawn up as a result of complaints and information laid before the king at his first curia. These decrees were issued 'pari consensu et communi omnium deliberatione', and the discussion and consent may have taken place at the curia earlier in the year, when the complaints were made, and the remedies may have been drawn up later; or there may have been a second assembly in July, with or without the representatives of the cities. These decrees increased the penalties for violence, laid down that satisfaction must be made for former crimes and the king also decreed 'de communi omnium consensu' that those who carried out justice were to be protected from violence. A final clause 'communi assensu et consilio baronum et curie mee' decreed that whoever recognised an illegitimate son was to be responsible for him as though he was legitimate.[78]

The text of the decrees of 1194 does not give the composition of the assembly, but the first clause, which re-enacted most of the precepts of 1188 concerned with the abuse of distraint, was decreed 'communi deliberatione'. Another, extremely important, clause instituted a procedure by which notorious thieves and robbers were indicted by a sworn jury in an inquisition held before the king, or by those who held land of the king, and had their names enrolled. These *raptores scripti* were thenceforth treated as outlaws, whom no one might protect, or receive as vassals, but who, on being captured, were handed over to justice. This procedure may be compared to Henry II's jury of indictment and the registering of fugitives from justice under the Assize of Clarendon. Other clauses were concerned with safeguarding regalian rights, and one forbade anyone to confer knighthood on those on royal demesne whose fathers were not knights. Three dealt with the temporal rights of the church: *jus spolii* was relinquished; those who had left church lands and gone elsewhere were to return; and lands donated to churches or monasteries were to retain the rights and liberties they had enjoyed before the donation was made. The decree of 1188 concerning illegitimate sons of nobles was re-enacted.[79]

The decrees promulgated at Benavente in 1202 took the form of *placita* or sentences pronounced by elected judges – 'ab electis iudicibus' – in matters at issue between the king and his subjects. As we have already seen, one question dealt with was the king's right to alter and to sell the coinage. The *placita* also defined the differences between ecclesiastical and secular lands, and enacted that lands held by nobles, knights, citizens or burgesses from bishops, abbeys or other religious orders, were to be held by the appropriate secular right. If a tenant of the church incurred the wrath of the king and was exiled, his lands

[78] *Ibid.* ɪɪ, no. 12.
[79] *Ibid.* ɪɪ, no. 84.

reverted to the church, but the usufruct belonged to the king until the tenant's death or return from exile. Lands held by a clerk, either by inheritance or by purchase, were not to be reckoned as *abadengo* or frankalmoin until donated to the church, but should pay the accustomed dues to the king.[80]

Another important code was that promulgated at Lugo in 1204. It has survived only in a cartulary under the heading 'Hec sunt decreta quae dominus Adefonsus, rex Legionis, posuit et statuit in Gallecia, apud Lucum, de Patronibus, raptoribus et malefactoribus.' The decrees follow immediately, without preamble of any sort, so that there is no information as to whether they were issued in an assembly, nor, if so, what was its composition, nor is there any reference to consent or consultation. The decrees were, however, closely akin to those of 1188 and 1194, and they re-enacted some of the earlier decrees including that protecting the beasts belonging to the rustic from seizure. The duties of the pursuit of thieves and robbers and the defence of the roads were laid on knights and town councils under threat of fine, loss of lands to the king and excommunication by the bishop of the diocese in the event of neglect of these duties. Heavy penalties were prescribed for interference with the course of justice and for false accusation. Regulations on buying and selling, designed to prevent the disposal of stolen goods, were also enacted, and butchers were forbidden to skin carcases except in the presence of two good men appointed for this purpose.[81]

The decrees promulgated at León in 1208 dealt exclusively with the temporal rights of the church. All right of spoil was renounced by the king and the goods of a deceased prelate were to be held for his successor by custodians appointed according to canon law. The clergy were to be exempt from the payment of *petitum*. Food and other necessities for the households of bishops and cathedral clergy were exempt from the payment of tolls. Lay tenants of the church who incurred the king's wrath and were exiled should not be reinstated in their lands without the king's permission. No suits reserved by canon law for the hearing of the ecclesiastical courts were to be tried by royal *merinos* or other secular judges. Those excommunicated by the church were also to be banished from the king's curia.[82] Most of this was not

[80] *Ibid.* II, no. 167; also in *Cortes*, I, no. VIII.
[81] González, *Alfonso IX*, II, no. 192; also publ. Vázquez de Parga, 'Decretos de Alfonso IX de León para Galicia publicados en 1204', *AHDE*, XIII, 265-8.
[82] González, *Alfonso IX*, II, no. 221.

new; former kings had renounced the right of spoil in privileges granted to individual prelates as, for example, had Alfonso VI to Bishop Osmund of Astorga in 1087, and Alfonso VII to Diego Gelmírez, archbishop of Santiago de Compostela, in 1128.[83] General renunciation of the right of spoil had been included in the decrees published in 1194, and the decree concerning tenants of the church who incurred banishment had appeared in a somewhat different form among the *placita* of 1202. Church courts had long functioned in León, and former kings had made no attempt to curtail their increasing jurisdiction. Exemption from the payment of *petitum* and *pedazgo* (toll) had been granted to particular churches in the past. The decrees of 1208, however, sum up the privileged position of the church.

Other legislation was of a more restricted application. Two laws concerned pilgrims. One was enacted in 1229 at the instance of the papal legate, John, bishop of Sabina, then presiding over a church council at Salamanca, and was promulgated in the presence and with the consent of Archbishop Bernardo of Santiago de Compostela and all the bishops of the kingdom summoned to the council by the legate 'nec non et baronibus regni nostri'. Presumably the law was promulgated by a great curia summoned to meet at the same time as the church council. This law allowed pilgrims to dispose of their goods by will and laid down a division in cases of intestacy. If the dead pilgrim was in the company of fellow countrymen, they were to swear to deliver his goods to his rightful heirs; otherwise the bishop of the diocese was to hold the goods in trust for up to two years and then, if they were unclaimed, one-third was to be given to the church where the dead pilgrim was buried and the remaining two-thirds were to be used for the war against the Moors.[84] The other law is undated, but has been assigned to 1229. It decreed that pilgrims were to be unmolested throughout the kingdom, laid down fines for landlords of hostelries or muleteers who ill-treated pilgrims and divided the goods of a pilgrim who died intestate between the king, the host of the hostelry where he died and the church where he was buried.[85] A single, undated, edict concerned with the administration of the archiepiscopal lands and the rights of the *perticarius* of Santiago was decreed by the king 'cum

---

[83] *ES*, xvi, *ap.* xxi (25 April 1087); *HC*, 466–8.

[84] González, *Alfonso IX*, ii, no. 519; López Ferreiro, *Iglesia de Santiago*, v, *ap.* xv.

[85] González, *Alfonso IX*, ii, no. 667; López Ferreiro, *Iglesia de Santiago*, v, *ap.* xiv; *DHILC*, no. lxxxvii, under date 1229. González places the undated law before that of 1229, *Alfonso IX*, i, 441, *et sqq.*

Archiepiscopo et cum tota curia mea'.[86] Thus, the curia in one form or another played an active part in legislation in the kingdom of León. Legislation increased in volume, particularly during the reign of Alfonso IX. This increase was a natural development in a kingdom where law was based on a written code – the *Forum judicum*, which was, however, antiquated – and not on custom. Alfonso IX carried on the work of Alfonso VII and Fernando II, but with increased impetus. Taken as a whole, the legislation of Alfonso IX's reign was impressive and it embraced a wide variety of subjects: the extirpation of violence and crime; the enforcement of law and order by the king; justice and judicial procedure; land tenure, the coinage and finance; and the liberties and privileges of the church. Thus it affected all classes of the population.

There was no fundamental change in the curia as a judicial tribunal during this period, but there are a number of developments of interest and a considerable volume of information about the curia's judicial activities. Although there are records of suits in which phrases such as 'in presentiam domini Fernandi' or 'coram domino rege Adefonso' occur, without any reference to the curia,[87] in the majority of cases specific reference to the *curia regis* is given.[88] Two interesting cases in which the king was one of the litigants occurred in 1207 and 1220. In the former year Alfonso IX claimed that the abbey of Corias was a royal abbey, that both the abbot and his tenants owed *petitum* to the king and that the king had the right to appoint the abbot. To this the abbot responded that the monastery was free from all royal services by its foundation charter. Alfonso IX, after consulting those present with him, cited the abbot to appear before a great curia at Toro, which was attended by the magnates of León, the archbishop of Compostela and many of the bishops. Here the charter of foundation was read before the curia and the king acknowledged the justice of the abbot's plea.[89] In 1220 a land suit between the king and the Order of Santiago was heard before the curia and decided in favour of the Order after an inquisition. In this case the

---

[86] González, *Alfonso IX*, II, no. 625; López Ferreiro, *Fueros*, I, 117. The *perticarius* was a secular official of the archbishop of Santiago.

[87] *DHILC*, no. XLIV (1168); González, *Alfonso IX*, II, nos. 358 (21 March 1218), 385 (9 Jan. 1220).

[88] E.g. González, *Alfonso IX*, II, nos. 158 (20 Aug. 1201), 403 (27 Sept. 1220), 419 (7 March 1222), etc.

[89] *Ibid.* II, no. 217 (1207).

king presided over the curia and judgment was given by royal judges
– 'adiudicatum fuit ante me, in mea curia, per meos iudices'.[90]
The growth of ecclesiastical jurisdiction and the efficiency of the
church courts inevitably affected royal justice, and suits between two
ecclesiastical litigants before the king's court became very rare, even in
proprietory and territorial cases though some, however, still occurred.[91]
The canon of the Fourth Lateran Council of 1215 which forbade
ecclesiastics to take proprietary cases before secular courts hastened this
tendency. Soon after 1215 the Order of Santiago obtained a papal bull
forbidding the Spanish bishops to cite the Order before secular courts,
and thence forward the Order appeared before the king's court only in
suits with the laity, concerned with such secular matters as land and
patronage.[92] Other orders continued to appear occasionally before the
royal court in suits against ecclesiastics. In 1220 an agreement was
reached in a land suit between Pedro Alvitiz, master of the Temple,
and García Sánchez, master of the Order of Pereiro and Alcántara, in
the presence of Alfonso IX and his curia; on a later occasion, the master
of the Temple and Bishop Pedro of Astorga entered into a concordat
about their rights in the *behetría* of Salas with the consent and by the
order of Alfonso IX, in his presence and that of the curia.[93]

Before 1215 suits between an ecclesiastic and a lay litigant before
the king's court were frequent. In 1168 a dispute arose between the
monastery of Sobrado and Don Pedro Muñoz about certain lands and
their inhabitants, and was brought before Fernando II at Lugo.
The king ordered an inquisition to be held by Bishop Juan of Lugo
and three other inquisitors, and the lands were divided between the
parties according to the results of the inquisition.[94] A suit between the
abbey of Eslonza and the inhabitants of Villa Savariego concerning
the patronage of the church of Villa Savariego was determined by
Fernando II in curia in 1178.[95] The monastery of Sobrado was involved
in another land suit before Alfonso IX in 1213 against Lope Núñez
who, it claimed, had unjustly seized certain lands which belonged to
the monastery. The suit was ended by an agreement, made by the
authority of the king and the nobles present with him – 'mea auctoritate

---

[90] *Ibid.* II, no. 391 (25 Feb. 1220); for an earlier suit in which Alfonso IX was the
plaintiff, see *Ibid.* II, no. 106 (4 Sept. 1197).
[91] E.g. *RC Cluny*, nos. 4326–8 (19, 24 July 1188); *ES*, xxxvi, *ap.* LVI (1167);
González, *Alfonso IX*, II, no. 158 (20 Aug. 1201).
[92] Lomax, *Orden de Santiago*, 26.
[93] González, *Alfonso IX*, II, nos. 403 (27 Sept. 1220), 419 (7 March 1222).
[94] *DHILC*, no. XLIV.
[95] *Cartulario del monasterio de Eslonza*, 33–4.

et uirorum nobilium qui mecum erant' – and with the consent of both parties.[96]

After 1215 such cases, as has been noted, were less frequent. On 9 January 1220 the king gave judgment in two cases in which the monastery of Ribas de Sil was a litigant. One was a land suit against Doña Sancha Fernández, her sons and other laymen. Here the case went by default as, on the day appointed for the hearing, only the proctor for the monastery was present, and none of the defendants appeared, either in person or by proxy; sentence was, therefore, given in favour of the monastery.[97] In the other, the men of Valdecerreda, Villouxe and Loona claimed to be able to withdraw from their allegiance to the abbot. The suit was settled after an inquisition, held by two ecclesiastics and two knights, which showed that the villages in question formed part of the *coto* of the abbey, and that the villagers were, therefore, vassals of the abbot.[98] In 1225 Alfonso IX, again after an inquest, and with the advice of the curia – 'habito consilio cum viris prudentibus curie nostre et aliis' – gave sentence in favour of the prior and monastery of Junquera, in its suit with the men of Cerdeira. The sentence included the *pesquisa* which gave a detailed enumeration of the possessions and rights of the monastery in the township.[99] It appears, therefore, that the king's court retained its jurisdiction in land suits and other suits concerned with secular rights, in which one party was ecclesiastical and the other lay, but that by the end of the period similar suits between two ecclesiastical litigants were usually heard in an ecclesiastical court. Thus, in León, the ecclesiastical courts encroached further on royal jurisdiction than they did in some other Western European kingdoms – for example, England, where land and proprietory suits were heard in the royal courts, even when both parties belonged to the clergy. There is, however, no evidence that the kings of León sought to combat this encroachment.

Another development during this period was the increasing frequency with which town councils (*concejos*) as such appeared as suitors before the king's court, a development which reflects their growing importance in the social and political life of the kingdom.[100] Ecclesiastical patronage, land and overlordship were the principal causes of such suits.

---

[96] González, *Alfonso IX*, II, no. 285 (3 Jan. 1213).
[97] *Ibid.* II, no. 387.   [98] *Ibid.* II, no. 385.
[99] *Ibid.* II, no. 455 (15 May 1225).
[100] See Procter, 'The towns of León and Castille as suitors before the king's court in the thirteenth century', *EHR*, LXXIV, 1–22.

In 1182 Bishop Manrique of León and the canons of the cathedral claimed the church of Santa María in Mansilla by royal donation, but the *concejo* contested this. The dispute was concluded by a compromise agreed on before Fernando II in curia at Astorga. By this agreement the rights of the church of León were acknowledged by the *concejo*, but the clerks who then possessed the church were allowed to retain half its revenues for their lives; as each one died, his share passed to the bishop. The rights of the bishop over churches existing, or to be built, within or without the walls of the town, were also laid down.[101] Another case heard before the king's court was that between Abbot Juan of Sahagún and the *concejo* of Mayorga, a town on royal demesne over certain lands in Siero and Villamaya. Six judges were appointed *ad hoc* who gave sentence of proof by inquest to determine who held the lands at the death of Alfonso VII. At this point the *concejo* decided to come to terms with the abbot, conceding his rights but asking for a grant of some of the land. The abbot granted the townsmen 'of grace' five jugates of land in Siero, on condition that they did not found a settlement there, nor molest the possessions of the monastery. This suit took place in 1186.[102] A compromise made before Alfonso IX, and with his approval, concerned the church of Santa María de Villacet which was claimed by both the abbot of Sahagún and the *concejo* of Villacet. By this agreement, the *concejo* acknowledged the abbot's rights, and in turn was granted a third of the tithes of the church for seventeen years, for the building of the town walls; after the end of this period the tithe reverted to the monastery of San Salvador of Villacet, a dependency of Sahagún.[103] In 1220 a land suit between the Order of Santiago and the *concejo* of Ledesma was heard at Zamora by Alfonso IX and the nobles and judges of his court. This was also ended by an agreement.[104] In 1226, in consequence of a suit between the master of Alcántara and the *concejo* of Coria, the boundaries of certain villages were determined.[105]

The first clear evidence of the appearance of *concejos* before

---

[101] Muedra Benedito, 'Textos para el estudio de la curia regia leonesa', *AHDE*, VI, 414–15.

[102] González, *Regesta*, no. 57 (17 March 1186); also publ. Escalona, *Sahagún, ap.* III, *esc.* CXCII.

[103] González, *Alfonso IX*, II, no. 310 (29 June 1214); Escalona, *Sahagún, ap.* III, *esc.* CCXVIII. González gives the abbot's name as Martin; Escalona prints M——; in fact, the abbot in 1214 was Miguel I de Grajal, abbot from 1213 to 1224. Villacet was later called Belver.

[104] González, *Alfonso IX*, II, no. 389 (13 Feb. 1220).

[105] *Ibid.* II, no. 495 (10 Oct. 1226).

the king's court by representatives also belongs to this period. For the twelfth century there is little evidence. *Assertores* or *advocati* presented the case for the parties involved, whether individuals or corporate bodies, as they had in the preceding period. In 1168, in the suit between the monastery of Sobrado and Pedro Muñoz, *assertores* stated the case for both parties, and in 1186, in the suit between the abbot of Sahagún and the *concejo* of Mayorga, Fernando II ordered both litigants to appoint advocates, but there is no evidence as to how the corporate bodies made their appearance. The agreement between the bishop of León and the *concejo* of Mansilla in 1182 was made 'de beneplacito domini episcopi nec non et totius concilii', but we do not know how the approval of the whole *concejo* was vouched for before the curia. Nor do we know who acted for the *concejo* of Villacet in the convention made between it and the abbot of Sahagún in 1214.

For the thirteenth century, however, there is evidence that the towns were being represented by proctors, although not generally under that title. The suit in 1220 between the Order of Santiago and the *concejo* of Ledesma was heard 'presentibus memorie comendatore regni dicti ordinis cum fratribus suis et alcaldibus et bonis hominibus cum cautione data concilio de Ledesma', and the agreement was witnessed by twelve members of the *concejo* who were presumably the *alcaldes* and the *boni homines* mentioned in the text. Three years later there was a clear case of representation. A dispute arose between the dean and chapter of the cathedral of Santiago de Compostela and the *concejo* of Santiago concerning the sale of the canon's wine. The case was first brought before the court of the archbishop as *dominus terrae*. The *concejo* refused to appear, and the suit was then brought before the king, who was at the time in Galicia. In these preliminary proceedings, the dean presented the case for the chapter and an unnamed advocate for the *concejo*. A day was fixed for the hearing of the suit, and the king ordered the *concejo* to appoint a representative (*personarius*). On the appointed day the chapter was represented by one canon, Juan Ibáñez, as *personarius*, while another canon, Pedro Odoaris, came as advocate, thus showing that the two offices were distinct. The *personarius* of the *concejo* was Pelayo García, who appears also to have acted as advocate for the *concejo*. The chapter continued to press for a hearing in the archiepiscopal court, but the *concejo* objected and was upheld by Alfonso IX and the curia. Finally, the chapter appealed *ad Librum*.[106] The title *personarius* which was used for the representa-

Ibid. II, no. 426 (7 March 1223); cf. López Ferreiro, *Fueros*, I, 182–4.

tives in this suit was that most frequently used for representatives of *concejos* in suits before the king's court for the rest of the thirteenth century, although *boni homines* and *procuratores* were also used.[107] The *personarius* of the chapter of Santiago came with letters sealed with the chapter seal, but there is no evidence as to whether the *personarius* of the *concejo* also brought sealed letters of appointment, although he may have done so. Thus, well before Alfonso IX's death and the reunion of the kingdoms, the cities of León were being represented in suits before the king's court by persons specially appointed for the purpose.

The inquest continued to be the method of proof most frequently used in suits before the king's court and we have already referred to a number of such cases. It was used especially in land suits, but also in patronage suits, and in cases concerning overlordship, services due to a lord and the status of persons. There is much more evidence of the procedure in this period than in the preceding one. The inquisitors were appointed by the king, in curia or by writ, but the consent of the parties to the persons appointed was sometimes mentioned. The inquisitors took an oath to the king to carry out the inquiry faithfully. There was no fixed number of inquisitors and the number appointed varied. Evidence was taken locally, generally from older persons, and on oath. Here again there was no fixed number, and in some cases the number questioned was very large. In one case it was specifically stated that the inquisitors selected those to give evidence on oath, and this may have been the usual procedure. The evidence thus obtained was written down and sent to the king; it was then read before the litigants in the curia and sentence was given in accordance with the inquest.[108] Many suits were also ended by compromise or agreement, and of this also we have already given examples. Documentary proof was produced more frequently than hitherto.

One result of the renewed study of Roman law in León, as in other western kingdoms, was that the royal curia increasingly became a court of appeal, as well as a court of first instance. Although there are no records of the hearing of appeals, there are references to this right to appeal to the king's court in a number of town *fueros*, including those of Milmanda (1199), Castroverde (1202), Puebla de Sanabria (1220)

---

[107] Procter, *EHR*, LXXIV, 8–9.
[108] Procter, 'The judicial use of "*pesquisa*" ', 1–19.

and Lobeira (1228).[109] Neither are there any records of sentences in criminal cases, but there is no doubt that Alfonso IX greatly increased royal control over such suits. As we have seen, his legislation in 1188, 1194 and 1204 dealt with justice, judicial procedure and the suppression of crimes of violence. Lucas of Túy noted the severity of Alfonso's justice and his attempts to prevent bribery of judges.[110] Crown pleas were among the regalian rights most frequently reserved to the crown in grants of immunities to ecclesiastical corporations, and in particular the *quatuor causae* of rape, robbery, *alevosía* (treachery) and destruction of roads were again and again reserved for the hearing of royal justices.[111]

Although there was no differentiation between the consultative and the judicial aspects of the curia and nothing to correspond to the separate development of the courts of common pleas and king's bench in England, yet there was a marked growth in the professional and legal elements in the curia. The title *judex regis* appeared from time to time in the lists of *confirmantes* as, for example, 'Pelagius Tabladellus et Petrus Captiuus, iudices regis', who confirm two documents of 4 May 1188, and 'Munnio Roderici de Cotes, iudex regis', who witnessed an agreement between the Orders of the Temple and Alcántara made before Alfonso IX in curia on 27 September 1220.[112] Although the appointment of *ad hoc* judges from among members of the curia still continued as, for example, in the suit between the abbot of Sahagún and the *concejo* of Mayorga in 1186 and also in that between Rodrigo Aprilis and Sancha Petriz in 1200,[113] there were also permanent and professional judges attached to the court, especially in the later years of the period, when there are a number of references to *judices curie*.

In 1219 Abbot Pedro of Celanova claimed the monastery of Arnoga from a certain knight, Pedro Fernández, and the case was heard in an ecclesiastical court before the bishop of Orense, who gave judgment in favour of the abbot; the knight then appealed to the archbishop of Braga, who confirmed the sentence given by the bishop of Orense. The abbot, because he failed to obtain possession of Arnoga, invoked

---

[109] González, *Alfonso IX*, II, nos. 126, 163, 401, 547. *DHILC*, no. LXXVIII, is a record of a suit in 1226 in which an appeal to the king's court was made.
[110] Lucas, *Chronicon mundi*, 110, 114.
[111] González, *Alfonso IX*, II, nos. 311 (7 Aug. 1214), 314 (16 Oct. 1214), 327 (7 Aug. 1215), 428 (5 April 1223), 460 (28 July 1225), 522 (24 April 1228), 532 18 May 1228), 589 (22 Oct. 1228).
[112] *Ibid.* II, nos. 5, 6, 403.
[113] González, *Regesta*, no. 57 (17 March 1186); *CDC Oviedo*, no. 215.

the royal power to see that the sentence was carried out. Alfonso IX, uncertain whether he was bound by the archbishop's judgment, summoned the bishops of León and Astorga 'et iurisperitos et curiam et judices curie et iudices Legionis' and asked their advice. After consultation and examination of the relevant documents, they advised the king to execute the sentence. The use of the title *iurisperiti* indicates that some of the king's advisers were learned in Roman law. In this case the *iurisperiti* and the *iudices curie* appear to have acted as assessors and advisers to the curia, whose spokesmen were the two bishops.[114] Again, a suit in 1200, in which the Order of Santiago was involved, was heard 'per dominum regem Adefonsum Legionis, et nobiles uiros et iudices eius curie'.[115]

To sum up the alterations in the judicial functions of the curia in León: the *curia regis* lost ground to the ecclesiastical courts and by the end of the period was rarely hearing proprietory suits between two ecclesiastical litigants and, although it continued to hear such suits when one of the parties involved was lay, yet these cases were often tried before ecclesiastical courts. The number of suits in which *concejos* were involved increased greatly and, before the end of Alfonso IX's reign, they as well as ecclesiastical corporations were being represented by *personeros*. The competence of the *curia regis* was extended by appeals from lower courts, and by the increased control over criminal jurisdiction exercised by the king. Finally, the curia as a court of law was becoming more expert and professional, and permanent judges, who were professional legists, were acting as assessors and advisers to the curia, and were also taking the place of the earlier *ad hoc* judges.

---

[114] González, *Alfonso IX*, II, no. 383 (4 Nov. 1219); also publ. Muedra Benedito, *AHDE*, VI, 418. The see of Orense formed part of the ecclesiastical province of Braga.
[115] González, *Alfonso IX*, II, no. 389 (13 Feb. 1220).

3

The *curia regis* in the separate kingdom of Castile
(1157–1230)

The use of the term *concilium* for the extraordinary meetings of the curia died out earlier in Castile than in León. There is plenty of evidence that *curia* was used there in this period for all kinds of meetings, from the small informal ones to the most formal and solemn assemblies.[1] In the treaty concluded in February 1158 between Sancho III of Castile and Ramón Berenguer IV, count of Barcelona and prince of Aragon, the former granted the disputed territory of Zaragoza, Calatayud, and certain other lands to the count's eldest son, Don Ramón, or to whoever inherited the kingdom of Aragon, on condition that whoever held the lands in question should do homage for them to King Sancho or his successors 'et faciat uel faciant ei inde tale seruicium, quod, quandocunque rex Sancius se coronaverit et eum vocaverit, veniat ad curiam suam et dum coronabitur ante ipsum teneat ensem'.[2] On five occasions during the reign of Alfonso VIII reference to the holding of a curia was added to the dating clause of royal privileges. In two cases we have no other evidence of this curia and know nothing of its purpose, but all five assemblies must have been specially summoned meetings of the great curia at which important business was transacted, or a reference of this sort would not have been made. On all five occasions *curia* was used without any attributive adjective.[3] The term was also used for great assemblies under Fernando III. Thus both Rodrigo of Toledo and the author of the *Crónica latina* use *curia* to describe the assembly held in Burgos on the occasion of the king's marriage to Beatrice of Suabia in 1219. The *Crónica latina* also

[1] For examples of *curia* applied to judicial sessions of the small curia, see González, *Reino de Castilla*, II, no. 461 (18 Oct. 1186); III, nos. 607 (2 Nov. 1192), 653 (31 March 1196), 1029 (29 Oct. 1196), 1034 (20 Nov. 1215).

[2] *Ibid.* II, no. 36; also in *Liber feudorum maior*, I, no. 31.

[3] González, *Reino de Castilla*, II, nos. 124, 125, 126 (Burgos, 11, 18, 19 Nov. 1169); nos. 295, 296 (Burgos, 29, 30 Jan. 1178); no. 398 (Medina de Río Seco, 25 Dec. 1182); no. 471 (San Esteban, 21 May 1187); no. 505 (Carrión, 4 July 1188).

used it for the assembly held at the marriage of Fernando's sister Berenguela to John of Brienne in 1224 and for the meeting at Carrión later in the year, summoned to prepare for war against the Moors.[4]

The form *tota curia* was used very occasionally, sometimes in lists of *confirmantes* where it appears, however, to refer to the small curia;[5] it was also used in the undertaking made by the Regent Alvaro Núñez de Lara not to misappropriate the ecclesiastical *tercias*, in what was, probably, a great assembly.[6] The ablative form *in plena curia* occurs very rarely. Rodrigo of Toledo, in his account of the Curia of Carrión in 1188, stated that Alfonso IX of León kissed the hand of King Alfonso VIII of Castile 'in plena curia', but in the rest of his account of this occasion he used 'curia'.[7] In a document of Fernando III of 11 June 1220, reference was made to a former judicial sentence given 'in conspectu meo plena curia mea'.[8] The phrase thus appears to have been used occasionally of judicial sessions, or of sessions in which homage was done to the king. This was also its use in León.

The same problem concerning the composition of the curia arises in Castile as in León – how far were the *confirmantes* of solemn documents actually present? The Castilian chancery adopted the *carta rodada* from 1165, a few years later than the chancery of León.[9] Differences in form between the privileges as issued in the two kingdoms were slight. In Castile the *signum* differed with the different persons who drew it, but towards the end of the period it usually took the form of a cross. The names of the *maiordomus curie regis* and the *alferez regis* (the term *signifer* was never used in Castile) were written round the outer circle of the *rueda*. From time to time the name of the chancellor was also written outside the *rueda*, but as a rule it was included in the notarial authorisation. The only other great official to appear regularly in these documents was the *merinus regis in Castella*. A majordomo of Queen Eleanor occasionally confirmed under Alfonso VIII; under Fernando III the majordomo of the queen-mother, Berenguela, appeared regularly until her death. For the first twenty-five years, at least, after the separation of the two kingdoms, the

---

[4] Rodrigo, *De rebus Hispaniae, lib.* IX, *cap.* x; *Crónica latina*, 78, 79–80, 82.

[5] González, *Reino de Castilla*, II, no. 88 (29 Sept. 1166); *Bullarium de Calatrava*, 6–7.

[6] González, *Reino de Castilla*, III, no. 995; and Fita, 'Cortes de Toro en 1216', *BRAH*, XXXIX, 529 (15 Feb. 1216).

[7] Rodrigo, *De rebus Hispaniae, lib.* VII, *cap.* XXIV.

[8] AHN, Clero, *carp.* 379/19 (11 June 1220); publ. Appendix, doc. 1, below.

[9] González, *Reino de Castilla*, II, no. 69 (15 June 1165), and thereafter.

chancellors of Castile were appointed by the king.[10] Alfonso VIII may
have granted the titular chancellorship to Gonzalo Pérez, archbishop of
Toledo from 1182 to 1191, but if so the diploma has disappeared.
The first extant grant is that of 1 July 1206 to Archbishop Martín.
By this grant Alfonso conceded that when Diego García, who had been
chancellor since 1192, died, the appointment of his successor should
lie with the archbishop, who should also appoint the notaries and
escribanos, but with the king's approval. This cession of the titular
chancellorship may have been confirmed by Alfonso VIII to Archbishop Rodrigo in 1213; it was certainly so confirmed by Fernando III
in 1230.[11]

Privileges in which the name of the archbishop of Toledo did not
occur were very few. If confirmations denoted presence, then the
archbishops must have been constantly at court. At the beginning of
the period the Castilian bishops numbered seven: those of Avila,
Burgos, Calahorra, Osma, Palencia, Segovia and Sigüenza. Two
bishoprics were added under Alfonso VIII – Cuenca in 1182 or 1183
and Plasencia circa 1190. Fernando III's early campaigns in Andalusia
led to the creation of the see of Baeza in 1228. Usually the names only
of the nobles were given, without any indication of the tenencias
which they held. Counts were more numerous in Castile than in León,
and the title continued to be used throughout the period. In a small
number of documents of Sancho III, Ordoño, prior to the Order of
the Hospital, was included among the confirmantes.[12] This, however,
was exceptional, and the masters of the Spanish military orders were
not mentioned in the documents of Alfonso VIII and his successors up
to 1230, although there is evidence that they attended meetings and
were consulted on affairs of state.[13] In Castilian documents, unlike
those of León, there was no substitution of the ablative for the nominative in the names of the confirmantes, and vacancies of bishoprics were
not noted until the reign of Fernando III. The variations in the number
of confirmantes were greatest at the beginning of the reign of Alfonso
VIII and it is possible that throughout his reign the confirmantes were
present, but from the accession of Enrique I onwards all the bishops

---

[10] For the chancellors from 1157 to 1182, see Millares Carlo, AHDE, III, 269–75.

[11] Ibid. 275–85; the documents of 1 July 1206 and 12 April 1230 are published
on pp. 277–8 and 284–5.

[12] González, Reino de Castilla, II, nos. 42, 43, 48, 49. Ordoño was also the king's
chaplain.

[13] Ibid. III, no. 995 (15 Feb. 1216): Curia of Soria held by the Regent Alvaro
Núñez.

were included whether present or not, and the confirmations denoted those customarily summoned to the great curia, not those actually present.[14]

There is a considerable amount of evidence of the intervention of the curia of Castile in affairs of state – much more than in the case of León. This, no doubt, is largely due to the nature of the narrative sources. Both the *De rebus Hispaniae* of Rodrigo of Toledo and the *Crónica latina* dealt mainly with the affairs of Castile, both were written during the first half of the thirteenth century and both authors were well informed.[15] Rodrigo Jiménez de Rada, bishop of Osma from 1208 to 1209 and thereafter archbishop of Toledo until his death in 1247, took an active and influential part in most of the important events of the first half of the thirteenth century. Various suggestions have been made about possible authors for the *Crónica latina* – such as Domingo, bishop of Plasencia, and even Rodrigo of Toledo himself,[16] this latter an inadmissable attribution which fails to meet the formidable objection that the *Crónica latina* is independent of, and at times contradicts, the *De rebus Hispaniae*. A more plausible suggestion is that the author was Juan, bishop of Osma from 1231 to 1240 and of Burgos from 1240 to 1246 and chancellor of Fernando III from 1217 to 1246.[17] Besides these two narrative sources there is also the *Primera crónica general*, the first of the vernacular general chronicles, compiled during the reign of Alfonso X from pre-existing sources. For the reigns of Alfonso VIII, Enrique I and Fernando III, it was based on the *De rebus Hispaniae*, but, besides the Latin text, the compilers also knew and drew on an amplified and extended vernacular translation which reached to the end of the reign of Fernando III.

On the death of Alfonso VII his eldest son, Sancho, brought the body for burial to Toledo and was there crowned. The *Primera crónica general* says that Sancho III took counsel about the affairs of the kingdom 'con los condes et los omnes buenos de Castiella', who are clearly here the nobles, before proceeding on a tour of justice. There is no specific reference to consultation with the nobles in *De rebus Hispaniae*, merely the statement that the king began to provide for the

[14] Gorosterratzu, *Don Rodrigo Jiménez de Rada*, 162–9.
[15] Sánchez Alonso, *Historiografía española*, i, 124–5, and 130–6.
[16] Cirot, 'Recherches sur la "Chronique latine" ', *Bulletin Hispanique*, xxi, 193–201; *Chrónica latina*, 10–11.
[17] Lomax, 'The authorship of the "Chronique latine des rois de Castille" ', *Bulletin of Hispanic Studies*, xl, 205–11.

affairs of the kingdom.[18] Most of the magnates must have been present with the army, and must also have attended the funeral of the dead king and the coronation of his successor. The first great council of a reign would, presumably, be mainly formal, and given up to the doing of homage, but general discussion might also take place. Alfonso VIII succeeded as a minor in 1158, before he reached the age of three years. Provision for the government of the kingdom during the minority was made by Sancho III and announced to the magnates – 'vocatis magnatibus' – shortly before his death. Land fiefs held from the crown, which were usually surrendered to a new king, were to be retained by their holders until Alfonso reached the age of fifteen; the already elderly Gutierre Fernández de Castro was appointed guardian and Manrique de Lara regent for the child king. By these measures and by the acquiescence of the curia, Sancho III hoped to balance the influence of the two great noble houses of Castro and Lara. These arrangements for the regency did not prove lasting; the guardianship of Alfonso VIII soon passed to Manrique de Lara and matters were complicated by the claims of Fernando II of León, as the child king's nearest male relative. The regent was forced to acknowledge Fernando's nominal guardian-ship of Alfonso VIII until he should reach the age of fourteen, although the count retained possession of the king's person and of the regency to which, on his death, his brother Count Nuño succeeded. In the chaotic conditions of the minority the curia did not play an effective part.[19]

Three donations passed at Burgos on 11, 18 and 19 November 1169 added to the date 'tunc temporis quo serenissimus rex Aldefonsus inibi primum curiam tenuit'.[20] Alfonso VIII was born on 11 November 1155, so that this extraordinary curia at Burgos must have been held to mark the king's majority and the beginning of his personal rule, and to carry out business arising therefrom. The question of his marriage to Eleanor, daughter of Henry II of England, may have been discussed there; of this there is no direct evidence, but the marriage took place in the following year.[21]

The marriages of Alfonso VIII's children were discussed at curias held at San Esteban de Gormaz in May 1187, and at Carrión in June

---

[18] *PCG*, II, *cap.* 985 (p. 664); Rodrigo, *De rebus Hispaniae*, *lib.* VII, *cap.* XII.

[19] Rodrigo, *De rebus Hispaniae*, *lib.* VII, *cap.* XV; cf. *PCG*, II, *cap.* 988; *Crónica latina*, 24–5. For the events of the minority, cf. González, *Reino de Castilla*, I, 150–79.

[20] González, *Reino de Castilla*, II, nos. 124, 125, 126.

[21] Queen Eleanor's name first appeared, added to the royal superscription, in a charter of 17 Sept. 1170; *ibid.* II, no. 148: 'cum uxore mea Alienor regina'.

and July 1188. At the former, the king of Castile received the envoy of the Emperor Frederick I sent to treat for the marriage of his son Conrad to a daughter of Alfonso VII.[22] These negotiations led to the Treaty of Seligenstadt of 23 April 1188, which arranged for the marriage of Conrad to Alfonso's eldest daughter, Berenguela, then aged eight and at that time his heir. The treaty was largely concerned with defining Berenguela's right to succeed her father, should he die without leaving a male heir, and with Conrad's rights as her husband.[23] The curia assembled at Carrión, in the church of San Zoil, in the second half of June.[24] More is known about it than about any other Castilian great curia of this period. Both Rodrigo of Toledo and the author of the *Crónica latina* gave accounts of it, and it was referred to in a number of documents.[25] By the end of June the young king of León, Alfonso IX, had arrived at Carrión,[26] and there he received knighthood from the king of Castile, and kissed his hand in token of vassalage.[27] On the same occasion proposals for a marriage between Alfonso IX and one of Alfonso VIII's daughters – presumably his third daughter, Urraca, since Berenguela, as we have seen, was already betrothed to Conrad of Suabia, and the second, Sancha, had died in 1184 – were discussed, although nothing was to come of it.[28] Before the end of July Conrad of Suabia had reached Carrión. He also was knighted by Alfonso VIII and, in fulfilment of the treaty of Seligenstadt, he was betrothed to his child bride and homage was done to the young pair as future sovereigns, should the king of Castile not have a male heir.[29] After the birth of such an heir, the Infante Don Fernando, on 29 November 1189, Conrad ceased to be interested in this marriage

---

[22] *Ibid.* II, no. 471: 'et ibidem cum nuncio domini imperatoris ad matrimonium contrahendum inter illustrem [filium Romani] imperatoris et illustrem filiam regis Castille tractauerunt'. This is the only evidence of the Curia of 1187.

[23] Rassow, *Der Prinzgemahl*, 1–6, for the text of the treaty.

[24] It was in session on 24 June 1188; *Bullarium de Calatrava*, 25–6: 'usque ad diem sancti Johannis, quando fuit Curia in Carrionem'.

[25] Rodrigo, *De rebus Hispaniae, lib.* VII, *cap.* XXIV (p. 166); *Crónica latina*, 27.

[26] González, *Alfonso IX*, II, no. 10 (Carrión, 27 June 1188).

[27] González, *Reino de Castilla*, II, no. 505 (4 July 1188): 'eo anno quo serenissimus rex prefatus Castelle A. regem Legionensem A. cingulo milicie in curia sua in Carrionem accinxit'; from AHN, Clero, *carp.* 904/4, original; *carp.* 904/5 is a contemporary copy which adds: 'et ipse rex legionensis deosculatus est manum dicti domini Aldefonsi Regis Castelle et Toleti'.

[28] *Crónica latina*, 27; *Annales compostellani*, ed. ES, XXIII, 322. On the children of Alfonso VIII, see González, *Reino de Castilla*, I, 194–212.

[29] A document of 28 July 1188, published in González, *Reino de Castilla*, II, no. 506, is the first to add the knighting of Conrad and his betrothal to the knighting of Alfonso IX. These events continued to be added to the dates of *cartas rodadas* until the end of 1190. For the homage to Conrad, see *Crónica latina*, 27.

which was later annulled by Archbishop Gonzalo of Toledo and the papal legate, Cardinal Gregory.[30]

Alfonso VIII was succeeded in October 1214 by Enrique I, his youngest and only surviving son, then aged ten years and six months. Provision for a regency had been made by Alfonso VIII. In his will, dated 8 December 1204, in the lifetime of his second son, Fernando, he left the kingdom to the latter and the guardianship and regency to his wife, Queen Eleanor. Fernando died in 1211, but later Alfonso VIII confirmed his will and made the same provision for Enrique.[31] Queen Eleanor died some three weeks after her husband, but before she died she remitted her rights as regent to her eldest daughter, Berenguela, the ex-queen of León.[32] In these provisions the curia took no part. Queen Berenguela retained the regency for barely three months before she was forced to relinquish it to Don Alvaro de Lara. She was, however, powerful enough to exact from Don Alvaro and the other magnates an oath that they would not confer or take away fiefs, nor make war on neighbouring kings, nor impose *pecta* on any part of the kingdom without her advice. The oath was administered by Archbishop Rodrigo of Toledo, and must have been taken in some form of curia.[33] The exact date is uncertain, but Rodrigo of Toledo clearly implies that the oath was taken at Burgos. Enrique I was still at Burgos on 15 February 1215, but he was at Palencia on 19 March, and the curia must have been held before the latter date.[34]

In August 1216 some sort of assembly was held at Valladolid. The narrative sources do not agree on its nature. According to the *Crónica latina* it was a meeting of all the magnates for an attempt to restore peace between the contending factions, but it ended in renewed dissension between the majority, who supported the regent, and the minority, who turned to Queen Berenguela.[35] The *Crónica* dates this curia about the feast of the Assumption (15 August), but it must have taken place rather earlier. The chancery passed documents from Valladolid on 12

---

[30] Rodrigo, *De rebus Hispaniae, lib.* VII, *cap.* XXIV.

[31] González, *Reino de Castilla*, III, no. 769.

[32] *Ibid.* III, nos. 963, 970.

[33] Rodrigo, *De rebus Hispaniae, lib.* IX, *cap.* I. The account in the *Crónica latina* (p. 64), is less specific. Sánchez-Albornoz, *España: un enigma histórico*, II, 84, calls this curia 'las Cortes de Burgos', but there is no evidence whatever of the presence of representatives of the cities and towns.

[34] González, *Reino de Castilla*, III, nos. 978, 979. González suggests that the curia took place at Palencia, but this contradicts Rodrigo of Toledo (*ibid.* I, 223–4, n. 302).

[35] *Crónica latina*, 65–6: 'cum convenissent omnes magnates apud Vallem oleti, ut de formatione pacis inter se tractarent'.

and 14 July and on 6 August, but by 12 August the court was already at Toro.[36] In the account given in *De rebus Hispaniae* this assembly, although Rodrigo calls it a 'curia', appears rather to be a junta of those nobles disaffected with the regent.[37] Both sources agree as to the names of the supporters of the queen. From then onwards the country declined into virtual civil war.

On the death of the young Enrique I on 6 June 1217 (after less than four years on the throne), the right of succession passed to his eldest sister, Berenguela, the ex-queen of León. The reign of Queen Urraca was a precedent, howbeit an unpropitious one, for the succession of a woman; Berenguela's rights had been duly acknowledged in the Treaty of Seligenstadt and homage had been done to her. Rodrigo of Toledo referred to this homage in support of her claims in 1217, and indeed stated that homage had been done to Berenguela twice, the first time, presumably, shortly after her birth, the second time at the Curia of Carrión in 1188.[38] The assembly at Valladolid, which first acknowledged Berenguela's rights and then received her renunciation of them in favour of her son, the Infante Don Fernando, was not a formally summoned curia. The state of virtual civil war at the time of Enrique's death precluded that. According to the *Crónica latina*, those present included Bishops Mauricio of Burgos and Tello of Palencia 'cum aliis viris religiosis', those magnates who favoured the queen and those who had rallied to her support after the death of Enrique I, together with many from Extremadura, a province which had hitherto supported the regent and whose support for Queen Berenguela was vital. All present acknowledged Berenguela's right to the throne, but then unanimously asked her to cede the kingdom to her son. To this she assented, and homage was done to Fernando as king in the church of Santa María of Valladolid.[39]

The marriage of Fernando III on 30 November 1219 to Beatrice of Suabia and that of his sister Berenguela to John of Brienne, king of Jerusalem, in 1224, took place during meetings of the great curia. Rodrigo of Toledo called the Curia of 1219 'curia nobilissima' and the author of the *Crónica latina* referred to it as 'celeberrima curia' and

[36] González, *Reino de Castilla*, III, nos. 1003, 1004 (12, 14 July), p. 891 (6 Aug.), nos. 1005, 1006 (12 Aug.).
[37] Rodrigo, *De rebus Hispaniae, lib.* IX, *cap.* II: 'Verum cum apud Vallemoleti curiam celebrassent magnates alii'. González, *Reino de Castilla*, I, 226, bases his narrative on Rodrigo of Toledo, without taking account of the *Crónica latina*.
[38] Rodrigo, *De rebus Hispaniae, lib.* IX, *cap.* V (p. 196).
[39] *Ibid.*; *Crónica latina*, 71-2. According to Rodrigo, the queen's abdication was voluntary and not required by the assembly.

opined that from ancient times such a curia had not been seen in Burgos. Both refer to the presence of *primores* of the cities and towns in 1219 and noted that noblewomen as well as noblemen were present.[40] Thus the Curia of 1219 appears to have been mainly ceremonial as was also that which graced the marriage of the king's sister to John of Brienne (1224).[41]

Fernando III's eldest son, Alfonso, was born on 21 November 1221 and in the following March homage was done to him as heir to the throne. The only evidence of this is the dating clause of a royal *carta* of 21 March 1222 which adds 'sequenti die videlicet postquam hominum de regno factum fuit infanti domino Alfonso solemniter apud Burgos'.[42] This was apparently the first occasion on which the oath of allegiance was taken to an heir as distinct from an heiress to the throne of Castile. There is no evidence that such an oath was taken to any of the three sons of Alfonso VIII, but only to his eldest daughter Berenguela. The version of the *Corónica de España* published by Florián de Ocampo in 1541 stated that such an oath was taken to Alfonso VIII's sons, but this version of the chronicle is too late for its statement to weigh against the absence of any contemporary evidence, narrative or documentary.[43]

Evidence of debates in the curia on questions of peace and war belongs almost entirely to the campaigns of Alfonso VIII against the Almohades in 1211 and 1212, and to Fernando III's campaign of 1224. There are frequent references to consultations and advice in 1211 and 1212 in the pages of the *De rebus Hispaniae* (whose author, Archbishop Rodrigo, himself took part) and also in the *Crónica latina*. Thus, after the capture of Salvatierra by the Almohades in September 1211 Alfonso VIII, 'habito cum Archiepiscopo, episcopis et magnatibus consilio diligenti', decided on a campaign in the following year, and called for a general muster of the kingdom.[44] In the following June the decision to continue to besiege Calatrava was taken 'post longos tractatus'.[45] Further consultation, in which opinion was divided, took

---

[40] Rodrigo, *De rebus Hispaniae, lib.* IX, *cap.* x; *Crónica latina,* 78.
[41] *Crónica latina,* 79–80.
[42] Manuel Rodríguez, *Memorias,* 331.
[43] *Corónica de España,* fol. cccxc. Its statement was accepted by Ibáñez de Segovia, *Memorias de Alonso el Sabio,* 337–8, who thought it was the chronicle commissioned by Alfonso X. It is the version to which Menéndez Pidal gave the name *Tercera crónica general.*
[44] Rodrigo, *De rebus Hispaniae, lib.* VII, *cap.* XXXVI. *Crónica latina,* 41. For the campaigns of 1211 and 1212, cf. González, *Reino de Castilla,* I, 989–1047.
[45] Rodrigo, *De rebus Hispaniae, lib.* VII, *cap.* VI.

place before the crossing of the Sierra Morena.[46] Again, there were discussions after the victory of Las Navas and in the concluding stages of the campaign.[47] It must, however, be remembered that in the campaign of Las Navas the kings of Aragon and Navarre and their nobles, who had joined the crusading army, took part in these deliberations, which were thus rather counsels of war between chiefs of armies than meetings of the Castilian curia. Fernando III's campaign against the Almohades in 1224 was first discussed in an augmented curia at Muño after Whitsuntide 1224, at which most of the magnates were present. There, at the instigation of the king, supported by the queen-mother, war against the Moors was decided on and a great curia was summoned to meet at Carrión in July, where final arrangements were made for the muster of the army at Toledo.[48]

Treaties with foreign rulers were also matters for discussion by the curia, and the text of two treaties with Aragon definitely referred to such deliberations. In the Treaty of Sahagún with Alfonso II of Aragon in 1170, Alfonso VIII stated that he made it 'consilio Cerebruni Toletani archiepiscopi, Palentini episcopi, comitum, aliorumque procerum curie mee' – a small or augmented curia rather than a great curia.[49] A later treaty between the same two kings, concluded during Alfonso VIII's siege of Cuenca in 1177, was confirmed 'communi consilio et consensu principum et baronum nostrorum'.[50] The conclusion of the treaty of peace between Enrique I of Castile and Alfonso IX of León at Toro in August 1216 was notified to Pope Innocent III. On 13 November 1216 his successor Honorius III replied referring to this 'pacem...de consensu et voluntate omnium episcoporum et baronum utriusque Regni adinvicem initam'.[51]

There is very little evidence in this period that the Castilian curia intervened in the relations of church and state. In 1180 Alfonso VIII issued some important decrees granting privileges to the church generally. These included a renunciation of *jus spolii*, an undertaking not to exact any pecuniary gift from archbishops, bishops or abbots or other ecclesiastics by violence, but only with their goodwill and with

[46] *Ibid. Crónica latina*, 46–7.
[47] Rodrigo, *De rebus Hispaniae, lib.* VIII, *cap.* XII; *Crónica latina*, 52; cf. also Alfonso's letter to Pope Innocent III, González, *Reino de Castilla*, III, no. 897.
[48] *Crónica latina*, 80–2.
[49] González, *Reino de Castilla*, II, no. 140 (4 June 1170).
[50] *Ibid.* II, no. 288 (Aug. 1177).
[51] For the text of the papal letter, see Fita, *BRAH*, XXXIX, 526–7. For the text of the treaty, González, *Reino de Castilla*, III, no. 1005.

the approbation of the archbishop (a decree which apparently applied to *petitum* and throws light on the way in which this supposedly free gift had been exacted) and exemption of all priests and clerks from the payment of *facendera*, *fossadera* and any other *pecta* to the crown.[52] These concessions were probably occasioned by the canons of the Third Lateran Council of the preceding year. They were similar to, but less far-reaching than, those granted by Alfonso IX to the prelates of León in 1208, and there was no reference in the text of the Castilian decrees to any consultation with the curia. Similarly, there was no reference to the counsel or consent of the curia in some decrees of May 1191, by which the king took under his protection lands and possessions which the Castilian churches held in the four Peninsular kingdoms of Aragon, Navarre, Portugal and León and also granted that any escaped prisoner who succeeded in taking refuge in any church or monastery of his kingdom should have security and right of asylum there.[53] At times, however, when a clash occurred between the ruler and the ecclesiastical authorities, the former sought the advice and support of the curia. Thus, in 1177, from his camp outside the walls of Cuenca, Alfonso VIII issued an angry edict 'consilio cum comitibus et principibus et baronibus nostris super hoc habito', confirming the *fueros* and constitutions of the clergy of Valladolid and annulling a decree against them pronounced by the papal legate, Cardinal Hyacinth, in an ecclesiastical council at Sahagún, 'nobis absentibus et inconsultis'.[54] Again, during the minority of Enrique I, when the regent, Count Alvaro, seized the ecclesiastical *tercias* and applied them to secular uses, it was on the advice of the curia that he finally gave in and undertook to restore the *tercias* and refrain from misappropriating them in future.[55]

Specific consent by the curia to donations in Castile was not frequent and, again, there was nothing to compare with the situation during the later years of the reign of Fernando II of León, when curial consent was the norm. In 1158 Sancho III granted the *fuero de infanzón* to the canons of Santa María de Husillos 'Consilio et auctoritate comitum meorum et principum regni mei'.[56] For the reign of Alfonso VIII, most

---

[52] González, *Reino de Castilla*, II, no. 344 (18 June 1180). A number of similar grants were addressed to individual bishops; see nos. 348 (12 July 1180), 351 (10 Nov. 1180), 368 (14 May 1181); and Colmenares, *Historia de Segovia*, I, 304–5 (20 Dec. 1180).

[53] González, *Reino de Castilla*, III, no. 570 (27 May 1191).

[54] *Ibid.* II, no. 275 (18 March 1177).

[55] *Ibid.* III, no. 995 (15 Feb. 1216); and Fita, *BRAH*, xxxix, 529.

[56] González, *Reino de Castilla*, II, no. 42 (4 May 1158); i.e. status of an *infanzón*.

of the references to consultation belonged to the minority or early years of his personal rule. A donation to the Order of the Hospital in 1162 was made 'voluntate, consilio et favore regni mei nobilium', and one to the bishop of Palencia in 1166 'tota curia regis presente, corroborante et testificante'.[57] Whether or no 'tota curia' here referred to the restricted or great curia, some grants were certainly made with the consent of the latter. Thus, at the assembly which marked the king's majority in November 1169, a thirty days' fair was granted to the Cluniac priory of San Zoil de Carrión 'Consilio et prelatorum sancte ecclesie et principum regni nostri'.[58] In June of the following year Alfonso VIII took the houses and flocks of the Order of the Hospital under his protection 'cum assensu comitum et principum et baronum nostrorum', and in September 1170 he confirmed to the cathedral of Osma its *collazos* (serfs) in Burgo de Osma and other places 'comunicato consilio cum baronibus meis et nobilibus curie mee'.[59] A year later he granted the castle of Oreja to the Order of Santiago on certain conditions 'cum consilio etiam episcoporum, comitum, et baronum meorum'.[60] After this, references to the consent of the curia become exceedingly rare. A grant to the monastery of San Juan de Burgos in 1178 was made 'consilio pariter et voluntate principum meorum',[61] and, in a small group of charters belonging to the year 1193, the formula 'hoc factum meum discretorum uirorum consilio approbatum' was inserted in the penal clause.[62] There were no examples of recorded advice and consent for the last twenty years of the reign, and very few for Enrique I and Fernando III.[63]

There is no evidence of any direct intervention of the curia in questions of taxation in Castile at this period. The story of Alfonso VIII's abortive attempt to tax the lesser nobles in order to meet the expenses of the siege of Cuenca first appeared in the Portuguese *Crónica geral de 1344* and is too late to be treated as historical fact. According to this story, Alfonso VIII, on the advice of Don Diego López de Haro, summoned the 'Cortes' of Burgos, which were attended by the *hidalgos*, and asked

---

[57] *Ibid.* II, no. 54 (Jan. 1162), 88 (29 Sept. 1166).
[58] *Ibid.* II, no. 124; also in *RC Cluny*, V, no. 4230 (11 Nov. 1169).
[59] González, *Reino de Castilla*, III, nos. 139 (3 June 1170), 148 (17 Sept. 1170).
[60] *Ibid.* II, no. 162 (11 Sept. 1171).
[61] *Ibid.* II, no. 306 (2 Sept. 1178).
[62] *Ibid.* III, nos. 609 (16 Feb. 1193), 612 (5 March 1193), 614 (3 May 1193), 616 (10 June 1193), 617 (26 June 1193), 618 (28 July 1193).
[63] E.g. *ibid.* III, no. 1010 (3 Feb. 1217); Manuel Rodríguez, *Memorias*, 335–7 (22 July 1222); *DA Madrid, 1a serie*, I, 65–9 (23 July 1222).

them to consent to a capitation tax of 5 *maravedies*, but Count Nuño de Lara put himself at the head of the *hidalgos* in opposition to the king, and left the assembly, together with three thousand knights. This narrative appears to have been intended to enhance the reputation of the house of Lara as against that of the house of Haro, and may have originated in some family history.[64]

The division of the kingdom in 1157 was less serious financially to the monarchy in Castile than in León. This was because of the large number of Castilian cities and towns on royal demesne, whose inhabitants paid taxes to the crown. Nevertheless, the development of *petitum* in Castile was much the same as in León. It apeared under the name of *petitio* early in the personal rule of Alfonso VIII, and under that of *petitum* from 1176. From 1178 to 1208 there was scarcely a year in which Alfonso VIII did not grant examption from *petitum* to some church or monastery.[65] As in León, so also in Castile, there is no evidence of consent being asked from the curia, and it seems probable, therefore, that consent was negotiated locally. There is, however, evidence that by the end of the twelfth century *petitum* was regarded as a customary and annual payment in some parts of the kingdom. In 1188 Alfonso VIII exempted the serfs of the Order of Santiago on its lands north of the Duero from 'pedido illo quod mihi annuatim secundum morem patrie solent persoluere', and in 1191 a grant of Sotoavellanos to the monastery of Oña referred to 'totum pedidum quod ibi solet dari annuum regi'.[66]

Of *moneda* in Castile we know even less than in León. There is no surviving decree testifying to the imposition of this tax with the consent of the curia and the towns, as in León in 1202, but the practice of selling the coinage in return for the payment of *moneda* was certainly followed early in the thirteenth century. In 1215 Enrique I exempted the tenants of the monastery of San Andrés de Arroya from all *pecho* except *moneda*, and in 1216 he granted the town of Torrecilla to the monastery of Nájera, with exception from all pecuniary tribute to the

---

[64] The *Crónica geral de 1344* is in process of publication by L. F. Lindley Cintra. The passage in question was published by Cirot, 'Appendices à la "Chronique latine" des rois de Castille', *Bulletin Hispanique*, XIX, 103–7. The 'Cortes' of Burgos of 1177 were accepted as genuine by, among others, Colmenares, *Historia de Segova*, I, 297, and Martínez Marina, *Teoría de las cortes*, II, 439. Guglielmi, *CHE*, XXVIII, 48, also accepted them but questioned the number of lesser nobles present. González, *Reino de Castilla*, I, 42–4, rejected the story.

[65] Sánchez-Albornoz, *Estudios*, 505–10; n.56 gives a lengthy list of such exemptions taken from documents published in González, *Reino de Castilla*, II and III.

[66] González, *Reino de Castilla*, II, no. 511 (1 Nov. 1188); III, no. 565 (1 April 1191).

king including *moneda*.[67] Fernando III, in 1219, conceded to the nunnery of Las Huelgas the right to take *moneda* in its lands whenever it was exacted by the king.[68] When, in 1225, he exempted the town of Lences from a number of tributes, including *portaticum*, *homicidium* and *fonsada*, he retained *moneda*.[69] When was *moneda* first introduced in Castile? Was it originally imposed by Alfonso VIII? The case for such a suggestion is that, on the face of it, it appears unlikely that an entirely new tax would be introduced in the first year of a minority. But possible indications of its existence under Alfonso VIII are scanty and uncertain. Nowhere in Alfonso VIII's privilege in 1180 to the church was there any mention of *moneda*, so it can be assumed that it was not in existence at that date. In the following year Alfonso VIII granted the church of Sigüenza a tenth part of all royal rents throughout the bishopric, specifically including 'decimam quoque monetarum partem', and in 1187 a similar grant of a third of all royal rents in Plasencia, including 'de monetis', was made to the bishop of Avila.[70] But were these grants of coinage or tax? Grants of a proportion of the coinage to bishops and churches were less frequent in Castile than in León, but they did occur. Thus, in 1170 Alfonso VIII granted to Bishop Rodrigo of Calahorra 'decimam omnium monetarum, quecumque regum arbitrio in episcopatu tuo in sempiternum fabricate fuerint', and in 1192 he granted Archbishop Martín of Toledo 'decimas de omni fabrica monete que nunc in Toleto fabricatur et ammodo fabricabitur in perpetuum'.[71] These two grants are completely unequivocable. The grants of 1181 and 1187 are more ambiguous, but the use of the plural (*monetarum* and *de monetis*) seems to indicate that coinage, not tax, was meant. There is one other grant which must be considered. In 1187 Alfonso VIII exempted a number of the *excusados* of the monastery of San Cebrián de Villamezquina 'de pecto, de petito, de moneta, et de fonsada, et de fonsadera, et de cada fratudera et ab omni regio gravamine et tributo'.[72] But this grant has survived in a confirmation of Alfonso X and it may have been interpolated. Thus, by itself it is not sufficient to prove the existence of this septennial tax under Alfonso VIII. The *Crónica de Alfonso X*, in its account of the revolt of the nobles in 1272, states that one of the demands of the

[67] *Ibid.* III, nos. 986 (4 Sept. 1215), 999 (6 March 1216).
[68] Manuel Rodríguez, *Memorias*, 297–8 (2 Dec. 1219).
[69] *Ibid.* 347–8 (18 March 1225).
[70] González, *Reino de Castilla*, II, nos. 376 (12 Aug. 1181), 464 (2 Jan. 1187).
[71] *Ibid.* II, no. 137 (10 March 1170); III, no. 606 (22 Aug. 1192).
[72] *Ibid.* III, no. 1023 (27 May 1187), from a confirmation of 22 May 1256.

84   CURIA AND CORTES IN LEÓN AND CASTILE

rebels was that *moneda* should be collected every seven years 'como la cogió su padre e su visabuelo'.[73] Alfonso X's great grandfather was Alfonso VIII of Castile, but although this part of the *Crónica* is based on a contemporary or near contemporary record of the revolt, it is still too late to be reliable evidence that *moneda* was taken during the reign of Alfonso VIII. Further, the statement of the demands of the Castilian nobles against Alfonso X which was made by Don Juan Núñez to Enrique I of Navarre contains the phrase 'de como la cojio su padre e el so auuelo', that is, Alfonso IX of León, so that the 'great grandfather' of the *Crónica* may be an error.[74] Thus, 1215 remains the first certain indication of the existence of *moneda* in Castile. It is not possible to say how consent to *moneda* was obtained, but in the absence of any evidence of consent by the curia, it is probable that it was negotiated locally by royal officials. Nor is it possible to say how soon it became a customary imposition.

A large number of *fueros* were confirmed or granted by the kings of Castile but, with few exceptions,[75] there were no specific references to advice or consent. A decree which gave protection to the persons and goods of those shipwrecked, which was included in the privileges granted to the church in 1180, contained no reference to the curia.[76] There was nothing in Castile in any way comparable to the series of general laws issued by Alfonso IX in León between 1188 and 1228. Some sort of edict was promulgated in the assembly held after the capture of Salvatierra by the Almohades in 1211. The text has not survived, but from the short accounts given by Rodrigo of Toledo and the author of the *Crónica latina* it appears to have been sent to all parts of the kingdom and to have directed both knights and foot soldiers to provide themselves with the necessary arms for a campaign against the Moors. Thus, it was of temporary application and was occasioned by the decision to attack in the following year.[77]

After the campaign of Las Navas, in December 1212, Alfonso VIII held an important curia in Burgos, in which he confirmed generally all the privileges and *fueros* granted to the towns by his ancestors, and commanded the *ricos hombres* and the *infanzones* of Castile to reduce their *fueros*, customs and franchises to writing, and submit them for

[73] *Crónica Alfonso X, cap.* XL.
[74] AGN, *caj.* 3/4; publ. Yanguas y Miranda, *Diccionario,* III, 42–3.
[75] E.g. *DA Madrid, 1a serie,* I, 65 (*Fueros* of Madrid); Manuel Rodríguez *Memorias,* 335–7 (*Fueros* of Uceda).
[76] González, *Reino de Castilla,* II, no. 344.
[77] Rodrigo, *De rebus Hispaniae, lib.* VII, *cap.* XXXVI; *Crónica latina,* 41.

revision and approval to the king. Pressure of other business seems to have prevented further action by Alfonso. Our evidence for this curia is very late, for it comes from the prologue to the version of the *Fuero viejo* drawn up in 1356, but the account is very circumstantial. The passage dealing with the confirmation of the privileges of the towns has every appearance of being based on a general charter of confirmation. It gives the exact date and place of the curia – on the feast of the Innocents (28 Dec.) 1212 in the Hospital Real at Burgos – and enumerates the names of some of those present.[78] Some other statements in this prologue can be substantiated and its account has, therefore, been accepted by modern legal historians.[79] From this curia, in all probability, stemmed the large number of extended, vernacular town *fueros* which were compiled during the first half of the thirteenth century and also some collections of territorial law and *fazañas*, which have not survived in their entirety, but which have passed in part into later collections, such as the *Libro de los fueros de Castilla*, and finally into the *Ordenamiento de Alcalá* of 1348 and the *Fuero viejo* of 1356.[80] Thus, the Curia of 1212 stimulated the collection and codification of existing customs and *fueros*, even though it enacted no legislation. There were also some laws promulgated then which have not survived, but which were referred to in later legislation. Thus, the preamble to Alfonso X's decrees of 1252 spoke of 'posturas que fizieron el Rey don Alfonso mio uisauelo et el Rey don Fernando mio padre', and one of these decrees, dealing with prohibited exports, specifically referred to earlier prohibitions by Alfonso VIII and Fernando III.[81] The latter also promulgated an edict against heretics, the text of which, again, has not survived.[82]

It remains to examine the *curia regis* of Castile as a judicial tribunal. For the period up to the death of Alfonso VII, most of the available documents concerning cases tried before the king's court dealt with suits arising in León. For the period of the separation of the two kingdoms,

[78] *PCG*, ii, *cap.* 1021 (p. 705), appears to refer to this curia which it places erroneously at Toledo. Alfonso VIII was at Burgos on 17,27 and 28 Dec. 1212; cf. González, *Reino de Castilla*, iii, no. 902, 903, 904.

[79] Sánchez, *AHDE*, vi, 279–81, who prints the relevant passage from the *Fuero viejo in extenso*; García Gallo, *AHDE*, xiii, 308–10; Sánchez-Albornoz, *CHE*, xxxv–xxxvi, 322–3.

[80] The articles cited above deal with some of these collections.

[81] García Rámila, *Hispania*, v, 205, 212; also *ap.* iv, preamble and cl. 19.

[82] *Registres de Grégoire IX*, ii, no. 3271; Mansilla Reoyo, *Iglesia castellano-leonesa*, 149–50.

however, there is ample evidence of the judicial activities of the Castilian curia, of its suitors, of the types of suits heard before it and of the procedure of the court. There are no records of suits in which the king was either plaintiff or defendant. Cases between two ecclesiastics were rare, as they were increasingly heard before ecclesiastical courts or before papal judges delegate.[83] There are, however, records of disputes between ecclesiastical bodies which were ended by conventions and agreements made before the king and with his approval. Thus, an agreement was reached, probably in 1181, between the chapter of the cathedral of Toledo and the Order of Calatrava on the parochial rights in new towns founded by the Order, in the presence of Alfonso VIII and the bishop of Avila and with the advice of the magnates. By this agreement the church was to receive the tenths of bread, wine and cattle, and the Order was to have the other ecclesiastical rights and the right of presentation to churches.[84] A further agreement on the division of the tithe in certain places was made between Archbishop Gonzalo of Toledo and the Order of Calatrava 'in praesentia Domini Aldefonsi Regis Castellae' in 1183.[85] In 1223 the monastery of San Pedro de Gumiel claimed lands from the monastery of Nuestra Señora de la Vid, and the abbot of the former obtained papal letters appointing the bishop, dean and cantor of Palencia as judges delegate to hear the case. The dispute was, however, ended by a compromise brought about by the arbitration of the royal chancellor, Juan, abbot of Valladolid, and Pedro Jiménez, one of the king's *alcaldes*, and was agreed to in the presence of Fernando III and approved by him. Presumably he intervened to bring about a solution, but we do not know why he did so.[86]

Cases concerning ecclesiastical patronage heard before the king's court were fewer in Castile than in León and most were probably heard before the ecclesiastical courts. Among those heard before the curia was one in 1210 between the abbot of Silos and the kin of Don Vicente Mayor, concerning the church of San Christóforo de Olmedo. In this case twenty *boni homines* of Olmedo gave sworn evidence that the church only paid certain dues annually to the abbey, as well as food rent when the abbot visited the church; that if there were a priest among the founder's kin, then he held the benefice; if there were not,

---

[83] See e.g. Serrano, *Obispado de Burgos*, III, nos. 167, 168, 175, 178, 215, 228, etc.
[84] González, *Reino de Castilla*, III, no. 932 (n.d.). The *carta* is addressed to Guillermo, prior of Toledo. In 1181 the archiepiscopal see was vacant.
[85] *Bullarium de Calatrava*, no. XXI (p. 20) (7 Dec. 1183).
[86] AHN, *Clero, carp.* 230/18 (21 Jan. 1223).

then a lay rector from among the kindred appointed a chaplain.[87] Another long-drawn-out case of ecclesiastical patronage was that concerning the church of Santa Eugenia de Cordobilla between the founder's kin, the abbot of Aguilar de Campóo, and the *concejo* of Cordobilla. The suit began in 1187, when Don Pedro de Santa Eugenia complained before Alfonso VIII that Abbot Andrés had dispossessed him of the church. Further complaints, including complaints of acts of violence committed both by the abbey and by the *concejo*, were made before Alfonso VIII on various occasions and finally before Fernando III in 1223.[88]

Most suits between an ecclesiastical and a lay litigant were land suits. In 1196 Bishop Gonsalvo of Segovia and the townspeople of Sepúlveda came before the king's court on the question of the ownership of the township of Navares, which the bishop claimed for the church but which the townsmen said they had purchased for money and other lands from his predecessor, Bishop Guillermo. To this, Bishop Gonsalvo responded that the transaction had been carried out without the knowledge or the sanction of the chapter. The case was heard 'coram rege et iudicibus curie' and judgment was given that if the consent of the chapter had not been obtained, then the action of the former bishop was void. Having ascertained by the testimony of good men that such consent had not been given, Alfonso VIII ordered the town to restore Navares to the church.[89] In 1201 the Order of Santiago and the *concejo* of Cuenca disputed the possession of the two villages of Valtablado and Villanueva; the case was ended by a compromise approved by the king, by which Valtablado was assigned to the Order and Villanueva to Cuenca.[90] Again, on 11 June 1220, Fernando III confirmed a sentence given in the presence of the king and the curia by his majordomo, Don Gonsalvo Rodríguez, and Don García Fernández, the majordomo of the queen-mother, Berenguela, in a case brought by Abbot Esteban and the canons of La Vid against Don Lope Díaz de Haro who, so the abbot contended, had seized 'Alcolia' and certain of its villages which belonged to the abbey. The sentence was in favour of the monastery.[91] Other cases concerned services due to ecclesiastical overlords, both by townships and by individuals, such as a suit between the bishop of

---

[87] *RC Silos*, no. 81 (20 March 1210); also in González, *Reino de Castilla*, III, no. 863.
[88] *Documentos lingüísticos*, no. 28 (4 April 1223).
[89] González, *Reino de Castilla*, III, no. 1029 (29 Oct. 1196).
[90] *Ibid.* III, no. 702 (17 May 1201).
[91] Publ. Appendix, doc. I, below.

Segovia and the *concejo* of Mojados on the payment of *fonsadera*, *pedido* and *pecho* by the *concejo*, in which judgment in favour of the bishop was given in the court of Enrique I in 1215,[92] and that between the abbey of Santillana and some of its tenants on dues owed to the abbey which 'fue iudgado enna cort del rei don Fernando'.[93].

As in León, so also in Castile, the *concejos* appeared with increasing frequency before the king's court.[94] The majority of the suits in which the towns were involved concerned rights in the *montes*, that is, in tracts of uncultivated, mountainous land covered by woods and scrub which afforded rough grazing for the flocks and herds of neighbouring centres of population. As well as grazing, the *montes* also afforded timber for building or for fuel. Rights in the *montes* roughly correspond to the rights in the wastes in England. In Castile, in the mountains between the valleys of the Duero and the Tagus, most of the inhabitants, both of walled towns and of scattered villages and hamlets, were engaged in pastoral pursuits, and these communities were dependent on rights in the *montes*. Suits about such rights might be between a monastery and a neighbouring town, as when, in 1186, Abbot Raimundo and the monks of Sacramenia asserted the right of the monks and their dependants to pasture their flocks and cut wood in the mountains, groves and pine forests belonging to the *concejo* of Sepúlveda,[95] or between a larger town and a smaller one within its *alfoz*. Thus a case in 1226 between the *concejos* of San Esteban de Gormaz and Alcózar turned on the question whether the latter was within the *alfoz* of the former and had common rights of pasture.[96]

The use of advocates to state a litigant's case before the king's court was exceptional – not normal – in Castile, and generally depended on a royal privilege or on an *ad hoc* arrangement during a suit. In 1166, when Alfonso VIII took the collegiate church of San Pedro de Soria under his protection, he granted the prior and canons the right, when involved in litigation, to appoint 'uocerum uel aduocatum quem eligant de Soria siue de foris'.[97] In the suit in 1196 between the *concejo* of Santa Cruz de Juarros on the one hand and the abbot of Ibeas and the prior of Santa Cruz de Burgos on the other, a certain Alvar García 'fuit in voce concilii Sancte Crucis' and the king appointed Fernando

[92] González, *Reino de Castille*, III, no. 1034 (20 Nov. 1215): 'Iudicatum fuit in curia mea'.
[93] *Documentos lingüísticos*, no. 6 (3 Dec. 1223).   [94] Procter, *EHR*, LXXIV, 1–22.
[95] González, *Reino de Castilla*, II, no. 461 (18 Oct. 1186).
[96] Manuel Rodríguez, *Memorias*, 352–4 (18 Feb. 1226).
[97] González, *Reino de Castilla*, II, no. 81 (6 June 1166).

Fernández de Castro to speak for the abbot and the prior.[98] There is little positive evidence as to how corporate bodies, especially towns, made their appearance before the king's court. In most cases in which a *concejo* was cited before the *curia regis* in this period, the documents merely state that such and such *concejo* was impleaded. It is probable that the *alcaldes* attended the court, but specific evidence is lacking. However, when in 1214 Alfonso VIII confirmed an agreement between the *concejo* of Las Barasas de Suso and the monastery of Ovila, Juan Marcos, 'pro parte concilii', and Brother Sancho, 'pro parte abbatis et monachorum', made the agreement before the king. Clearly these two persons must have been representatives, having powers to bind their principals.[99]

One important difference between procedure in the *curia regis* in Castile and that in León was that, as the *Forum judicum* was not recognised in Castile, except in the province of Toledo, there was no proof *ad librum*. Otherwise, all the methods of proof used in the Leonese court were also used in the Castilian curia. Documentary proof was adduced in a suit between the *concejo* of San Esteban de Gormaz and Bishop Martín of Osma, concerned with the buying and selling of land and houses, by which the bishop increased the number of his *collazos* (serfs) in the Burgo de San Martín and three nearby villages. The bishop produced a charter of Alfonso VII in support of his case.[100] In 1196 the *concejo* of Santa Cruz de Juarros denied the right of the *collazos* of the abbey of Ibeas and the priory of San Juan de Burgos, who dwelt in San Adrián, to pasture their beasts and cut wood on the lands of the *concejo*. The judges of the king's court ordered the abbot and the prior to produce privileges in support of their case 'in curia coram rege'.[101] Documentary proof was not always considered sufficient in itself. In the suit between Abbot Raimundo of Sacramenia and the *concejo* of Sepúlveda, the abbot brought documents to prove his case, but the king ordered an inquisition to be held.[102] Proof by oath was used in a suit between the *concejo* of Agusejo and the monastery of San Martín de Albelda in 1192 and in the one between the abbey of Silos and the kindred of Don Vicente Mayor in 1210. Both these were patronage suits.[103]

An example of judicial combat occurred in 1184 in a suit between

[98] *Ibid*. III, no. 653 (31 March 1196).   [99] *Ibid*. III, no. 922 (22 June 1214).
[100] *Ibid*. II, no. 557 (25 Aug. 1190).
[101] *Ibid*. III, no. 653 (31 March 1196).
[102] *Ibid*. II, no. 461 (18 Oct. 1186).
[103] *Ibid*. III, no. 607 (2 Nov. 1192); *RC Silos*, no. 81 (20 March 1210).

the men of Villagonzalo and of Madriz concerning the ownership of three *majadas* (buildings on the *montes*, where shepherds and their flocks sheltered at night). Each party was ordered to provide a champion to fight on foot with staves, and as the champion of Villagonzalo was the victor, the *majadas* were assigned to that village.[104] Certain treaties, which among other things dealt with violence committed along the frontier, provided that in some cases such questions should be settled by *duellum*. Thus, in the treaty of Cabreros of 1206 between Castile and León, it was laid down that, if a complaint was made against an *hidalgo* living in a frontier town and the damage was valued at more than 500 *solidi*, the suit was to be heard in the court of the defendant's king and proof was to be by battle.[105] A similar provision was made in the treaty of Guadalajara of 1207 between Castile and Navarre.[106] In this connection it is perhaps worth noting that, when in 1177 the kings of Castile and Navarre submitted their boundary disputes to the arbitration of Henry II of England, they each sent, with their respective embassies, an armed champion, should trial by battle be decided on.[107]

The method of proof most frequently used in the Castilian court was, as in León, the inquisition or *pesquisa*.[108] It was a method particularly well suited to cases concerned with rights in the *montes*, but it was used in all types of cases. The procedure in Castile did not differ from that used in León, but the evidence available for Castile includes a number of detailed records of the evidence collected locally. These records show that the inquiries might be held at a single centre or in several neighbouring villages, and evidence obtained from a variable number of *boni homines* of the locality, who answered questions put to them on oath. These jurors included knights, priests, clerks, vine-dressers and shepherds. They gave record, not only from their own knowledge, but also hearsay evidence, based on what they had heard from their parents, grandparents or others of an older generation. These answers were written down, sealed with the seals of the inquisitors and remitted to the king. They were then read before the king and the suitors in the curia, and sentence was given in accordance with the evidence.[109]

---

[104] González, *Reino de Castilla*, II, no. 429 (12 Dec. 1184).
[105] *Ibid.* III, no. 782 (p. 371) (26 March 1206).
[106] *Ibid.* III, no. 813 (p. 428) (29 Oct. 1207).
[107] *Gesta Henrici* I, 129.   [108] See Procter, 'The judicial use of "*pesquita*" ',1–19.
[109] Examples of *pesquisas* published *in extenso* include: González, *Reino de Castilla*, III, nos. 751 (14 Aug. 1203), 905 (5 June 1213), 934 (n.d.); *CD Oña*, I, no. 369 (1207); II, no. 458 (1229?); *Documentos lingüísticos*, nos. 4 (1210), 165 (before 1215); Manuel Rodríguez, *Memorias*, 352–4 (18 Feb. 1226).

A large number of cases were also ended by compromise between the parties. Such conventions were made in the king's presence, before the curia, and were specifically approved by the king. In 1200 Bishop Rodrigo of Sigüenza and the *concejo* of Atienza made an agreement about the village of Cabanillas which had been purchased by a former bishop. By this agreement the bishop's men in Cabanillas were not to acquire messuages in Atienza, nor the men of Atienza in Cabanillas; further, the men of Cabanillas were no longer to pay certain dues and services such as *fonsadera, posta* and *petitum* with the *concejo*, although they were still bound to contribute to the upkeep of the walls of Atienza; and the inhabitants of both town and village were to have common rights over waters, pasture and the *montes*.[110] Conventions between two *concejos*, generally concerned with such matters as pasturage rights, rights in the *montes* or the boundaries between the lands of contiguous towns, were numerous in the earlier years of the thirteenth century. The records, however, do not always make clear whether such agreements arose out of litigation before the king's court, or whether the parties reached agreement without litigation, and then sought approval from the king.[111]

The professional lawyer element appeared in the Castilian curia at this time, as it did in the curia of León. *Ad hoc* judges were still appointed in some cases as, for example, in 1192 in the patronage suit between the *concejo* of Agusejo and the monastery of Albelda when García Ruiz gave judgment in the king's court,[112] or in 1220 when Fernando III's majordomo, Gonsalvo Rodríguez, and García Fernández, the majordomo of the queen-mother, gave sentence in the suit between the abbot and canons of La Vid and Lope Díaz de Haro.[113] There are, in fact, no references in judicial record to *jurisperiti* as such and, although there was certainly knowledge of Roman law among the Castilian clergy, Roman lawyers may not have penetrated secular justice at this time as far in Castile as they did in León. There are, however, a number of references to *iudices curie* who must have held some sort of permanent office and have been professional legists.[114] The names of a number of persons described as *alcaldes* of the king or of the king's

[110] González, *Reino de Castilla*, III, no. 691 (25 Oct. 1200).
[111] E.g. *ibid.* III, nos. 815 (30 Nov. 1207), 818 (16 March 1208), 822 (25 July 1208), 909 (8 Aug. 1213), etc.
[112] *Ibid.* III, no. 607 (2 Nov. 1192).
[113] AHN, Clero, *carp.* 379/19 (11 June 1220); publ. Appendix, doc, 1, below.
[114] E.g. González, *Reino de Castilla*, III, no. 1029 (29 Oct. 1196): 'Coram rege et iudicibus curiae', and 'Supredictae curiae iudices iudicaverunt.'

court have also come down to us. These were presumably men learned in the customary law of Castile and holding office on a regular or permanent basis. Four such alcaldes – Gonzalvo Pérez de Torquemada, Gutierre Díaz de San Boal, Don Ordoño de Torme and García Pérez de Toledo – gave judgment with Alfonso VIII in the suit between the monastery of Ibeas and the concejo of Santa Cruz de Juarros in 1196.[115] Two others who served Alfonso VIII as alcaldes were Minaya and Pedro Vidas.[116] Pedro Jiménez, described by Fernando III as alcaldus meus, appeared in documents of 1220 and 1223.[117]

There are no documentary records of appeals to the king's court from lower courts, nor to criminal cases tried in the king's court, but some information about such cases can be obtained from other sources. Thus, in a concord between the citizens and clergy of Cuenca in 1207, which was approved by Alfonso VIII, it was laid down that lay servants of the clergy were to be justiciable before the alcaldes of the town but with the right of appeal to the curia regis.[118] Some town fueros, granted or compiled in the late twelfth or early thirteenth century, allow for appeals to the king in certain cases. Thus, the fuero of Cuenca (c. 1190) laid down that appeals could only be made in suits in which more than ten mancales were involved. It also gave considerable details on the time allowed during which the appeal must be made and on other matters of procedure.[119]

Treason trials and cases against magnates for maladministration in their tenencias were certainly heard before the great curia, but we have no documentary evidence in such cases, and have to rely on the not always precise accounts given in narrative sources. After the accession of Fernando III in 1217, the ex-regent for Enrique I, Alvaro de Lara, was taken prisoner and brought to Valladolid. No formal trial took place but, after discussion, an agreement was reached by which Count Alvaro undertook to hand over his castles in return for his liberty.[120] In 1219 Fernando III cited Rodrigo Díaz, 'ut ad curiam veniens', he should make answer to charges of wrongdoing in the lands committed

115 Ibid. III, no. 653 (31 March 1196).
116 Ibid. III, nos. 809 (20 July 1207), 822 (28 July 1208), 828 (12 Dec. 1208), 868 (16 May 1210); AHN, Clero, carp. 230/11 (18 July 1219): 'Miennaya alcaldus curie auei mei'.
117 AHN, Clero, carp. 379/19 (11 June 1220); carp. 230/18 (21 Jan. 1223): 'P. Xemeni alcaldus meus'.
118 González, Reino de Castilla, III, no. 795 (6 March 1207).
119 Fuero de Cuenca, cap. XXVII: 'De Appellantibus ad Regem', 600–8.
120 Rodrigo, De rebus Hispaniae, lib. IX, cap. VIII; PGG, II, cap. 1032; Crónica latina, 75.

to his administration. He appeared before the curia, but then withdrew, whereupon the king declared his lands forfeit – 'abstulit ei terram
suam'. Finally, Rodrigo handed over his castles in exchange for
fourteen thousand gold pieces. This is the version of Rodrigo of Toledo.
The *Primera crónica general* follows Rodrigo, but adds that the king
confiscated his lands in curia – 'tolliole la tierra por corte'. This
addition turns the action of Fernando III into a judicial sentence, but
the king had the undoubted right to confiscate lands held from the
crown without recourse to the curia in such circumstances. When
Gonsalvo Pérez de Molina rebelled and devastated the country surrounding Molina, Fernando III resorted to force and the matter was
finally settled by compromise.[121] These examples show that during the
early years of Fernando's reign judicial action against nobles was ineffectual and such revolts as these were ended in practice by force of
arms or by compromise.

[121] *Ibid. lib.* IX, *cap.* XI; *PCG*, II, *cap.* 1035; *Crónica latina*, 79, refers shortly to
these matters.

4

The towns of León and Castile in the
thirteenth century

It is now necessary to describe briefly the main characteristics of the towns on royal demesne. These towns alone sent representatives to the cortes, and, by the end of the twelfth century, were to all intents and purposes self-governing corporations under the crown. The municipalities of Christian Spain differed in various ways from those in other kingdoms in Western Europe; they also exhibited different characteristics in different parts of the Peninsula, though these differences do not correspond with the political divisions into separate kingdoms. It is, however, only with the towns in León and Castile that we are here concerned.

Broadly speaking, the towns of both kingdoms can be divided into those to the north of the valley of the Duero, those of the centre from the Duero to the Guadiana and, in the case of Castile, those of Andalusia and Murcia. It was only in the north of the Peninsula that the eleventh-century revival of trade which occasioned the rapid growth of the towns in most of Western Europe had much effect. In the towns to the north of the Duero the eleventh century saw the settlement of traders and merchants in the suburbs (*burgos*) of the towns, but this occurred only where French influence was strong, and most of these traders and merchants came from north of the Pyrenees. Such influence and settlement were found along the pilgrimage routes to Santiago de Compostela: from the passes of the Pyrenees, or from La Coruña, where pilgrims who came by sea disembarked, or from Portugal, where there was considerable French influence. French influence was also found in monastic towns, such as Sahagún, Santo Domingo de Silos or San Zoil de Carrión, where the monasteries had been reformed by, or had been granted to, Cluny, or in episcopal sees whose first bishop after restoration had been French, as in the case of the Castilian bishoprics of Burgo de Osma and Sigüenza. It is only in relation to such cities and towns that the terms *burgo* and *burgueses* were used in this period.[1] Many of the towns of the north, however, were not royal towns but were subject to the overlordship of bishops or abbots. The Galician towns of Santiago de Compostela, Orense, Lugo and Túy and the Castilian town of Burgo de Osma were all subject to their bishops; towns such as Sahagún, Santo Domingo de Silos and Oña were monastic towns of which the abbot was lord.

From the valley of the Duero to the valley of the Guadiana the towns were restored, founded and colonised during the course of the reconquest, especially during the last years of the eleventh century and during the twelfth century. The growth of these towns was not much affected by mercantile considerations; they were inhabited mainly by warriors, husbandmen and herdsmen. They were, as we shall see when we consider the social status of their inhabitants, markedly military. Most of these towns were on royal demesne. They included such Leonese towns as Salamanca, Ledesma, Alba de Tormes and Ciudad Rodrigo and such Castilian towns as Avila, Cuéllar, Cuenca, Madrid, Segovia, Sepúlveda and Soria. Toledo had its own characteristics and was an exception. Unlike the others it had had a continuous existence from Visigothic times and a large Mozarabic population. After its reconquest in 1085 many Moslems remained in the city, and foreign, as well as Castilian, settlers were added to the Mozárabes and Mudéjares.[2]

The reconquest of Andalusia and Murcia during the thirteenth century added another group of cities and towns, including Seville, Córdoba, Jaén, Murcia and Cartagena, whose characteristics differed from those of the north and the centre. Like Toledo, they, too, had existed continuously since the Visigothic period and, under Moslem rule, they had traded extensively with the states of North Africa and the Eastern Mediterranean. At the time of the earliest appearances of town representatives in the curia, they were still under Moslem rule and their entry into the cortes took place after the reunion of León and Castile.

One marked characteristic of the towns of Castile and León was that their jurisdiction extended far beyond the town walls and the suburbs, to cover considerable tracts of land known as the *término*, *tierra* or *alfoz* of the town concerned. The *término* thus included villages (*aldeas*) and other smaller centres of population and in some cases even other, but smaller, towns. The *términos* subject to the towns

[1] García de Valdeavellano, *Burgos y burgueses*, 74–5, 85–7, 105–10, 116–28; Defourneaux, *Les Français en Espagne*, 35–7, 230–8, 239–40, 244–5.
[2] García de Valdeavellano, *Burgos y burgueses*, 137–41.

which had been colonised during the reconquest were often very extensive indeed, and some corresponded in area to modern provinces.
In the north the *términos* were generally much smaller, and some towns
had none. In Andalusia they were, as in the centre, very extensive, but
lands and villages granted by the crown at the time of the conquest
to the military orders, to churches and to nobles were interspersed
within the boundaries of the *término* and were not subject to the
town.[3]

The inhabitants of the town and *término* were divided into *vecinos*,
who enjoyed full rights of citizenship, and *moradores*, who did not.
The qualifications of the *vecino* were possession of house and land,
residence within the town or *término* and payment of dues and taxes
(*pechos*) to the crown and to the town government although, in course
of time, both the privileged and the very poor were exempted from
pecho. Within the walls of the town the majority of the inhabitants
were *vecinos*; in the rural *término*, however, they formed a minority.
The *vecinos* shared in the possessions and rights held in common, such
as rights in the *montes*, and in the enclosed pastures they had greater
protection than those who were not *vecinos*, and they participated in
town government.[4]

It is probable that at the time of colonisation there was equality
among the *vecinos*, but social classes tended to reappear and to become
more marked with time and with the extension of the *término* administered by the town. By the end of the twelfth century the towns exhibited a complex social structure. Lesser nobles – *infanzones, hidalgos*
and knights of noble origin (*caballeros hidalgos*) – often held land
within the jurisdictions of the towns, as the result of royal donations.
They did not as a rule live within the walls, but in the rural *tierra*, and
were often lords of villages; they were subject to the town *fueros*, but
took no part in town government.[5] In Andalusia, however, nobles were
granted houses and messuages by the crown within the walls of cities.
In Seville two hundred knights of noble lineage, and in Jerez, Baeza,
Carmona and Arcos lesser numbers, were established with houses to
act as garrisons.[6]

By the end of the twelfth century a town patriciate had grown up.

---

[3] Carlé, *Del concejo*, 163–71.
[4] *Ibid.* 81–90; Gilbert, *Concejo de Madrid*, 37–44.
[5] For references to nobles in town *fueros*, see González, *Alfonso IX*, II, nos. 163
(p. 230) (Castroverde), 523 (p. 624) (Bonoburgo de Caldelas); in royal documents, see e.g. *MHE*, I, nos. XXXIII, XL, LV, LXIII, etc.
[6] *Repartimiento de Sevilla*, I, 291–3.

The most important element in this was that composed of knights of non-noble origin – the *caballeros villanos* or *caballeros de las villas*. This class had originated in the early days of the reconquest from those freemen who had possession of horses and weapons of war and had obtained lands in unpopulated districts. Alfonso VI had granted special privileges to such knights who settled in Toledo after its recapture, and these privileges were confirmed by Alfonso VII and became known as the *fueros de los caballeros de Toledo*.[7] During the period of the separation of the two kingdoms, the kings of both León and Castile pursued a definite policy of encouraging the growth of this class within the towns, by granting to all those who possessed horses and arms some of the privileges which belonged to knights of noble origin. The most important of these privileges were exemption from all *pechos* except *fonsadera* (a payment in lieu of miiltary service) and a similar exemption for a certain number of *excusados* from among the dependants of each knight. All the *fueros* granted by Fernando III to the towns of Andalusia included the *fueros* of the knights of Toledo.[8] Under Alfonso X this policy reached its apogee. Throughout his reign he made frequent grants to the knights of individual towns of such privileges.[9] In the Cortes of Seville of 1264 he granted extensive privileges to the knights of the towns of Extremadura generally.[10] There are also references in documents to those who owned the best houses and to *mayores*.[11] These, who might include others besides knights, also belonged to the town patriciate and were presumably persons of substance. By degrees the knights of the towns began to monopolise municipal government and this too was encouraged by the crown during the thirteenth century.[12]

The bulk of the population, especially out in the *tierra*, was formed by the *pecheros*, who owed dues to the king and the *concejo*. They were also referred to as *peones* and *pobladores*. This was a composite class. It comprised craftsmen and artisans (*menestrales*), such as smiths,

---

[7] For the early development of the *caballeros villanos* up to 1157, see Pescador, 'La caballería popular en León y Castilla', *CHE*, XXXIII–XXIV, 137–61.

[8] *Ibid*. 163–8; 173–87.

[9] E.g. *MHE*, I, nos. XLIII (to Peñafiel, 19 July 1256), XLIV (to Buitrago, 23 July 1256), LXXXIII (to Escalona, 5 March 1261), CXII (to Requena, 11 Aug. 1268), etc.

[10] BL, Add. MS. 9916, fols. 250–9; publ. Appendix, doc. VII, below.

[11] E.g. *MHE*, I, nos. XL (to Seville, 23 Jan. 1256), XLIII (to Peñafiel, 19 July 1256); *CD Cuéllar*, no. 16 (21 July 1256); *CD Murcia*, I, no. XLIV (30 April 1271); Colmenares, *Historia de Segovia*, I, 413 (27 Sept. 1278).

[12] Bó and Carlé, 'Cuando empieza a reservarse a los caballeros el gobierno de las ciudades castellanas', *CHE*, IV, 120–4.

carpenters, shoemakers, armourers and tanners; the traders and shop-keepers of the town, such as butchers, bakers and vintners, most of whom were also, to some extent, engaged in agriculture; and the villagers of the *término*, who were mainly shepherds and agricultur-alists. The artisans and traders were a growing class, and were begin-ning to combine in guilds and associations (*cofradías*). Such associations were, however, viewed with suspicion both by the crown and by the knights of the town, and both Fernando III and Alfonso X forbad them, except for religious purposes. These distinctions between social classes are clearly seen in the allotment of lands in Seville after its capture by Fernando III; *peones, caballeros villanos* and *caballeros hidalgos* received estates varying with their rank – single, double or special.[13] So, too, in a licence granted by Alfonso X in 1257 to the Christians who garrisoned the citadel of Requena, permitting them to buy lands from the Mudéjares (who still inhabited the town and the surrounding countryside), knights and squires of noble lineage were licensed to buy lands to the value of 150 *maravedíes*, knights of the town up to 100 *maravedíes* and *peones* up to 50 *maravedíes*.[14]

Trade was carried on mainly in the weekly markets which catered principally for local needs, and there are many references in the *fueros* to these markets and to the enforcement of the peace of the market by fines.[15] Most towns of any importance also had the right to hold an annual fair which in some cases lasted for several weeks. Enrique I, for example, granted Brihuega a fair on St Peter's day, with a safe-conduct to those coming to and going from it valid for fifteen days before and after the feast.[16] Under their *fueros*, Cáceres held a fair from mid-April to mid-May, and Sepúlveda one for eight days before and after Pentecost.[17] At the beginning of his reign Alfonso X granted to the Order of Santiago, for the services it had rendered him in his conquest of the kingdom of Murcia before his accession, a ten days' fair in the town of Montiel, starting on St Luke's Day.[18]

Such fairs served not only local trade but also national and foreign

---

[13] Carlé, *Del concejo*, 168–9.
[14] *MHE*, I, no. LV.
[15] E.g. *Fuero de Salamanca*, cl. 39, 149–50; *Fuero de Ledesma*, cl. 96, 223, 309; both publ. in *Fueros leoneses*; González, *Alfonso IX*, II, no. 49 (*Fuero of Villafranca*), no. 126 (*Fuero of Milmando*); *Fuero de Miranda de Ebro cl.* 28; González, *Reino de Castilla*, III, no. 579 (*Fuero of Arganzón*), no. 633 (*Fuero of Navarrete*).
[16] González, *Reino de Castilla*, III, no. 987.
[17] González, *Alfonso, IX*, II, no. 596; *Fueros de Sepúlveda*, 68.
[18] AHN, Santiago, *caj*. 214/11.

commerce and were frequented by itinerant merchants from other parts of the kingdom and also by foreign merchants. Foreign trade was mostly seaborne and entered the Peninsula either by the ports of the Biscayan coast, which were the places of entry for trade with France, Flanders, England and Germany, or in the south by way of the Andalusian and Murcian ports or by cities on navigable rivers, such as Seville, through which city in particular trade with the Italian cities was carried on.[19] There was also trade across the land frontiers with Portugal, Aragon and Navarre. In 1253 Alfonso X granted a safe-conduct to the men of the Burgo de San Cernin of Pamplona which was to hold good whether there was peace or war between the kings of Castile and Navarre and, in 1281, a safe-conduct was granted by him to the merchants of Pamplona generally.[20] After the conquest of Andalusia many foreigners settled in some of the southern towns. In 1248 Fernando III granted a ward in Seville to the Genoese, who also settled in Almería, Cádiz, Jerez, Córdoba and other cities.[21]

Native merchants grew in number and wealth during the thirteenth century and were sufficiently important to be summoned to the Cortes of Jerez in 1268 to give advice on economic questions.[22] Not much is known of the social situation of the merchants in the towns at this time; it is not possible to say whether they were included among the *mayores*, although they may have been, nor whether they intervened actively in town government.[23] Jews and Mudéjares had special wards in the towns. The Jews were *menestrales* and many of them were money-lenders. In Andalusia most of the Moors had been driven from the towns, but many remained in the open country. Neither Jews nor Mudéjares took part in town government.

The governing body of the town with its *término* was the *concejo* – the assembly or town council. In its largest form – the *concejo abierto* – it comprised all the *vecinos*, whether they lived in the town or the *tierra*. In this form it must have met at least once a year for the election of officials, but it is probable that at most other periodic meetings all the *vecinos* were not present. The *concejo mayor* met weekly, generally – but

---

[19] G[arcía] de Valdeavellano, *Instituciones españolas*, 277–8.
[20] AM Pamplona, *caj.* B and *caj.* A, no. 14. The city of Pamplona was divided into five *burgos*.
[21] G[arcía] de Valdeavellano, *Instituciones españolas*, 279–80; Carlé, *Del concejo*, 61.
[22] *Cortes*, I, no. XIV.
[23] Carlé, *Del concejo*, 80.

not in all towns – on Sunday after Mass. Special meetings were summoned to deal with particular business. The additional *fueros* granted by Alfonso X to Medina del Campo confirmed that the *concejo* should meet on Sundays but added that if a royal *carta* should be received, or other special circumstance arise, the *concejo* might be summoned on any other day.[24] Besides the appointment of officials, the business transacted by the *concejo* included purchases, sales and donations of the goods and possessions of the *concejo*; questions concerning boundaries, common pastures, permission to found villages in the *término*; the fixing of prices, weights and measures, until fixed for the whole kingdom by Alfonso X; and the elaboration of the *fuero*.[25]

The names and numbers of the officials varied from town to town, but in general the principal officials were the *juez* or mayor, who was the head of the town government, and the *alcaldes* or magistrates. The right of the town to elect its own officials was conceded by the crown at various dates, in many cases in the second half of the twelfth or first half of the thirteenth century. Thus, Sancho III granted Miranda de Ebro the right to elect its *alcaldes* annually when he confirmed its *fuero* in 1157, and Fernando III granted the annual election of its *alcaldes* to Pancorbo in 1219.[26] The *juez* summoned meetings of the *concejo* and probably presided over them; if absent, he appointed a deputy to carry out his functions; he accompanied the town militia on military expeditions and carried the town banner. The main function of the *alcaldes* was judicial; in the *Fuero* of Belbimbre they are referred to as 'iudices que uulgo alcaldes uocantur'.[27] The court of the town – the *corral de alcaldes* – was generally held weekly, but in some cases more often. The additional *Fueros* of Medina del Campo laid down that the *alcaldes* should hold the pleas three days a week, on Mondays, Wednesdays and Fridays.[28] In some *fueros* persons described as *jurados* were joined with the *alcaldes* and had certain judicial functions. Lesser functionaries included the summoner (*pregonero*) who summoned special meetings of the *concejo*, messengers (*andadores*) at the orders of the *alcaldes*, the *almotacén* who inspected weights and measures and the *escribano* or notary who kept records of suits and sentences, sales and purchases and acted generally as secretary to the *concejo*. In many

[24] Muedra Benedito, 'Adiciones al Fuero de Medina del Campo', *AHDE*, v, 448–50.

[25] Carlé, *Del concejo*, 92–100.

[26] *Fuero de Mirando de Ebro*, 57, cl. 42; Manuel Rodríguez, *Memorias*, 295.

[27] González, *AHDE*, xvi, 636–9.

[28] Muedra Benedito, *AHDE*, v, 449, ley v.

towns from the second half of the twelfth century the *juez* and the *alcaldes* and, often lesser officials had to be knights of the town.[29] Towards the end of the twelfth century the *concejos* began to use seals. The earliest surviving impression is of a seal of León in 1214, but the city must have been using one earlier. Zamora had a seal in 1189.[30] Moya was using one before 1214.[31] In 1231, in the suit between the abbey of Sahagún and the town of Belver, the town representatives brought with them 'carta de procuracion, abierta et seellada', and the agreement reached on the occasion was sealed with the seals of both parties.[32] Similarly, an agreement between the abbey and the town of Mayorga in 1254 was sealed with the seals of the abbey and the *concejo*.[33] In the second half of the thirteenth century references to municipal seals become increasingly frequent.

The law administered by the *alcaldes* in the town court was that contained in the *fuero* of the town.[34] The *fueros* granted in the eleventh and first half of the twelfth centuries were short; they were drafted in Latin and contained rules of public law only. *Fueros* belonging to the end of the twelfth century and to the thirteenth century were long, and were increasingly redacted in the vernacular; they dealt with municipal organisation and private and penal law and procedure, and were very comprehensive. Some were granted by the king but others, especially those belonging to the thirteenth century, were compiled by the *concejo* which later sought the approval of the king. Among the long *fueros* some of the most important were the Leonese ones of Zamora, Salamanca and Ledesma and those of the Castilian towns of Cuenca and Soria. *Fueros* granted to one town were granted to or adopted by other towns, generally with variations, omissions and additions, and thus families of *fueros* arose. The conquests of Fernando III in Andalusia raised new problems; the existing *fueros* of Leonese and Castilian towns were not readily applicable. Fernando extended to the

---

[29] Carlé, *Del concejo*, 126–9.
[30] Gonzáles, 'Sellos concejiles de España en la Edad Media', *Hispania*, v, 341, 375.
[31] AHN, Santiago, *caj.* 100, II, no. 25, Sentence of Fernando III: 'et ui los privilegios que tenie el Maestro de uos el conceio [de Moya] e seelados con vestro seello e otorgados de mio auuelo' (Alfonso VIII).
[32] AHN, Clero, *carp.* 913/10; publ. Appendix, doc. II, below.
[33] AHN, Clero, *carp.* 916/11 (25 June 1254, inserted in a royal *carta* of 20 Jan. 1255): 'seelada con el sello del abbate e del conuento e con el seello del conceio de Maorga'.
[34] On the municipal *fueros*, see García Gallo, 'Aportación al estudio de los fueros', *AHDE*, XXVI, 387–446; Gibert, 'El derecho municipal de León y Castilla', *AHDE*, XXXI, 695–753.

Andalusian cities the *Forum judicum*, translated into the vernacular under the title *Fuero juzgo*, which was by this period also partly inapplicable and partly incomprehensible. Each city introduced special characteristics and to each was also granted the *fuero* of the knights of Toledo. Alfonso X added the *Fuero real* in some cases.[35]

An obligation to serve in the army on military expeditions was laid by the *fueros* on all heads of households, except when dispensation was allowed for certain specific reasons – such as old age or infirmity, when a son or other male relation went instead, if a man's horse or his wife had died at the time of summons or if he were absent on pilgrimage. Service was for a fixed period, generally for three months in the year (as, for example, at Sepúlveda) and often only if the king himself led the host. At Uceda and Madrid the militia had to serve with the king outside the kingdom only once in any given year, but within the kingdom whenever the king had need. In some cases, a proportion of the knights remained to garrison the town.[36] From the mid-thirteenth century, when Fernando III and Alfonso X began the creation of a royal fleet, the men of some coastal towns could be called upon to serve in the fleet instead of the army. The inhabitants of Cartagena thus served for one month in the year with the host in Murcia, or did service with the fleet, if so required, but not both in the same year, while those of Alicante had both to provide ships and to serve with the fleet.[37]

The town militias comprised both cavalry, composed of the town knights, and infantry. There were also crossbowmen who might either be mounted, or who might fight on foot. The number of a knight's *excusados* and his share of the plunder both depended on the extent of his equipment; so, too, the foot soldier's share of the booty depended on the number of his weapons. Once a year the town militia was assembled for a view of arms (*alarde*) and an inspection of the equipment of each person was carried out.[38]

The military strength of the towns made them particularly important to the monarchy in times of civil disorder and in wars against the

---

[35] Gibert, *AHDE*, xxxi, 747–9.

[36] *Fuero de Cuenca*, cap. xxx, títs. iv, v; *Fuero de Ledesma*, cl. 386; González, *Alfonso IX*, ii, no. 126 (*Fuero* of Milmanda); Manuel Rodríguez *Memorias*, 375, 276. On military service, see Palomeque, 'Contribución al estudio del ejército en los estados de la reconquista', *AHDE*, xv, esp. pp. 230–40; *Fueros de Sepúlveda*, 457–9; Gibert, *Concejo de Madrid*, 111–17.

[37] Manuel Rodríguez, *Memorias*, 483–5 (16 Jan. 1246); *Colección de privilegios de la corona de Castilla*, vi, no. cclvii (p. 102) (25 Oct. 1252).

[38] Palomeque, *AHDE*, xv, 271–6; Gibert, *Concejo de Madrid*, 117–18.

Moors. Fernando III was materially helped at the time of his accession to the throne of Castile by the towns and duly acknowledged his debt to the *concejos* of Burgos and Avila. He also acknowledged the help given him by Salamanca when he claimed the throne of León in 1230.[39] The *concejo* of Ledesma aided Alfonso IX in the capture of Mérida, and the part played by the militias of the cities and towns in Fernando III's sieges of Córdoba and Seville was noted in the narrative sources.[40]

The political importance of the towns is illustrated by the reliance laid on them in some of the treaties between León and Castile. The Treaty of Toro of 1216, which dealt with the prevention of violence on the frontier between the two kingdoms, laid down that amends for damages were to be made 'per decem juratos ad hoc electos in singulis civitatibus et villis', and the treaty between Alfonso IX and Fernando III, concluded in the winter of 1217–18, provided that ten good men of every city and town on the frontier were to swear to keep the peace.[41] The growing independence of the towns, too, was seen in the formation of *hermandades* or leagues between individual towns. The earliest of these were a series of four agreements made by Escalona with three other towns of the Castilian Extremadura – Avila, Segovia and two separate agreements with Plasencia. It was not, however, until the end of the reign of Alfonso X, during the rebellion of his son, the Infante Don Sancho, that these *hermandades* became an important political force.

By the time of the reunion of Castile and León the towns on royal demesne in both kingdoms were recognised as corporate bodies who elected their own officials, had their own seals, could sue and be sued in the royal court and who were used to electing *personeros* to represent them in suits or to bring petitions before the king. Government was concentrated in the *concejo* or assembly of *vecinos*, and the name *concejo* had become synonymous with the town and its *término*. The *concejo* was responsible for the maintenance of law and order and administered justice according to the town *fuero* throughout the *término*, which formed an administrative district centred on the walled town. The *concejos* provided contingents of both horse and foot for the royal army and paid taxes to the king. Social classes within the *concejo*

[39] Manuel Rodríguez, *Memorias*, 253–4, 291–2; *Fueros leoneses*, 70–1.
[40] *Fuero de Ledesma*, cl. 357; *Crónica latina*, 119; *PCG*, II, caps. 1046, 1075, 1118.
[41] González, *Reino de Castilla*, III, no. 1005; *Alfonso IX*, II, no. 352.

were complex, but the most important element was composed of the knights of the town, who participated in many of the privileges of knights of noble origin and who were monopolising power within the *concejo* with the encouragement of the crown. Administratively, militarily and financially, the towns were thus of the utmost importance for the maintenance of royal power, and for the efficient government of the kingdom.

5

Early appearances of representatives of the towns in great assemblies in León and Castile before 1250

León

We have already noted that citizens and townsmen attended the great curia in León on three occasions during the reign of Alfonso IX – in 1188, 1202 and 1208. Of these appearances there can be no doubt, for they are referred to in the decrees promulgated in those assemblies. The presence of elected citizens was thus attested in the preamble of the decrees of León (1188):

Ego dominus Aldefonsus, Rex Legionis et Gallecie, cum celebrarem curiam apud Legionem cum archiepiscopo et episcopis et magnatibus regni mei et cum electis civibus ex singulis civitatibus, constitui et iuramento firmavi quod omnibus de regno meo, tam clericis quam laicis, servarem mores bonos, quos a predecessoribus meis habent constitutos.

Again, in the final confirmation at the end of the code, it was stated: 'omnes etiam episcopi promiserunt et omnes milites et cives iuramento firmaverunt quod fideles sint in consilio meo ad tenendam iustitiam et suadendam pacem in toto regno meo'.[1] Many from every town of the kingdom were similarly stated to have been present at Benavente in 1202: 'presentibus episcopis et uasallis meis et multis de qualibet uilla regni mei in plena curia'.[2] Finally, the preamble to the laws in favour of the church promulgated in 1208 also referred to the presence of citizens with the king, the prelates and the magnates:

conuenientibus apud Legionem, regiam civitatem, una nobiscum uenerabilium episcoporum cetu reuerendo et totius regni primatum et baronum glorioso colegio, ciuium multitudine destinatorum a singulis ciuitatibus considente, ego Alfonsus, illustrissumus rex Legionis, Gallecie et Asturiarum et Extremature, multa deliberatione prehabita, de uniuersorum consensu hanc legem edidi mihi et a meis posteris omnibus obseruandam.[3]

---

[1] González, *Alfonso IX*, II, no. 11.
[2] *Ibid.* II, no. 167.
[3] *Ibid.* II, no. 221.

Thus, the presence of citizens and townsmen in the curia on these three occasions is incontestable. But was 1188 the earliest example, or were citizens already summoned by Fernando II? It has been claimed that they were present in 1170, when a charter suposedly of that date states that Fernando decided to move the site of the city of Túy further from the Portuguese frontier 'bonorum hominum consilio, pontificum, militum, burgensium'.[4] However, this document, which exhibits various peculiarities, has now been shown to have been falsified in the reign of Alfonso IX, when disputes arose between the bishop and the citizens of Túy, so that its wording cannot be relied on.[5]

There are no other specific references than the three cited to the presence of the citizens or townsmen at the enlarged curia during the reign of Alfonso IX. The three certain attendances were at assemblies at which decrees were promulgated. Were they summoned to the curia on other occasions when decrees were issued? Those of 1194, 1204 and 1229 make no mention of their presence. The first clause of the decrees of 1194 was agreed 'communi deliberatione', but the composition of the assembly was not given; the Lugo decrees of 1204 have survived in a truncated form without preamble. Both confirmed some of the laws issued in 1188 when citizens were present, but there is nothing to prove their presence in either 1194 or 1204. The law on pilgrims promulgated in 1229 stated explicitly that it was issued with the consent of the bishops summoned by the papal legate, John, bishop of Sabina, to attend the ecclesiastical council of Salamanca and with that of the barons of the kingdom, which seems to preclude the representatives of the *concejos*.[6] If the towns were represented at any of these three other assemblies in Alfonso IX's time, the most likely occasion would be in 1194, but of this there is no proof.

We have already noted that homage was twice done to the Infante Don Fernando, Alfonso IX's eldest son by his second wife Berenguela of Castile as heir to the throne of León, at the instigation of Alfonso VIII of Castile, but there is no evidence in either case as to how, when or where. Professor O'Callaghan has suggested that the first time was at the Curia of Benavente in 1202 and the second at that held in Toro in 1207.[7] The first of these suggestions is very probable. The date fits

---

[4] Fernández Rodríguez, 'La entrada de los representantes de la burguesía en la curia regia leonesa', *AHDE*, XXVI, 757–66, with a photograph of the document.
[5] Sánchez-Albornoz, '¿Burgueses en la curia regia de Fernando II de León?', *Revista Portuguesa de História*, XII, 18–29.
[6] González, *Alfonso IX*, II, nos. 84 (1194), 192 (1204), 519 (1228).
[7] O'Callaghan, *AHR*, LXXIV, 1520–1.

- Fernando was born before 5 August 1201, and homage had been done to him before June 1203 when Innocent III complained about it.[8] The second suggestion has less to commend it. As O'Callaghan admits, our only knowledge of the Curia of Toro is the sentence pronounced there in the suit between Alfonso IX and the abbot of Corias, which gives the following description of the composition of the curia: '[Rex] dixit quod idem abbas accederet ad Taurum, ubi magnates regni Legionis et multi episcopi cum Compostellano archiepiscopo conuenire debebant uocati ab eodem rege'. There is no evidence whatever, either that homage was done there to the heir to the throne, or that representatives of the cities were present.[9] Another possibility is that the homage of the towns was performed locally. It is known that, after Fernando III's accession to the throne of León, he spent the early months of 1231 on progress through part of his newly acquired kingdom receiving homage from the cities.[10] The same procedure may therefore have been followed on the earlier occasion, as he was brought up in the kingdom of León.

Another suggestion of Professor O'Callaghan is that the towns were represented at Zamora in November 1221.[11] Here, again, we have a single document which attests the homage done to the king by Gil Manríquez for the castle of Villalobos 'in plena curia domini regis et in concilio'.[12] The phrase used denotes a great curia, but unless we assume that 'in plena curia' also always implies the presence of the representatives of the towns – and this is emphatically not the case – then there is nothing to indicate that they attended this assembly.

Thus, there are only three occasions for which we have any certain evidence of the attendance of the representatives of the cities and towns at a great curia in León before 1230. From what cities or towns did these representatives come? In 1188 and 1208 they were referred to as *cives* but in 1202 as 'many from every town of the kingdom', which appears to denote a wider representation. Presumably the towns

[8] *Documentación pontificia hasta Inocencio III*, nos. 276, 305.
[9] González, *Alfonso IX*, ii, no. 217.
[10] Rodrigo, *De rebus Hispaniae, lib.* ix, *cap.* xv; *PCG*, ii, *cap.* 1040. Both give Fernando's itinerary as Zamora, Salamanca, Ledesma, Ciudad Rodrigo and Alba de Tormes. There is documentary evidence of his presence in all these towns, except Ledesma, between 31 Dec. 1230 and 12 March 1231; cf. AHN, Clero, *carp.* 913/7, 8, 9 (Zamora, 31 Dec. 1230, 4, 5 Jan. 1231); *carp.* 913/10, 11 (Alba de Tormes, 6 March 1231); *Fueros leoneses*, 70–1 (Ciudad Rodrigo, 26 Feb.); documents published by Manuel Rodríguez, *Memorias*, 376–85, and those cited by Ballesteros, *Historia de España*, iii, 144, n. 20.
[11] O'Callaghan, *AHR*, lxxiv, 1526, n. 102; 1533.
[12] González, *Alfonso IX*, ii, no. 415.

referred to in the latter document were those on royal demesne, but there is no evidence as to which towns actually were represented. Nor do we know how they were represented – by how many persons, how selected (in 1188 they were called 'elected citizens') and with what powers. The phrases 'many from every town' and 'a multitude of citizens' used in 1202 and 1208 suggest considerable numbers. There are no writs of summons from the king, nor mandates granted by the towns, extant for this period, so that we do not know for what purposes they were summoned, nor what powers or instructions, if any, were given them. It seems likely that they were chosen in the *concejo abierto* (which at this period included the whole body of the *vecinos*) as were the officials of the town, but, again, there is no evidence.

Some of the legislation enacted on these three occasions – such as the general decrees against violence in 1188 – had particular interest for the citizens. Townsmen were obviously interested parties in the *placita* of 1202; one of the clauses on land law referred specifically to cases in which 'ciuis uel burgensis aut aliquis alius qui non sit miles' held lands from ecclesiastical persons or bodies. They were also clearly interested parties in the questions relating to the coinage and to the imposition of *moneda*, and it may be that it was specifically for the purpose of consenting to the latter that the representatives were summoned. It is more difficult to account for their presence in 1208, when the decrees promulgated were concerned exclusively with ecclesiastical privileges. At the same time, evidence seems to suggest that they did not take part in all the business transacted by the curia, and that their position was in some ways a subordinate one. A notification of Alfonso IX to the archbishop of Compostela, which concerned the revocation of Fernando II's grants in the Curia of León of 1188, referred only to the presence of the ecclesiastical and lay magnates.[13] An exemption from *portazgo* granted to the canons of the cathedral of León during the curia of 1208 was also assented to solely by the archbishop, bishops and nobles.[14]

Castile

Evidence of the attendance of representatives of the towns at the Castilian curia is less specific than in the case of León. Their supposed presence in the Curia of 1169, when Alfonso VIII celebrated his majority, was based on the version of the general chronicle published by

[13] *Ibid.*, II, no. 662 (undated).
[14] *Ibid.* II, no. 223 (Feb. 1208).

Ocampo in the sixteenth century, but this is too late to have any authority in face of the silence of earlier sources.[15] It has been claimed with greater probability that they attended either the curia held at San Esteban de Gormaz in 1187, or that held at Carrión in 1188, or both. These assertions rest ultimately on the text of the marriage treaty of Seligenstadt, of 23 April 1188, which ends with the names of certain bishops and nobles and of fifty cities and towns whose chief men (*mayores*) had taken the oath to fulfil the treaty.[16] In the text the perfect tense – 'iurauerunt' – was used, and it has also been pointed out that Diego Jiménez, one of the nobles named, ceased to appear among the confirmantes of royal documents after November 1187 and presumably died at that time.[17] For these reasons, attendance at the earlier curia seems the more probable, but all we know of this curia is contained in the statement attached to the dating clause of a document of 21 May 1187 to the effect that the envoy of the Emperor Frederick Barbarossa there negotiated a marriage between the Emperor's son and Alfonso VIII's daughter, but without any reference to the presence of the *mayores* of the cities and towns.[18] The chief men of the cities and towns may also have been among those who did homage to Conrad and Berenguela at Carrión in July 1188, but none of the sources, narrative or documentary, mentions their presence.[19] Another very tentative suggestion made by Professor O'Callaghan is that a decree of Alfonso VIII made in 1191, guaranteeing the security of the church and its possessions, may have been promulgated in an assembly in which townsmen participated, but the decree makes no reference to any assembly or to any consultation or consent, and appears to be a royal edict.[20] This suggestion can be dismissed.

The next two occasions on which the representatives might have been summoned fall within the thirteenth century; these are the

15 *Corónica de España*, fol. ccclxxxvii. Their presence in 1169 was accepted by, among others, Ibáñez de Segovia, *Memorias de Alonso el Noble*, 51, and Martínez Marina, *Ensayo sobre la antigua legislación*, 72. It is also accepted by García Rámila, 'Cortes de Castilla', *RABM*, xlix, 92.
16 Rassow, *Der Prinzgemahl*, 5–6.
17 Carlé, *Del concejo*, 252.
18 González, *Reino de Castilla*, ii, no. 471.
19 Sánchez-Albornoz, *España: un enigma histórico*, ii, 81, assumes that the *mayores* of the towns were present at Carrión; Carlé, *Del concejo*, 252, is in favour of San Esteban de Gormaz; O'Callaghan, *AHR*, lxxiv, 1512–13, 1516, 1533, thinks they were probably present on both occasions.
20 O'Callaghan, *AHR*, lxxiv, 1516. O'Callaghan does not include this occasion among his list of 'possible' occasions on p. 1533. For the document, see González, *Reino de Castilla*, iii, no. 570.

assembly held after the loss of Salvatierra in 1211, and that at Burgos in December 1212, after the campaign of Las Navas. The first can be rejected as against the admittedly scanty evidence. The *Crónica latina* states that Alfonso VIII, 'habito tractatu et deliberatione' with his son, the Infante Don Fernando, Diego López, the archbishop of Toledo, and other magnates, decided on an expedition to take place in the following year, and issued an edict concerned with the muster of the army.[21] This was a council of war with some of the leaders of the army present with the king, not a specially summoned cortes or even a great curia. There is more to be said for the possibility that the towns took part in the assembly at Burgos in 1212, as the king confirmed their *fueros* there but, as we have already seen, the evidence is very late, and it makes no reference to the presence of the representatives.[22]

There is much stronger evidence for the presence of representatives of the towns at the time of the accession of Enrique I in 1214 and of that of Fernando III in 1217. Of the former the author of the *Crónica latina* wrote: 'Henricus, filius eius, sublimatus est in regem, et receptus ab omnibus castellanis et prelatis ecclesiarum et populis civitatum, et fecerunt ei omagium manuale.'[23] There is no specific reference to the curia here, but the wording implies that the cities did homage, presumably through their chief men, together with the nobles and prelates at the time of Enrique's recognition as king, so that this assembly may be accepted as a meeting of the cortes. Again, in connection with the accession of Fernando III to the throne of Castile, the *Crónica latina* refers to the homage done by citizens and townsmen, together with the nobles, in the church of Santa María within the walls of Valladolid: 'et ibidem Deo agentes fecerunt omagium manuale omnes qui aderant, tam magnates quam populi civitatum et aliarum villarum, regi domino Fernando'.[24] Those present at Valladolid were the bishops and nobles who had supported Queen Berenguela against the Regent Don Alvaro, and the people of the towns of Extremadura and others.[25]

Some time shortly after Fernando III's accession it was decided in curia that 'nullum arduum negotium quod tetigerit ipsum regnum'

---

[21] *Crónica latina*, 41; O'Callaghan, *AHR*, LXXIV, 1523. Not included in his list on p. 1533.

[22] *Fuero viejo, prólogo*; O'Callaghan, *AHR*, LXXIV, 1523, 1533.

[23] *Crónica latina*, 64; O'Callaghan, *AHR*, LXXIV, 1524, 1533.

[24] *Crónica latina*, 71; Rodrigo, *De rebus Hispaniae, lib.* IX, *cap.* V: 'ibidem omnes ei fecerunt hominium'; Lucas of Túy, *Chronicon mundi*, 112, refers only to nobles. O'Callaghan accepts this as a meeting of the cortes, *AHR*, LXXIV, 1525, 1533.

[25] *Crónica latina*, 71: 'Extremadurani et alii'.

was to be dealt with until after the king had reached the age of twenty.[26] It is possible that it was at this curia that Fernando III made the promise to confirm the *fueros* of the towns to which he referred in the preamble to the *cuadernos* of the Cortes of Seville in 1250.[27] It is also possible that both decisions were taken in the assembly in which homage was done at the time of the accession, but a separate assembly seems more likely, in which case we know neither the exact date nor the composition of this curia.[28]

There is, however, firm evidence that the chief men of the cities – 'primores civitatum' – attended the curia held at the time of Fernando III's marriage to Beatrice of Suabia. The *Crónica latina* describes the reception of the bride at Burgos where the king was 'cum magnatibus suis et aliis nobilibus multis et primoribus civitatum et villarum regni sui', and then, after describing Fernando's assumption of knighthood on 28 November 1219 and his marriage on 30 November, goes on to say 'Celeberrima curia tunc habita est Burgis, magnatum et militum et primorum civitatum multitudine convocata' and opines that 'a diebus antiquis non fuit visa talis curia in civitate Burgensis'. Rodrigo of Toledo used similar language: 'Et fuit ibi curia nobilissima celebrata, assistentibus totius regni magnatibus, dominabus, et fere omnibus regni militibus et primoribus civitatum.' The general impression given by these two narrative sources is of a very numerous assembly of a predominantly ceremonial character.[29] The king's assumption of knighthood and his marriage were added to the dating clause of royal privileges during the succeeding year.[30]

There are two further occasions before 1230 on which O'Callaghan thinks that representatives may have been present. He considers that they were 'almost certainly summoned' to the assembly which did homage to the heir to the throne in March 1222, and that they possibly attended the curia in 1224 for the marriage of John of Brienne to Fernando III's sister, Doña Berenguela. Our sole knowledge of the first

[26] Manuel Rodríguez, *Memorias*, 256–7.

[27] *Fuero de Cuenca*, 859; publ. Appendix, doc. III, below.

[28] O'Callaghan, *AHN*, LXXIV, 1525, suggests that the reference in the *cuadernos* of 1250 is to the assembly at the king's accession.

[29] *Crónica latina*, 78; Rodrigo, *De rebus Hispaniae*, lib. LX, cap. X; cf. *PCG*, II, cap. 1034; O'Callaghan, *AHR*, LXXIV, 1525–6, suggests that the bishops, nobles and townsmen were summoned to pledge allegiance to their new queen and that the representatives were 'probably *caballeros villanos*' and 'it is possible that they had proctorial powers', but this goes beyond the documentation.

[30] E.g. AHN, Clero, carp. 379/18 (13 Dec. 1219); carp. 379/19 (11 June 1220); Manuel Rodríguez, *Memorias*, 296, 298, 299, 300, 301, 304 (12 and 21 Dec. 1219, 25 Jan., 2 March, 4 and 16 April 1220).

event is the addition to the dating clause of a document of 22 March 1222 'sequenti die videlicet post quam hominum de regno factum fuit infanti domino Alfonso solemniter apud Burgos',[31] but the phrase 'hominum de regno' may well include the homage of the cities and towns. The events leading up to the marriage of John of Brienne and Doña Berenguela are given in some detail in the *Crónica latina* which ends its account: 'Celebrata est igitur curia Burgis, et tradita est puella predicta regi sepedicta [sic] solempniter in uxorem'; but nowhere is mention made of the towns.[32]

We can, then, conclude that the cities and towns did homage to Enrique I on his accession, that those of Extremadura and some others did homage to Fernando III on his accession in 1217 in a somewhat anomalous assembly and that the *primores* of the cities and towns took part in the curia held on the occasion of Fernando III's marriage in 1219. Of the other suggested occasions, the most probable appear to be 1187 or 1188 and 1222. For the rest, the evidence is either completely lacking, insufficient or too late to be reliable.

The available evidence for the attendance of representatives of the cities and towns in both kingdoms in this period suggests that their role differed in the two kingdoms. In León they took part in legislative assemblies, although their presence was not essential to the promulgation of legislation, and they gave their consent in 1202 to the levying of *moneda*. In Castile they were present at the ceremonial court of 1219 summoned to grace the king's marriage and the other occasions on which they were, or may have been, present were concerned with the doing of homage to the monarch at his accession, or to the heir to the throne.

After the union of the two crowns

Professor O'Callaghan has continued his survey of early assemblies beyond the union of León and Castile up to and including the Cortes of Seville, held by Fernando III in November 1250. Because of this, but also because the Cortes of 1250 began a series of frequent assemblies and enacted legislation dealing with some of the subjects which were to figure in greater detail in decrees promulgated in Alfonso X's reign, it

---

[31] Manuel Rodríguez, *Memorias*, 331. O'Callaghan, *AHR*, LXXIV, 1526. Martínez Marina, *Teoría de las cortes*, II, accepted the presence of the representatives. The detailed description of the ceremony given by Ballesteros, *Alfonso X, el Sabio*, 51–2, is a piece of historical fiction.

[32] *Crónica latina*, 80.

is convenient to continue our survey in this chapter up to, but excluding, the Cortes of 1250.

Shortly after the recognition of Fernando III as king of León, the cortes were summoned to Benavente, in November and December 1230, to complete the union of the two kingdoms. At this meeting the Pact of Benavente was ratified, by which Alfonso IX's two daughters by his first wife – Sancha and Dulce – renounced all claims to the throne of León, and restored to Fernando III, for an annual rent of 30,000 *maravedíes*, all towns and castles of which they had possession.[33] They were also granted the usufruct of the stronghold of Castrotorafe, in which they had taken refuge after the failure of their bid for the crown of León, although this grant was unsuccessfully opposed by the Order of Santiago, who then held Castrotorafe.[34] The text of the treaty does not give the composition of the assembly but, according to the *Crónica latina*, those present were the king, his half-sisters, the two former queens of León, the archbishops of Toledo and Compostela 'et baronibus multis et consiliis'.[35] The Pact of Benavente was dated 11 December 1230 and Fernando III remained in the city until near the end of the month. By 31 December he was at Zamora so that the cortes must have been dismissed before that date.[36]

For the twenty years between the Cortes of Benavente and those of Seville in 1250, the evidence for possible meetings of the cortes is scanty and uncertain. Documents are of little help, except for fixing the king's itinerary. The *Crónica latina*, the *Chronicon mundi* of Lucas of Túy and the *De rebus Hispaniae* of Rodrigo of Toledo all end about 1236, although Rodrigo, who finished his work in 1243, included a brief reference to Fernando III's second marriage in 1237. For the rest of the reign, we have to rely on the *Primera crónica general* which reproduced a vernacular continuation of the *De rebus Hispaniae*.

Professor O'Callaghan considers that 'there is reason to believe that in 1232 and 1233 the king convened assemblies in which townsmen participated'.[37] In this he relies on the *Crónica latina*, according to which at Carrión:

[33] For the text of the treaty, see Serrano, 'El canciller de Fernando III de Castilla', *Hispania*, i; v, 29–33.
[34] Lomax, 'The Order of Santiago and the kings of León', *Hispania*, xviii, 26–8, 32–7.
[35] *Crónica latina*, 105; cf. O'Callaghan, *AHR*, lxxiv, 1526–7.
[36] Millares Carlo, *AHDE*, iii, 298 (Benavente, 14 Dec. 1230); Manuel Rodríguez, *Memorias*, 375 (Benavente, 20 Dec. 1230); *AHN*, Clero, *carp.* 913/7 (Zamora, 31 Dec. 1230).
[37] O'Callaghan, *AHR*, lxxiv, 1527.

Convenerunt autem ibidem ad eum multi de populis regni Legionis et multi nobiles de Gallecia et de Asturiis, quorum quosdam expedivit, alios secum duxit Burgis.

Confluxit ad eadem civitatem maxima hominum multitudo populorum et nobilium, tan de Castella quam de Gallecia et de aliis partibus regni, ubi longam protraxit moram, rex expediendo negocia multiformia cum consilio bonorum virorum.[38]

Fernando III was at Carrión early in July 1232. At the end of the month he was in Burgos, where he may have remained during August and September. In October he moved south to Segovia and Avila but then returned to Burgos in mid-November. By the end of November he was in Toledo where he remained for the rest of the year.[39] The assembly at Carrión must, therefore, have taken place early in July, that at Burgos may either have begun at the end of July and have continued during the two following months, or may have taken place in November. The former appears the more probable. The narrative of the *Crónica latina* implies that the assembly at Burgos followed directly on that at Carrión, without any intermission, and that Fernando III remained in Burgos for some time, but his itinerary does not allow time for a stay of any length at Burgos in November. From January to July 1233 he was engaged in the siege of Ubeda.[40] By October he was again at Burgos, where he made a protracted stay 'dum quedam magna negocia tractaret, que tocius terre continebant utilitatem'.[41]

Do these passages from the *Crónica latina* denote meetings of the cortes? O'Callaghan considers it reasonable to suppose that they do, although he admits that the language of the chronicle is 'imprecise'.[42] Imprecise it certainly is, and it is worthwhile to consider more carefully certain phrases used. At Carrión we have the odd juxtaposition 'multi de populis regni Legionis, et multi nobiles de Gallecia et de Asturias'.

[38] *Crónica latina*, 106–7.
[39] Carrión, 2 July 1232 (Ballesteros, *Historia de España*, III, 145, n. 22); Burgos, 26 July (Manuel Rodríguez, *Memorias*, 400); Segovia, 17 Oct., Avila, 31 Oct., 2 Nov. (*ibid.* 401–5); Muñó near Burgos, 6 Nov. (*ibid.* 406); Burgos, 20 Nov. (O'Callaghan, *AHR*, LXXIV, 1527); Toledo, 27 Nov., 3 Dec. (Ballesteros, *Historia de España*, III, 145, n. 23); Toledo, 24 Dec. (AHN, Clero, *carp.* 380/5).
[40] *Crónica latina*, 107.
[41] *Crónica latina*, 108. Fernando III was at Burgos on 10 and 19 Oct. 1233 (AHN, Clero, *carp.* 369/8; Manuel Rodríguez, *Memorias*, 407, 409) and on 12 Nov. (AHN, Clero, *carp.* 369/9); at Muñó near Burgos on 15 Nov. (Manuel Rodríguez, *Memorias*, 410).
[42] O'Callaghan, *AHR*, LXXIV, 1527.

At Burgos there were present 'populi et nobiles' from Castile, Galicia and other parts of the kingdom. In the third instance, at Burgos in 1233, there is no reference to those present, but only the statement that the king dealt with business which was to the profit of the whole land. In no case is there any specific mention of the cities and towns, and this omission should be contrasted with the language used by the author of the *Crónica latina* when referring to the homage done to Enrique I in 1214 and to Fernando III in 1217 as well as to the curia held at the time of Fernando's marriage in 1219. The terms used on these three occasions are 'populi civitatum' in 1214, 'populi civitatum et aliarum villarum' in 1217 and 'primores civitatum et villarum regni sui' in 1219 – terms which are precise and unambiguous.[48] One other phrase needs examination. At Burgos in 1232 the king dealt with many matters 'cum consilio bonorum virorum'; 'boni vires' like 'boni homines' could be used of all classes of society and was not used exclusively of townsmen. In this instance it seems to refer to the members of the curia whose advice the king sought. The two assemblies in 1232 *may* have been meetings of the cortes, or they may simply have been military assemblies concerned with preparations for the campaign in the following year. That at Burgos in 1233 may have been a judicial session of the curia.

Another assembly, at which O'Callaghan suggests that the representatives of the towns 'probably' participated, was that held on the occasion of Fernando III's marriage to his second wife, Jeanne of Ponthieu, at Burgos in 1237. Rodrigo of Toledo makes no mention of them; the *Primera crónica general* says that Jeanne was raised to the dignity of queen 'ante toda la corte', which seems to indicate a meeting of the great curia but without the town representatives.[44] Another assembly before 1250, which O'Callaghan also considers to be a meeting of the cortes, rests on a single sentence in the *Primera crónica general*, referring to the beginning of the revolt of Don Diego López: 'legando el rey don Fernando a Burgos et estando y librando sus pleitos con sus ricos omnes et con los de la tierra, acaescio que se ouo a desauenir Diego Lopez, sennor de Vizcaya, con el rey'. O'Callaghan equates 'those of the land' with the representatives of the towns but, although the phrase can be interpreted in this sense, it is ambiguous, and it appears more probable that this was a judicial session of the curia and that 'those of

---

[48] *Crónica latina*, 64, 71, 78.
[44] Rodrigo, *De rebus Hispaniae*, lib. IX, cap. XVIII ; *PGG*, II, cap. *1048;* O'Callaghan, *AHR*, LXXIV, 1527.

the land' were suitors.[45] From the king's itinerary it can be deduced that this assembly took place in July 1241.[46]

Professor O'Callaghan distinguishes scrupulously between those cortes which he considers certain, and those which he considers 'probable' or 'possible', and from his final list of possibilities he has eliminated the most dubious of the asesmblies he has considered, such as those of 1191 and 1211 in Castile.[47] His certain examples are: 1188, 1202 and 1208 for the kingdom of León, 1217 and 1219 for the kingdom of Castile and 1230, 1241 and 1250 after the union of the kingdoms. Of these, I would reject 1241, which appears to me to be a judicial session of the great curia, but I would add to the list the assembly which did homage to Enrique I of Castile in 1214, which O'Callaghan includes among his 'probable' cases. Among these uncertain cases he lists 1187, 1188, 1212, 1214, 1221 and 1222, all for Castile, except 1221 and, after the union, the two assemblies at Carrión and Burgos in 1232 and those at Burgos in 1233 and 1237. Of these, 1221 should certainly be rejected, and those of 1212, 1232, 1233 and 1237 appear very dubious; the rest are much more probable although conclusive evidence in their favour is lacking.

For the period from 1187 to 1230, when León and Castile were separate kingdoms, O'Callaghan surveys the various assemblies in both kingdoms together in strictly chronological order. As the certain cortes in León were in 1188, 1202 and 1208, and the best authenticated ones in Castile in 1187, 1188, 1214, 1217, 1219 and 1222, this approach gives a greater appearance of continuity than the evidence warrants, and serves to obscure the fact that, up to 1230, such occasions in both kingdoms were few and occurred at irregular intervals with some very long gaps. If we consider the kingdoms separately, this fact becomes self-evident. In León there is no certain evidence of the attendance of the representatives of the towns during the fourteen years between

---

[45] *PCG*, II, *cap.* 1058; O'Callaghan, *AHR*, LXXIV, 1528, 1533. Guglielmi, *CHE*, XXIV, 159, assumes that it was a judicial session.

[46] The king was in Burgos on 8 July 1241 (Muedra Benedito, *AHDE*, VI, 419–20), 12 and 21 July (Manuel Rodríguez, *Memorias*, 455–6). O'Callaghan, *AHR*, LXXIV, 1528, n. 111, cites C. Fernández, *Memorias, de la ciudad de Zamora* (1883), IV, 7, and U. Alvarez Martínez, *Historia de la provincia de Zamora* (1965), 190, for a meeting of the cortes at Benavente in 1240. Like O'Callaghan, I have found no further evidence of these cortes, nor have I found any evidence that the king was at Benavente in 1240. For most of that year he was in Andalusia (Ballesteros, *Historia de España* III, 146, n. 41; *PCG*, II, *cap.* 1057, states that Fernando spent 13 months in Córdoba, presumably from February 1240 to March 1241).

[47] O'Callaghan, *AHR*, LXXIV, 1533.

1188 and 1202, nor any during the twenty-two years from 1208 to the death of Alfonso IX in 1230. In Castile, even if we accept their presence in 1187, 1188 and 1222, we are still left with intervals of twenty-six years between 1188 and 1214 and eight years from 1222 to 1230. Evidence may come to light which may confirm some or all of the possible instances, or prove the existence of others, but, unless or until that happens, we can only conclude that the summoning of representatives of the cities and towns to the great curia in either kingdom was an occasional expedient.

The picture is much the same after the union of the two kingdoms. For the twenty years between the Cortes of Benavente in 1230 and those of Seville in 1250, all the possible instances put forward by O'Callaghan fall before 1241, so that even if we accept them all, we are left with a gap of nine years from 1241 to 1250. If, as I think we should, we reject them all, then we have a gap of no less than twenty years – from 1230 to 1250. Thus, throughout the whole period from 1187 to 1250, the summoning of the cortes presented an exceptional expedient, employed at irregular and often very long intervals. This is the familiar pattern of the development of representative assemblies in other Western European kingdoms – a more or less lengthy period of only occasional assemblies to which representatives were summoned, followed by a period of frequent meetings and rapid development. It is with such a period of development which we shall now deal.

6

The attendance of representatives of the cities and towns in the cortes (1250–1295)

Before we can analyse the composition, functions and powers of the cortes in the second half of the thirteenth century, it is necessary to survey the various assemblies to which representatives of the cities and towns were, or have been said to have been, summoned. If we assume, as a broad definition, that the cortes were assemblies specially summoned by the king, at which the constituents of the king's curia or *corte* in its largest form were joined by representatives of towns on royal demesne, throughout the kingdom, then we shall find that some of the assemblies reviewed do not in all respects measure up to this yardstick. In some cases only towns from one or other province of the kingdom are known to have been present, but separate cortes for either León or Castile continued to be summoned from time to time during the early years of the fourteenth century. On two occasions, in 1282 and 1283, the writs of summons were issued not by the king, but by the rebel heir to the throne. Other assemblies were anomalous for other reasons, but have some of the characteristics of the cortes, while in other cases where assemblies have been called cortes, there is no conclusive evidence of the presence of the representatives. In the following survey an attempt will be made to establish the place, date and the available evidence for those assemblies which approximate to our definition of the cortes.

The sources

The most important sources for the cortes are the *cuadernos*. Few writs of summons have survived for this period and no *cartas de personería* (mandates) given to the representatives by the towns, although there are references to them. The principal chronicles for the reigns of Alfonso X and Sancho IV are the *Crónica de Alfonso X* and the *Crónica de Sancho el Bravo*, which, together with that for the reign of Fernando

118

IV, are often referred to as *Las tres crónicas*. They have been ascribed to the chronicler Fernán Sánchez de Valladolid, but the ascription is conjectural, and they are best considered as anonymous.[1]

The general prologue to *Las tres crónicas* states that they were written at the orders of Alfonso XI, and includes the town of Algeciras among the king's titles.[2] This would assign the date of compilation to some time between March 1344, when Algeciras was captured, and the Alfonso's death in March 1350. The reference to Algeciras may, of course, be a later interpolation, but there are a number of time references in the chronicles of both Alfonso X and Sancho IV which show that they were compiled long after the events they describe, and one, at least, of these references indicates a date after 1343. The *Crónica de Sancho el Bravo* thus enumerates the three sons of Charles II of Anjou, held as hostages in Aragon: 'el uno, que despues fué obispo de Tolosa e fué calonisado por santo, que dicen Sant Luis, e el otro que ovo nombre Felipe, que fué rey de Pulla, e el otro que le dijeron Remon Berenguel'.[3] Saint Louis of Toulouse was canonised in 1317, Robert (not Philip, as the compiler mistakenly called him) was king of Naples from 1309 to 1343. The perfect tense is used, so the sentence cannot have been written until after Robert's death.

The *Crónica de Alfonso X* is, generally speaking, a most unsatisfactory source for this very important reign, but its value varies in different parts of the narrative and it can best be considered in three separate sections. The first (chs. i–xix) covers the years 1252 to 1269, and it is chiefly remarkable for its amazing mistakes in chronology and wholesale omission of facts. There are occasional, but very few, references to sources.[4] The middle section (chs. xx–lviii) deals with one subject only, the revolt of the nobles in 1272 and 1273. This section differs in every respect from the preceding one. It is extremely full and detailed, it gives many names and titles, it inserts a large number of documents *in extenso* and summarises others.[5] It is favourable to the

---

[1] All three are published in BAE, lxvi. On the chronicles of Alfonso X and Sancho IV, see Puyol y Alonso, *El presunto cronista Fernán Sánchez de Vallodolid*; Procter, 'Materials for the reign of Alfonso X of Castile', *Transactions of the Royal Historical Society*, xiv, 52–7; Rivero, *Indice de las personas, lugares y cosas notables que se mencionan en las tres crónicas*, 7–33; Sánchez Alonso, *Historiografía española*, i, 223–6.

[2] BAE, lxvi, 3.

[3] *Crónica Sancho IV*, cap. ix (p. 87).

[4] *Crónica Alfonso X*, cap. x (p. 8): 'dice la estorial'; cap. xiii (p. 10): 'segund lo que falló en escripto', etc.

[5] *Ibid.* caps. xl (pp. 30–1), xli (pp. 31–2), xliii (pp. 32–3), li (pp. 38–41).

king; thus it condemns as unreasonable – 'cosa muy sin razon' – the demand of the nobles to come armed and under truce to the Cortes of Burgos, and the robberies and burnings perpetrated by them 'sin derecho é sin razon' on their way to Granada, after they had withdrawn from their allegiance to the king. It also condemns the prelates who supported the malcontent nobles, and made demands and petitions which former kings were not accustomed to grant.[6] This section has all the characteristics of a contemporary or near contemporary record, written by someone with access to the royal archives, and which the fourteenth-century compiler has incorporated more or less *verbatim* into his chronicle. This narrative is of especial value for our purpose, because it is the only source for the Cortes of Burgos at Michaelmas 1272.[7] The third and last section of the *Crónica* (chs. LIX–LXXVII) covers the period from Alfonso X's visit to Beaucaire in 1275 (to meet Pope Gregory X) to his death in April 1284. In length, accuracy and value it stands between the first and second sections, far superior to the first, but less valuable than the second. Although the author inserted no documents, he had some written records before him to which he referred from time to time.[8] He made some mistakes, but he did not commit such blunders as those which disfigure the first section. He was also biased in favour of the Infante Don Sancho. This section contains an account of some cortes held, according to the *Crónica*, at Segovia in 1276, which present difficulties and which we shall have to examine later. It also gives accounts of the Cortes of Seville in 1281, and of the Infante Don Sancho's Cortes of Valladolid in 1282, but in neither of these cases is it our sole evidence.[9] Of the *Crónica de Sancho el Bravo* far less need be said. It is short, but is reasonably reliable, and is far less controversial than the *Crónica de Alfonso X*. It provides the only evidence of the Cortes of Seville in 1284 and those of Zamora in 1286.[10] It gives no reference to the other cortes of the reign.

Of the minor historical works the most important is the *Crónica de los reyes de Castilla* of Jofré de Loaisa.[11] The author belonged to a family closely connected with the Castilian court. His father, Jofré de

---

[6] *Ibid. caps.* XXV (p. 21), XXVI (p. 23), XXVII (p. 23).
[7] *Ibid. caps.* XXV–XXVI (pp. 21–3).
[8] *Ibid. cap.* LXVII (p. 53): 'en el escripto que se falla desde aquel tiempo'; *cap.* LXVIII (p. 53): 'Non se falla más en escripto'; *cap.* LXXII (p. 56): 'la estoria de lo que se falló en escripto de este fecho'.
[9] *Ibid. caps.* LXVIII, LXXV, LXXVI.
[10] *Crónica Sancho IV, caps.* I (p. 70), II (p. 72).
[11] References to the *Crónica de Jofré de Loaisa* are to the edition by Ubieto Arteta.

Loaisa, had come to Castile with Violante of Aragon in 1249, and was a frequent recipient of gifts from Alfonso X. His brother, García Jofré de Loaisa, was *copero mayor* (butler) at the end of Alfonso X's reign, and was one of the executors of the king's second will; under Sancho IV he became *adelantado mayor* of Murcia. The author himself was abbot of Santander from 1272 and archdeacon of Toledo from 1280. We do not know the date of his death, but he was still alive in 1307. The work was written in the vernacular and was intended as a continuation of *De rebus Hispaniae*. It was translated into Latin, at the author's request, by Armand of Cremona, canon of Córdoba and later *socius* of the cathedral of Toledo. The vernacular text has disappeared and it is the Latin version which has survived. The chronicle covers the years 1248 to 1305 and was probably written shortly after the latter date.[12] It is very short and concise, but it contains some facts not found elsewhere, and where it contradicts the later vernacular chronicles it is to be preferred to them. Other minor chronicles, from which a few facts may be gleaned, include the *Anales toledanos*, III, which were known to Jofré de Loaisa, the *Crónica de la población de Avila* and the second *Crónica anónima de Sahagún*. The last named has survived only in what appears to be a fourteenth-century translation of a lost Latin chronicle, written by a monk of Sahagún who was eyewitness of some of the events which he described.

The various legal codes connected with the court of Alfonso X are also valuable sources for this period. The *Setenario* is the earliest of them, and most of it was written in the reign of Fernando III. It was completed early in his son's reign, and it was drawn on by the revisers of the later codes, but it has little relevance for our purpose. More important for us are the three codes generally known as the *Fuero real*, the *Espéculo* and the *Siete partidas*, all of which show in greater or lessor degree the influence of Roman law.[13] The *Fuero real*, the most traditional and least romanised, was completed by 1255, and from then onwards it was granted by Alfonso X, at various dates in the reign, to a large number of individual Castilian towns, either to supersede or to supplement their existing *fueros*. It was clearly the king's purpose by

---

[12] See Jofré de Loaisa, 'Chronique des rois de Castille', ed. Morel-Fatio, *Bibliothèque de l'Ecole des Chartes*, LIX (325–34), for information about the author. Further references are to be found in Gaibrois de Ballesteros, *Sancho IV*, III, nos. 174, 265, 270, 543; and *Memorias de Fernando IV*, II, nos. 196, 222, 378. Armand of Cremona was employed in Fernando IV's chancery (*ibid.* II, nos. 438, 472).

[13] A new edition of the *Espéculo* is in preparation by Professor R. A. Macdonald.

this means to bring some sort of unity into the disparate laws administered by the municipal courts. The two codes known as the *Espéculo* and the *Siete partidas* are two widely divergent versions of one code of which, as Alfonso García Gallo has convincingly shown, the *Espéculo* is the earlier and, in his view, represents the earliest form of Alfonso's *Libro de los fueros* or *Libro de las leyes*, while the *Partidas*, as they appear in the printed editions and in most of the manuscripts, represent a greatly revised and in parts wholly rewritten redaction.[14] The *Siete partidas* were promulgated in 1348 in the *Ordenamiento de Alcalá* and, according to the opinion of the legists who drafted the ordinance, they had not hitherto been received as law.[15] There is, certainly, no evidence that the *Espéculo* or the *Siete partidas* in any form were promulgated in any of Alfonso X's cortes, but, on the other hand, there are indications that the *Espéculo* was promulgated and recognised as law by the king's court in the earlier years of Alfonso X's reign. The prologue of the work affirms: 'nos el sobre dicho rey don Alfonso... feziemos estas leyes que son escriptas en este libro, que es espeio del derecho porque se judguen todos los de nuestros regnos e de nuestro señorio'. It also states that sealed copies of the book were sent to every town, and that all appeals from local courts to the king's court were to be judged by it.[16] In the judicial ordinance of 1274 reference was made to the chancery fees contained in 'el su libro que fue fecho por corte en Palencia en el anno que caso Don Doarte'. If, as is probable, this 'book' was the *Espéculo*, then the code was published in the *corte* which was held in May or June 1255.[17] There is also evidence of its use in the royal court in the early years of the reign. The instructions sent to the *alcaldes* of Valladolid, on 31 August 1258, on the manner of holding the pleas, were largely based on some of the laws of the *Espéculo*.[18] The form of oaths to be sworn by Christians, Moors and Jews in certain transactions, which were sent to the towns in the spring of 1260, and which were later incorporated in the decrees promulgated

[14] García Gallo, 'El "Libro de las leyes" de Alfonso el Sabio', *AHDE*, xxi–xxii, 345–528.

[15] *Ordenamiento de Alcalá*, tít. xxviii, *ley* 1: 'fasta aqui non se falla que fuesen publicadas por mandado del Rey nin fueron auidas nin rescibidas por leyes'.

[16] *Espéculo*, prólogo, 1–2.

[17] *Cortes*, I, no. xvi, cl. 40. Edward of England married Eleanor, half-sister of Alfonso X, on 30 Nov. 1254. A reference to the marriage was included in the dating clauses of *privilegios rodados* from December 1254 to December 1255 inclusive. During this period Alfonso X was in Palencia from 2 May to 22 June 1255; see Ballesteros, *Itinerario*, 113–20.

[18] García Gallo, *AHDE*, xxi–xxii, 385–6, and *cuadro décimo*, 513–28.

in the Cortes of Jerez in 1268 and included in the Burgos collection known as *Las leyes nuevas*, were also taken from the *Espéculo*.[19] Again, much of the *Espéculo, lib.* IV. *tít.* XI ('De los pesquisidores') was incorporated *in extenso*, or else summarised, as part of a long arbitral sentence pronounced by Alfonso X on 21 February 1261, in a suit between the archbishop and chapter of Santiago de Compostela on the one hand, and the *concejo* of the city on the other.[20] The *Espéculo* has survived in an incomplete form consisting of five books, although there are references to a sixth and a seventh book, but we do not know whether these were even written.

The compilation of the *Siete partidas* was begun as early as 1256. There are two distinct versions of the *Primera partida*. One is contained in most of the manuscripts and in the printed editions and is that recognised in the *Ordenamiento de Alcalá* of 1348. The other is contained in the British Library's Add. MS. 20787, which is the earliest surviving manuscript. In this manuscript the prologue is, broadly speaking, a revision of the prologue of the *Espéculo*, in which the title 'el libro de fuero de las leyes' is given to the work and the first two titles are also taken from the *Espéculo*.[21] The coincidence between the *Espéculo* and the *Partidas* varies in different parts of the two works. Much of books IV and V of the *Espéculo* reappears, often verbatim, in the *Tercera partida*, although the latter draws on other sources besides the *Espéculo*.[22] On the other hand, books II and III of the *Espéculo* differ markedly from the *Segunda partida*. There is nothing surviving of the *Espéculo* which corresponds with the subject matter of *Partidas cuarta* to *séptima*. The *Espéculo* was rescinded during the revolt of the nobles from 1272 to 1273 and ceased to be the law used in the king's

---

[19] *Ibid.* 386–8; and López Ortiz, 'La colección conocida con el título "Leyes nuevas"', *AHDE*, XVI, 14–26.

[20] Procter, *The judicial use of 'pesquisa'*, 32–3; Bermejo Cabreno, 'En torno a la aplicación de las *Partidas*, fragmentos del *Espéculo* en una sentencia real de 1261', *Hispania*, XXX, 169–77, publishes the parallel passages from the sentence and the *Espéculo*.

[21] Alfonso X, *Primera partida* (*manuscrito Add. 20,787 del British Museum*), ed. Juan Antonio Arias Bonet. The MS. is late thirteenth-century, written after the death of Alfonso X, probably for the chamber of Sancho IV. On it, see Herriot, 'A thirteenth-century manuscript of the *Primera partida*', *Speculum*, XIII, 278–94. Another MS. of this version, but with variations, is the Hispanic Society of America's, MS. HC 397/573; see García y García, 'Un nuevo códice de la *Primera partida*', *AHDE*, XXXIII, 267–345. This version was printed as a variant in italics at the foot of the pages in the 1807 edition from a MS. now lost. Arias Bonet's view is that both versions were completed during Alfonso X's reign and that the generally accepted version may be the older of the two. On this last point I do not find his reasoning wholly convincing.

[22] See García Gallo, *AHDE*, XXI, 423–45, for the sources of the *Tercera partida*.

court.[23] It does not deal with the cortes, but it treats, among other subjects, of the nature of law, the king's rights as legislator, royal officials, justice and judicial procedures. As the law administered in the king's court from 1255 to 1273, it is important for our subject.[24]

Great assemblies, 1250–1274

In the autumn of 1250 Fernando III summoned the cortes to meet in Seville. Our knowledge of these cortes comes exclusively from the *cuadernos*, three of which, addressed to the *concejos* of Segovia, Uceda and Cuenca on various dates in November, have been published. In all three cases, the editors wrongly considered them to be privileges granted to the individual town.[25] They are, however, identical, apart from the address and minor variations, and they exhibit all the characteristics of *cuadernos* of the cortes.[26] They state explicitly that the king had sent his writ to the *concejo* concerned, ordering it to send 'good men' to speak with him on matters concerning the good estate of the town or, in the case of the *carta* to Cuenca, 'of Extremadura'; that after this business had been concluded, the good men petitioned the king to confirm those *fueros* and customs which they had had at the time of the death of Alfonso VIII, and which Fernando himself, when he was king of Castile – that is, before 1230 – had promised to keep 'ante mi Madre e ante mios ricos omnes, e antel Arçobispo e ante los Obispos, e ante caueros de Castilla e de Estremadura e ante toda mi corte'. The king also acknowledged that 'quando yo era mas ninno' – presumably, therefore, during his minority – he had granted away certain villages from the towns, and these he would restore. The rest of the *cuaderno* consists of a number of miscellaneous articles dealing, *inter alia*, with the payment of representatives sent to the king, *cofradías* (guilds) and wedding feasts. There is also a *cuaderno* in the municipal archives of Alcaraz, which is closely connected with the other

---

[23] *Crónica Alfonso X*, caps. XXIV, XL, XLVII, LIV, LV.

[24] In *Alfonso X of Castile*, 71–5, I put forward the theory that the *Espéculo* was probably compiled after 1276 but that its first book was based on the version of the *Primera partida* contained in BL, Add. MS. 20787. I have since been convinced by the arguments of García Gallo that the *Espéculo* represents the earliest version of Alfonso X's *Libro de las leyes*, cf. Procter, 'The judicial use of "pesquisa"', 28–9, 32–3.

[25] Colmenares, *Historia de Segovia*, I, 380–2 (22 Nov. 1250); Manuel Rodríguez, *Memorias*, 520–1 (18 Nov. 1250); *Fuero de Cuenca*, 859–60 (12 Nov. 1250). Piskorski, *Cortes*, 54, 62, who only knew the one to Segovia, also thought it was a privilege to that city.

[26] This has been recognised by O'Callaghan, *AHR*, LXXIV, 1529.

three, but which has one disconcerting feature – it is dated a year later: 'Ffacta carta apud Sibillam rege exprimente XXV^a die de Novembris, Michael Petri scripsit, era M^a CC^a LXXX^a nona', that is, A.D. 1251. It is an original, and although it has lost its seal, it still retains the red and yellow strands to which the seal was attached.[27] It begins by stating that the king had sent his *cartas* to the *concejos* of the Extremadura of Castile (Cuenca, Segovia and Uceda were all towns of the Castilian Extremadura) and that the *concejo* of Alcaraz had sent its good men to the king. The rest of the *cuaderno* is identical with the other three, apart from minor verbal variations. It is difficult to account for the difference in date; it is, perhaps, possible that Alcaraz failed to send its good men to Seville in the autumn of 1250, but that they were summoned before the king at a later date and then received the *cuaderno*. All the extant *cuadernos* were addressed to towns of the Castilian Extremadura, none were addressed to Leonese towns. The first two clauses of these *cuadernos* granted petitions made by the *concejos* which referred back to the beginning of Fernando III's reign as king of Castile and before he succeeded to the kingdom of León. Thus these two clauses concerned only the *concejos* of Castile. Unless *cuadernos* addressed to Leonese cities come to light, we cannot be certain whether or no the rest of the decrees were general for all the towns of Fernando III's dominions.

Alfonso X was proclaimed king on 1 June 1252 and the first cortes of his reign were sitting in the autumn of the same year.[28] A number of *cuadernos* have survived and they fall into two distinct groups according to their date of issue. Those addressed to Nájera, Burgos and Alcalá belong to October 1252.[29] Those addressed to the archbishop of Santiago and the inhabitants of the Tierra de Santiago (which was, of course, subject to the archbishop), to Astorga and to Escalona were

---

[27] AM Alcaraz, *leg.* 1/22. My thanks are due to Professor D. W. Lomax who drew my attention to this *cuaderno* and provided me with a transcript of it. It is published in full in Appendix, doc. III, below. The *cuadernos* to Cuenca and Uceda are also originals. That to Cuenca has lost its seal, but retains the ties; that to Uceda has the leaden bull; see the editions quoted above.

[28] See Ballesteros, *Alfonso X el Sabio*, 68–74, for these cortes.

[29] To Nájera (12 Oct.), publ. Ballesteros, *Cortes de 1252*; to Burgos (12 Oct.), publ. García Rámila, *Hispania*, v, 204–22; to Alcalá (6 Oct.), cited by Portilla y Esquivel, *Historia de la ciudad de Compluto*, I, 306. There are two transcripts of an abbreviated version of the Burgos *cuaderno*, omitting clauses 11–16, 19–39, in BL, Add. MSS. 9916, fols. 8–14v, and 21448, fols. 8–12, the latter said to be taken from an original in AM Talavera. Ballesteros, *Alfonso X el Sabio*, also referred to another transcript of this shortened version. He also cites (p. 69) *cuadernos* to Calatañazor and Ubeda.

dated on various days in February 1253.[30] This four months' gap poses a problem. During November Alfonzo X left Seville and visited Badajoz, whence he returned to Seville. It is unlikely that the cortes remained in session during the king's absence. It may be that the chancery held up the *cuadernos* addressed to the towns of León and Extremadura for some reason, or it is possible that the assembly in October 1252 included only representatives of the *concejos* of Castile and that towns of the other provinces of the kingdom were summoned early in 1253. The contents of the *cuadernos*, which are mainly economic, are, however, so similar that they can be treated together, as though they emanated from one assembly.

The cortes met again in March 1254 at Toledo. There are no surviving *cuadernos*, probably because there was no legislation, but reference was made to these cortes in a document of Alfonso X of 2 March 1254, inserting and confirming the general privilege of Fernando III of 21 January 1237 to the city of Toledo,[31] and also in a private *carta* of Pedro Núñez de Guzmán to Fernando, abbot of La Vid, dated 4 March 1254.[32] The composition and object of these cortes can be learnt from a document of the following year. In 1255 Alfonso X was engaged in negotiations for the marriage of his eldest daughter, Berenguela, to Louis, eldest son of Louis IX of France.[33] On 5 May, from Palencia, Alfonso issued a solemn document, at the request of the French king, redacted in Latin, attesting that, according to Spanish custom, the king's eldest daughter succeeded her father in the absence of a legitimate male heir, and also stating that, in order to guard his daughter Berenguela's rights, he had caused the prelates, nobles and proctors of the cities and towns to come to Toledo to do homage to Berenguela and take the oath to receive her as their queen should Alfonso have no legitimate son.[34] The Infanta Doña Berenguela was born shortly before 6 December 1253, and between that date and

---

[30] To Santiago (15 Feb. 1253), publ. López Ferreiro, *Fueros*, I, 347–72. To Astorga (5 Feb.), publ. Rodríguez Díez, *Historia de Astorga*; I have not been able to consult this book. BL, Add MS. 9916, fols, 172–89v, is a transcript of a *cuaderno* to Escalona, misdated 27 Feb. 1256 for 1253; publ. Appendix, doc. IV, below. Ballesteros, *Alfonso X el Sabio*, 69, also cites a *cuaderno* to Ledesma.

[31] BN, MS. 13094, fol. 143: 'cuando vin a Toledo a facer hy mis Cortes vinieron ami los cavalleros e los omes bonos del conceio de Toledo e amostraron me sus Privillegios'.

[32] Cited by Ballesteros, *Alfonso X el Sabio*, 90; 'quando el rey don Affonso ffizo las primeras cortes en Toledo'.

[33] Daumet, *Relations*, 1–9. The marriage was not carried out, as Prince Louis died in 1259.

[34] Publ. *ibid.* 143–6, no. 1, and Piskorski, *Cortes*, 196–7.

5 May 1255 Alfonso X was at Toledo from 3 February to 19 May 1254 and at no other time. The *curia generalis* of the document of 5 May 1255 must, therefore, have taken place in the preceding year between those dates and must be the cortes which we know to have been in session in March 1254.

The only evidence for a meeting of the cortes held in December 1255 or January 1256 at Vitoria is a single sentence in *Los miráculos romanzados* of Pere Marín, prior of Santo Domingo de Silos, a work containing a collection of miracles performed by the saint between 1232 and 1293. In one of these miracles, the author narrated how Alfonso X visited the monastery when he was at war with both Navarre and Aragon and was also faced by a revolt of some of his nobles, who were supported by Jaime I of Aragon; how the saint appeared to him in a vision, and promised him that his prayers would be granted within three months; and how the rebels submitted and peace was restored, first with Teobaldo of Navarre at Vitoria, and then with Jaime I at Soria.[35] Pere Marín was well informed and most of the facts given in the narrative can be substantiated from documents. The sentence of importance to us is that concerning the restoration of peace with Navarre: 'et el rey venose dessa pressa a Victoria; e el seyendo y, veno a el don Tibalt, rey de Navarra, a sus cortes e tornose su vasallo'. Alfonso X was at Vitoria from 2 to 14 December 1255 and again from 1 to 23 January 1256. The text of the treaty with Navarre has disappeared, but it was concluded on or before 1 January 1256, for it is referred to in a letter patent of Alfonso X of that date, by which the king of Castile granted to the king of Navarre the two towns of San Sebastián and Fuenterrabía for life.[36] There is no evidence that Teobaldo became Alfonso's vassal for the kingdom of Navarre, and he was never included among the *vasallos del rey* whose names appeared in Alfonso's *privilegios rodados*, but San Sebastián and Fuenterrabía were granted to Teobaldo as life-fiefs and he may have done homage for them at Vitoria.

Colmenares is the source of a statement that the cortes met in Segovia in July 1256.[37] His account is here based on the *Crónica de*

[35] The only edition of *Los miráculos romanzados* is in P. Sebastián de Vergara, *Vida y milagros de Santo Domingo de Silos* (Madrid 1736), 131ff. I have not been able to consult this, but the relevant passage is reproduced in *RC Silos*, 226–7; cf. also Ballesteros, *Alfonso X el Sabio*, 123–5, 146.
[36] AGN, *caj.* 3/3 (1 Jan. 1256), publ. Appendix, doc. v, below.
[37] Colmenares, *Historia de Segovia*, I, 398. He is followed by Ortiz de Zúñiga, *Anales de Sevilla*, 84, who added a quotation from a document of 1256 which referred to the scarcity of cloth; Ibáñez de Segovia, *Memorias de Alonso el Sabio*.

Alfonso X, which does not mention the cortes but states that complaints of scarcity of consumer goods were made to the king who, therefore, fixed prices; as a result merchants and others held back goods from sale so that the king was obliged to rescind the tariffs he had set and allow free sale again.[38] Complaints of scarcity had already been made, and prices of many goods had been fixed in 1252 and 1253. These were re-enacted on a fresh basis, because of the fall in the value of money, and in far greater number, in 1268, and there is no evidence, other than the statement of the *Crónica*, that the regulations of 1252 were rescinded, or that prices were fixed in 1256. Colmenares also referred to a *fuero* granted to Cuéllar on 21 July 1256. This was a grant of the *Fuero real* which was described as 'aquel fuero que yo fiz con consejo de mi corte escripto en libro e sellado con mio seello de plomo', and a number of additional privileges to the knights of the town.[39] It is possible that Colmenares misinterpreted the reference to the *corte* to mean that the cortes were in session at Segovia. The *Fuero real* had been completed in the previous year. During July 1256 a large number of *fueros* were confirmed or granted, including grants of the *Fuero real* to Soria, Peñafiel, Buitrago, Alarcón, Trujillo and Burgos.[40] Ballesteros saw in this legislative activity an additional proof that the cortes were assembled at Segovia,[41] but town *fueros*, including the *Fuero real*, were granted at many times during the reign, when the cortes were not in session, so that, by itself, this granting of *fueros* in July 1256 is not sufficient evidence that representatives of towns were summoned to cortes at Segovia at that time. Definite evidence may come to light, but unless it does, the meeting of the cortes at Segovia in July 1256 must be deemed non-proven.

There are fewer problems about the Cortes of Valladolid of January 1258, as they are attested by a number of surviving *cuadernos* which include those given to Ledesma, Ponferrada, Burgos, Sepúlveda, Escalona, Lorca and León.[42] The contents of the *cuadernos* were, like

128–9; Colmeiro, *Introducción*, 155; Ballesteros, *Itinerario*, 171, and *Alfonso X el Sabio*, 167–8.

[38] *Crónica Alfonso X*, cap. v (p. 6).

[39] *CD Cuéllar*, No. 16.

[40] *MHE*, I, nos. XLIII, XLIV, XLV: grants of the *Fuero real* to Peñafiel, Buitrago and Burgos; for references to these and grants to other towns, see Ballesteros, *Itinerario*, 160–2.

[41] Ballesteros, *Alfonso X, el Sabio*, 168.

[42] *Cortes*, I, no. XIII (from AM Ledesma, 18 Jan. 1258, with variants from a *cuaderno* to Ponferrada); García Rámila, *Hispania*, v, 224–35 (from AM Burgos, 15 Jan. 1258); *CD Sepúlveda*, I, no. 8 (from a fragment in AM Sepúlveda); BL, Add. MS. 9916, fols. 218–30, is a transcript from an original in AM Escalona,

those of 1252 and 1253, essentially economic. Many of the clauses re-enacted decrees laid down in 1252 and 1253.[43]

The cortes were again summoned to Toledo sometime in 1259. These cortes are known only from references in documents. The essential document is a *carta abierta* of 6 February 1260 to the knights and good men of Toledo confirming their exemption from *posada* (lodging), which the king had contravened when he held his cortes in Toledo 'sobrel ffecho del Imperio', and when the city had been commanded to give lodgings to the *infantes*, bishops, nobles and good men of the towns who had been summoned to the cortes.[44] Another document of the same date referred to a *moneda* granted 'por ayuda del fecho del Imperio'.[45] There are further references to these cortes in Toledo on the matter of the Empire in two *cartas* of 20 and 25 June 1264.[46] The exact date of these cortes is not known. Alfonso was in Toledo from 26 January 1259 to 6 February 1260, but the most probable date for them was during the spring of 1259. In June 1259 Pope Alexander IV knew of Alfonso's intention to visit Rome to claim the imperial crown. It seems likely that this decision, and its financial implications, were announced to the cortes at that time.

Spanish historians from Ortiz de Zúñiga onwards have postulated a meeting of the cortes in 1260.[47] Ortiz de Zúñiga based his opinion on two documents, one of Archbishop Juan Arias of Santiago and the other of Archbishop Sancho of Toledo. Both dealt with a dispute with Archbishop Remondo of Seville, who had protested that the entry of the other two archbishops into the ecclesiastical province of Seville, with their archiepiscopal crosses carried before them, transgressed his rights. Both letters also refer to a royal summons to attend

and Add. MS. 21,448, fols. 16–29, is a transcript from an authentic copy of the Ponferrada *cuaderno*. Both these transcripts are misdated 18 June (for 18 Jan.) 1258, but their contents are identical with the rest of this group of *cuadernos*: Ballesteros, *Alfonso X el Sabio*, 201, cites in addition *cuadernos* to Lorca (13 Jan.) and León (18 Jan.).

[43] Ballesteros, *Alfonso X el Sabio*, 201–6, quotes at length from these decrees.

[44] Publ. Ballesteros, *Alfonso X, Emperador*, 71; and *MHE*, I, no. LXXI.

[45] Publ. Ballesteros, *Alfonso X, Emperador*, 69–71. This document does not mention the cortes.

[46] The two letters are identical. That addressed to Bishop Pedro Lorenzo of Cuenca is published in part in Ballesteros, *Alfonso X, Emperador*, 72, and 'Itinerario', *BRAH*, CVIII, 17–23, with a running commentary The other, addressed to Bishop Andrés of Sigüenza, is published in Minguella, *Historia de Sigüenza*, I, 599

[47] Ortiz de Zúñiga, *Anales de Sevilla*, 89; Ibáñez de Segovia, *Memorias de Alonso el Sabio*, 215; Colmeiro, *Introducción*, 157–8; Ballesteros, *Alfonso X el Sabio*, 290–5.

a curia or *corte*.[48] That of Archbishop Juan Arias, in Latin, stated that he had been summoned to Seville by the king, 'ut ad Curiam quam apud Ispalensim Civitatem ordinauerat ueniremus' and was dated from Seville, on 22 February A.D. 1260. That of Archbishop Sancho, in the vernacular, stated that he had come to Seville 'a Corte de nuestro hermano' and was also dated from Seville, but on 14 December 'era mill CCLXXXXVIII annos' (A.D. 1260). Both letters are taken to refer to the same assembly, but there were more than nine months between their accepted dates. Alfonso X was certainly not in Seville during the first half of 1260. Ballesteros placed the cortes at the end of 1260, and suggested that they probably opened on St Clement's Day (25 November), but he made no attempt to explain why the archbishop of Santiago should have been summoned to attend in the previous February. An obvious explanation is that the chancery of Archbishop Juan Arias, which in this letter used the style of the Incarnation, began the year in March, not January, so that the letter belongs to 1261, modern style. This would reduce the time between the two letters to less than three months, and would place the assembly between December 1260 and February 1261. That the archbishop of Santiago's letter did in fact belong to 1261, not 1260, is proved by the final paragraph of the letter, which referred to the election of Fernando, canon of Coria, to the bishopric of Coria and to a disputed election to the see of Avila, both of which took place while the archbishop was in Seville. These elections took place early in 1261 not in 1260, as is shown by the lists of *confirmantes* in the *privilegios rodados*.[49] The cortes, in fact, met in January 1261, as is proved by the only *cuaderno* known to have survived, that sent to Astorga, which, although it has been in print more than sixty years, has been overlooked by recent Spanish historians.[50] The *cuaderno* was passed at Seville on 24 January 1261; the preamble spoke of the cortes as taking place in the month of January.[51] The

---

[48] Both publ. Ballesteros, *Sevilla*, nos. 107, 144.

[49] Ballesteros, *Alfonso X, Emperador*, 70 (6 Feb. 1260): 'Don Benito Obispo de Avila', 'Don Pedro Obispo de Coria'; Ballesteros, *Sevilla*, no. 110 (21 Nov. 1260): 'La eglesia de Avila uaga', 'La eglesia de Coria uaga'. ANTT, *Liv. Afonso II*, III, fol. 3 (8 April 1261): 'Don fferando electo de Coria', 'La eglesia de Avila vaga.'

[50] Publ. Rodríguez Díez, *Historia de Astorga*, 715–20, which I have been unable to consult. I am indebted to Dr Richard Fletcher for a xerox copy of the *cuaderno* taken from the copy of the book in the Cathedral Library of Astorga. The original *cuaderno* is, presumably, in the municipal archives but Dr Fletcher was unable to obtain access to them. Ballesteros knew of the existence of this *cuaderno* but does not appear to have examined it (*Alfonso X el Sabio*, 295).

[51] 'fiziemos nuestras cortes en Sevilla en el mes de Enero'.

cuaderno, like those of 1252 and 1258, was largely economic and re-enacted many of the regulations of the earlier codes.

In April 1264 the knights and good men of the *concejos* of Extremadura were assembled in Seville, together with those prelates, nobles and masters of the military orders who were then with the king. Our primary evidence for this assembly consists of two *cuadernos*, one addressed to Peñafiel, and dated 15 April 1264, the other addressed to Cuéllar, dated 29 April 1264. The *cuaderno* to Cuéllar has been published, but its editor considered it to be a petition granted to the town and did not recognise it as a *cuaderno* granted to the *concejos* generally.[52] That to Peñafiel survives in three eighteenth-century transcripts, one of which is contained in the British Library Add. MS. 9916.[53] In this manuscript the transcriber has entitled the *cuaderno* 'Peticiones de los pueblos de Extremadura respondidas en las cortes de Sevilla de 1264'. Is this description of 'cortes' justified? Clearly they were not general cortes for the whole realm. There is no evidence of the presence of representatives of towns of the other regions of the kingdom, but they can be considered to be provincial cortes for Extremadura. Both *cuadernos* state that all the *concejos* of Extremadura were represented, and the petitions and answers are identical – only the address to the individual town differs. What appear to be extracts from a similar *cuaderno* to Avila dated 22 April 1264 have been published, as has also a petition from the *concejo* of Escalona, concerned with the government of that town and granted during the assembly.[54] The only other source is the *Crónica de Alfonso X* which, under the erroneous year 1263, gives some account of an 'ordenamiento' granted by Alfonso X to the towns of Extremadura.[55]

The cortes were next assembled at Jerez early in 1268. On 25 March, while the gathering was in session, Alfonso X granted petitions which had been presented to him by the representatives of Burgos at Christmas 1267 and which were mainly concerned with administration and

[52] *CD Cuéllar*, no. 21. Published from a confirmation of Sancho IV.
[53] Publ. Appendix, doc. VII, below. The other two transcripts are: RAH, 'Colección de Martínez Marina', II, 94; and Biblioteca Colombina, Seville, *ley* B, col. 1; all three are cited by Ballesteros, *BRAH*, CVII, 398. Ballesteros knew the Martínez Marina transcript but made little use of it.
[54] Ariz, *Historia de la grandezas de la ciudad de Avila, 3a parte*, 18; and Carramolino, *Historia de Avila*, II, 491. These extracts are printed as supplements to the grant of the *Fuero real* to Avila on 30 Oct. 1256, and correspond to cls. 5, 6, 7 and part of cl. 12 of the *cuaderno* of 1264. *MHE*, I, no. XLVI (8 April 1264).
[55] *Crónica Alfonso X*, cap. XII (p. 10).

justice in the city.[56] There is only one known *cuaderno* – that addressed to Seville and the other *concejos* of the archbishopric of Seville – and it was not passed by the chancery until 30 July from Seville, more than two months after Alfonso X had left Jerez.[57] This delay was probably accounted for by the detailed nature of the contents. The reason for summoning the cortes was clearly stated in the preamble of the *cuaderno*. Many complaints of the great scarcity from which the country suffered had reached the king, and for this reason he had sent for merchants and other good men of Castile, León, Extremadura and Andalusia, and he had taken counsel with them and with the *infantes*, prelates and nobles on the measures to be taken to remedy the scarcity and restore the good estate of the land. The forty-six clauses of the *cuaderno* were overwhelmingly economic in character. Many of them re-enacted clauses in the decrees of 1252, 1258 and 1261 but often at greater length and in more detail. Certain matters appeared for the first time. This was the last and the most important of Alfonso X's economic codes.[58]

On 30 November 1269 Alfonso X's eldest son and heir, the Infante Don Fernando de la Cerda, was married to Blanche of France at Burgos.[59] The cortes were summoned to assemble at the same time,[60] thus recalling the ceremonial curia held in Castile for Fernando III's marriage in 1219. The cortes of 1269, however, were not wholly ceremonial, but were largely concerned with financial matters. They voted six subsidies (*servicios*) for the defence of the frontier,[61] probably also a special tax on migrating flocks and herds for the expenses of the Infante's marriage,[62] and they authorised Burgos to impose a local tax

---

[56] *Opúsculos legales*, ii, 205–8, dated Sunday 30 March 1268; in 1268 the 30th fell on a Friday, Sunday was 25 March. The document states that Burgos had been ordered to send knights to the king at Christmas (1267). BN, MS. 13075, fol. 26v, gives the date correctly as 25 March.

[57] *Cortes*, i, no. xiv.

[58] Ballesteros, *Alfonso X el Sabio*, 438–45, gives a detailed analysis of the contents of the *cuaderno* with copious quotations.

[59] For the date of the marriage, see *Cronicón de Cardeña*, i, in *ES*, xxiii, 370. The account in *Crónica Alfonso X*, *cap.* xviii, is extremely inaccurate; e.g. it places the knighting of Edward of England at this marriage, instead of at his own marriage to Eleanor of Castile in 1254, and calls him Alfonso's nephew instead of his brother-in-law. It also places the marriage of don Fernando in 1268 instead of 1269.

[60] Ballesteros, *Alfonso X el Sabio*, 483, 489, citing *carta* of the *gran comendador* of the Hospital, dated 12 Nov. 1269.

[61] *Cortes*, i, no. xv (p. 86).

[62] *MHE*, i, no. cxl (p. 314): 'Servicio de los ganados que fué demandado por toda la tierra pora las bodas del Infante don Fernando'.

on sales (*alcabala*) for the completion of the city walls.[63] The *Crónica*'s account does not use the word *cortes*, but it states that the nobles, knights and those of the *concejos* of the cities and towns of the kingdom granted the subsidies, thus implying a meeting of the cortes.

Our only account of the Cortes of Burgos in 1272 is that contained in the narrative of the revolt of the nobles, which the fourteenth-century author of the *Crónica de Alfonso X* incorporated in his work. The *Crónica* is annalistic in form, and the author has inserted dates in the narrative of the revolt. The first two of these both antedate events by a year. Under 1270 is recorded the Confederation of Lerma, which took place during the king's absence in Murcia, and in which his brother, the Infante Don Felipe, many nobles and knights and 'others of the towns' conspired against the king.[64] In 1270 Alfonso was in Castile, but he went to Murcia in February 1271 and remained there until June 1272. The king's itinerary from Murcia to Burgos, as given in the *Crónica* under 1271, corresponds with his known itinerary from June to September 1272.[65] It is, then, in the autumn of 1272, not in the preceding year, that the cortes of Burgos took place.

Alfonso had reached Burgos by 6 September 1272, and his first negotiations with the malcontent nobles were held outside the city. The demands of the nobles were mainly directed against Alfonso's legislative and administrative reforms; they also demanded some remission of the taxation imposed at the Cortes of 1269, and complained of the royal policy of founding new towns and centres of population. Alfonso was prepared to make some concessions and the nobles then demanded that the cortes should be assembled so that these concessions could be solemnly promulgated in them.[66] This demand for the summoning of the cortes shows not only their growing importance, but also indicates that the nobles knew that they could count on support from some of the towns. As a result the king summoned nobles, prelates and the proctors of the *concejos* to assemble in Burgos at Michaelmas.[67] In these cortes the nobles put forward additional demands, including many personal grievances and, not placated by further concessions

---

[63] *Crónica Alfonso X*, cap. XXIII (p. 20): 'el pecho que daban en Burgos que dicen alcabala'.

[64] *Ibid. cap.* XX (p. 15); other references to support given by some towns to the rebels occur in *cap.* XXVIII (p. 24), and *cap.* XLV (p. 35).

[65] *Ibid. cap.* XXII (p 18).

[66] *Ibid. cap.* XXIII (p. 20), for the nobles' demand, and *cap.* XXIV (pp. 20–1), for the king's reply.

[67] *Ibid. caps.* XXV–XXVI (pp. 21–3), for the cortes; cf. Ballesteros, *Alfonso X el Sabio*, 579–87, with copious quotations from the *Crónica*.

from Alfonso X, then withdrew to Campos. At this point some of the bishops put forward grievances and petitions of their own. The *Crónica* neither names the bishops nor specifies their grievances. Ballesteros, by a process of elimination, concluded that the bishops implicated were, most probably, those who held Galician and Leonese sees.[68] To deal with the petitions of both the nobles and the prelates, a commission of no fewer than forty-two persons was set up, including Queen Violante, the Infante Don Fadrique, nobles, knights, prelates, other clergy, members of the Franciscan and Dominican Orders and seventeen proctors from nine towns.[69] We have no knowledge whether the commission ever met. Probably it did not, for the noble malcontents renounced their allegiance to the king as Castilian law allowed them to do, and asked for the customary forty-two days' truce while they retired to Granada; thus the cortes ended in open revolt.

It is not necessary for us to follow the events of the rebellion, which are narrated in great detail in the *Crónica*,[70] but during the course of 1273 two further assemblies took place which, although they were not themselves cortes, need to be considered since they are of interest for the development of the institution. These were the *ayuntamientos*, as they were called by the *Crónica*, of Almagro and Avila. The *ayuntamiento* of Almagro took place some time before 28 March 1273, on which date Alfonso X, from Toledo, attested that, at the request of Queen Violante, the Infante Don Fernando, the Infantes Don Fadrique and Don Manuel, the masters of the Orders of Uclés, Calatrava, Alcántara and the Temple and those nobles, *infanzones*, *caballeros* and *hidalgos* who were loyal to him and were with him at Almagro, he had remitted two of the remaining four of the six *servicios* granted at Burgos in 1269 and that he would withdraw the customs duties on imports and exports after a period of six years.[71] To these financial concessions the *Crónica*, whose account tallies closely with the royal *carta* but is not solely based on it, added a general confirmation of the 'fueros, e usos e costumbres' enjoyed under former

---

[68] Ballesteros, *Alfonso X el Sabio*, 584.

[69] *Crónica Alfonso X, cap.* xxvi (p. 23); the nine towns were Avila, Segovia, Arévalo, Medina (del Campo), Cuéllar, Valladolid, Palencia, Burgos and Sepúlveda.

[70] *Ibid. caps.* xxvii–lviii; Ballesteros, *Alfonso X el Sabio*, 591–671, 677–82, incorporates the greater part of the narrative of the *Crónica* interspersed with comments.

[71] *Cortes*, I, no. xv; Ballesteros, *Alfonso X el Sabio*, 637–8, noted that there is a gap in the king's itinerary from 22 Feb. to 27 March, during which time the *ayuntamiento* must have taken place.

kings.[72] This assembly, as has been mentioned, was not a cortes. Many nobles were absent, in open rebellion in Granada; none of the bishops was present; and although the *Crónica* speaks of 'caballeros fijosdalgo de las cibdades e villas quel Rey mandó llamar para esto', these knights of noble lineage were not there as representatives of the *concejos*, but had probably been summoned for military reasons. Yet it is noteworthy that the king in this assembly abrogated *servicios* granted in cortes in 1269 and made concessions which he had refused to make at the Michaelmas Cortes of 1272. It will thus be seen that the part of the cortes in the business of government was still ill-defined and, in spite of their special name, which indicated some degree of differentiation, they were still in fact regarded as a variant form of the king's curia, so that acts performed in cortes could still be rescinded by an anomalous body such as the *ayuntamiento* of Almagro.

The second *ayuntamiento*, that of Avila, took place between 21 April and 28 May 1273, when Alfonso was in that city.[73] To it were summoned the representatives of the *concejos* of León and of the Extremaduras, but not apparently those from the other provinces of the kingdom. Although the *Crónica* called this assembly an *ayuntamiento*, it approached more nearly the norm of the cortes than had the assembly at Almagro, and bore some resemblance to the provincial cortes for the Extremaduras at Seville in 1264. The business transacted at Avila was concerned with the war against Granada and the revolt of the nobles.[74]

The conclusion of peace with Granada, and the return of the rebels to their allegiance, left the way open, at last, for Alfonso X's projected expedition to Italy in support of his pretensions to the imperial crown. The cortes were summoned to Burgos early in 1274 to further this purpose. The only reference to them occurs in a privilege of Alfonso X of 13 April 1274 from Palencia 'en el anno de la era de mill et trezientos et doze annos' (A.D. 1274) 'quando feziemos las cortes de Burgos sobre fecho de enbiar caualleros al imperio de Roma'.[75] There are, however, a number of *cartas* addressed to towns and passed by the chancery at various dates from April to October 1274 which, while they do not mention the cortes, refer to 'el seruiçio de dos annos. . .que era cosa que

---

[72] *Crónica Alfonso X*, *cap*. XLVII (pp. 35-6); see Ballesteros, *Alfonso X el Sabio*, 638-41, for a summary of the differences between the *carta* and the *Crónica*.
[73] Ballesteros, *Alfonso X el Sabio*, 646, and *Indice de documentos*, nos. 887-92.
[74] *Crónica Alfonso X*, *cap*. L (p. 37); *cap*. LII (p. 38); royal *carta* to the Infante Don Fernando inserted in the *Crónica*. Another version of this letter was published by Ibáñez de Segovia, *Memorias de Alonzo el Sabio*, 306-11.
[75] Publ. Ballesteros, *Alfonso X, Emperador*, 72-3.

auiemos mucho mester pora fecho del imperio'. It seems logical to suppose that this *servicio* needed for 'the matter of the Empire' was granted by the Cortes of Burgos, summoned for the same purpose and, if this be so, then the cortes must have met before 20 March 1274, the date of the earliest *carta* to refer to the *servicio*.[76]

The *Crónica de Alfonso X* does not mention these Cortes of Burgos, but, under the year 1275, it records an assembly held at Toledo, at which Alfonso X made provision for the government of the kingdom during his absence. The account of the proceedings is very circumstantial. Some of the most important persons present are given by name, including Alfonso's sons, his brother the Infante Don Felipe, Archbishop Sancho of Toledo, the masters of the military orders and a number of *ricos hombres*, and the list ends with the words 'e todos los otros ricos omes e infanzones e caballeros de los reinos de Castilla e de León'. This is followed by a summary of the king's speech, in which he informed the assembly that his brother the Infante Don Manuel was to accompany him to Italy; his heir the Infante Don Fernando was to be regent and Don Nuño de Lara, *adelantado mayor de la frontera*. The appointments of the *merinos* in Castile, León and Galicia were to be made by the Infante, but the letters of appointment were to be sealed with the king's seal, left for the purpose, and issued in the king's name. *Cartas* concerned with justice and other matters were to be sealed with the Infante's personal seal.[77] Both date and place as given in the *Crónica* are manifestly incorrect. We know that Alfonso left Castile at the end of 1274 and spent Christmas with his father-in-law, Jaime I of Aragon, at Barcelona before proceeding to Beaucaire for his meeting with Pope Gregory X. Moreover, his itinerary for the year 1274 does not allow for a visit to Toledo. Ballesteros, therefore, suggested that these provisions were made, not at Toledo, but at the Cortes of Burgos in 1274.[78] This is a plausible solution, and the references in the king's speech to embassies from his north-Italian supporters and 'la ida que avia de ir al Imperio' seem to indicate a date early in 1274, when Alfonso still intended an expedition to Italy but before he had changed his purpose to that of a meeting with Pope Gregory X in the south of

[76] *DA Madrid, 1a serie*, I, 119, 121 (20 March, 27 Oct. 1274); *Colección de privilegios de la corona de Castilla*, v, no. LIX (to Oviedo, 15 April); *Ballesteros, Alfonso X, Emperador*, 74–7 (to Túy, 15 April 1274, to Cuéllar, 17 April, to León, 27 April, to Toledo, 13 May, to Alcalá, 28 Aug.). AC León no. 1121 (2 July); *CD Murcia*, I, no. LXIV (16 Oct.). The cartas to Túy and León refer to 'otros conceios del Regno de León'; those to Madrid and Cuéllar to 'los otros concejos de Castiella e de Estremadura'.
[77] *Crónica Alfonso X, cap.* LIX.   [78] Ballesteros, *Alfonso X el Sabio*, 684–6.

France, where the Pope held the Council of Lyons in July 1274. There is a point which, however, requires explanation: Don Nuño de Lara does not appear as *adelantado* of the frontier in the *privilegios rodados* of the summer of 1274, but his appointment to this office may well have been made late in the autumn, immediately before Alfonso's departure from Castile.[79]

Some three months after the Cortes of Burgos, in June and July 1274, an assembly was held at Zamora, which is known only from an important ordinance on the administration of justice, dated from that city.[80] The original of the ordinance has been lost, but it survives in a sixteenth-century copy in an Escorial manuscript and in various transcripts taken from this manuscript.[81] The title uses the word *cortes*: 'Siguense las leyes e ordinamientos quel Rey don Alonso Decimo llamado Sabio fizo e ordeno para abreviar los pleitos en las cortes que tuvo en Zamora con acuerdo de los de su regno en el anno del sennor de mill e dozientos e setenta e quarto annos', etc., but this heading is not original and there is no use of the word *cortes* in the text. The preamble, which appears to be abbreviated and which is in the third person, as is the whole ordinance, begins:

Sobre el consejo quel Rey demando a los prelados e alos religiosos e alos ricos omes e alos alcalles tambien de Castilla como de Leon, que eran conel en Zamora en el mes de junio que fue en la era de mill e trezientos e doze annos, en razon delas cosas porque se embargavan los pleitos porque se non libravan ayna, ni como devian.

The preamble then goes on to state that the king instructed the *alcaldes* to confer together on the causes of the delays in justice; that each gave the king his reply in writing, and that the scriveners and advocates also gave written replies, although the king had not ordered them to do so. Colmeiro called this assembly 'cortes verdaderas' and likened the *alcaldes* of the ordinance to the 'majores civitatum et villarum' whom he thought had attended the Curia of Carrión in 1188, but whom he did not consider to be representatives because he confused them with the royal *merinos*.[82] Ballesteros twice refers to them as cortes for the

---

[79] E.g. Ballesteros, *Sevilla*, no. 183 (6 June 1274); *MHE*, I, no. cxxxv (3 Aug. 1274).

[80] *Cortes*, I, no. xvi. The preamble refers to 'el mes de Junio'; cl. 48 gives the date 'viernes veynte dias de Jullio'.

[81] Zarco Cuevas, *Catálogo de los manuscritos castellanos en la Real Biblioteca de El Escorial*, III, 110, MS. Z, II, 6, item 1. There are two eighteenth-century transcripts taken from this manuscript in BL, Add. MSS, 9915, fol. 379, and 9916, fol. 289.

[82] Colmeiro, *Introducción*, 164.

kingdom of León, although those present were clearly not limited to Leonese.[83] But were cortes in the correct sense of the term held at Zamora, or was the assembly there simply an extraordinary meeting of the *corte*? The towns frequently included some of their *alcaldes* among those sent to represent them, but there is no other instance in which the representatives were collectively called *alcaldes*. These *alcaldes* of Castile and León must have included, as well as *alcaldes* appointed by the *concejos*, those appointed by the king and, as the greater part of the ordinance dealt with the constitution of a judicial tribunal within the *corte*, those alcaldes attached to the king's court. Thus, the *alcaldes* were not present as representatives of the *concejos* but were experts summoned to give advice and information on matters of justice. The *Ordenamiento de Zamora* was of importance in the history of the development of a central court of justice but not in the development of the cortes.

The succession dispute

Alfonso returned from his abortive interview at Beaucaire with Gregory X towards the end of 1275, after an absence from his kingdom of just over a year.[84] During his absence, Andalusia had been invaded by Ibn Yuçef of Morocco, in concert with the king of Granada. The Infante Don Fernando had died on his way south to the frontier; Don Nuño González had been defeated and killed at Ecija; and Archbishop Sancho of Toledo had also been killed in a skirmish with the invaders. As a result of these disasters, the conduct of affairs had fallen into the hands of Alfonso's second son the Infante Don Sancho. Alfonso's first action was to summon some towns to send representatives to Alcalá. Here the king laid before them the state of the kingdom and the matter of the war (*el fecho de la guerra*) and they granted him in aid the equivalent of a *moneda* each year for three years. It is probable that this assembly was for Castile and the Extremaduras which are specifically mentioned in the only document referring to it.[85] It is, indeed, difficult to see how representatives from Galicia and León could have reached Alcalá in the time available. Most of the nobles must have been

[83] Ballesteros, *Alfonso X el Sabio*, 683, 692.
[84] The earliest known royal document after the king's return is dated 10 Dec. 1275, from Brihuega; publ. Ballesteros, *Sevilla*, no. 195.
[85] Royal *carta* to Burgos (22 Dec. 1275), partly published in Ballesteros, 'Burgos y la rebelión del Infante Don Sancho', *BRAH*, cxix, 118–19. Ballesteros omitted this assembly in *Alfonso X el Sabio*, 778. The *carta* refers to 'los de Castilla como los de Estremadura' and 'todos los otros de todos los concejos que a mi uinieron'.

with the army on the frontier and could not have attended. The three aids were also granted by the bishops on behalf of their vassals, so some of the bishops may have been present.[86]

The question of the succession remained to be dealt with – whether the heir to the throne was the king's eldest grandson Don Alfonso de la Cerda, then a child of five, or his second son the Infante Don Sancho. The narrative sources give contradictory accounts of the part played by the cortes. According to the *Crónica de Alfonso X* the claims of Don Sancho were put to the king at Toledo by Lope Díaz de Haro, and there the king consulted with his brother the Infante Don Manuel and other advisers. Don Manuel supported the claim of Alfonso's son as against his grandson and, as a result, writs of summons were despatched to all the cities and towns of the kingdom to send their proctors to the cortes at Segovia to do homage to the Infante Don Sancho as heir to the throne, and this was done.[87] This account has been accepted by historians up to and including Daumet.[88] Alfonso X was certainly in Toledo in January 1276 but, as Ballesteros pointed out as long ago as 1922, he was not in Segovia at any time during 1276 or 1277 although he was there in the summer of 1278.[89] Ballesteros, therefore, concluded that the cortes took place at Segovia in 1278. On the other hand, according to the chronicle of Jofré de Loaisa, the cortes were held at Burgos to decide the question of the succession; there the cause of Don Alfonso was upheld by Juan Núñez and Nuño González de Lara but the Infante Don Fadrique, Lope Díaz de Haro and many other *ricos hombres* and prelates 'et omnia concilia seu comunitates Castelle et Legionis voluerunt et petierunt ut preffatus infans dompnus Sancius regnaret, et eidem tamquam futuro regi homagium prestiterunt'. These cortes Loaisa placed in 1276, in the same year in which King Jaime I of Aragon died.[90] Loaisa's account of the Cortes of Burgos has support from contemporary documents. Until the last quarter of the nineteenth century, a writ of summons, dated from Burgos, 30 April 1276, addressed to the *concejo* of Salamanca and ordering it to send two 'good men' to Burgos, was conserved in the Municipal Archives of Salamanca. This writ has now disappeared, but in 1870 it was cited by

[86] *Documentos lingüísticos*, no. 201 (24 July 1276), which refers to 'las tres ayudas'.
[87] *Crónica Alfonso X*, caps. LXVII, LXVIII (p. 53).
[88] E.g. Colmenares, *Historia de Segovia*, I, 411–12; Ibáñez de Segovia, *Memorias de Alonso el Sabio*, 331–2; Colmeiro, *Introducción*, 165–6; Daumet, *Relations*, 22–6.
[89] Ballesteros, *Historia de España*, III, 23–4.
[90] Jofré de Loaisa, *Crónica*, 20–1. Cf. also *Anales toledanos*, III (VIII), 419, which states that the magnates did homage to the Infante Don Sancho in 1276.

J. Sánchez Ruano in his edition of the *Fuero* of Salamanca, among a list of royal documents then to be found in the municipal archives, and it is on his description of it that we have to rely. Sánchez Ruano's summary of its contents is as follows:

Otra [carta de Alfonso X] en Burgos, 30 de Abril, era de 1314 [A.D. 1276], mandando que esta ciudad nombrase dos hombres buenos de su Concejo que fueran a Burgos, para señalar Principe heredero de estos reinos, y responder al rey de Francia que pretendia tener derecho a ellos D. Alfonso, nieto del mismo Alfonso X.[91]

Alfonso X remained at Burgos from 30 April until the end of July 1276, during which time the cortes must have taken place. Further evidence that Don Sancho was recognised as heir to the throne during the summer of 1276 is provided by the Convention of Vitoria which was agreed on 7 November 1276 between Robert of Artois, on behalf of Philip III of France, and Alfonso X. By one clause of this convention Alfonso undertook to do all in his power to procure the revocation of the oath and homage to the Infante Don Sancho, both by the nobles who had made them and by Don Sancho, and also undertook to assemble a curia within a year from Christmas, at which the prelates and nobles should judge the case between the Infante Don Sancho and Don Alfonso de la Cerda, and that the king of France might appoint jurists to plead the cause of his nephew Don Alfonso. Alfonso X further agreed that, if he were unable to obtain the revocation of the oaths and homage, other barons and prelates, the best and wisest who could be found, who had not taken the oath to the Infante Don Sancho, should judge the case.[92] Thus, the question of the sucession was to be submitted to a judicial inquiry and sentence in the king's court.

The Convention of Vitoria was not ratified by Philip III, and it remained a dead letter, but its text showed clearly that some of the prelates and nobles had done homage to the Infante Don Sancho as heir to the throne in the summer of 1276. Who were the 'alii barones et prelati' of the Convention? Did they include the members of the house of Lara who by September 1276 had already fled the country and become pensioners of Philip?[93] Were there other supporters of the king's grandson who had refused to take the oath to the Infante Don

---

[91] *Fuero de Salamanca,* ed. Sánchez Ruano, xxiv. Professor D. W. Lomax, who visited these archives in 1958, could find no trace of this writ.

[92] The text of the convention is published by Francisque Michel in his edition of Anelier, *Guerre de Navarre,* 652. Cf. Daumet, *Relations,* 45–7.

[93] Daumet, *Relations,* 30–3, and nos. VII, VIII.

Sancho? Or were they nobles and bishops who had been prevented from attending the Cortes of Burgos because they were needed on the frontier, or for other reasons? We have no means of knowing who, or how many, of the magnates were still uncommitted to Don Sancho. Ballesteros made no use of the chronicle of Jofré de Loaisa in his treatment of the succession question, and in his earlier works he made no mention of the Cortes of Burgos of 1276. In his last work he referred to the lost writ to Salamanca, to the Cortes of Burgos and to the Convention of Vitoria, but he played down the importance of the Cortes of Burgos. He considered that their principal business was the granting of subsidies and that, although the question of the succession was discussed there, it was not decided. He admitted that some of the magnates must have done homage, as was shown by the Convention of Vitoria, but he maintained that the *concejos* had not done so, and he tried to explain away the importance of the evidence in order to retain his view that the account given by the *Crónica de Alfonso X* of the Cortes of Segovia was correct in all save the date, which should be 1278 instead of 1276.[94] In support of his view that Don Sancho was not recognised as Alfonso's heir in 1276, Ballesteros also pointed out that the chancery did not give him the title of heir in *privilegios rodados* of 1276 and most of 1277. This is so: in royal privileges for more than a year after the Cortes of Burgos the title given to Don Sancho was 'fijo mayor del Rey y su mayordomo'. But, as Ballesteros himself showed, from the autumn of 1276 the Infante Don Sancho was himself using the title 'fijo mayor e *heredero*' in his own documents and, from November 1277, the royal chancery was giving him the same title, several months before the possible date of the Cortes of Segovia.[95] This considerably weakens Ballesteros's argument from the form of title used in the royal privileges. To the question whether the cortes met at Segovia in 1278 and, if so, for what purpose, we shall have to return later.

Ballesteros has also postulated another meeting of the cortes at Burgos in 1277. Evidence for this is provided by what appears to be a rough draft of a petition to Pope John XXI, to absolve Alfonso X from his oath to maintain for the rest of his life the coinage known as

[94] Ballesteros, *Alfonso X el Sabio*, 789–90, 805.
[95] AHN, Santiago, caj. 102/10 (14 July 1276); Ballesteros, *Sevilla*, no. 205 (7 July 1277); Ballesteros, *Alfonso X el Sabio*, 824, citing documents of the Infante Don Sancho of 14 Nov. 1276 and 3 March 1277; *ibid.* 841, citing a royal document of 11 Nov. 1277; *Sevilla*, no. 211 (26 April 1278). The number of royal privileges for the years from 1276 to 1278 is small.

the *dineros prietos* (presumably a reference to that minted in 1271), so that he might be free to issue a new and more plentiful coinage to meet the expenses of the war against the Merinid king, Ibn Yuçef. This petition was not a petition from the cortes, but was in the name of a long list of individuals who, although they included the king's brother, the Infante Don Manuel, his son, the Infante Don Juan and ten nobles, were most of them ecclesiastics: the archbishop of Seville, six bishops, eight abbots and numerous archdeacons and cathedral clergy. The text, however, states that the king had consulted with prelates, nobles and 'los otros omes buenos de los conceios de su tierra que eran y con el' on the defence of the frontier, so that the matter seems to have been discussed in cortes. This draft was dated 9 May 1277, so that the cortes must have been in session before that date.[96] There is also evidence that Alfonso X was granted an annual subsidy for the rest of his life at this time. With this we shall deal later.

We must now return to the question whether the cortes were, or were not, summoned to Segovia in 1278. Alfonso X was at Segovia from June to September of that year; Ballesteros transferred to 1278 the account given in the *Crónica* under 1276 of the homage done to Sancho, as heir to the throne, in cortes at Segovia.[97] There are, however, serious difficulties in the way of this simple solution. The discussion at Toledo and the Cortes of Segovia, as recounted by the *Crónica*, were two stages in a single procedure, in which the second depended on the first. Alfonso X was at Toledo and Camerena in January 1276, but he was not in Segovia in 1276 or 1277. In 1278 he was not at Toledo but in Castile, and he reached Segovia early in June. Thus, we are left with a gap of two and a half years between the preliminary discussion at Toledo and the Cortes of Segovia, where homage was done to Don Sancho as heir, if we accept Ballesteros's solution. There is irrefutable evidence that the cortes were summoned to Burgos in 1276, to resolve the succession question. The events which took place in the summer and autumn of 1276 – the flight of the chief supporters of Don Alfonso de la Cerda to France; the muster of the French army, which began at the end of July, so that by October it had reached Sauveterre in Béarn; the Convention of Vitoria in November and its prescriptions for the revocation of the oath and homage done to

---

[96] This draft is published by Escudero de la Peña, *RABM*, 1a época, II (1872), 58–9. Cf. Ballesteros, *Alfonso X el Sabio*, 835–41, and O'Callaghan, 'The cortes and royal taxation during the reign of Alfonso X', *Traditio*, XXVII, 390–1.
[97] Ballesteros, *Alfonso X el Sabio*, 852–3.

Don Sancho by the barons – all presuppose a definite recognition of the Infante Don Sancho as heir, and support the account of the Cortes of Burgos in 1276 given by Jofré de Loaisa.[98]

There are two other scraps of evidence which should be taken into account. One is a writ of Alfonso X of 8 December 1278 to the *concejo* of Santo Domingo de Silos, to the effect that the king was sending his son through the country to receive homage and ordering the *concejo* to send two good men with *cartas de personería* to Don Sancho, when and where he should appoint for this purpose.[99] Silos was subject to the abbey, and would not have been represented in the cortes. If homage was done locally by towns not on royal demesne, the procedure would have been carried out gradually, as Don Sancho visited various parts of the kingdom, but the gap between the summer of 1276 and the end of 1278 is a long one and this writ gives some support to the theory that homage was done to Sancho in cortes at Segovia in 1278. The second piece of evidence, which was overlooked by Ballesteros, brings up a fresh consideration. It is the statement made by a contemporary, the Franciscan, Juan Gil de Zamora, in his *Liber de preconiis civitatis Numantine*, that Spain was ruled by many noble kings 'usque ad regem Allefonsum in regem Romanorum electum et illustrem Sancium filium eius, qui iam eidem incipit coregnare sub anno Domini MCCLXXVIII'.[100] This does not imply that the Infante Don Sancho was recognised as heir to the throne in 1278, but that in that year he began to reign together with his father. Alfonso X's health was precarious; the country was threatened from the south by Ibn Yuçef and from the north by Philip III of France; it may be, therefore, that Sancho was in some way regarded as associated with Alfonso X in the government of the kingdom. There is no other evidence for this, but it was certainly from 1278 that Don Sancho began to exercise a predominant part in policy, and was entrusted with much business by his father. It is, then, possible that the *Crónica* has confused two separate cortes – those at Burgos in 1276 when Don Sancho was recognised as heir, and those at Segovia in 1278 when he was associated in government with Alfonso X.

---

[98] On the French evidence, see Daumet, *Relations*, 40–7.
[99] *RC Silos*, no. 230; cf. Ballesteros, *Alfonso X el Sabio*, 874.
[100] Gil de Zamora, 'De preconiis civitatis Numantine', ed. Fita, *BRAH*, v, 146.

'Las Leyes nuevas'

Ballesteros has also assumed that the so-called *Leyes nuevas* were promulgated in cortes at Segovia in 1278.[101] The *Leyes nuevas* are not, as used to be thought, an official revision of parts of the *Fuero real*, but an unofficial collection compiled at Burgos from answers to queries and petitions from the *alcaldes* of Burgos, together with a number of royal letters.[102] The core of the collection consists of a number of *leyes* headed 'Estas son las cosas en que dubdan los alcaldes: xxix leyes', followed by some unnumbered *títulos*. These laws are prefaced by a *carta* of Alfonso X, with a general address, dealing with debts to Moors and Jews. In the *Opúsculos legales* this *carta* is undated, but in the 1781 edition, which was taken from a manuscript now lost, the place and day were given as Almazán, 21 April, without the year.[103] The *títulos* are followed by a number of letters of Alfonso X to Burgos, of various dates from 7 March 1263 to 13 April 1279, and one of Sancho IV of 23 April 1295 with a general address. These letters are not in chronological order and the one immediately following the *títulos* is dated 16 May 1278, without place of issue. In it reference is made to 'las leyes que me enviastes seelladas con vuestro seello, en que me pidiestes merced que yo que vos las otorgase, et vos las diese por fuero'. Then follows the formula of consent, 'tengo por bien e mando que vos usedes destas', and the *carta* goes on to forbid clerics to act as advocates in suits in the town court, or as judges of appeal; lays down the procedure in cases of rape; deals with the issue of royal *cartas* which contradicted existing *fueros* and with the division of inheritances among heirs.[104] Ballesteros took a sentence from the initial, undated, *carta* referring to 'muchos bonos omes de nuestra corte', which he considered indicated a meeting of the cortes, and assumed that the *Leyes nuevas* were promulgated in cortes on 16 May 1278, the date of the first *carta* following the laws. This argument is untenable. The undated letter on usury belongs, not to 1278, but to 1260, and is identical, except for the address and some

---

[101] Ballesteros, *Alfonso X el Sabio*, 853–4.

[102] Publ. *El fuero real de España*, ed. Alvaro Díaz de Montalvo (1781), iii–xvii, and *Opúsculos legales*, II, 181–209, on which later editions are based. I have here used the edition in *Opúsculos legales* as did Ballesteros. For a detailed study of the collection, see López Ortiz, *AHDE*, xvi, 5–70.

[103] The order of the *leyes* and the number of additional titles differ in different MSS. and editions. There is a transcript of the lost Campomanes MS. of the *Leyes nuevas* in BL, Add. MS. 9916, fols. 189–206.

[104] *Leyes nuevas*, 199–201. In my opinion the *leyes* approved by Alfonso X in this letter are those enumerated in it, not the preceding *leyes*.

minor variations, with other letters despatched to individual towns on varying dates in April and May 1260, some of which Ballesteros himself had cited in his earlier *Itinerario de Alfonso el Sabio*.[105] The 'good men' of these letters were members of the *corte*, not representatives sent by the towns to the cortes. The *carta* of 16 May 1278 has no reference to the cortes. Ballesteros also considered that the *Ordenamiento de la Mesta* of 22 September 1278 was promulgated in the cortes at Segovia, but there is nothing in the ordinance which supports this.[106] Whether the cortes met at Segovia in 1278 and, if so, for what purpose, remains an open question, but it seems probable that the *Crónica*'s Cortes of Segovia of 1276 were the Cortes of Burgos of that year wrongly located.

In the autumn of 1279 the Infante Don Sancho summoned to Valladolid the representatives of the *concejos* of Castile for St Luke's Day (18 October) in order to consider matters raised with Alfonso X by the papal legate, Peter, bishop of Rieti. Few of the *concejos* sent representatives, possibly because the time allowed was too short, and those who attended refused to reply without further consultation, and asked for another assembly at some town in Castile. On 17 November Don Sancho again summoned the representatives, not to a Castilian town, but to Salamanca, on 1 December, later postponed to 10 December. Don Sancho may have been acting with the knowledge of, possibly on orders from, his father, then at Seville, as the summons stated that the king was sending his messengers to him on certain matters. At the end of December, however, before the assembly at Salamanca had completed its discussions, Alfonso summoned his son to join him at Badajoz, on the Portuguese frontier, and Sancho ordered the representatives to accompany him thither. The sole evidence for these two assemblies at Valladolid and Salamanca are three *cartas* of the Infante Don Sancho of 17 and 28 November and 26 December 1279 addressed to Burgos.[107] It is possible that the cortes met at Badajoz under the presidency of the king in February 1280, when we have no evidence of his whereabouts.[108] The whole episode is a curious one. Only *concejos* of Castile appear

[105] *BRAH*, cvii, 29. For one of these *cartas*, see Appendix, doc. vi, below (AHN, Clero, *carp.* 918/15, to Sahagún, 29 April 1260).
[106] Ballesteros, *Alfonso X el Sabio*, 855. The ordinance is published in *MHE*, i, no. cxlviii. It is incorrectly dated from Seville, but Alfonso X was not in Seville in 1278.
[107] The first and last of these were published, apparently *in extenso*, except for the initial and final protocols, by Ballesteros, *BRAH*, cxix, 142–4, and *Alfonso X el Sabio*, 909, 911; the second letter changed the date of the assembly at Salamanca.
[108] See Ballesteros, *Alfonso X el Sabio*, 912, 1119, for Alfonso's itinerary.

to have been summoned to Valladolid; the second assembly, as it took
place at Salamanca, a Leonese city, may have been attended by representatives from towns and cities of León, but they are not mentioned in
the available documents. These assemblies were not cortes; only representatives of towns were present and they were summoned by the heir
to the throne, but Don Sancho's letters give very precise instructions as
to the powers to be given to the representatives, and for this reason they
are important.

We are better informed about the purpose of the legate's mission.
He was sent to expostulate with Alfonso X on the latter's treatment of
the Castilian church, and was provided with a *memoriale secretum* of
matters which he was instructed to make known to Alfonso X privately.
The indictment contained in these instructions was severe and far-
reaching. It included Alfonso's retention of the *tercias*, his custody of
vacant cathedral and monastic churches, his treatment of Archbishop
Gonzalvo of Santiago de Compostela, then in exile at the papal court,
and of Bishop Martín of León, together with a long list of grievances
put forward by the Castilian episcopate. Some of these grievances
accused the king of using menaces and threats to influence episcopal
elections, of extorting subsidies from the clergy and of forcing bishops
to seal blank charters; others dealt with attacks on ecclesiastical
jurisdiction, by which clerks were subjected to secular courts, as were
testamentary causes and those concerned with usury; sentences of excommunication and interdict were forbidden; apostolic indulgences
were not suffered to be published in the kingdom; prelates were not
permitted to meet together or refer their grievances to the Holy See;
Jews, it was claimed, were exalted above Christians.[109] It seems unlikely
that such matters would have been discussed with the town representatives.

Great assemblies, 1281–1293

The cortes were again summoned in the autumn of 1281. During the
early summer the war against Granada had been prosecuted with
vigour; the Christian army had entered the Vega de Granada and
inflicted a defeat on the enemy which led the king of Granada to sue for
peace.[110] During the campaign the knights and good men of the towns
present with the army approached the Infante Don Sancho and asked

[109] *Registres de Nicolas III*, no. 743 (23 March 1279); cf. Linehan, *The Spanish
church and the papacy*, 218–20.
[110] Ballesteros, *Alfonso X el Sabio*, 942–3.

him to represent to the king, on their behalf, the poverty of the people and the weight of the taxes. As a result, Alfonso X ordered his sons, the nobles, prelates and good men who were present to assemble and take counsel together. On their advice, he then issued writs of summons to every town on royal demesne to send representatives to Seville on St Martin's Day (11 November).[111] The *Crónica de Alfonso X* says nothing of these preliminaries but it states that the king returned from the Vega de Granada to Córdoba and from there summoned the cortes to assemble at Seville. In cortes he proposed a new coinage of two types, one of silver and one of copper, as an alternative to fresh taxation. To this the representatives agreed 'mas con temor que con amor' and, before they were dismissed, laid their complaints against the king before the Infante Don Sancho.

The Cortes of Seville in 1281 were the last cortes summoned by Alfonso X. In the spring of 1282, on the eve of the Infante Don Sancho's open revolt, the king put forward a proposal for some sort of assembly at either Toledo or Villarreal, at which he would meet his son and redress the grievances of the land. The evidence for this project is provided by some Latin documents, where the word *curia* can mean either *corte* or cortes. Thus, on 1 April 1282, Pedro III of Aragon wrote to Alfonso X to the effect that he had intended to send his envoy to Villarreal – where he understood that the Castilian king would be a fortnight after Easter 'celebrare curiam' – with an offer that he himself should come in person to mediate between father and son. But, he went on, as Alfonso had now changed both place and date of the assembly, and as Pedro's presence was necessary with his fleet, he found himself obliged to abandon this offer of personal mediation.[112] A fuller account of this proposed assembly is given in Alfonso X's sentence of disinheritance, launched against his son on 8 November 1282. In this it was stated that when Alfonso learnt of Don Sancho's tour of Castile, stirring up disaffection, the king had offered to meet his son at Toledo, or Villarreal or any other place he should select, where Alfonso with the advice of the prelates, nobles and other good men would redress grievances and re-establish peace and tranquility. The phrase used in

---

[111] *Ibid.* 946–8, based on two *cartas* of 26 and 28 August 1281 from the Infante Don Juan and Bishop Suero of Cádiz to the *concejo* of Burgos, with copious quotations from the former. The *carta* of Don Juan gives St Peter's Day in error; the correct date, St Martin's Day, is given in Bishop Suero's letter.

[112] *MHE*, II, no. CXCVII; also ACA, Reg. 47, fol. 117, Pedro III to R[amón] de Muntayana (not Rodrigo de Matallana as Ballesteros, *Alfonso X el Sabio*, 963, mistranscribed the name) recalling him from his mission to Alfonso X.

this document, 'iuxta suum, et Praelatorum ac Baronum et aliorum virorum bonorum consilium', without any definite reference to the towns, suggests that Alfonso X intended to summon the *corte* in its extraordinary form, rather than the cortes. The assembly in any case never took place. As the sentence went on to relate, the Infante Don Sancho detained his father's envoys with violence and himself summoned a *curiam generalem* to meet at Valladolid, while Alfonso X remained at Seville.[113]

These cortes, held by Don Sancho at Valladolid from mid-April to mid-May 1282, are well documented. The writ of summons addressed to Salamanca, which survived in the city's archives till the end of the nineteenth century, has disappeared, but it was summarised by Sánchez Ruano.[114] There are also numerous *cartas* and privileges granted by Don Sancho during the cortes, and *cartas de hermandad* concluded between various groups of his supporters, besides the narrative accounts given by the *Crónica de Alfonso X* and by Jofré de Loaisa.[115] The king's sentence disinheriting his son also gives details of the assembly.

By the autumn of 1283 the tide had begun to turn against Don Sancho, and many of his supporters, including his brothers, the Infantes Don Juan and Don Jaime, had made their peace with the king. Further, in August Pope Martin IV had declared himself against the rebels.[116] In these circumstances Don Sancho, after consulting those present with him in Burgos, summoned an assembly of his supporters to meet at Palencia, on the feast of All Saints, to consider proposals for a reconciliation with Alfonso X. Our only evidence for this little known assembly consists of a writ of summons and a short reference in the *Crónica*.[117]

The cortes of Sancho IV

Of the first three cortes of the reign of Sancho IV we know scarcely anything. In the summer of 1284 at Seville, the new king received the

---

[113] Zurita, *Indices*, 171–4. Ibáñez de Segovia, *Memorias de Alonso el Sabio*, 409–13, gives a translation of the sentence from Zurita's Latin version. It is probable that the sentence was drafted in both Latin and Castilian and that the Latin version was sent to foreign kings.
[114] *Fuero de Salamanca*, ed. Sánchez Ruano, xxvii.
[115] E.g. *MHE*, II, nos. CXCIX, CC, CCII, CCIII, CCV, etc.; *Crónica Alfonso X, cap.* LXXVI (p. 61); Jofré de Loaisa, *Crónica*, 22. Cf. Ballesteros, *Alfonso X el Sabio*, 970–4, who gives a long list of Don Sancho's grants.
[116] *Registres de Martin IV*, no. 479 (9 Aug. 1283).
[117] Ballesteros, *Alfonso X el Sabio*, 1039–40, with quotations from a writ of 12 Oct. 1283; *Crónica Alfonso X, cap.* LXXVII (pp. 64–5).

submission of Andalusia and 'in cortes' revoked many of the unwise and lavish gifts which he had made to his supporters during his rebellion, and had the privileges granting them destroyed – although many have survived.[118] At the end of the year he held cortes at Valladolid, for which the sole evidence is the dating clause of a royal document: 'en las nuestras Cortes de Valladolit, cinco dias del mes de deciembre, era de mill et trezientos et veinte et dos annos' (A.D. 1284).[119] On 6 December 1285 Sancho's eldest son, the Infante Don Fernando, was born at Seville and early in the following year was taken to Zamora, where the magnates and representatives of the cities and towns did homage to him as heir to the throne.[120]

We are better informed about the Cortes of Palencia in November and December 1286 for, although the *Crónica de Sancho IV* does not refer to them, a number of *cuadernos* have survived.[121] The first of the fifteen clauses provided for a further resumption of grants of crown lands made by Sancho IV, both as *infante* and as king. The former resumption at Seville must, therefore, have been of partial application only. The king also promised that no further such grants should be made – a promise which was certainly not kept. The remaining clauses dealt with a variety of subjects, including the coinage, justice, administration, military service and the payment of various monetary dues such as *yantar*.

The Cortes of Haro in 1288 took place under very exceptional circumstances. On 8 June 1288 Don Lope Díaz, Count of Haro, who had come to exercise an almost complete domination over Sancho IV, was assassinated at Alfaro, and his death was followed by the siege of his principal stronghold of Haro by the king. By 20 June, Haro had been taken. Sancho IV remained there or, more probably, at Villabuena, outside the walls, which had been the headquarters of the besieging army, until 2 August.[122] Thence he went to Miranda and Vitoria, where he remained from 8 August to mid-September.[123] Though it is

---

[118] *Crónica Sancho IV, cap.* I (p. 70).

[119] Cited by Gaibrois de Ballesteros, *Sancho IV*, II, 213–14, n. 1.

[120] *Crónica Sancho IV, cap.* II (p. 72); Sancho IV was at Zamora on 27 and 29 Jan. 1286 (Gaibrois de Ballesteros, *Sancho IV*, III, no. 102; Marcos Rodríguez, *Catálogo del Archivo Catedralicio de Salamanca*, no. 401).

[121] *Cortes*, I, no. XVII. The editors used the *cuaderno* in AM León collated with that in AM Avilés; Gaibrois de Ballesteros, *Sancho IV*, I, 127, n. 1, cited also those in the municipal archives of Toro, Badajoz and Cuenca, BL, Add. MS. 9916, fols. 402–8, is a transcript of that to Toro.

[122] Gaibrois de Ballesteros, *Sancho IV*, I, 188–95.

[123] *Ibid.* III, nos. 210–15.

from Vitoria that the *cuadernos* of the cortes were dated, the *cuadernos* granted to the towns of Castile in the cortes of Valladolid in 1293 refer back to the ordinance 'que fiziemos en Villabona' and the *Crónica de Sancho IV*, which does not mention the cortes under the year 1288, later also refers back to a grant of *servicios* for ten years 'en la hueste de Haro'.[124]

The main purpose of the cortes held in the summer of 1288 was to revoke the farming out of the royal revenues to a Catalan Jew, Abrahem el Barchilón, which had taken place in the preceding year, and to remit all outstanding debts to the crown, in return for an annual *servicio* for ten years. Presumably the cortes had been assembled at Haro after the fall of the stronghold, and the grant of the *servicios* made in return for the king's promises. Later, from Vitoria, the *cuadernos* containing the full details of the remission of debts were despatched.[125]

The cortes again assembled during May 1293 at Valladolid. Royal *cartas* dated 12, 14, 20 and 28 May referred to these cortes.[126] On this occasion the proctors of the *concejos* were asked to present their grievances, most of which were redressed. The towns of Castile, León and the Extremaduras presented separate petitions, but all three sets of petitions dealt mainly with judicial and administrative grievances and included such matters as the confirmation of *fueros*, law and order, the collection of taxes and customary impositions, the administration of justice, the appointment of town officials and matters concerning Jews and Moors.[127] Sancho IV left Valladolid on 21 May and the *cuadernos* were passed by the chancery on the two following days.

In this chapter we have surveyed the evidence for thirty-two different

---

[124] *Cortes*, I, no. XIX, cl. 17; *Crónica Sancho IV, cap.* VIII (p. 86).

[125] *Cortes*, I, no. XVIII. The editors used *cuadernos* from AC Burgos and Archivo del Monasterio de Santa María de Aguilar de Campóo. One from AC Avila is published in *Documentos lingüísticos*, no. 141. Gaibrois de Ballesteros, *Sancho IV*, I, 194, no. 1, cited in addition *cuadernos* in the archives of the collegiate church of Santo Domingo de la Calzada and in AM León. AC Pamplona, Arca BB, no. 54, is an authorised copy of 1292 of a *cuaderno* with a general address.

[126] Gaibrois de Ballesteros, *Sancho IV*, III, nos. 471, 472; Gaibrois de Ballesteros, 'Tarifa, y la política de Sancho IV de Castilla', *BRAH*, LXXVI, 422, no. 3; *Memorias de Fernando IV*, II, no. CLXXX, *carta* of Sancho IV, inserted in one of Pedro I.

[127] *Cortes*, I, no. XIX (pp. 106–7). Petitions of Castile (from a *cuaderno* in AM Aguilar, collated with those in the archives of Briones and Carrión): *ibid.* I, no. XX (pp. 117–30). Petitions of León (from a *cuaderno* in AM Cáceres collated with one in AM León and with variants from the petitions of Extremadura from *cuadernos* in AM Madrid and Segovia): *DA Madrid, 1a serie*, I, 139–50. Petitions of Extremadura: Martínez Marina, *Teoría de las Cortes*, I, 180–1, cites a *cuaderno* to Plasencia.

assemblies. Not all of them fulfil our tentative definition of the cortes, nor do some of them provide us with relevant information. There is no convincing proof to support the opinion that any such assembly took place in July 1256 at Segovia, nor, again, is there any evidence that representatives of the cities and towns were summoned to Zamora in July 1274. The cortes placed at Segovia in 1276 by the *Crónica de Alfonso X* may be either a reference to the Cortes of Burgos of 1276 wrongly located, or else to the cortes which indeed took place in 1278 at Segovia, but were summoned for a reason other than that given by the *Crónica*. Possible cortes of Badajoz in 1280 are purely conjectural; if they took place, we know nothing about them. The two assemblies in 1273 at Almagro and Avila were anomalous, and are best considered as *ayuntamientos*. Four assemblies were summoned by the Infante Don Sancho – those at Valladolid and Salamanca in 1279 appear to have been assemblies of representatives only. Those of Valladolid in 1282 and Palencia in 1283 took place while Don Sancho was in open revolt against his father and were not, therefore, strictly speaking cortes, although they were clearly modelled on them. All four of these assemblies give valuable information about the powers granted to the representatives by the towns. Three of the assemblies were provincial, not general, cortes – those of Seville in 1264 for Extremadura; those of Alcalá in 1275 for Castile and Extremadura; those of Seville in 1284 for Andalusia. The remaining nineteen were all general cortes for the whole realm. From the available evidence about the general and provincial cortes and about the assemblies summoned by the Infante Don Sancho in 1279, 1282 and 1283, it is possible to deduce information concerning the composition, procedure and functions of the cortes during the second half of the thirteenth century and, particularly, of the part played by the representatives of the cities and towns.

7

The composition and procedure of the cortes in the second half of the thirteenth century

When, in the mid-thirteenth century, the vernacular ousted Latin as the official language of the Castilian chancery, the word *curia*, which had previously been used for the court, whatever its size or composition, was replaced by two vernacular terms, the singular form *corte* and its plural, *cortes*. By the end of the thirteenth century, the plural form was employed consistently to refer to specially summoned assemblies in which nobles, prelates and other members of the king's court were joined by representatives of the cities and towns on royal demesne.

From the accession of Fernando IV in 1295, the term *cortes* appeared regularly in the preambles of the *cuadernos*, in such phrases as 'nos Don Fernando...estando en las Cortes en la villa de...'.[1] In the reigns of Alfonso X and Sancho IV this was not the normal usage; the word *cortes* appeared in the preambles of the *cuadernos* of only two assemblies, in 1261 in the sentence 'nos fiziemos nuestras cortes en Sevilla en el mes de Enero',[2] and in 1293 when 'acordamos de fazer nuestras Cortes en Valladolit' occurs.[3] A number of assemblies were, however, called cortes in *cartas* of Alfonso X and Sancho IV. There are six *cartas* of Alfonso X in which the term is used. These are: the *carta* of 2 March 1254: 'cuando vin a Toledo a facer hy mis cortes';[4] that of 6 February 1260 and two *cartas* of June 1264, all three of which refer to 'nuestras Cortes en [la Noble Cibdad de] Toledo sobrel ffecho del Imperio', which were held in 1259;[5] that of 28 March 1273 by which the king remitted two of the six *servicios* granted 'en las Cortes de Burgos, quando casó el infante Don Fernando con fija del rey de Francia' in November 1269;[6] and that of 13 April 1274 in the year

---

[1] See *Cortes*, I, nos. XXI, XXIII, XXIV, XXV, etc.
[2] Rodríguez Díez, *Historia de Astorga*, 715.
[3] *Cortes*, I, nos. XIX, XX.   [4] BN, MS. 13094, fol. 143.
[5] Ballesteros, *Alfonso X Emperador*, 71, 72; and Minguella, *Historia de Sigüenza*, I, 599.
[6] *Cortes*, I, no. XV.

'quando feziemos las cortes de Burgos sobre fecho de enbiar caualleros al imperio de Roma'.[7] The Infante Don Sancho, in a *carta* of 4 June 1282 addressed to the *concejo* of Burgos, referred to the request of the representatives for the reissue of the coinage of Fernando III made 'quando agora uinieron a mi a Valladolit, a las Cortes que y fiz'.[8] A *carta* of Sancho IV of 5 December 1284 added to the date 'en las nuestras Cortes de Valladolit';[9] four royal *cartas* of 12, 14, 20 and 28 May 1293 all mentioned 'estas Cortes que yo agora fiz en Valladolit', as did also the royal accounts for the year 1293–4.[10] Letters of Pedro Núñez de Guzmán and the Grand Commander of the Hospital also used the term *cortes*.[11] Among narrative sources, the *Crónica de Alfonso X* employs the term in respect of four different assemblies: those of Burgos in 1272, Segovia in 1276, Seville in 1281 and the Infante Don Sancho's Cortes of Valladolid in 1282.[12] In the *Crónica de Sancho IV* it is used only once – in reference to the otherwise unknown assembly in Seville in 1284.[13] Among literary sources, *Los miráculos romanzados* used the term to describe the assembly held at Vitoria in 1256 and Alfonso X's own *Cantiga* 386 describes some cortes held at Seville – probably those of 1281.[14] These examples involve altogether, twelve different assemblies and there is evidence of the presence of the representatives of the towns at all but three of them – those of Vitoria in January 1256, of Seville in 1284 and of Valladolid in the same year, for none of which is there any evidence either way. Taken as a whole, this evidence justifies the assumption that the plural form *cortes* was commonly used in the vernacular, from the beginning of Alfonso X's reign, to denote assemblies at which the representatives were present. This differentiation of nomenclature thus presupposes a differentiation of institution. In the occasional Latin documents of Alfonso X's reign which refer to the cortes, either *curia* or *curia generalis* was used.[15]

[7] Ballesteros, *Alfonso X, Emperador*, 72–3.
[8] Cited by Ballesteros, *Alfonso X el Sabio*, 977, and *BRAH*, cxix, 164–5.
[9] Cited by Gaibrois de Ballesteros, *Sancho IV*, ii, 213, n. 1.
[10] *Ibid.* iii, nos. 471, 472; Gaibrois de Ballesteros, *BRAH*, lxxvi, *Memorias de Fernando IV*, ii, no. clxxx, inserting *carta* of Sancho IV. Gaibrois de Ballesteros, *Sancho IV*, i, lxv.
[11] Cited in Ballesteros, *Alfonso X el Sabio*, 90 (4 March 1254), 483, 489 (12 Nov. 1269).
[12] *Crónica Alfonso X*, caps. xxiv–xxvi, lxviii, lxxv, lxxvi.
[13] *Crónica Sancho IV*, cap. i (p. 70).
[14] Quoted in *RC Silos*, 226–7; Alfonso el Sabio, *Cantigas*, iii, 331–3.
[15] Daumet, *Relations*, *pièce just.* no. i (5 May 1253); *MHE*, ii, no. cxcviii; Zurita, *Indices*, 173.

It is customary among historians to speak of the cortes as composed of 'the three estates' of the realm: clergy, nobles and representatives of the towns.[16] However, the term 'los tres estados' does not occur in thirteenth-century documents relating to the cortes. It is not until late in the fourteenth century that it is used in this connection.[17] The description was probably borrowed from France, as was the case in England. The thirteenth-century cortes appear rather to have been seen as consisting of a number of groups. There are no lists of those who attended any particular assembly, but the groups or classes of persons present were enumerated in the preambles of most of the *cuadernos* and in other documents in such sentences as: 'et a estas cortes vinieron don Alfonso de Molina nuestro tio, et nuestros hermanos, et los Arçobispos et los Obispos, et todos nuestros Ricos omes de Castiella et de Leon, et muchos omes bonos de todas las villas de nuestros Regnos'.[18] In the *cuaderno* of 1261 a longer list is given: 'con nuestros hermanos e con los arçobispos e con los obispos e con los Maestres de las ordenes e con los abades benitos e con los Ricos ommes e con otros nuestros fijos dalgo cavalleros e ommes bonos de las villas de Castilla e de Leon e de todos los otros nuestros Regnos e de nuestro sennorio'.[19] The forty-two persons appointed to a commission of inquiry, set up in 1272, were arranged in six groups under the following headings: (i) 'de la parte del Rey', under which appeared the names of Queen Violante, the Infante Don Fadrique and six nobles; (ii) 'caballeros'; (iii) 'prelados'; (iv) 'clerigos'; (v) 'de las ordenes'; (vi) 'de las villas'.[20]

We know more of the composition of the cortes which met during the reign of Alfonso X than of those of his son. For Sancho IV's reign there are no *cartas* which give any information about this aspect of the matter. Of the *cuadernos*, those of 1286 refer specifically only to the good men of the towns of Castile, León and Extremadura while those of 1288 are addressed to all classes of the population from the bishops to the tenants on the lands of the nobles (*solariegos*) and the men of the

[16] Colmeiro, *Introducción*, 15–19; Piskorski, *Cortes*, 13ff.; G[arcía] de Valdea-vellano, *Instituciones españolas*, 472–5.

[17] *Cortes*, II, no. XLII (p. 527) (1393): 'Los tres estados que deven venir a vuestras Cortes'; III, no. III, cls. 18, 19 (1419), etc. In Navarre 'los tres estados' was first used of the cortes in a *carta* of 11 June 1319, AGN, *caj*. 5/98, publ. Yanguas, *Diccionario*, III, 67–73; in Portugal it was not used until the mid-fifteenth century, see Gama Barros, *Histórica da administração pública em Portugal*, III, 127, n 2.

[18] Ballesteros, *Alfonso X, Emperador*, 71.

[19] Rodríguez Díez, *Historia de Astorga*, 715.

[20] *Crónica Alfonso X*, cap. XXVI.

behetrías, but do not give details about those who were present at the assembly itself.²¹ The *cuadernos* to the towns of Castile in 1293 state, in the preamble, that the king 'con acuerdo de los prelados e de los maestres de las Ordenes et de los ricos omes e inffançones et otrossi con los caualleros e los omes bonos de Castiella que nos tomamos pora nuestro consseio' commanded those of Castile to present their grievances. Similar statements occur in the *cuadernos* to the towns of León and Extremadura.²²

The four groups usually enumerated were, as we have seen, the princes of the blood royal, the prelates, the *ricos hombres* and the representatives of the towns, but the number of groups noted might at times be as many as seven or eight. The *infantes* were generally referred to collectively as 'mis hermanos' in the *cuadernos* and *cartas* and as 'los infantes' in the chronicles. Sometimes, however, the names of those actually present were enumerated individually. Thus, Fernando III's brother, the Infante Don Alfonso of Molina, and his son, the future Alfonso X, were both described as present at Seville in 1250.²³ Alfonso X's uncle, Don Alfonso of Molina, and his brothers, the Infantes Don Fadrique, Don Felipe and Don Manuel, were present in 1252.²⁴ The Infante Don Sancho's Cortes of Valladolid in 1282 were attended by his uncle, Don Manuel, and his brothers, Don Pedro, Don Juan and Don Jaime.²⁵ Alfonso X's wife, Queen Violante, was certainly present at the provincial cortes for the Extremaduras in 1264, where she received petitions, and the *Crónica de Alfonso X* also noted her presence at the Cortes of Burgos in 1272 and at the Infante Don Sancho's cortes in 1282.²⁶

The ecclesiastical and lay magnates had, of course, been accustomed to attend the enlarged curia in the preceding period, and, as one would expect, the names of the bishops and *ricos hombres* were given in the lists of *confirmantes* subjoined to the *privilegios rodados* of Alfonso X and Sancho IV.²⁷ These lists did not, at this period, indicate presence; they were concerned to give the names of the bishops, nobles and great officials who together formed the natural counsellors of the king, and

---

²¹ *Crónica Sancho IV, cap.* II (p. 72); *Cortes,* I, nos. XVII, XVIII.
²² *Cortes,* I, nos. XIX, XX; *DA Madrid, 1a serie,* I, 141.
²³ *Fuero de Cuenca,* 859.
²⁴ García Rámila, *Hispania,* V, 205; Appendix, doc. IV, below.
²⁵ *MHE,* II, no. CCIX.
²⁶ BL, Add. MS. 9916, fol. 252 (1264); publ. Appendix, doc. VII, below; *Crónica Alfonso X, caps.* XXVI, LXXVI.
²⁷ The description *privilegios rodados* was substituted for *cartas rodadas* from 1260.

whose obligation it was to attend the court when summoned to do so. In the later Middle Ages, the lay magnates were to take precedence over the prelates in the cortes.[28] In the thirteenth century, however, the bishops preceded the *ricos hombres* in most, but not in all, the lists of groups attending the cortes. We shall, therefore, consider them next.

Their presence was noted collectively as 'los arçobispos e obispos', or 'los obispos', or 'los prelados' at all the cortes of the two reigns for which any indication of composition exists, except for the cortes at which homage was done to Sancho IV's heir, the Infante Don Fernando, where their presence is not mentioned, although they could scarcely have been absent on such an occasion.[29] The conquests of Fernando III in Andalusia added a third archbishopric – that of Seville – to the traditional two, Toledo and Santiago de Compostela, and led to the creation of five new bishoprics – those of Baeza, Córdoba, Jaén, Mérida and Cartagena. Under Alfonso X the see of Mérida was transferred to Badajoz. The see of Cádiz was founded in 1266. At the beginning of his reign Alfonso X also restored and endowed the see of Silves in the Portuguese Algarve, a province to which he laid claim, and the usufruct of which had been granted to him by Afonso III of Portugal. In 1267, by the Treaty of Badajoz, which settled the frontier between Portugal and Castile, Alfonso X renounced his claims to the Algarve but Afonso III undertook not to interfere with the obedience owed by the see of Silves to that of Seville as metropolitan.[30]

The relations of the first four bishops of Silves to the kings of Castile and Portugal require further elucidation. The Dominican Frey Roberto was consecrated bishop of Silves before 20 August 1253, on which date Alfonso X granted 'ffrey Roberto obispo de Silves' the town of Lagos.[31] On 22 January 1254 Afonso III of Portugal protested against this grant, as Alfonso X enjoyed only the usufruct of the Algarve, the dominion over it belonging to the Portuguese king.[32] In spite of this protest, the name of Roberto, bishop of Silves, appeared regularly in Alfonso X's *privilegios rodados* from 1253 until Roberto's death, while his name does not occur in the documents of Afonso III. Roberto was, in fact, a trusted servant of the Castilian king, and in 1258 he was sent by Alfonso X on embassy to Henry III of England.[33] Early in 1261 his

[28] Piskorski, *Cortes*, 23.   [29] *Crónica Sancho IV*, cap. II (p. 72).
[30] Publ. Brandão, *Monarchia lusitana*, parte IV, escs. XXXIV, XXXV.
[31] ANTT, *liv. Afonso III*, III, fol. 6v.
[32] Brandão, *Monarchia lusitana*, parte IV, esc. XXX (pp. 539–40); Silva Lopes, *Memórias*, 160; Sánchez-Albornoz, *Curia regia portuguesa*, ap. I.
[33] *Calendar of Close Rolls, Henry III, 1256–9*, 315.

successor, García, also appeared as bishop-elect of Silves in a *privilegio rodado* of Alfonso X and on 8 April 1261 Alfonso confirmed to him all the grants made to Roberto, together with further extensive donations.[34] García, too, was clearly *persona grata* with the Castilian king; in 1263 he was appointed ambassador to Pope Urban IV.[35] It is also significant that his name was not included among the Portuguese bishops who petitioned the Pope to ratify Afonso III's marriage to Beatriz of Castile.[36] However, from 1266 Bishop García also begins to appear in Portuguese documents, although he still continued to appear in those of Alfonso X.[37] He died sometime between 27 January 1268, when he was last named in a Castilian privilege, and 9 April 1268, when the Portuguese chancery noted that the see of Silves was vacant.[38] The third bishop of Silves, and the first to be elected after Alfonso X had renounced his rights to the Algarve, was a Portuguese, Bartolomeu, monk of Alcobaça and physician of Afonso III, to whose influence he owed his elevation.[39] He appeared as bishop-elect of Silves in a Portuguese document of 4 July 1268.[40] In 1270 he made a solemn declaration acknowledging that Afonso III of Portugal was 'verus dominus ac patronus' of the Algarve and all its churches.[41] Either then, or later, Bishop Bartolomeu formally renounced all the endowments made by Alfonso X to the see.[42] Yet the name of Bartolomeu of Silves continued to appear among the *confirmantes* of the *privilegios rodados* not only of Alfonso X but also of Sancho IV of Castile, and the fourth bishop of Silves, one Frei Domingo, also appeared in Sancho IV's privileges.[43] The question therefore arises: were these four bishops summoned to attend the *corte* and cortes of Alfonso X and Sancho IV? There is no definite proof one way or the other. It is probable that Bishop Roberto, who owed his bishopric to Alfonso X, would have

[34] *MHE*, I, no. LXXXIV (24 March 1261); ANTT, *liv. Afonso III*, III, fol. 3 (8 April 1261).
[35] Silva Lopes, *Memórias*, 166.
[36] Publ. Brandão, *Monarchia lusitana, parte* IV, 418–19 (May 1262).
[37] ANTT, *liv. Afonso III*, I, fols. 82v (Aug. 1266), 84 (13 Nov. 1266).
[38] *MHE*, I, no. CIX; ANTT, *liv. Afonso III*, I, fol. 89: 'Ecclesia Siluensis vacat.'
[39] On Bishop Bartolomeu, see Gaibrois de Ballesteros, *Sancho IV*, II, 224.
[40] ANTT, *liv. Afonso III*, I, fol. 90: 'Dominus Bartholomeus Electus Siluensis conf.'
[41] ANTT, *liv. Afonso III*, III, fol. 10, publ. Brandão, *Monarchia lusitana, parte* IV, *esc.* XXXI (p. 540) (28 March 1270), and Silva Lopes, *Memórias*, 550.
[42] ANTT, Extras, *gav.* 14, *mac.* I, no. 11. From an authentic copy of 31 Jan. 1285. The instrument itself is not dated, but as it refers to Alfonso X as king of Castile, it must date from before his death on 4 April 1284.
[43] E.g. Gaibrois de Ballesteros, *Sancho IV*, III, nos. 484 (23 May 1293), 594 (24 April 1295).

attended his patron's court; it is also probable that Bishop García attended at least until 1266, when his name first appeared in Portuguese royal documents, but it seems exceedingly unlikely that Bishop Bartolomeu attended the Castilian court, especially after his recognition of Afonso III's rights over the Algarve and his renunciation of Alfonso X's donations.

There is much less information about the attendance of the abbots. Only one *cuaderno*, that to Astorga in 1261, specifically mentions their presence.[44] Some seem to have been present in 1277.[45] A very large number were certainly summoned to Valladolid by the Infante Don Sancho in 1282; the *hermandad* drawn up there on 2 May 1282, during the meeting of the cortes, was concluded between thirty-seven abbots of Benedictine, Cistercian and Praemonstratensian houses, 'ex edicto generali convocati per...D. Santium...apud Vallemoleti in simul congregati'. On the following day twenty-four abbots – twelve Benedictine, eight Cistercian and four Praemonstratensian – concluded an *hermandad* with the bishops of Astorga, Zamora, Mondoñedo, Túy, Badajoz and Coria.[46] As only seven houses occur in both lists, the number of abbots who attended the cortes must have been fifty-four. The protest of the bishops of Burgos and Palencia against the sentence depriving Alfonso X of his regalian rights was made before three Dominican priors.[47] The king's sentence disinheriting his son also referred in general terms to 'praelatos saeculares ac religiosos' at Valladolid.[48] It is possible that Don Sancho, who could not count on the support of all the bishops, summoned a larger number of heads of religious houses than was customary.

Some or all of the masters of the military orders were present on at least six occasions, as well as at the *ayuntamiento* of Almagro.[49] In some cases they were named individually but they were usually referred to generically by the phrase 'los maestres de las órdenes'. In the document of 1264 the words 'con consejo...delos maestres, et de los otros omes de orden' may indicate that representatives of the knights of the orders also accompanied the masters. On some occasions

[44] Rodríguez Díez, *Historia de Astorga*, 715.
[45] Publ. Escudero de la Peña, *RABM*, 1a época, II (1872), 58–9.
[46] *MHE*, II, nos. CCII, CCIII.
[47] *Ibid.* II, no. CXCVIII.
[48] Zurita, *Indices*, 173.
[49] In 1250, 1261, 1264, 1269, 1282 and 1293. They took part in the negotiations with the rebels after the end of the Cortes of Burgos in 1272, so were probably at the cortes. The *Crónica de Alfonso X* mentions their presence at the Cortes of Segovia which it places in 1276.

'de las órdenes' was used alone and in such cases it is not certain whether the orders referred to were military or monastic, or whether heads of houses or proctors of the knights or monastic chapters were meant. For example, in the commission set up in 1272 'de las órdenes' was the heading of a group consisting of the minister-general of the Franciscans in Spain, two Franciscan and two Dominican friars; it therefore follows that the use of the phrase 'de las ordenes' without further qualification is ambiguous.[50] As to the attendance of proctors of cathedrals and monasteries or of the parochial clergy, there is little evidence. The commission of 1272 included under the heading 'clericos', the secular abbot of Cuevasrrubias, the dean of Seville, the archdeacon of Cuéllar and a certain Master Stephen. These references, together with those to the Franciscans and Dominicans noted above, imply some representation of chapters and parochial clergy. Presumably, too, the archdeacons and cathedral dignitaries whose names occur in the draft petition to Pope John XXI were representatives of parochial clergy and cathedral chapters who were in attendance at the Cortes of 1277.[51] The survival of *cuadernos* of some cortes in cathedral or monastic archives may also indicate representation. Certainly in 1282 the protest of the bishops of Burgos and Palencia already alluded to referred to discussion 'cum aliquibus aliis praelatis ac cum procuratoribus aliquarum ecclesiarum'.[52]

The *ricos hombres* constituted the highest rank of the nobility and their attendance is noted at all the cortes of which there is evidence of composition. The *Siete partidas* defined them as those who in other countries were called counts and barons, and stated that they had to counsel the king in great matters and adorn the court and the kingdom.[53] They held their lands and money rents from the crown. They correspond to the *nobiles*, *barones* and *optimates* of the Latin documents of the earlier period, and these titles continued to be used in the occasional Latin *cartas* of the second half of the thirteenth century, and in the chronicle of Jofré de Loaisa.[54] Evidence of the attendance of the lesser nobles is scanty. The presence of *infanzones* was noted at the

[50] *Crónica Alfonso X, cap.* xxvi.
[51] Publ. Escudero de la Peña, *RABM*, *1a época*, II (1872), 58–9.
[52] *MHE*, II, no. cxcviii.
[53] *Part.* IV, *tít.* xxv, *ley* 10; *Part.* II, *tít.* IX, *ley* 6. There is nothing in the *Espéculo* which corresponds to these two passages.
[54] E.g. Daumet, *Relations, pièce just.* no. 1; Zurita, *Indices*, 173; Jofré de Loaisa, *Crónica*, 20.

ayuntamiento of Almagro, by the *Crónica de Alfonso X* in its account of its cortes at Segovia in 1276 and in the *cuadernos* of the Cortes of Valladolid in 1293.[55] The *hidalgos* were present at Burgos in 1272.[56] *Caballeros* are mentioned more frequently. Knighthood, however, was a profession, not a social class, and the distinction has to be made between knights of noble birth and the non-noble knights of the towns. The former are usually distinguished from the latter in the available sources. In the *cuaderno* of 1261 and in the *Crónica*'s account of the assembly at Almagro, they were specifically called 'fijosdalgo cavalleros' – knights of noble origin.[57] On other occasions their position in the list of groups present indicated that noble knights were meant. Thus, in the *cuadernos* of 1252 and 1253 *caballeros* were listed between *ricos hombres* and *las ordenes*.[58] In 1272 they were placed immediately after *ricos hombres* and before the *hidalgos*.[59] The majority of the lesser nobles – *infanzones*, *hidalgos* and *caballeros hidalgos* – were direct vassals of the *ricos hombres* and prelates. It was only those who held lands from the king, or had some special relationship with him or connection with his court as office holders or household knights, who were summoned to attend the cortes.[60]

One group which attended once, and once only, in the thirteenth century were the merchants, who were especially summoned to Jerez in 1268 to advise the king and the cortes. They are referred to in the preamble of the relevant *cuaderno*, but we do not know how many were sent for, whether they were summoned as individuals or whether they were elected by groups of merchants in various towns to represent them. The latter is possible, as in 1281 the merchants of Castro Urdiales, Laredo, Santander, Burgos, Vitoria, Aguilar de Campóo and Medina del Pomar sent one or two proctors from each town with *cartas de personería* to Alfonso X, to compound for fines incurred for breaches of customs regulations and laws prohibiting certain exports.[61] The ordinance promulgated at Jerez, as well as fixing prices for a wide

---

[55] *Cortes*, I, no. xv, and *Crónica Alfonso X*, caps. xl.vii, lxviii; *Cortes*, I, nos. xix, xx.

[56] *Crónica Alfonso X*, cap. xxv.

[57] Rodríguez Díez, *Historia de Astorga*, 715; *Crónica Alfonso X*, cap. xlvii.

[58] García Rámila, *Hispania*, v, 205; López Ferreiro, *Fueros*, I, 348; Appendix, doc. iv, below.

[59] *Crónica Alfonso X*, cap. xxv.

[60] See Rodríguez Díez, *Historia de Astorga*, 715: 'otros nuestros fijosdalgo Cavalleros'; *MHE*, II, no. ccix, *Ordenamiento de Cuéllar*, in which the Infante Don Sancho referred to 'los cavalleros de mio señorio'. For the fourteenth and fifteenth centuries, see Piskorski, *Cortes*, 26–7.

[61] BL, Add. MS. 9916, fols. 382–5 (15 Feb. 1281).

range of consumer goods, laid down detailed regulations on imports and exports. It was on such matters, doubtless, that the merchants were consulted.[62]

The cities and towns summoned to send representatives to the cortes were only those on royal demesne, as reference to 'cada villa de sso ssennorio' shows, and which had an autonomous municipal organisation and jurisdiction over the surrounding *tierra*.[63] Towns on ecclesiastical lands, or on the land of the nobles, were represented at the cortes by their overlords. The name most usually applied to the representatives of the towns in the second half of the thirteenth century was *hombres buenos*, but as this term could be used of many other groups who were not townsmen, those so described in this context were generally specifically stated to be 'of the towns'. Thus, in 1252 Alfonso X in cortes took counsel with the *infantes*, bishops, nobles, knights, 'et de omnes buenos de las villas et de otros omnes buenos que se azercaron conmigo', a phrase which clearly denotes that there were 'good men' other than those of the towns present.[64] In 1258 he took counsel with 'omnes bonos de villas de Castilla e de Extremadura e de tierra de León'.[65] In 1259 'muchos omes bonos de todas las villas de nuestros Regnos' were present.[66] In 1261 'ommes bonos de las villas de Castilla e de León e de todos los otros nuestros Regnos e de nuestro sennorio' attended the Cortes of Seville.[67] In 1286 Sancho IV, in the preamble of the *cuaderno*, stated 'yo ffablé agora en Palencia con omes buenos que eran conmigo delas villas de Castiella e de Leon e de Extremadura'.[68] Similar phrases continued to be used in the first half of the fourteenth century.[69] Sometimes in royal documents or in chronicles references were made to the *concejos* (or municipalities) as such. Thus, Alfonso X referred to 'los concejos de tierra de Leon e de las Extremaduras' as present at the assembly at Avila in 1273.[70] Jofré de Loaisa used the term *concilii* in his description of the Cortes of Valladolid in

---

[62] *Cortes*, I, no. XIV.
[63] Ballesteros, *Alfonso X el Sabio*, 947 (quoting from ꞔarta of 26 Aug. 1281).
[64] García Rámila, *Hispania*, v, 205.
[65] *Cortes*, I, no. XIII.
[66] Ballesteros, *Alfonso X, Emperador*, 71.
[67] Rodríguez Díez, *Historia de Astorga*, 715.
[68] *Cortes*, I, no. XVII.
[69] E.g. *ibid.* I, preambles to nos. XXVI (1299), XXVII (1301), XXVIII (1301), XXIX (1302), XXXII (1305), etc.
[70] *Carta* of Alfonso X to the Infante Don Fernando, inserted in *Crónica Alfonso X*, *cap.* LII.

1282.[71] The *Crónica de Sancho IV* included 'çibdades e villas de los reinos' among those who did homage to the heir to the throne at Zamora in 1286.[72]

As well as the description 'good men of the towns', the representatives were occasionally called *personeros* or *procuradores* (proctors). The term *personeros* was used, for example, in 1282 in the Infante Don Sancho's *Ordenamiento de Cuéllar* with reference to those who had attended his Cortes of Valladolid.[73] In the reign of Fernando IV the same word was used of the town representatives to the cortes in *cartas* addressed to the towns. In some of the *cuadernos* and in the *Crónica de Fernando IV* both terms are combined – for example, 'hombres buenos por personeros de las villas'.[74] From 1325 onwards in the *cuadernos* the representatives were usually called *procuradores*. Colmeiro claimed that the earliest example of the use of the latter term in a *cuaderno* was in 1305, and Professor Post, repeating him, added 'we therefore have no clear evidence of corporate proctorial representation until 1305'.[75] This, however, is incorrect, for *procurador* was employed earlier than 1305 in official documents relating to the thirteenth-century cortes, although not in the *cuadernos*. It was used, as Piskorski has pointed out, by Alfonso X in 1255 with reference to the representatives who took the oath to his daughter Doña Berenguela at Toledo in 1254.[76] Sancho IV, in various letters to the city of León, referred to its proctors sent to the cortes of Valladolid in 1293.[77] The *Crónica de Alfonso X* also used *procuradores* for the representatives at the Cortes of Burgos in 1272, at the cortes which it (the *Crónica de Alfonso X*) places at Segovia in 1276 and at the Cortes of Seville in 1281. The *Crónica de Fernando IV* used *procuradores* as well as *personeros* for the representatives at the Cortes of Valladolid in 1295, but these instances from the chronicles may reproduce fourteenth-century usage rather than that of the thirteenth century.[78]

The titles *procuradores* and *personeros* were evidently synonymous.

[71] Jofré de Loaisa, *Crónica*, 22.
[72] *Crónica Sancho IV, cap.* II (p. 72).
[73] *MHE*, II, no. CCIX.
[74] *Memorias de Fernando IV*, II, nos. V, XIV; *Cortes*, I, nos. XXVII, XXVIII, XXXII, XXXIII; *Crónica Fernando IV*, caps. II (p. 107), III (p. 111), etc.
[75] Colmeiro, *Introducción*, 28, 203; Post, *Studies in medieval legal thought*, 71.
[76] Piskorski, *Cortes*, 196–7, n. 1.
[77] Gaibrois de Ballesteros, *Sancho IV*, III, nos. 471, 472; and *BRAH*, LXXVI, 422, no. 3.
[78] *Crónica Alfonso X*, caps. XXV, XXVI, LXVII–VIII, LXXV; *Crónica Fernando IV*, cap. I (p. 95).

In law suits before the king's court the two words were often used of the same person in the same document.[79] Master Jacobo de las Leyes, writing in the second half of the thirteenth century, clearly equated the *personero* with the *procurator*. In his *Doctrinal* he wrote: 'Procurador [procurator] en latin tanto quiere dezir como personero en romance', and in his *Flores de derecho* he heads his title on this subject: 'De los personeros que son dichos en latin procuratores'.[80] Both terms, then, have a definite legal meaning: in law suits the *personero* or *procurador* stood in place of someone or some community impleaded, whom he had power to represent and to bind in accordance with the mandate given him by his principal.[81] If the *personero* and the *procurador* were representatives in the legal sense, what of the less precise term *hombres buenos* ('good men')? When the thirteenth-century *cuadernos* and other documents concerned with the cortes use it, do they intend to imply that the latter were not true representatives? Such a conclusion does not necessarily follow, for on some occasions the *hombres buenos* were also called *personeros* (as in 1282), or *procuradores* (as in 1293).

In the fourteenth century the proctors of the towns brought with them mandates or *cartas de personería* which defined their powers to act on behalf of their towns. None of these mandates has survived for the thirteenth century, but in some cases specific reference is made in the documents to such mandates, and in these instances some indication of the scope of the powers was given. Thus, in 1275, the representatives of Burgos refused to grant the three aids asked for by Alfonso X, and granted by the other representatives present, because they said that the powers given them by the *concejo* did not authorise them to do so.[82] In 1279 the Infante Don Sancho instructed the representatives, whom he had summoned to Salamanca, to bring with them 'uestra carta de personeria en que diga que otorgades, et auedes por firme todo lo que ellos fizieran conmigo'. When, a few weeks later, he ordered them to proceed with him to Badajoz to join the king, similar instructions were given, and they were also ordered to bring with them blank *cartas* sealed with the seal of the *concejo* 'para afirmar las cosas que acá ffueren ffechas' – to confirm the decisions made there.[83] The Infante Don

---

[79] See López Ferreiro, *Fueros*, I, 276–80 (three documents of 30 Jan. 1264).
[80] Jacobo de las Leyes, *Obras: Doctrinal*, lib. II, tít. I, cap. 2 (p. 219); and *Flores*, lib. I, tít. III (p. 27).
[81] *Espéculo*, lib. IV, tít. VIII, leyes 11, 9, 18–19; cf. *Part.* III, tít. V, leyes 1, 14, 19.
[82] Ballesteros, *BRAH*, CXIX, 119.
[83] *Ibid.* 143; Ballesteros, *Alfonso X el Sabio*, 909 (17 Nov. 1279), 911 (26 Dec. 1279).

Sancho's writ of summons to his assembly at Palencia in the autumn of 1283 also contained similar instructions.[84] According to the *Crónica de Alfonso X* the proctors of the towns sent to the Cortes of Seville in 1281 brought with them 'personerias cumplidas para otorgar todo lo que fuese librado antel'.[85] The two assemblies summoned by the Infante Don Sancho were not strictly speaking cortes, but they exhibited some of the characteristics of the cortes and their evidence concerning *cartas de personería* is relevant. It corroborates the evidence given in Alfonso X's *carta* to Burgos of 22 December 1275, and that of the *Crónica de Alfonso X* on the cortes of 1281.

All these instances of representatives of the towns bringing with them *cartas de personería* come from the last decade of the reign of Alfonso X, but there are indications that such mandates were required by the king and issued by the *concejos* for earlier meetings of the cortes. In December 1255, when Alfonso X ordered the *concejo* of Orense – an ecclesiastical city – to send three good men to him at Candlemas, wherever he should be, to do homage to his eldest daughter Berenguela, he also instructed the *concejo* to send a mandate (*poderío*) with the representatives, and also to seal with the seal of the *concejo* a declaration of the rights of Doña Berenguela that had been drawn up by the chancery and sent to the *concejo* for this purpose; it was to be brought to the king by the representatives.[86] We may, therefore, assume that the proctors sent by the towns on royal demesne to do homage to Doña Berenguela at the Cortes of Toledo in 1254 were provided with similar powers.

There are also close similarities between the representation of towns as suitors in cases tried before the king's court, and their representation in the cortes. Documents connected with suits in which cities and towns were impleaded before the *curia regis* prove that their *personeros* brought with them mandates from the towns at least as early as the union of the kingdoms, if not earlier. In 1231, when the Abbot of Sahagún charged the *concejo* of Belver with riot against the abbey, the 'good men' of the town who were also referred to as 'proctors' brought with them 'carta de procuración abierta et seellada', which gave them power to come to an agreement with the abbot and proctor of the monks and also to accept terms dictated by the king.[87] In 1250

[84] Ballesteros, *Alfonso X el Sabio*, 1039–40 (12 Oct. 1283).
[85] *Crónica Alfonso X, cap.* LXXV.
[86] Sánchez-Albornoz, 'Señoríos y ciudades', *AHDE*, VI, 456–7.
[87] Appendix, doc. II, below.

Túy sent as its *personero* its justiciar, Martín Fernández Boquero, who brought with him a 'carta del concejo que estaria el concejo por quanto el ficiese' and who, after Fernando III had pronounced sentence in favour of the bishop's claim to lordship over the city, did homage to Bishop Gil and took the oath of allegiance to him in the name of the city.[88] In the same year the *concejo* of Santiago sent four *personeros* with a *carta de personería* in which the concejo gave them full power – *lleno poder* – to bind the city.[89] *Cartas de personería* were also brought by the *personeros* of Cuenca and Moya in suits with the Order of Santiago in November 1250.[90] From then onwards references to *cartas de personería* in law suits are numerous. The Order of Calatrava was involved in law suits with Córdoba in 1255, with Bolaños in 1261 and with Zorita in 1264, and in all three cases the towns were represented by *personeros* who brought with them *cartas de personería*.[91] In some cases these mandates were called *cartas complidas de personería*, in others a longer description was given, such as 'con carta de personeria e sellada con el sello de concejo que por quanto él fesiese que lo otorgarian ellos e lo tenian por firme'.[92] An early example of a *carta de personería*, issued by the concejo of Seville to its *personero* in a suit with the archbishop of Seville, has survived incorporated in the *Tercera partida*, where it served as a model for such mandates issued by corporations, whether lay or ecclesiastical. The date has been omitted, but internal evidence shows that it belonged to the years 1260 to 1264. It gave the *personero* power to do all that a true representative could do, and the *concejo* undertook to abide by what he did. It appears to be based on ecclesiastical letters of procuration.[93] Although the earliest references to *cartas de personería* brought by town representatives to the cortes belong to the final decade of Alfonso X's reign, yet the fact that towns had by then been accustomed to give such mandates in connection with suits before the king's court for forty years or more makes it probable that their representatives also brought

---

[88] *ES*, XXII, *ap.* XVIII.

[89] López Ferreiro, *Fueros*, I, 216–18. Nearly all the documents concerned with this case and with later cases in 1253, 1261, 1263 and 1264 mention *cartas de personería*; ibid. 235, 248, 266, 274, 276, 277, 278.

[90] AHN, Santiago, *caj.* 99/26, *caj.* 100, II, no. 25. The second document is published by Manuel Rodríguez, *Memorias*, 522.

[91] AHN, Calatrava, R. 103 (20 June 1255); Esc. Calatrava, IV, fol. 2 (28 March 1261); Calatrava, R. 143 (2 Jan. 1264).

[92] E.g. *MHE*, I, nos. LXXIX (11 Sept. 1262), XC (30 Dec. 1262); *ES*, XXXV, *ap.* XII (10 Oct. 1269); Ballesteros, *Itinerario*, 32, n. 1 (17 July 1253). On *cartas de personería* in suits, see Procter, *EHR*, LXXIV, 9–12.

[93] *Part.* III, *tít.* XVIII, *ley* 98.

such mandates to the cortes throughout the second half of the thirteenth century. The suits between the Order of Santiago and the *concejos* of Cuenca and Moya referred to above were heard in November 1250, when the cortes were in session. Both towns were on royal demesne. Cuenca was certainly represented at the cortes, as the *cuaderno* addressed to it shows; Moya presumably also was. It therefore seems reasonable to suppose that their representatives to the cortes on this occasion were the same as those who appeared for them in the law suit, and that their *cartas de personería* covered both contingencies.

On a number of occasions the representatives of the *concejos* were knights, and this was encouraged, and at times even required, by the king. The *cuaderno* of 1250 thus laid down that when the king sent for good men from the towns, or when they wished to send them to him, they should send knights.[94] The *concejos* of Extremadura sent knights to Seville in 1264.[95] Burgos, and presumably other towns, were ordered to send knights to Alcalá in 1275 and to Seville in 1281.[96] In 1250 Fernando limited the number of knights to be sent to three or four, unless he particularly specified more. Two was, however, the more usual number. We know that Burgos sent two knights to Alcalá in 1275; Alfonso X's writ to Salamanca in 1276 as well as the Infante Don Sancho's writs of 1279 and 1283 all provided for the attendance of two representatives.[97] The general *Hermandad*, when it met early in Sancho IV's reign, and not long before it was dissolved, laid down that when the king wished to hold a cortes each town should send 'dos omes de los buenos mejores e mas entendidos e sin sospecha'.[98] During the fourteenth century, however, the numbers continued to vary.[99] In some cases separate representatives were sent from the villages and inhabited places of the *términos*. Thus, in 1264, the *concejos* of Extremadura sent 'caballeros et omes bonos de los pueblos'.[100] In 1268 'cavalleros de vuestra villa, e omes buenos de los pueblos' were present from Burgos, and in 1281 the great towns were ordered to send four knights and six good men from the *pueblos* (villages) and the lesser towns two knights,

94 *Fuero de Cuenca*, 860; see Appendix, doc. III, below.
95 Appendix, doc. VII, below.
96 Documents quoted by Ballesteros, *BRAH*, CXIX, 118 (Dec. 1275), and *Alfonso X el Sabio*, 947 (26 Aug. 1281).
97 Ballesteros, *BRAH*, CXIX, 118 (22 Dec. 1275); *Fuero de Salamanca*, ed. Sánchez Ruano, XXIV (30 April 1276); Ballesteros, *Alfonso X el Sabio*, 909, 1040.
98 Cited by Ortiz de Zúñiga, *Anales de Sevilla*, 139 (8 Sept. 1284).
99 Piskorski, *Cortes*, 54–6.
100 Appendix, doc. VII, below.

two good men and four *pecheros*.[101] There is no evidence how such representatives were chosen, but it seems probable that they too were elected, as were the town officials and *personeros* in law suits, in the open *concejo*, which at that time included all the *vecinos*, whether they lived in the walled city itself or in its surrounding *tierra*.

The town and the *término* together, as we saw in an earlier chapter, formed an administrative district of which the walled town was the centre, and over which the town magistrates and other officials and functionaries exercised justice, maintained law and order and collected royal and municipal dues. The knights of the towns, who with increasing frequency represented these districts in the cortes, tended to become socially indistinguishable from the knights of noble origin. If we compare these town representatives of León–Castile with the two classes who made up the English commons, it becomes obvious, however, that the Castilian proctors of the towns did not correspond closely either to knights of the shire or to burgesses, but combined some of the characteristics of each.

The *concejos* were responsible for the payment of the expenses of their representatives to the cortes. The rate laid down in 1250 for the towns of Extremadura was half a *maravedí* a day for attendance at assemblies as far away as Toledo and a *maravedí* a day for those held further south.[102] Presumably the rate was higher for those who had to come from north of the Duero. When in 1279 the Infante Don Sancho ordered the assembled representatives to proceed with him from Salamanca to Badajoz, those from Burgos were unable to do so until they had communicated with the city, because they had only been granted expenses up to Salamanca.[103]

There were, as we have seen, no regular times of meetings and the cortes were summoned as need arose. There were, however, in the second half of the thirteenth century, no long periods during which the body did not meet. There are some gaps of three or four years but the longest is a gap of nearly five years between Sancho IV's Cortes of Haro in July 1288 and those of Valladolid in May 1293. This presents a very different picture from the infrequent meetings in the first half of the century.

[101] *Leyes nuevas*, 205 (30 March 1268); Ballesteros, *Alfonso X el Sabio*, 947 (26 Aug. 1281).
[102] *Fuero de Cuenca*, 860. This rate was confirmed to Cuenca on 23 Aug. 1256 (*ibid.* 862). It was also confirmed to Escalona on 23 June 1262 (*MHE*, I, no. LXXXVI).
[103] Ballesteros, *Alfonso X el Sabio*, 911–12.

The cortes usually assembled in one of the larger cities or towns. Those at which most assemblies took place were Seville, where the cortes met six times and which, besides being a favourite place of residence of Alfonso X, was also the obvious seat of government during periods of hostility with the Moors; Burgos, where they met five times; and Valladolid, where four cortes were held. Meetings of the cortes and, to a lesser extent, also those of the *corte* in its augmented form, entailed a large concourse of people: there were present the king and his immediate entourage, the bishops and magnates with their retinues and, at the cortes, the representatives of the cities and towns – all of whom required lodging (*posada, hospedaje*). The obligation on the local people to provide *posada* was an onerous and an unpopular one.[104] Exemptions from forced *posada* were often granted to towns, but were also sometimes disregarded as when, in 1259, the good men of Toledo were ordered by the king to give lodgings to those summoned to the cortes, in spite of exemptions granted by former kings and by Alfonso himself.[105] The exemption from *posada* granted to the canons of Toledo cathedral, on 29 December of that year, may have been occasioned by the meeting of the cortes in the city, although the privilege does not refer to them.[106] In March 1261 Alfonso X granted to all the inhabitants of the city of Seville, both clerks and laymen, that no one should lodge in their houses, except with their consent, and against payment for man and beast accommodated. This, too, may have been a result of *posada* enforced during the Cortes of Seville in January of that year, though the exemption was drawn very widely, and a similar exemption was granted two months later to the canons and other members of the chapter of the cathedral of Córdoba, where no meeting of the cortes had been held.[107] Large cities also, of course, could easily provide buildings such as royal palaces, monasteries and cathedral chapter houses and cloisters, where sessions of the cortes could take place, but on this point there is no specific evidence for the period, apart from the statement in the *Crónica de Alfonso X* that the cortes of Burgos held at Michaelmas in 1272 met in the Hospital del Rey, outside the walls of Burgos, because the malcontent nobles refused to enter the city.[108]

The participants in the cortes were summoned by writs of summons

---

[104] On *posada*, see Nilda Guglielmi, 'Posada y yantar', *Hispania*, xxvi, 5–29.
[105] Ballesteros, *Alfonso X, Emperador*, 71 (6 Feb. 1260).
[106] BN, MS. 13075, fol. 26 (29 Dec. 1259): 'Otorgamos que...ninguno non sea osado de posar en sus casas sin su plazer.'
[107] *MHE*, i, nos. LXXXIV (24 March 1261), LXXXV (30 May 1261).
[108] *Crónica Alfonso X, cap.* xxv.

(*cartas convocatorias*), few of which have survived for the thirteenth century, probably because they were written on paper and were of temporary validity only. We have only Sánchez Ruano's short and inadequate summaries of the lost writs ordering Salamanca to send representatives to the Cortes of Burgos in 1276 and to the Infante Don Sancho's Cortes of Valladolid in 1282.[109] The two writs of summons to Burgos concerned with the assemblies of representatives called by the Infante Don Sancho in 1279 were examined and transcribed by Ballesteros in the municipal archives of Burgos before the civil war of 1936–9 and were published by him, apparently *in extenso*, apart from the initial and final formulas, in 1946; they are also included in his posthumous *Alfonso X el Sabio*.[110] Finally, there is the Infante Don Sancho's writ of summons to the assembly at Palencia in 1283, which was also partly published by Ballesteros.[111] The *cartas convocatorias* of the Infante Don Sancho in 1279 and 1283 began with long explanatory preambles, but it is possible that the normal writ was a much simpler document, as appears to be indicated by the brief summaries given by Sánchez Ruano of the writs of 1276 and 1282 – that is, if we can assume that he did not suppress in his summaries all reference to such preambles. All these writs have this in common: they give the specific business for which the representatives were being summoned: in 1276, the succession question and the reply to the king of France; in 1279, the mission of the papal legate; in 1282, the redress of the grievances of the towns, then much concerned with the king's breach of their *fueros*; and, in 1283, the question of a possible reconciliation between Alfonso X and his son. It should be noted that the reason given for the summons in 1282 was the breach of the *fueros*, not the sentence against Alfonso, which was, in fact, the real reason for summoning the cortes. Because of the loss of most writs of summons we do not know in many cases exactly why the cortes were held.

As so few writs have survived, there is also little information available as to the actual date of assembling of the various cortes, or the length of time allowed between the despatch of the writ of summons and the opening of the session. The writ for the Cortes of Burgos in 1276 was dated 30 April but, unfortunately, Sánchez Ruano omitted the date of assembly in his summary. It was, however, probably towards the end of June. The Infante Don Sancho's writ for the assembly at Salamanca

[109] *Fuero de Salamanca*, ed. Sánchez Ruano, xxiv, xxvii.
[110] Ballesteros, *BRAH*, cxix, 142–3, 143–4; *Alfonso X el Sabio*, 909, 911–12.
[111] Ballesteros, *Alfonso X el Sabio*, 1039–40.

was dated 17 November 1279, for an opening on 1 December. On 28 November this date was postponed until 10 December. His writ for the Cortes of Valladolid in 1282 was dated 9 March, with the opening fixed for Easter Day (29 March); in 1283 the writ of summons was despatched on 12 October and the date of assembly was to be All Saints Day. In neither 1282 nor 1283, however, did the meetings open on the date specified; in the first case Don Sancho did not reach Valladolid until 15 April, and in the second he was not at Palencia until 18 November.[112] In all these cases the length of time between the passing of the writ of summons and the day set for the opening of the cortes was surprisingly short – two to three weeks or less – and it must have been difficult for the representatives from the more distant parts of the kingdom to arrive in time.

There are also a few cases in which the date of assembly is known from other sources. The Cortes of Burgos in 1269 coincided with the marriage of the Infante Don Fernando de la Cerda, which took place on 30 November.[113] Those of Burgos in 1272 met on Michaelmas Day and those of Seville in 1281 were summoned for St Martin's Day.[114] In the case of the Cortes of Burgos in 1272, the time allowed for the assembling of the cortes was also very short. Alfonso's first document from Burgos was dated 6 September; some days must have been taken up with negotiations with the discontented nobles before they demanded, and the king agreed, that the cortes should be summoned to meet at Michaelmas.[115] It is true that the only occasions when the length of time between the date of the writ and the date of assembly is known were instances when the cortes were summoned under exceptional circumstances. In the fourteenth and fifteenth centuries the time allowed was one or two months or more.[116]

Of the actual procedure of the cortes in the thirteenth century we have little knowledge. In the fourteenth century the session certainly opened with a speech from the throne,[117] and indications of such speeches are to be found in documents of the period under review. In 1250 Fernando III spoke to those assembled 'aquellas cosas que entendi que

---

[112] AHN, Santiago, *caj.* 372/3 (Burgos, 29 March 1282); *RC Silos*, no. 240 (Burgos, 31 March); AHN, Calatrava, R. 130 (Valladolid, 15 April); Ballesteros, *Alfonso X el Sabio*, 1041.
[113] *Cortes*, I, no. XV.
[114] *Crónica Alfonso X*, *cap.* XXIV; Ballesteros, *Alfonso X el Sabio*, 948.
[115] *Crónica Alfonso X*, *caps.* XXIII–XXIV.
[116] Piskorski, *Cortes*, 74.
[117] *Ibid.* 78.

eran buen paramiento de la tierra'.[118] In 1275 a summary of events was given by Alfonso X: 'todas las cosas que pasaron e todos los fechos de la tierra como eran. Otrossi fecho de la guerra en que estado estaua'.[119] The *Crónica de Alfonso X*, in its account of the Cortes of Seville in 1281, also summarised briefly the king's speech in which he outlined the dangers of the war with Granada and the financial straits of the kingdom, before proposing an alteration of the coinage in lieu of further taxation.[120] Thus, the speech from the throne took the form of a survey of the state of the realm, followed in some cases by requests for financial aid. During the reign of Sancho IV the representatives of the towns seem to have deliberated separately from the magnates about their grievances and petitions, and this may have been so during the preceding reign.[121]

Of the duration of the various cortes there is little definite evidence. The general *cuadernos* were issued towards the end of the meeting, but those intended for individual towns bore various dates over two or three weeks. Thus, the surviving *cuadernos* of the Cortes of Seville in 1250 were dated 12, 18 and 22 November; those of Palencia in 1286, 2, 20 and 25 December. In some cases the *cuadernos* were not passed by the chancery until after the end of the cortes, and from another city than that where the assembly had taken place. The only surviving *cuaderno* for the Cortes of Jerez, which took place in the winter and spring of 1268, was thus dated from Seville on 30 July. The *cuadernos* of the Cortes of Haro in July 1288 were all passed from Vitoria on various dates in August. At times the king's itinerary provides evidence for the longest possible duration of a meeting, but Alfonso X spent several very lengthy periods amounting to months or even years in certain cities, with only occasional brief visits to other towns. In such cases his itinerary is useless for our purpose. Sometimes, however, the king's movements do set terms to the length of the cortes. In 1269 when the cortes met in Burgos at the end of November, he remained in that city until 18 December. In 1272 Alfonso's last *carta* dated from Burgos was one of 10 December, some ten weeks after the assembling of the cortes at Michaelmas. The Infante Don Sancho's Cortes of Valladolid in 1282 cannot have begun before 15 April nor lasted after 10 May, the dates of the first and last *cartas* of the Infante dated from that town.

[118] *Fuero de Cuenca*, 859.
[119] Ballesteros, *BRAH*, cxix, 118.
[120] *Crónica Alfonso X, cap.* lxxv.
[121] *Cortes*, I, preambles to nos. xvii, xix, xx.

Ballesteros, who considered that certain legislative or quasi-legislative acts, such as the granting, confirmation or amendment of *fueros*, the pronouncement of arbitral sentences and ordinances dealing with judicial procedure, generally took place in the cortes, was inclined to stretch the length of the meetings to cover the dates of such acts. But, although some *fueros* were granted when the cortes were meeting, they were often granted at other times, and the settlement of judicial suits was a matter for the *corte*, not the cortes, although the hearing might coincide with a meeting of the latter. Such acts by themselves, therefore, are not necessarily evidence that the cortes were in session. Thus, Ballesteros thought that the Cortes of Seville of 1261 began in the preceding November and lasted up to March 1261.[122] He considered that the arbitral sentence of 21 February 1261, given in the dispute between the archbishop and the *concejo* of Santiago with the advice of the *infantes*, the nobles 'et con nuestros alcaldes, et los otros omes buenos de nuestra corte, clerigos et legos que se acercaron y' was pronounced in these cortes.[123] Other privileges which Ballesteros considered indicated the continued sitting of the Cortes of Seville included the grant of a fair to Alba de Tormes, the confirmation of the *fuero* of Escalona and the grant to the inhabitants of Seville of freedom from forced *posada*, all on various dates in March;[124] perhaps also the privilege to Toledo concerning weights and measures, and, presumably, that to León on 4 April, which is identical.[125] None of these documents mentioned the cortes. The 'otros omes buenos' of the judicial sentence were, as the document stated, 'de nuestra corte', not representatives of the towns summoned to the cortes. Some of the privileges mentioned by Ballesteros may, of course, have arisen out of the holding of the cortes, without necessarily being granted while they were still assembled. Thus, one of the decrees of the cortes was that weights and measures were to be the same throughout the kingdom,[126] and *cartas* to Toledo and León were concerned with the carrying out of this decree, but they were not necessarily despatched before the dismissal of the cortes. The only surviving *cuaderno* was dated 24 January 1261 and the preamble referred to 'our cortes in Seville in the month of January'. The representatives of the cities and towns would hardly have remained

[122] Ballesteros, *Alfonso X el Sabio*, 294–5.
[123] Text publ. López Ferreiro, *Fueros*, I, 248–61.
[124] *MHE*, I, nos. LXXXIII, LXXXIV.
[125] [Burriel,] *Informe sobre pesos y medidas*; and Alvarez de la Brāna, 'Igualación de pesos y medidas', *BRAH*, XXXVIII, 134–7.
[126] Rodríguez Díez, *Historia de Astorga*, 720.

long in Seville after the issue of the *cuadernos*. In the case of the Cortes of Seville of 1261, there is reason to believe that the prelates and nobles who attended the *corte* in its largest form assembled earlier than the representatives and remained after the latter had been dismissed.

Ballesteros also thought that the Cortes of Seville in 1264 for the Extremaduras had already assembled early in February, because on the sixth of that month the king granted the *Fuero real* to Requena;[127] but the only documents which can definitely be connected with these cortes were all dated in April.[128] There are other instances of the Spanish scholar's tendency to assume lengthy meetings of the cortes in order to include quasi-legislative acts. The most striking instance is, however, the suggestion made by Ballesteros that the Cortes of Burgos, which met in November 1269 and which must have ended before the king left the city shortly before Christmas, were reconvened in the March of the following year and remained in session until June 1270.[129] Ballesteros admitted that neither the *Crónica* nor any document during that time mentioned the cortes, and he based his conjecture on the nature of some of the privileges granted in these four months. He cited a number of privileges granted in March to Logroño and other towns of La Rioja, which region Alfonso had visited early in the year, and which Ballesteros thought were held back so that they might be granted with accustomed solemnity in the cortes. It was not, however, unusual for the king to promise some favour during a visit to a town or monastery, while the actual grant was made at a later date. The exemption from *martiniega* granted to the abbot of Silos on 19 February 1256 had been promised when Alfonso visited the abbey in the previous November.[130] The vernacular version of the *fuero* of Palencia, given to the city on 20 July 1256, was the result of a petition made to the king when he had visited Palencia in the previous year.[131] A privilege to Sepúlveda of 16 October 1257 was also granted because of a request from the *concejo* made during a former visit, the date of which is unknown.[132]

From among the many royal privileges and *cartas* issued during these four months which he cited, Ballesteros singled out some which

[127] Ballesteros, *Alfonso X el Sabio*, 366.
[128] *MHE*, I, no. xcvi (8 April 1264); BL, Add. MS. 9916, fol. 257v (15 April); Ariz, *Historia de Avila, 3a parte*, 18 (22 April); *CD Cuéllar*, no. 21 (29 April).
[129] Ballesteros, *Alfonso X el Sabio*, 510–13.
[130] *RC Silos*, no. 194.
[131] 'El fuero romanceado de Palencia', *AHDE*, xi, 503–22.
[132] Ballesteros, *Itinerario*, 184–6.

he considered indicated the presence of the representatives of the towns. Thus, one dated 1 May granted to those good men of Palencia who had horses and arms the privileges of *caballería*, but this grant was in line with Alfonso's policy of increasing the military potential of the towns and did not differ from other similar privileges granted to various cities and towns on various dates during the course of his reign.[133] Two, dated 21 and 25 June, dealt with disputes between the lay and ecclesiastical authorities of Badajoz and laid down certain rules for the division of jurisdiction between them. The first reserved for lay justices disputes in testamentary cases, the second conceded to the city the administration of justice in Iguala and Campomayor against the claims of the bishop and chapter. Without definite references to the cortes, such documents are an insufficient basis for an hypothetical four months' session of the cortes from March to June 1270.

For the reign of Sancho IV, the king's itinerary is much more helpful for establishing the duration of the cortes. Sancho IV was always on the move and rarely spent long periods in any one place. Thus, in 1284 he was in Seville from 20 June to 24 August and in Valladolid from 18 November to 6 December and it was within those dates that the Cortes of Seville and Valladolid of that year must have taken place.[134] In 1286 there are two royal documents dated from Zamora – on 27 and 29 January – and there is no evidence of the king's whereabouts earlier in the month; in the previous December he had been at Badajoz and on 12 February he was at Benavente.[135] In all probability, therefore, the cortes at which homage was done to the newly born heir to the throne was of short duration and had no other purpose. The Cortes of Palencia in 1286 must have taken place between 25 November and 23 December; those of Haro in 1288 between 20 June, when Haro surrendered, and 3 August, when Sancho IV went to Miranda and thence to Vitoria.[136] The itinerary also shows that the Cortes of Valladolid of 1293 were held between 13 April and 23 May.[137] Thus, none of Sancho's cortes can have lasted for more than two months. Piskorski held that the duration of the sessions of the cortes held during the fourteenth and early fifteenth centuries varied from some weeks to

---

[133] Pescador, 'La caballería popular en León y Castilla', *CHE*, xxxiii–xxxiv, 188, gives a list of such privileges granted by Alfonso X.
[134] Gaibrois de Ballesteros, *Sancho IV*, I, 12; III, nos. 6–13, 28–36.
[135] *Ibid.* III, nos. 99–103; Marcos Rodríguez, *Catálogo de documentos del archivo catedralicio de Salamanca*, no. 401.
[136] Gaibrois de Ballesteros, *Sancho IV*, III, nos. 137–43; 206–10.
[137] *Ibid.* III, nos. 458, 460–2, 468, 471–81, 483–4.

two months and that not until the second half of the fifteenth century did longer meetings become common.[188] The evidence for the reign of Sancho IV leads to a similar conclusion for the late thirteenth century and it seems improbable that Alfonso X's cortes lasted much longer.

[138] Piskorski, *Cortes*, 104.

8

The cortes and questions concerning the succession to the throne, and home and foreign policy

In the second half of the thirteenth century the cortes participated from time to time in most of the functions of government. In the later Middle Ages it was customary for the cortes to be assembled soon after the accession of a new king, in order to acknowledge him and take the oath of allegiance to him. As we have already seen, in Castile citizens and townspeople had done homage to Enrique I on his accession in 1214, and to Fernando III in 1217. For the accession of Alfonso X there is little definite evidence. Piskorski asserted that the oath of allegiance was taken to Alfonso X in cortes held at Toledo in 1252.[1] This assertion was based on Martínez Marina, who relied on the king's confirmation of the privileges of Toledo which referred to cortes held in that city, and which Martínez misdated 2 March 1253 instead of 1254. He admitted that nothing was known of these cortes, but assumed that the oath of allegiance was taken there.[2] Alfonso's first visit to Toledo took place from early February to mid-May 1254, by which time he had been on the throne for nearly two years and, as we have already seen, the oath was taken at the Cortes of Toledo to Alfonso's eldest daughter Berenguela as his heiress in default of a male heir, not to the king himself. The oath of allegiance may have been taken to Alfonso during the Cortes of Seville, in the autumn of 1252, but there is no evidence that this was so. Again, there is no definite evidence of the taking of the oath of allegiance to Sancho IV. Don Sancho was at Avila when the news of his father's death at Seville reached him; there he was proclaimed king, his wife Doña María queen and his daughter Isabel his heiress, if he should have no son. Presumably the prelates, magnates and others with him at Avila did homage to him there. By 3 May 1284 he was in Toledo, where he and the queen were crowned. At Córdoba his brother the Infante Don Juan and those

---

[1] Piskorski, *Cortes*, 111.
[2] Martínez Marina, *Teoría de las cortes*, II, 30–1.

prelates and magnates who had formed the dead king's court at Seville met him and acknowledged him as king. Sancho IV had reached Seville by 20 June; up to that date, then, no cortes could have been assembled. The *Crónica de Sancho IV* gives us two relevant pieces of information: that at Seville those of the kingdom of Seville (that is, of Andalusia) received Sancho 'for the king and for lord', and that the king revoked 'in cortes' the grants which he had made during his rebellion.[3] Those of Andalusia may, therefore, have done homage and taken the oath in these cortes which appear to have been partial cortes for Andalusia, and possibly for Murcia too.[4] If this was so, then the cortes held at Valladolid in December 1284 may have been for the kingdoms of León and Castile and homage may have been offered there by those who had not already done so. Given the circumstances in which Sancho IV succeeded to the throne, his recognition as king may well have taken place in such successive stages.

We are rather better informed about the procedure for taking the oath of allegiance to the heir to the throne. The right of the eldest son or, in the absence of a male heir, of the eldest daughter, to succeed to the undivided kingdom was clearly enunciated in the attestation on the rights of the Infanta Doña Berenguela sent to Prince Louis of France in 1255, in connection with the treaty for his marriage to her. In this it was stated that the kingdom was indivisible and that, according to the custom of Spain ('iuxta generalem totius Ispanie consuetudinem aprobatam'), it descended to the eldest son or, if there were no sons, to the eldest daughter; if there were both sons and daughters, to the eldest son even if a daughter was the eldest born. For this reason Alfonso X, it explained, had summoned to Toledo the archbishops, bishops and magnates of his court and the proctors of the cities, strongholds and towns and had caused them to do homage to his eldest daughter Berenguela as his successor, should he have no male heir.[5] This homage had been done at the Cortes of Toledo in 1254.

Alfonso X's eldest son, the Infante Don Fernando, was born on 23 October 1255.[6] There is no documentary evidence of the doing of homage to him as heir to the throne, and the only reference to such an

---

[3] *Crónica Sancho IV, cap.* 1 (pp. 69–70); cf. Jofré de Loaisa, *Crónica*, 24, who does not mention the cortes. For the king's itinerary, see Gaibrois de Ballesteros, *Sancho IV*, I, 9–12; III, nos. 1–13.

[4] See Gaibrois de Ballesteros, *Sancho IV*, I, 15, for the suggestion that these were partial cortes for Murcia as well as Andalusia.

[5] Daumet, *Relations*, 4–5, and *pièce just.* no. 1 (pp. 142–6).

[6] *Ibid.* 11.

act is contained in the *Crónica de Alfonso X*, in its account of the measures taken for the government of the kingdom before the king's journey to Beaucaire in 1275. Reference is there made to 'el pleito e omenage' which had been done to the Infante.[7] Ballesteros suggested that this homage was done to the Infante in the Cortes of Vitoria in January 1256, two months after his birth. This suggestion is plausible and may very well be correct but, as Ballesteros himself admitted, it is purely conjectural.[8] At the same time Alfonso X was engaged in exacting from some ecclesiastical cities homage to his daughter Berenguela in fulfilment of his treaty with Louis IX of France. Certainly in the case of Orense (and possibly of other cities) he went over the heads of the ecclesiastical overlords for this purpose and, on 14 December 1255, ordered the city directly to send three good men with powers to do homage. They were not summoned to attend the cortes but were ordered to come before the king wherever he might be on Candlemas Day, which in the event was at Belorado. This procedure occasioned a sharp protest from the bishop and chapter of Orense who claimed that only they, as overlords, could do homage on behalf of the city.[9] Later the king admitted the justice of the bishop's claim.[10] At San Esteban de Gormaz on 10 February homage was also done by the proctors of the archbishop and chapter of Santiago on behalf of the towns of Santiago and Pontevedra.[11] None of this correspondence makes reference to homage done to the Infante Don Fernando.

The situation which arose on the death of Alfonso X's eldest son in 1275 was a complicated one, since it entailed a decision as to who was the heir – the king's grandson or his second son. The history of the kingdoms of León and Castile afforded no exact precedent; in no former case had the heir to the throne died, leaving issue, in the lifetime of his father. The treaty of 1255 with France had not foreseen this eventuality. The legal position was obscure. The *Espéculo* enunciated a theory of the succession similar to that in the attestation of 1255, argued at length and in detail. It did not specifically refer to the possibility of the heir's death before his father's, but it concluded with a clear declaration that only if the direct line died out entirely did the

<hr/>

[7] *Crónica Alfonso X*, cap. LIX (p. 48).
[8] Ballesteros, *Alfonso X el Sabio*, 146.
[9] Sánchez-Albornoz, *AHDE*, VI, 454–9. Sánchez-Albornoz stated that the city was to send proctors to the cortes but none of the documents he published in fact refers to the cortes.
[10] Ballesteros, *Itinerario*, 151 (14 Feb. 1256); *Alfonso X el Sabio*, 149.
[11] López Ferreiro, *Iglesia de Santiago*, V, 221, and ap. XXXI.

right of succession revert to a collateral branch.[12] The *Segunda partida*, as it appears in the printed editions, deals specifically with the eventuality of the heir's death before his father. It laid down that in such a case the dead man's eldest son should succeed – the so-called 'right of representation'.[13] It is inconceivable that this unequivocable enunciation of the right of representation can have been added after the recognition of the Infante Don Sancho as Alfonso X's heir; it must, therefore, be an early revision, representing the views of Alfonso X and his legal advisers. At least one manuscript of the *Segunda partida*, however, substituted for the right of the grandson an assertion of the right of the second son – pero si, fincare otro fijo varon del rey, que aquel lo herede et non el nieto' – a variant which, as Professor Macdonald points out, must have been influenced by the events of 1276.[14] In any case, Alfonso's code had been abrogated during the rebellion of 1272–3 and was not, therefore, legally binding in 1276. The question of the succession was now a matter of political expediency rather than of legal right, of whether the threat of internal rebellion or of foreign invasion was the greater danger. We have already dealt (pp. 139–40) with the facts, so far as they can be ascertained, concerning the Cortes of Burgos of 1276 and the recognition of the Infante Don Sancho as heir to the throne. In the present context the main interest of this event lies in the differing role assigned to the cortes by the two available narrative sources. According to the *Crónica de Alfonso X*, they were summoned solely to take the oath of allegiance to the Infante as heir – the decision that he was heir having already been reached. According to Jofré de Loaiso, however, the cortes were summoned to advise Alfonso X on the succession question and in the ensuing debate the *concejos* supported the claims of the Infante Don Sancho.[15] In view of Jofré's evidence, it is difficult to deny that the cortes took a definite part in the decision on the succession. No uncertainties arise in the case of Sancho IV's eldest son, Fernando, to whom the magnates and 'las ciudades e villas' did homage at Zamora in 1286.[16]

The cortes also intervened in a more general way in internal politics. In this respect they were to reach the height of their power during the

---

[12] *Espéculo*, II, *tít.* XVI, *leyes* 1, 3.

[13] *Part.* II, *tít.* XV, *ley* 2.

[14] Macdonald, 'Alfonso the Learned and the succession', *Speculum*, XL, 651. This manuscript is quoted in the footnotes to the edition, II, p. 133, and also by Professor Macdonald, p. 651, n. 12.

[15] *Crónica Alfonso X*, caps. LXVII, LXVIII; Jofré de Loaisa, *Crónica*, 20–1.

[16] *Crónica Sancho IV*, cap. II (p. 72).

minorities of Fernando IV and Alfonso XI, when disputes between various members of the royal family about the regency gave the cortes an opportunity to intervene in affairs of state. But in the preceding half century, also, the cortes had played a part in politics. Three assemblies – the Cortes of Burgos in 1272, the Infante Don Sancho's 'Cortes' of Valladolid in 1282 and of Palencia in 1283 – were summoned for political reasons. The Cortes of Burgos were summoned by Alfonso X at the request of the malcontent nobles, in order that the concessions promised by him might have the additional sanction of promulgation in cortes.[17] The main object of the nobles then was to force the king to rescind his legislative codes with their strong predilection for the principles of Roman law and to restore, in their stead, the ancient, pre-Alfonsine *fueros*. One of the demands put forward by the nobles, which was granted by the king and promulgated at Burgos, was, thus, that *hidalgos* who lived within the jurisdictions of the towns should not be judged by *fueros* which had been granted the towns by the king.[18] This demand was principally directed against the *Fuero real*, which Alfonso had given to a number of towns on royal demesne. This concession granted by the king in 1272 limited the application of Alfonso's *Fuero real*, but it did not abrogate it. Many towns continued to use it, and it was also used in the king's court in cases of appeals from the municipalities, as is proved by references to it in the *Leyes del estilo*.[19] Much more damaging to Alfonso's legal reforms was his concession that the *ricos hombres*, knights and *hidalgos* should in future be judged according to the *Fuero antiguo*, for this involved the rescinding of the provisions of the *Espéculo* and the restoration of customary law in Castile. The demand for the restoration of the *Fuero antiguo* continued to be put forward at later stages of the revolt of the nobles, during the protracted negotiations between the king and the rebels before and after their withdrawal to Granada. The restoration of the *Fuero antiguo* was conceded to the loyal supporters of the king at Almagro and also confirmed to the rebels in the final agreement with them.[20] Among other demands put forward before and during the Cortes of Burgos was one, also conceded, that the nobles should be judged only by their peers and for this purpose the king was to have two judges of noble birth at his court (*alcaldes fijosdalgo*).[21]

[17] *Crónica Alfonso X*, cap. xxiv (p. 21).
[18] *Ibid. caps.* xxiii–xxiv (p. 20).
[19] E.g. *leyes* l, lii, lxvi–lxxii, etc.
[20] *Crónica Alfonso X*, *caps.* xxiv, xl, xlvii, liv, lv.
[21] *Ibid. caps.* xxiii, xxiv, xxv.

The Infante Don Sancho's Cortes of Valladolid in 1282 was also summoned for purely political reasons, in this case to give some cloak of legality to his open rebellion against his father, much as the last parliament of Edward II gave a constitutional backing to his deposition. The forms were carefully observed. The writs were, of necessity, issued in the name of the Infante Don Sancho, as at no time did the insurgents have possession of the king's person, nor were they able to control his actions, as were the rebels against Edward II. It must, however, be remembered that Don Sancho had already issued the writs for the assemblies of representatives in 1279, presumably then with his father's knowledge. If he had, indeed, been recognised as co-regnant with Alfonso X in 1278, then he could claim some legality for his actions. The principal business of the Cortes of Valladolid was the pronouncement of the sentence depriving Alfonso of the exercise of his regalian rights, including the control of the strongholds of the kingdom, the royal revenue and the administration of justice, and transferring them to Don Sancho. There was no formal trial; the king was neither present nor represented, as he himself complained in the document disinheriting his son for rebellion. The sentence against Alfonso X was read out by his younger brother, the Infante Don Manuel, and the deed was sealed by those present. This must have taken place before 21 April 1282, on which date Bishop Fernando of Burgos and Bishop Juan Alfonso of Palencia issued a formal protest, stating that they had been summoned without warning to hear the sentence read behind locked doors, and had been forced to seal it against their will.[22]

These cortes also dealt with the question of Alfonso X's non-observance of the *fueros*, usages and customs of the towns. Most of the *cartas de hermandad* concluded during or after the assembly referred to the maintenance of the ancient customs as the principal objective of the revolt.[23] Some of them mention the privilege granted by Don Sancho at Valladolid confirming the *fueros*.[24] During the cortes the Infante confirmed, for services rendered, the privileges of (and made many

[22] *MHE*, II, no. CXCVIII; the details of the sentence are also given in Alfonso's sentence disinheriting his son, Zurita, *Indices*, 173–4 and by Jofré de Loaisa, *Crónica*, 22. The *Crónica de Alfonso X, cap.* LXXVI, adds that the cortes offered the title of king to Don Sancho, who refused it.
[23] E.g. *MHE*, II, nos. CCII, CCIII, CCV (2, 3, 10 May 1282); Escalona, *Sahagún, ap.* III, *esc.* CCLXVI (8 July 1282).
[24] AHN, Santiago, *caj.* 260/10, 11; *caj.* 326/30 (10, 12 July 1282): 'assi commo diçe el privilegio que nos dio nuestro sennor el Inffante Don Sancho en Valladolit'.

grants to) individual churches, monasteries, the military orders and towns.[25] In the general confirmation of all the privileges of the monastery of Sahagún, Sancho not only promised on the cross and the Gospels to maintain all the *fueros*, uses and customs of the monastery and all its privileges and did 'pleito e omenage' that he would never act against them, but also declared that he would aid the abbot against the king or any other person.[26] Finally, he made sure of support by wholesale promises to the nobles and by dividing much of the royal revenue among them.[27]

The reason for the assembly summoned by Don Sancho to Palencia in 1283 was also political: to bring about some sort of reconciliation between the king and his son, which would guarantee the rights of both of them and maintain the *fueros* of the towns. As a result envoys were sent to Alfonso X at Seville, but without any immediate result; on 10 January 1284 King Alfonso, in his second will, confirmed the disinheritance of his son.[28] Attempts at mediation were, however, still being carried out by Pedro III of Aragon and Queen Eleanor of England.[29] Finally, in March 1284, shortly before his death, Alfonso pardoned the rebel prince, and informed Pope Martin IV, and possibly other foreign rulers, as well as his own subjects, of this decision. His death on 4 April, however, prevented any meeting of reconciliation with the Infante.[30]

From time to time the cortes intervened in the administration of the royal demesne lands. At the Cortes of Burgos in 1272, the nobles even unaccountably demanded that new towns founded by the king in Galicia, León and Castile should be destroyed; as these were on royal demesne they could not affect the rights of the nobles, but the king offered an inquiry into the practice of former kings. Here he was on

---

[25] E.g. *RC Silos*, no. 242; *MHE*, ii, nos. cxcix, cc; AHN, Esc. Calatrava, iv, fols. 104, 105, 108. Cf. Ballesteros, *Alfonso X el Sabio*, 970–3, 1124–6.

[26] AHN, Clero, *carp.* 919/24 (28 April 1282); publ. Appendix, doc. viii, below.

[27] Zurita, *Indices*, 173; *Crónica Alfonso X, cap.* lxxvi; cf. Ballesteros, *Alfonso X el Sabio*, 966–7.

[28] The two wills have survived both in the vernacular (*MHE*, ii, nos. ccxxviii–ccxxix) and in Latin (Daumet, 'Les testaments d'Alphonse X', *Bibliothèque de l'Ecole des Chartes*, lxvii, 70–99). On the dates of the wills, see Daumet's article. There is a copy of the second will in ANTT, Extras, fol. 229, where the date, 10 Jan. 1284, agrees with the Latin version.

[29] ACA, Reg. 47, fol. 122: Pedro III to Queen Eleanor, 6 Feb. 1284.

[30] *Foedera*, i, ii, 640: letter of Alfonso X to Pope Martin IV, 23 March 1284. Jofré de Loaisa, *Crónica*, 24; *Cronicón de Cardeña*, ii, 379; *Crónica Alfonso X, cap.* lxxvii.

strong ground, as a similar policy of colonisation had been carried out extensively by his predecessors in both León and Castile.[31] Sancho IV's two acts of resumption, when he revoked *cartas* granting lands to his supporters during his revolt and after his recognition as king, both took place in cortes, at Seville in 1284 and at Palencia in 1286.[32] In this he was following the example of Alfonso IX of León who had revoked his father Fernando II's donations in the Curia or Cortes of 1188. Such gifts had been necessary to buy support during Sancho's revolt, to reward his supporters and buttress his position at the beginning of his reign. The initiative to resume the alienated lands came from the king, who doubtless found it convenient to do so with the support of the cortes. The whole question of changes in land tenure which adversely affected the crown, especially the passing of land into mortmain, came to the fore in Sancho IV's reign. Among the decrees of 1286 was one forbidding nobles to purchase lands belonging to *realengo*.[33] In 1288, however, all previous changes as a consequence of which *realengo* had passed to churches, nobles and corporations (or *vice versa*) were recognised as valid as part of a general amnesty on debts to the crown, and this was confirmed at the petition of the *concejos* of Castile at the Cortes of Valladolid in 1293.[34]

It was not until the second half of the thirteenth century that there is clear evidence of the intervention of the cortes in questions of foreign policy. The first definite reference to consultation with the cortes was in 1259, when Alfonso X held his Cortes of Toledo 'sobrel ffecho del Imperio'.[35] The imperial venture was again the reason for the Cortes of Burgos in 1274, before Alfonso X's unsuccessful journey to Beaucaire in 1275 to meet Gregory X.[36] Relations with North Africa and Granada were also from time to time debated in the cortes. Alfonso had inherited from his father a project for the invasion of North Africa; this was shelved during the earlier years of the reign, but was revived early in 1260; in the autumn of that year Salé on the Atlantic coast of North Africa was taken and sacked by a Castilian fleet.[37] Advice on this question was sought from the Cortes of Seville in January 1261;

[31] *Crónica Alfonso X, caps.* XXIII, XXIV, XXV. There is no evidence whether such an inquiry took place.
[32] *Crónica Sancho IV, cap.* I; *Cortes,* I, no. XVII, cl. I.
[33] *Cortes,* I, no. XVII, cl. 2.
[34] *Ibid.* I, no. XVIII, cl. I, 2; no. XIX, cl. 17.
[35] Ballesteros, *Alfonso X, Emperador,* 71 (6 Feb. 1260).
[36] *Ibid.* 72–3 (13 April 1274).
[37] Ballesteros, *Alfonso X el Sabio,* 274–80.

the preamble of the resulting *cuaderno* referred to 'el conseio que nos davan en el fecho de Africa que aviemos començado' – proof that, at that date, the king had in mind a full-scale invasion across the Straits.[38] Fourteen years later, at the meeting at Alcalá in December 1275, Alfonso X addressed those assembled on 'el fecho de la guerra', that is, again, the war with the Moors.[39] It is probable that the war with Morocco and Granada was also discussed in the cortes held in 1277 and 1281. During the last decade of the reign relations with France were at times also considered in the cortes; for example, one of the reasons for the summoning of the Cortes of Burgos in 1276 was, as we have already seen, to make answer to King Philip III of France, who supported the rights of his nephew, Don Alfonso de la Cerda, to be declared heir to the Castilian throne.[40]

Thus, during the reign of Alfonso X, foreign policy was undoubtedly brought before the cortes on some occasions, but this does not prove that the king considered himself bound to consult the cortes about foreign affairs. On several of these occasions, for example, in 1274, 1275 and 1277, the king asked for and obtained financial aid to carry out his policy. To obtain such aid, it was necessary to make clear the state of affairs and engage the support of the cortes, but it was need of money, rather than need of advice on, or consent to, the policy as such, which led to the consultation. Such consultations were also very intermittent and on many occasions involving foreign relations no recourse was made to the cortes; Alfonso did not summon the cortes when he abandoned his North African designs in favour of an attack on the tiny Moorish subject kingdom of Niebla and the cortes did not meet between January 1261 when *el fecho de Africa* was considered and February 1262, when Niebla was besieged and taken.[41] Again, there is no evidence that the cortes were consulted during the long and tortuous negotiations with Pedro III of Aragon from 1279 to 1281, which led up to the Treaty of Campillo in March 1281. Indeed, the cortes were not summoned at all between the possible meeting at Segovia in the summer of 1278 and that which took place at Seville in the autumn of 1281.[42]

[38] Rodríguez Díez, *Historia de Astorga*, 715.
[39] Ballesteros *BRAH*, cxix, 118.
[40] *Fuero de Salamanca*, ed. Sánchez Ruano, xxiv.
[41] On the date of the siege of Niebla, see Ballesteros, *Seville, ap. E*, cclxxxix; *Alfonso X el Sabio*, 314–17.
[42] Ballesteros, in his account of the negotiations with Pedro III, overlooked the fact that the Aragonese chancery, which used the style of the Incarnation, began the year on 25 March. He therefore antedated by one year all Aragonese documents

There were also occasions on which Alfonso consulted with anomalous bodies, in which some *concejos* might be represented, but for which no general summons had been issued. This generally happened during times of war or rebellion, when the king consulted those available, because they were present with the army. In 1265, during war with Granada, when the king of Granada proposed a truce, Alfonso X consulted the *infantes*, nobles and knights who were with him and some of the representatives of the *concejos* whom he had summoned to the discussion (*fabla* is the word used by the *Crónica*) and accepted their advice that he should meet the king of Granada.[43] Again, at the *ayuntamiento* of Avila in May 1273, Alfonso X informed those of León and the Extremaduras, whom he had summoned to meet him there, of the course of the rebellion of the nobles and the war with Granada, and ordered a general muster of the kingdom.[44] Sancho IV, throughout his reign, showed a marked preference for consultation on foreign affairs with the *corte*, in either its augmented or restricted form, rather than with the cortes.

passed between 1 Jan. and 25 March in 1279, 1280, and 1281 (*Alfonso X el Sabio*, 848–50, 861, 876–82, 913–14). The same mistakes in date were made by the editors of *MHE*, I and II, who published some of the documents from the Villanueva transcripts in the Real Academia de la Historia. All the documents are contained in ACA, Reg. 47. Ballesteros's transcripts of Aragonese documents are often faulty.

[43] *Crónica Alfonso X*, cap. XV.
[44] *Ibid. cap.* L.

9

The cortes and the voting of subsidies

'Moneda'

We have already traced (Chapters 2 and 3) the history of the tax called *moneda* in the separate kingdoms of León and Castile. After the reunion of the kingdoms in 1230, for the rest of Fernando III's reign references to *moneda* are scanty, but they occur from time to time in grants of royal rents in which *moneda* was reserved for the crown. An example occurs in 1245 when the king granted the as yet unconquered towns of Pego and Alcaudete with their rents to the Order of Calatrava, but reserved to the crown both *moneta* and *prandium*.[1] Under Alfonso X grants in which *moneda* was reserved were frequent in all periods of the reign. Many such grants were made to the military orders. Thus, during the revolt of Andalusia, the king granted to the Order of Calatrava the castle of Osuna with its rents, but retained *moneda*: 'Sacado ende que retenemos para nos e para todos los que regnaren despues de nos en Castiella e en Leon para siempre moneda e iusticia e yantar e las otras cosas de nuestro sennorio assi como las abemos e las debemos aber en todos los otros logares de la Orden.'[2] *Moneda* was also reserved to the crown in grants of the castle and town of Medina Sidonia to the Order of Santa María de España in 1279 and of the castle and town of Cieza to the Order of Santiago in 1281.[3] The same reservation was made when the castle of Hinosa was given to the Order of Calatrava.[4]

In donations to towns and other communities which included grants of fiscal rights, *moneda* was generally reserved. Alfonso X's confirma-

---

[1] Manuel Rodríguez, *Memorias*, 479–82 (31 Dec. 1245).
[2] AHN, Esc. Calatrava, IV, fol. 21 (29 Dec. 1264); publ. *Bullarium de Calatrava*, 123–5.
[3] AHN, Santiago, *caj.* 222/4 (10 Dec. 1279); *caj.* 90/2 (24 April 1281). The Order of Santa María de España, which was founded by Alfonso X, was later incorporated in the Order of Santiago.
[4] AHN, Esc. Calatrava, IV, fol. 103 (14 May 1281).

tion of the *Fueros* of Valle de Fenar in 1254 included exemption 'de todo pecho...salvo moneda'.[5] In 1255 he granted the inhabitants of Seville the royal rents in Constantina and Tejada except *moneda* and *martiniega*.[6] In 1265 the widows and orphans of the knights of Ciudad Rodrigo were excused all *pechos* except *moneda*.[7] Among privileges granted to those who colonised Arcos de la Frontera in 1268 was exemption from all tributes except *moneda* and *yantar*.[8] Later in the reign, in 1278, a similar exemption from all *pechos* except *moneda* and *yantar* was allowed to those of Segovia who inhabited the best houses in the city, together with their families and households.[9]

The Infante Don Sancho, during his rebellion, also reserved *moneda* in grants to his supporters. Thus, during the Cortes of Valladolid he gave to the Order of Calatrava Villarreal with Alarcos and its villages and all its rights: 'Salvo que retengo para mí e para todos los otros que despues de mí vinieren justicia si la vos non facieredes e moneda forera e yantar.'[10] *Moneda* was also excluded from a comprehensive grant made by the Infante to the chapter of the collegiate church of Valladolid, which excused its clergy from every other sort of payment.[11] Many similar reservations of *moneda* occurred in grants made by Sancho IV during the course of his reign.[12]

There are also some examples of exemption from the payment of *moneda*, generally made to the church. Under a decree of 1202 the members of the chapters of the Leonese cathedrals had been granted a general exemption. In spite of this, Alfonso X, in the early years of his reign, specifically confirmed such exemption to a number of individual Leonese chapters, including those of León itself in 1254, 1255 and again in 1258, and to those of Astorga and Salamanca in 1255.[13] These confirmations suggest that *moneda* had been demanded from

---

[5] Díez Canseco, 'Sobre los fueros del Valle de Fenar, Castrocallón y Pajares: notas para el estudio del Fuero de León', *AHDE*, I, 373.

[6] *MHE*, I, no. XXXI (17 June 1255).

[7] Ballesteros, *BRAH*, CIX, 382 (22 June 1265).

[8] *MHE*, I, no. CIX (27 Jan. 1268).

[9] Colmenares, *Historia de Segovia*, I, 413–15 (27 Sept. 1278).

[10] AHN, Esc. Calatrava, IV, fol. 104 (3 May 1282); for other similar privileges of 15 April and 3 May, see fols. 105, 108.

[11] *MHE*, II, no. CCXXX (26 March 1284).

[12] Gaibrois de Ballesteros, *Sancho IV*, III, nos. 69 (21 April 1285), 92 (16 Nov. 1285), 111 (1 May 1286), 133 (1 Oct. 1286), 137 (25 Nov. 1286), 154 (24 April 1287), 335 (26 Jan. 1291), 400 (15 Feb. 1292), 447 (10 Feb. 1293), 462 (25 April 1293), 486 (12 July 1293), 591 (24 Feb. 1295).

[13] AC León, no. 1114 (15 Oct. 1255); Ballesteros, *Itinerario*, 55 (4 April 1254), 210 (18 July 1258); to Astorga, *ibid.* 132 (15 Oct. 1255); Marcos Rodríguez, *Catálogo del archivo catedralicio de Salamanca*, no. 260 (15 Oct. 1255).

members of cathedral chapters in spite of the exemption of 1202.
Many exemptions were also granted to the cathedrals of Castile, to
whose clergy no general exemption had been conceded. Alfonso X
exempted from the payment of *moneda* the cathedral clergy of Toledo
in 1253 and again in 1256.[14] Similar exemptions were granted to the
chapters of Cuenca and Palencia in 1255.[15] In November 1255 the
chapter of Córdoba was exempted: 'que ninguno que sea persona, o
canonigo, o Racionero, o capellan, o clerigo del coro tambien losque
agoro son, como losque seran daqui adelante pora siempre, que non
pechen moneda ami nin a quantos despues demi vinieren'.[16] The
members of the chapters of the cathedrals of Segovia and Avila were
exempted in the following year.[17] The clergy of the collegiate church of
Santo Domingo de la Calzada were also exempted in 1256 and those of
Covarrubias in 1260.[18] Some of these privileges, including those to the
chapters of Toledo, Avila and Santo Domingo de la Calzada in 1256
and of Covarrubias in 1260, specifically stated that, although former
kings had granted them many privileges, 'franqueza de moneda non les
dieron'. The parochial clergy of the city of Seville were exempted in
1271, and in 1283 the Infante Don Sancho exempted the cathedral
clergy of Cartagena from *moneda* and other *pechos*.[19] Other exemptions were granted or confirmed during the reign of Sancho IV.[20]

The decree of 1202 had also excused the knights of the kingdom of
León and their households from payment of *moneda*. There was no
such general exemption in Castile but, during the second half of the
thirteenth century, exemption was sometimes granted to knights and
others of the Castilian towns. The *caballeros hidalgos* and squires of
Toledo were given this privilege early in 1259.[21] In 1273 knights of
noble origin, squires and all citizens of Seville who had horses and arms
were excused and, in 1280, a similar grant was made to the knights and
good men of Córdoba exempting them from 'la moneda forera que nos

---

[14] *MHE*, I, no. IV (21 Feb. 1253). BN, MS. 13075, fol. 38v, is a transcript of this
document, misdated 1259; the *confirmantes* are those of 1253. *Documentos lingüísticos*, no. 284 (24 May 1256).
[15] Ballesteros, *Itinerario*, 93 (28 Jan. 1255), 95 (2 Feb. 1255).
[16] BN, MS. 13077, fol. 46 (2 Nov. 1255).
[17] Colmenares, *Historia de Segovia*, I, 398 (6 May 1256); *Memorias de Fernando
IV*, II, no. CCXXI, 13 Sept. 1256, inserted in a *privilegio rodado* of 1302.
[18] Martínez Marina, *Teoría de las cortes*, III, no. V (14 Jan. 1256); *Fuentes de
Castilla*, II, no. LVIII (11 March 1260).
[19] *MHE*, I, no. CXXIV (5 Nov. 1271); II, no. CCXIX (6 March 1283).
[20] E.g. Gaibois de Ballesteros, *Sancho IV*, III, nos. 163 (1 July 1287), 208 (29
July 1288), 274 (20 Dec. 1289), etc.
[21] Ballesteros, *Alfonso X, Emperador*, 25, 69–70; *Alfonso X el Sabio*, 227.

an a dar de siete en siete años'.[22] The knights of Madrid were excused
moneda by the Infante Don Sancho during his rebellion.[23] At some
time also the inhabitants of Salvatierra de Alava were quit of *moneda*
for, at the Cortes of Valladolid in 1307, their *personeros* complained
that *moneda forera* had been demanded of them, although they were
not liable for its payment.[24]

From the beginning of Alfonso X's reign, and probably earlier,
moneda had become a customary payment, taken periodically without
renewed consent. It was treated as a *pecho* and frequently coupled
with *yantar*, a customary payment rarely granted away. Some time
between August 1257, when the German embassy arrived in Castile to
notify Alfonso X of his election to the imperial crown, and the beginning of 1259, the Castilian king imposed a *moneda* at double the usual
rate, because it was the normal time for the collection of the tax and
because he needed the additional amount for the expenses of the
imperial affair. On 6 February 1260 the king confirmed his earlier
exemption from *moneda* to the knights of Toledo because, in spite of it,
they had paid the double *moneda*. This privilege nowhere refers to the
cortes and it specifically states that *moneda* was due at that time by
right – *por derecho*; however, the double rate was probably an innova-
tion, and may have been granted by the Cortes of Valladolid in 1258.[25]
Of this, however, there is no proof.

There is evidence of the continued levying of *moneda* at unaccustomed times and rates and that this practice encountered opposition. In 1265 Alfonso X promised the *concejo* of Salamanca that, in
return for their services in the war against Granada, in future *moneda*
should be demanded of them only as it had been in the time of
Alfonso IX and Fernando III, a clear indication that the king had
abused his right.[26] One of the demands put forward during the revolt
of the nobles in 1272 and 1273 was that Alfonso X should not levy
moneda 'sinon de siete en siete años, asi commo la cogio su padre e su
visabuelo e los del su linaje, e que nunca demande otros pechos, nin

---

[22] *MHE*, I, no. cxxxii (3 June 1273); II, no. clxxvii (3 Aug. 1280).
[23] *DA Madrid*, 1a serie, I, 127 (3 March 1283).
[24] BL, Add. Charter 12766 (4 Dec. 1307): 'non ouieren nin an de fuero, nin de vso,
nin de costumbre de pechar moneda forera nin quela non pecharan en tiempo de
los Reyes ende nos uenimos'.
[25] The privilege of 6 Feb. 1260 is published in Ballesteros, *Alfonso X, Emperador*,
69–70; in *Alfonso X el Sabio* (227–8) Ballesteros gives extracts from both privileges. Cf. O'Callaghan, *Traditio*, xxvii, 383, for the possible grant in 1258.
[26] *Fuero de Salamanca*, ed. Sánchez Ruano, xxi (2 July, 1265).

aya cabeza la moneda'.²⁷ The account given in the *Crónica* is substantiated by the manifesto presented by Don Juan Núñez to Enrique I
of Navarre, detailing the grievances of the nobles against Alfonso X,
and which included the demand 'e que coia la moneda de siet en siet
ayños de como la cojio su padre e el so auuelo'.²⁸ The attempt to return
to the connection between the tax and the maintenance of the value of
the coinage was also an aim of the general *Hermandad* formed in July
1282 by the cities and towns of León and Castile in support of the
Infante Don Sancho. The document of association included in the list
of recognised regalian rights 'moneda a cabo de siete annos do la
solien dar, et como la solien dar, non mandando los Reyes labrar
moneda'.²⁹ During the last years of Alfonso X's reign the tax became
known as *moneda forera* and from 1291 onwards it was generally
referred to in Sancho IV's documents as 'moneda forera de siete en
siete annos'.

'*Servicios*'

The most important extraordinary direct tax which appeared in the
second half of the thirteenth century was the *servicio*. The term can
mean any service, pecuniary or otherwise, and, as a financial exaction,
it was often used of a sum obtained by way of gift and negotiated
directly with individual churches, monasteries or towns. Thus, in
1255 Alfonso X acknowledged that a *servicio* obtained from the bishops
and chapters of León, Burgos, Oviedo, Palencia and possibly other
cathedrals for the repayment of a sum owed by Fernando III to the
papacy was granted by grace and not taken by right, and would not
henceforth be taken by custom or force but only at the donors' good
pleasure.³⁰

So far as we know, the first occasion on which a general *servicio*
or subsidy was granted by the cortes was not until those held at Burgos
in 1269, when six *servicios*, each equal in value to the product of a
moneda, were granted for the defence of the frontier. These were

---

²⁷ *Crónica Alfonso X, caps.* XL, LIV. This demand appears to have been first made
after the dismissal of the cortes, either at the end of 1272 or early in 1273.
²⁸ AGN, *caj.* 3/64; publ. Yanguas, *Diccionario*, III, 42–3.
²⁹ Escalona, *Sahagún, ap.* III, *esc.* CCLXVI.
³⁰ AC León, no. 1092 (16 Oct. 1255); Ballesteros, *Itinerario*, 135–6 (30 Oct. 1255);
   García Larragueta, *Catálogo de los pergaminos de la catedral de Oviedo*, no.
   364 (16 Oct. 1255); Fernández del Pulgar, *Historia de Palencia*, II, 340. Cf.
   Linehan, *The Spanish church and the papacy*, 123, and O'Callaghan, *Traditio*,
   XXVII, 381–2.

agreed to by the nobles on behalf of their vassals – an unprecedented
occurrence since the vassals of the nobles were normally exempt from
royal taxation. This taxation was clearly unpopular. One of the
demands put forward by the nobles in September 1272 was that fewer
than six *servicios* should be collected and that the king should
acknowledge that they were not taken *por fuero*; while Alfonso
refused any concession on the first point, he agreed to the second.
Among the further demands made at the Cortes of Burgos was one
that the *servicios* should not be taken from the vassals of the nobles,
and this also the king was prepared to grant. As we have already seen,
two of the six *servicios* were excused to the king's supporters at the
ayuntamiento of Almagro in 1273, by which time two had been paid.[31]

We next hear of *servicios* in 1274, when Alfonso X was preparing for
an expedition to Italy. The Cortes of Burgos, early in that year, granted
the king a double *servicio* 'for the affair of the Empire', payable in the
current year. During the following months a number of towns and
monasteries were exempted, because of their poverty, from the payment of an annual *servicio*, evidently granted for as long as the king
required it, on condition that they paid the two *servicios* intended for
the imperial venture.[32] In July, at the request of the Infante Don
Fernando, the clergy of the bishopric of León were excused from 'este
servicio que me agora dan que es tanto commo dos monedas'.[33]
In some cases, to meet the fears of the *concejos* for their privileges,
cartas were granted to the effect that neither the king nor his successors would demand such subsidies 'por pecho ni por fuero'.[34] We do
not know when the annual *servicio* mentioned in some of these letters
had been granted. Professor O'Callaghan believes that it was agreed to
by the towns only, during the Cortes of Burgos in 1272, and that the
price paid for it by the king was the restoration and confirmation of the
fueros of the towns.[35] This is a plausible suggestion but, again, there is
no proof.

The three aids granted to Alfonso X in December 1275 were also
equal to a *moneda* each year for three years and were therefore
servicios under another name. In the following July, to meet the doubts

---

[31] *Crónica Alfonso X, caps,* xxiii, xxv; *Cortes,* i, no. xv.
[32] Ballesteros, *Alfonso X, Emperador,* 74–7 (*cartas* of 15, 17, 27 April and 13, 23
   May 1274).
[33] AC León, no. 1121 (2 July 1274).
[34] Ballesteros, *Alfonso X, Emperador,* 77 (28 Aug. 1274), to Alcalá de Henares;
   CD Murcia, i, no. lxiv (16 Oct. 1274, to Murcia).
[35] O'Callaghan, *Traditio,* xxvii, 387. This annual *servicio* was also granted by the
   monasteries. Cf. Ballesteros, *Alfonso X, Emperador,* 74, 76 (17 April, 23 May).

of the bishops, the king promised that when the vassals of the churches had paid these three aids, granted for the war with the Moors, he would not take any further *servicio* without their consent – 'sin su plazer'.[36] The collection of these aids was pushed ahead during the next two years. The first two were both referred to in a grant of 2 October 1276 farming out royal rents and debts; the third was being collected in the summer of 1277, as is shown by a mandate of that time instructing the collectors of the third aid not to exact it from the vassals of the church of Cuenca.[37]

The Cortes of Burgos in May 1277 appears to have granted Alfonso X an annual *servicio* for the rest of his life. The evidence for this consists of a series of *cartas*, addressed to various towns of León, Castile and Extremadura, all of which referred to 'este servicio que nos prometieron de dar cada aña por en toda nuestra vida'. None of these documents refers specifically to any part played by the cortes in connection with the grant, but some of them state that 'good men' were sent to the king at Burgos, where the cortes met. The contents of the letters varies: some promised that the *servicio* would not be held to be customary, nor payable after the king's death; others excused individual towns from *pecho*, or from debts owed to the king in exchange for the subsidy; in others knights or their sons, or clergy, were exempted from payment.[38]

Professor O'Callaghan has suggested that Alfonso X obtained some kind of subsidy or levy from almost every cortes which he summoned.[39] This supposition does not hold good for the early years of Alfonso's reign when, indeed, there is little evidence of grants of taxation by the cortes. Ballesteros thought that a subsidy was granted at Toledo in 1254 but gave no evidence, and it seems probable that the cortes were summoned on that occasion for the sole purpose of doing homage to the

---

[36] *Documentos lingüísticos*, no. 201 (24 July 1276). Ballesteros, *Alfonso X el Sabio*, 793, thought this document referred to subsidies granted in 1276, but it refers specifically to 'las tres ayudas'. O'Callaghan, *Traditio*, XXVII, 390, suggests that the king probably obtained full consent to this levy from the Cortes of Burgos, which he places in May 1276.

[37] Ballesteros, *Alfonso X el Sabio*, 838, cites this document.

[38] *MHE*, I, nos. CXL, CXLI; Colmenares, *Historia de Segovia*, I, 412–13; *CD Cuéllar*, nos. 32, 33; *Fuero de Salamanca*, ed. Sánchez Ruano, xxiv; Minguella, *Historia de Sigüenza*, I, no. 240; Ballesteros, *Alfonso X el Sabio*, 838, also cites and quotes from *cartas* to the *concejos* of Alarcón, Ledesma, Benavente, Oviedo, Ciudad Rodriga, Toro, Alba de Tormes and others. AC León, no. 1126, excused the cathedral clergy from the tax. These documents are of various dates from 20 June to 25 Oct. 1277.

[39] O'Callaghan, *Traditio*, XXVII, 395.

Infanta Doña Berenguela.[40] The double rate for *moneda* for the 'affair of the Empire' may have been sanctioned by the Cortes of Valladolid in 1258, and the Cortes of Seville in 1261 may have granted a subsidy for the 'affair of Africa', but both these suggestions rest on conjecture.[41] From 1269 onwards, however, the picture is very different and there is documentary evidence for a series of subsidies: the six *servicios* granted in 1269 for the defence of the frontier; the annual *servicio* for as long as the king required it, granted some time before 1274 – possibly in the Cortes of Burgos in 1272; the double *servicio* for the imperial venture in 1274; the three aids granted at the end of 1275 for the war against Ibn Yuçef of Morocco and, finally, the annual *servicio* voted in 1277.[42]

On various occasions during his rebellion the Infante Don Sancho obtained grants from his supporters. Some time in 1282, possibly at the Cortes of Valladolid, he was granted *moneda forera*, although it was not due; he was also promised an aid by 'those of Castile' for the sieges of Seville, Badajoz and other towns and castles which still supported his father.[43] At the assembly of Palencia in November 1283 the *hermandad* of the towns also granted him a *servicio* (referred to in a document of 1285) and some accounts for 1284 also contain references to *servicios* promised in Toro and Palencia and to the 'servicio de tierra de Leon'.[44]

Some documents of the early years of Sancho IV's reign contain references to aids and subsidies which do not appear to have been granted by the cortes. Such an aid was imposed to meet the threat of rebellion by the Infante Don Juan which, however, did not materialise. This aid cannot have been agreed to by the cortes as it is mentioned in a *carta* of 3 May 1284, and there is no evidence that the cortes could have met before Sancho IV reached Seville in June.[45] It is possible that we have to do here with a demand made of individual towns and

---

[40] Ballesteros, *Alfonso X el Sabio*, 90–1.
[41] O'Callaghan, *Traditio*, xxvii, 383, 385.
[42] *Crónica Alfonso X, cap.* xviii, states that in 1268 the cortes granted Alfonso two *servicios* annually until the affair of the Empire was completed. This may be an error for the six *servicios* granted in 1269 or for the annual *servicio* for as long as the king required it.
[43] Ballesteros, *BRAH*, cxix, 169 (28 Dec. 1282).
[44] Gaibrois de Ballesteros, *Sancho IV*, iii, no. 83: 'lo servicio que ahermandade derron al Rey don Sancho en palencia quando era Inffante [sic]'. *Ibid.* i, clvii, clxxiii. O'Callaghan, *Traditio*, xxvii, 394, n. 61, suggests that the *servicio* of Toro was granted by the *hermandad* of the towns of León and Galicia which met in Toro in July 1283.
[45] Gaibrois de Ballesteros, *Sancho IV*, iii, no. 1 (3 May 1284).

monasteries. In the following year Sancho IV required money to repel the threatened invasion of Andalusia by Ibn Yuçef of Morocco, and there is some puzzling evidence of *servicios*. The royal accounts for May, June and December 1285 contain references to two *servicios* granted in Burgos. In December, also, one of two *servicios* promised in Seville was excused to the inhabitants of a number of ports on the Atlantic seaboard – Vivero, Puentedeume, Ferrol, Coruña, Pontevedra, Bayona and La Guardia.[46] Sancho IV was in Burgos from 18 March to 25 April and in Seville from 8 September to 27 November.[47] It is possible that selected towns were asked to send representatives to meet the king at these two places and that they undertook to give him financial assistance. The subsidies granted in Seville were also taken from the vassals of the churches of León and Toledo, as references in three writs of 1286 and 1287 indicate.[48] One of these, dated 16 April 1286 and concerned with the collection of the tax from the vassals of the cathedral of León, refers to the subsidies granted in Seville and also to 'estos dos servicios de Castiella e de León' – phrases which suggest that these were general taxes and also hint at the possibility of an otherwise unknown meeting of the cortes in the autumn of 1285. There is, however, no more positive evidence that the cortes met at any time or place during 1285.

With the Cortes of Haro in 1288 we are on surer ground. There the king was granted an annual *servicio* for ten years in return for a general remission of all the debts to the crown which had been farmed out to the Catalan Jew, Abrahem el Barchilón.[49] These *servicios* were collected expeditiously. The first five were taken between 1288 and 1292; the sixth was in process of collection in May 1293 and was used for Sancho IV's successful siege of Tarifa.[50] The seventh and eighth *servicios* were both collected in 1294.[51] Additional extraordinary taxation, however, became necessary and before this, in 1292, an aid had been granted in Zamora for the expenses of the siege of Tarifa by some, possibly all, the cities of the kingdom of León. We do not know how the grant was made.[52]

---

[46] *Ibid.* I, clxii, clxiii, clxvii.
[47] *Ibid.* III, nos. 53–72, 85–98.
[48] *Ibid.* III, nos. 108 (16 April 1286), 117 (15 June 1286), 156 (26 April 1287).
[49] *Cortes,* I, no. XVIII, preamble.
[50] Gaibros de Ballesteros, *BRAH,* LXXVI, 422, no. 3.
[51] See Gaibrois de Ballesteros, *Sancho IV,* I, xxx, xxxvii, li, lv, lxiii, lxvi, lxix, lxxi, lxxxvii–lxxxviii, for references to 'el servicio seteno' and 'el servicio ochavo' in the *cuentas* for 1294.
[52] *Ibid.* I, lxxx. Sancho IV was in Zamora from 15 to 20 April 1292.

Originally both *moneda* and *servicio* had been capitation taxes of 1 *maravedí per capita*, but by the end of the thirteenth century they had both become taxes on moveables. Thus, the aid for three years granted at Alcalá in 1275 was at the rate of 10 *sueldos* on every 10 *maravedíes*.[53] The annual *servicio* granted for the rest of Alfonso X's reign in 1277, however, was a fixed capitation tax taken at the rate of $5\frac{1}{2}$ *maravedíes* in the depreciated *moneda de la guerra*.[54] This was regarded as a retrograde step and the decrees of the Cortes of Palencia in 1286, to restore the situation, laid down that both *moneda* and *servicio* were taxes on moveables and the rate of tax was fixed at a tenth.[55] At the Cortes of Haro in 1288, at the request of the *concejos*, Sancho IV confirmed that the ten *servicios* there granted to him were to be taken at the same rate as *moneda* and not *per capita*, and that new assessments were to be made each year.[56]

Other taxes

Besides the general *servicio*, there were other forms of taxation which appeared in the thirteenth century. Of these, most important were the *servicios de los ganados* and the customs duties on imports and exports known as the *diezmos de los puertos*. The *servicio de los ganados* was a royal tax on all flocks and herds, distinct from, and in addition to, the *montazgo*, which was a local tax levied by religious orders, lay lords and *concejos* for the use of their *montes*, and for the passage through their lands of migratory flocks. The *servicio de los ganados* is said to have been granted originally by the cortes and to date from *circa* 1270. A royal document of that year was addressed to the collectors of it in the kingdom of León.[57] There is, however, little evidence that it was granted by the cortes. In the autumn of 1276 Alfonso X farmed out a number of taxes, impositions and debts due to the crown to five money-lenders. Two of these separate contracts (*cartas de arrendamiento*) made reference to the *servicios de los ganados*. One, dated 9 October 1276, included this tax among a number of taxes farmed out for the next two years. Another, dated 13 October, farmed out debts which had accrued to the king from the time of the siege of Niebla (1262); among these were 'el servicio de los ganados que fué demandado por

---

[53] Ballesteros, *BRAH*, cxix, 118–19.
[54] *MHE*, i, no. cxli.
[55] *Cortes*, i, no. xvii, cls. 10, 13.
[56] *Ibid.* i, no. xviii, cl. 20.
[57] *Colección de privilegios de la Corona de Castilla*, vi, no. cclviii, 117–18. Cf. Klein, *Mesta*, 256; G[arcía] de Valdeavellano, *Instituciones españolas*, 269, 606.

toda la tierra pora las bodas del Infante don Fernando' and also 'el servicio de los ganados que vos dieron los pastores de toda la tierra despues que Don Alfonso García lo dejo fasta este Sant Johan que agora paso'.[58] These references must relate to two separate impositions. The one, for the wedding of the Infante Don Fernando, appears to be an extraordinary tax for a special purpose – the marriage expenses – and it may well have been granted by the cortes which met in November 1269 at Burgos. The other was an annual payment which had already been farmed out at an earlier period, and there is nothing to connect it with any particular meeting of the cortes. It was probably the tax referred to in 1270; the flocks of the monastery of Oña were exempted from it in 1272.[59] In 1287 it was described as one of the taxes farmed out by Sancho IV to Abrahem el Barchilón.[60] One concession relating to it was obtained by the cortes. In the Cortes of Valladolid in 1293, at the petition of the *concejos* of León and Extremadura, non-migratory flocks (*estantes*), mainly those belonging to sheep-owners in the west and south of the country, where pasture was available throughout the year, were exempted from the *servicio*, which thereafter became a tax levied only on migratory flocks.[61]

The *diezmos de los puertos* were closely connected with a system by which the export of certain articles was forbidden. These prohibitions were in force under Alfonso VIII and Fernando III, so that it is probable that import and export duties originated in Castile early in the thirteenth century. Clauses referring to prohibited exports occurred in all Alfonso X's economic codes. The *cuadernos* of 1252 and 1253 thus laid down that the export of horses, mules (except those used to carry merchandise), skins and hides, grain, rope, mercury and all the articles whose export had been forbidden by Alfonso VIII and Fernando III was to remain prohibited. These earlier ordinances have not survived, but it is probable that they were occasioned by the Moorish wars, as most of the specified articles had military uses. Another clause in the *cuadernos* prohibited the export of cattle, pigs and goats. In all cases the penalty was double the value of the articles exported plus a fine of 1,000 *maravedíes* – the largest pecuniary penalty laid down in these *cuadernos*.[62] In 1258 similar prohibitions

---

[58] *MHE*, I, 308–10; 314–20, both inserted in no. CXL (20 June 1277).
[59] *CD Oña*, II, no. 604 (1 Aug. 1272): 'nin el servicio que yo deuo auer de los ganados'.
[60] Gaibrois de Ballesteros, *Sancho IV*, I, clxxxv.
[61] *Cortes*, I, no. XX, cl. 8; cf. Klein, *Mesta*, 258–9.
[62] García Rámila, *Hispania*, V, 212–13, cls. 19, 20, and Appendix, doc. IV, below.

were reimposed at the express petition of the *concejos* and it was provided that anyone who connived at such exportation should suffer the loss of lands held from the king.[63] In the *cuaderno* of 1261 the prohibition of the export of horses and other livestock was limited to ten years.[64]

In 1268 the system was reorganised and much more detailed regulations concerning imports and exports were included in the *cuaderno* of the Cortes of Jerez of that year. Because the country had need of gold, silver, copper and cloth from abroad, merchants importing these commodities were allowed to export merchandise to the same value, except gold, silver, horses, cattle and other livestock, silk, flax, grain, wine or foodstuffs, hawks or falcons. If anyone was found exporting such commodities, he was to be seized and held at the nearest town, until the king's pleasure concerning him was known. The names of authorised ports through which goods could be imported or exported were given as were, in most cases, the names of the customs officials who superintended the loading and unloading of merchandise in them. The duties of such officials were also described in detail: they had to check the amount of goods and make sure that it corresponded with the amounts given in the *cartas* of those who were sureties (*fiedores*) for the merchants. They also had to check that the value of imports and exports tallied. When the ships' masters were foreigners, the laws of the kingdom governing imports and exports must be explained to them. Most of the ports named were those on the Galician and Biscayan coasts – from Túy on the Portuguese frontier to Fuenterrabía on the border with France – eighteen ports in all. The Andalusian ports named were Huelva, Cádiz, Vejer, Seville and Jerez, and those in the kingdom of Murcia were Elche, Cartagena and Alicante.[65] Customs posts on the land frontiers with Navarre, Aragon and Portugal were not included in the *cuaderno*. It should be noted that these decrees regulated the collection of the *diezmos*, but not their imposition, which was a matter for the king. Occasionally exemption from payment of the *diezmos de los puertos* was granted. Thus, in 1271 Alfonso X, then residing in the city of Murcia, granted to the *vecinos* of the city that merchandise brought into Murcia for sale there, either by native or by foreign merchants, was to be exempted from payment of the *diezmos*.[66]

---

[63] *Cortes*, I, no. XIII, cl. 12.

[64] Rodríguez Díez, *Historia de Astorga*, 717: 'Otrossi pusiemos que ninguno non saque cavallos nin ganados de nuestros regnos fasta diez annos.'

[65] *Cortes*, I, no. XIV, cls. 21–5. Cl. 21 is imperfect at the beginning, but some of the missing places are supplied in cl. 22, which gives the names of the port officials.

[66] *CD Murcia*, I, no. XLIV (30 April 1271).

One of the additional demands put forward by the nobles at the Cortes of Burgos in 1272 was that the king should give up the *diezmos de los puertos*. This request was put forward on several occasions during the course of the negotiations between the king and the rebels after the end of the cortes, and it was also included in the manifesto presented by Don Juan Núñez to Enrique I of Navarre.[67] At the *ayuntamiento* of Almagro Alfonso X promised to surrender the customs duties after six years, athough he protested his right to exact them.[68]

This undertaking was not kept, for there are references to customs on exports and imports during the last years of the reign and under Sancho IV. Thus, the privilege granted to foreign and native merchants in 1281 laid down, among other matters, that the *diezmos* were to be paid at the port of embarkation or disembarkation, that no further demands for import duties were to be made to those merchants who produced the quittance (*carta de pagamiento*) given them at the port, nor were duties to be levied on objects of personal use.[69] On the same occasion foreign merchants and the merchants of Burgos, Castro Urdiales, Laredo, Santander, Aguilar, Vitoria and Medina de Pomar compounded (for a sum of 100,000 *maravedíes* in the coinage minted during the first war with Granada plus 1,000 *maravedíes* chancery fee) the fines and penalties they had incurred on account of frauds and evasions concerned with customs duties and exports. These crimes had been brought to light by an inquiry carried out in the northern ports from Vicente de la Barquera to Fuenterrabía.[70] Customs duties for two years were also included in the royal revenues farmed out to Abrahem el Barchilón by Sancho IV in 1287.[71] In 1290 Sancho granted a safe-conduct to foreign merchants crossing Castilian territory on their way from the port of Fuenterrabía to the kingdom of Navarre as well as a licence to buy or sell in Castile on their way to and from the Navarrese frontier, provided that they paid the *diezmos*.[72] The royal accounts for the year 1294 include the customs collected at the Biscayan ports as well as those collected at the inland customs posts along the Portu-

---

[67] *Crónica Alfonso X, cap.* xxv (p. 22); *cap.* xl (pp. 30–1); *caps.* liv–lv (pp. 42–3). AGN, *caj.* 3/64.
[68] *Crónica Alfonso X, cap.* xlvii (p. 35); *cap.* lv (p. 43). *Cortes,* i, no. xv (pp. 85–6).
[69] *MHE,* ii, no. clxxix (p. 29) (13 Feb. 1281).
[70] BL, Add. MS. 9916, fols. 382–5 (15 Feb. 1281).
[71] Gaibrois de Ballesteros, *Sancho IV,* i, clxxxix.
[72] AM Pamplona, *caj.* A, no. 17 (1 Dec. 1290), inserted in *carta* of 8 May 1291; publ. Appendix, doc. ix, below.

guese frontier.[73] So much for the undertaking extracted from the crown in 1272.

Tax farming

Although the consent of the cortes was necessary for the imposition of a general *servicio*, their control over such taxes was far from complete. The practice of granting *servicios* for a number of years or for the king's lifetime obviously weakened the position of the cortes. When once the *servicio* had been granted the cortes had no control over its use. Nor had they any real control over its collection. It was, of course, common practice to farm out taxes and other royal revenues, and this practice was indulged in at all levels – from the king down to the local tax collectors. The two most notorious examples of the farming of the royal revenue in the thirteenth century took place in 1276 and 1287. In the former year Alfonso X entered into a series of agreements, dated from Vitoria on various dates from 2 October 1276 to 3 January 1277, with a number of mostly Jewish individuals. These were Isaac de la Malea (the Don Zag of contemporary documents), at that time the king's treasurer (*almojarife mayor*), Isaac and Yuçef, the sons of Don Mayer (a former king's treasurer), Abraham Ibn Yugen and Roy Fernández of Sahagún. Most of the royal revenues were farmed out to them. Those so leased included the *servicios de los ganados*, fines incurred for trespass of flocks on enclosed pastures, for misuse of the sheep walks and for the manslaughter of shepherds and *pechos* or customary payments for the whole kingdom except Andalusia and Murcia, described as outstanding since the date of the capture of Niebla (1262) – an item which throws light on the difficulty of collecting customary payments. The payments so farmed included *fonsadera*, *martiniega* and *pedido* but excluded the revenues from the royal monopolies of coinage, salt, iron and mines, which were already farmed out. Also included were the *tercias reales* and a long list of fines owed to the king, such as those incurred by knights of the towns who took the king's wages to join the host, but either did not go or went insufficiently armed, by royal officials who took *yantar* or other payments unlawfully or by merchants who exported goods the export of which was forbidden.[74]

---

[73] Gaibrois de Ballesteros, *Sancho IV*, I, xxii, xl–xli, xliii–xlv.
[74] *MHE*, I, no. CXL (pp. 308–24). Five *cartas de arrendamiento* of 2, 9, 13 Oct., 18 Dec. 1276, 3 Jan. 1277, inserted in a *carta* of 20 June 1277 to the *concejo* of Aguilar de Campóo. Cf. O'Callaghan, *Traditio*, XXVI, 390–1.

The farm of the revenues in 1287 to Abrahem el Barchilón was also far-reaching. It, too, comprised the *servicio de los ganados* and the customs duties on imports and exports as well as a large number of other revenues: the profits from the coinage, including the right to mint gold coins in the kingdoms of León, Castile, Andalusia and Murcia; the special taxes paid by the Jews; the possessions of those who died without heirs; fines for exporting prohibited goods; the rents of the chancery; profits arising from the royal monopolies of mercury, iron and salt; fines imposed after inquiries into the conduct of royal officials; and other outstanding debts to the crown. In most cases the period of the farm was for two years, either from January or May 1287. The contract also referred to earlier farms of some of these items made to Don Lope Díaz, to Fernan Pérez, archbishop-elect of Seville, and to others.[75]

Under Sancho IV the cortes made various attempts to limit the classes of persons who might be appointed by the king to collect dues and taxes. The Cortes of Palencia in 1286 thus decreed that tax collectors were to be good men of the towns, who were neither *alcaldes* nor other office-holders.[76] At the Cortes of Haro in 1288 the king, at the express request of the *concejos*, agreed to appoint good and suitable persons to collect taxes, and *not* to appoint Jews either as collectors at any level, or as tax farmers.[77] At the Cortes of Valladolid in 1293 the *concejos* of Castile petitioned that nobles, knights, *alcaldes* and *merinos* should not be tax collectors or farmers in their own districts; that collectors must be men resident in the principal town of the *merindad*; that rents were not to be farmed out; that collectors should be given a quittance when they paid in sums collected.[78] On the same occasion the *concejos* of Extremadura, for their part, petitioned that all taxes should be collected by the appointed tax collectors, who should not farm them out, and that the collectors should be good men and natives of the towns.[79] Both petitions were acceded to, but with little permanent effect.

Additional sources of revenue

The king had other means by which he could obtain additional revenue.

[75] Publ. Gaibrois de Ballesteros, *Sancho IV*, I, clxxxv–ix.
[76] *Cortes*, I, no. XVII, cl. 10.
[77] *Ibid.* I, no. XVIII, cls. 20, 21.
[78] *Ibid.* I, no. XIX, cl. 9.
[79] *DA Madrid*, 1a serie, I, 143.

One such was by extraction of forced loans or 'gifts' from individual towns. In 1248, during the siege of Seville, Fernando III sent his *portero* (messenger) with royal letters to the towns of Galicia, including the ecclesiastical towns of Santiago, Orense, Túy and Lugo, demanding a loan from the inhabitants, based on the value of their property both in land and moveables. The amount of the loan was fixed at 50 *maravedíes* on every 1,000 *maravedíes*, 25 on every 500 and 15 on every 300 *maravedíes* – that is, a loan of 5 per cent. Those whose property was less than 300 *maravedíes* in value were exempt. The king argued his pressing need for funds to achieve the capture of Seville and undertook to repay the loans when he next levied *moneda*; the loans were enforced by fines on those who refused to pay.[80]

In the early years of his reign Alfonso X also exacted *empréstitos* (forced loans) from individual towns. Thus, he took enforced gifts from Burgos and Valladolid in 1255, but promised that they should not be obliged to make grants against their will in future.[81] Similar promises were made to Salamanca on 7 April 1256 and to the merchants of Ribadavia on 30 June 1256. The king also exacted 1,000 *maravedíes* from the *concejo* of Oviedo for the expenses of the fleet which took part in the capture of Cádiz in 1262.[82] During the later years of the reign, when Alfonso was obtaining general subsidies and aids granted by the cortes, he no longer resorted to the expedient of demanding forced loans and gifts from individual towns.

The main source of additional revenue was, however, the church, and it was the church which paid most of the expenses of the wars against the Moors. In 1236 Gregory IX ordered the Castilian bishops to aid Fernando III in the siege of Córdoba with an annual grant of 20,000 *áureos* for three years.[83] In 1247 Innocent IV made the first papal grant to the king of a portion of the ecclesiastical *tercias*, again for a period of three years.[84] In spite of papal remonstrances, Alfonso X continued to take this tax, as though it were a customary payment,

[80] Grassotti, 'Un empréstito para la conquista de Sevilla', *CHE*, xv–xvi, 191–247. The text of Fernando III's letter is printed on pp. 202–4.
[81] *MHE*, I, no. xxxiii (Palencia, 18 June 1255); Ballesteros, *Itinerario*, 138 (Burgos, 6 Nov. 1255). O'Callaghan, *Traditio*, xxvii, 381 says that Alfonso 'apparently made this pledge in a cortes at Valladolid' but gives no reference; Alfonso was at Valladolid from 3 July to 21 October 1255, but there is no evidence that the cortes met there.
[82] *Fuero de Salamanca*, ed Sánchez Ruano, xx (7 April 1256); Ballesteros, *Itinerario*, 158 (30 June 1256), and *BRAH*, cvii, 414.
[83] *Registres de Grégoire IX*, II, no. 3315.
[84] *Registres d'Innocent IV*, I, no. 2538 (15 April 1247).

without specific papal grant.[85] He referred to it in a *carta* of 1265 as 'la nuestra tercia de los diezmos que nos auemos e deuiemos auer en las eglesias de Ossuna e de todo su termino', and the tax soon became known as *las tercias reales*.[86] Wars against the Moors were, of course, regarded as crusades, and it was therefore generally possible to obtain from the papacy grants of crusading tenths, and the privileges of crusaders for those who took part. Such grants were made by Innocent IV to Fernando III in 1246 and to Alfonso X by Alexander IV in 1259, and, in 1264, Alfonso made use of these by then expired bulls at the time of the revolt of the Moors of Andalusia.[87] In the following year Clement IV granted Alfonso X a tenth of clerical revenues for five years and this was again granted for six years in 1275 by Gregory X.[88] This spoliation of the church was continued under Sancho IV, especially during the last four years of the reign. In 1291 the king assembled the bishops of his kingdom at Medina del Campo and there asked for 'servicio e ayuda' for his projected siege of Algeciras. In the following years when Tarifa was substituted for Algeciras as the prime Christian objective, 35,000 *maravedies* were obtained from the sees of Palencia, Burgos and Calahorra and the total receipts from the church towards the campaign amounted to 800,000 *maravedies*.[89] As long as the king could drain the Castilian church of its wealth to such an extent, the financial control exercised by the cortes was bound to be intermittent and ineffectual.

[85] On the *tercias reales*, see Mansilla Reoyo, *Iglesia castellano–leonesa*, 56–8; Lineham, *The Spanish church and the papacy*, 111–12.
[86] AHN, Calatrava, R. 114 (30 Dec. 1264).
[87] *Registres d'Innocent IV*, I, no. 1832; *Registres d'Alexandre IV*, III, no. 862; Minguella, *Historia de Sigüenza*, I, 599–601; Ballesteros, *Alfonso X el Sabio*, 371.
[88] *Registres de Clément IV*, no. 16; *Registres de Grégoire X*, II, no. 838.
[89] *Crónica Sancho IV*, cap. VIII; Gaibrois de Ballesteros, *BRAH*, LXXVI, 75, 431, 432; Lineham, *The Spanish church and the papacy*, 243, n.3.

IO

The cortes and legislation

The first *título* of the first book of the *Espéculo* is headed 'De las leyes' and defines the nature of law. In thirteen short *leyes* it deals with such subjects as who had power to make laws, why they were called laws and how they should be obeyed. The compilers' theory of legislation was derived from Roman law, and it envisaged the king as the sole source of legislation: 'Ninguno non puede facer leyes sinon emperador o rey o otro por su mandamiento dellos. E si otros las fezieren sin su mandado non deven aver nombre leyes nin deben seer obedecidas nin guardadas por leyes nin deven valer en ningun tiempo.'[1] The last *ley* of this title was written in the first person and elaborated the grounds on which Alfonso X claimed the right to make, and add to or delete from, or change laws.[2] The obligations and responsibilities of kings were, however, recognised. It was also stressed that all men, and especially the king, must obey the law.[3] The whole of this title as it appears in the *Espéculo* was retained, with only slight verbal alterations, in the version of the *Primera partida* contained in the British Library manuscript.[4] In the version in most of the other manuscripts of the *Partidas*, and in the printed editions, however, this conception of the king as legislator is modified. In them his sole right to make laws is asserted, but other laws are included which somewhat limit his legislative rights. If laws needed to be amended, the king must take counsel 'con homes buenos, entendudos et sabidores del derecho'; laws could be rescinded, but only 'con grant consejo de todos los homes buenos de la tierra, los mas buenos et honrados et mas sabidores' and, if it were necessary to add to the law, then again 'debe ayuntar el rey homes sabidores et entendudos para escoger el derecho, porque se acuerde conellos en qué manera deben

---

[1] *Espéculo, lib.* I, *tít.* I, *ley* 3.
[2] *Ibid. lib.* I, *tít.* I, *ley* 13.
[3] *Ibid.* I, *tít.* I, *ley* 9: 'Todos los omes deven seer tenidos de obedecer las leyes, e mayormiente los reyes.'
[4] BL, Add. MS. 20787, fols. 1–2, ed. Arias Bonet, 5–10.

ende facer ley'.[5] A title defining use, custom and *fuero* is also included.[6] It is noticeable that there is no specific reference to the cortes in any of these laws; those with whom the king must consult are the *sabidores del derecho*. But the reference is at any rate clear that the king cannot alter existing law without advice. Sancho IV's chancery, however, occasionally made use in grants of phrases which seem to claim for the king the right to make, add to or amend the law: 'Sauida cosa es quelos Reyes e los emperadores son sennores e façedores de Leyes e las pueden fazer de nueuo e acreçentar las e hemendar las alli do entendieren que las deuen acrecentar e emendar.'[7] Yet, in spite of the *Espéculo*'s enunciation of the theory that the king was the sole legislator, legislation was certainly one of the functions of the cortes during the second half of the thirteenth century, although not all legislation was promulgated in the cortes. It is with the intervention of the cortes in legislation that we must now deal.

In the first half of the fourteenth century, two different kinds of legislation were transacted in the cortes and included in the *cuadernos*. Firstly, there were ordinances emanating from the king and his council which were promulgated in cortes, such as the *Ordenamiento de Alcalá* of 1348. Secondly, there were collective petitions presented by the cortes as a whole, or by one of the 'estates' which, in so far as they were accepted by the king, then had the force of law. At times one legislative act might comprise both these kinds of legislation. In the earlier ordinance of 1312, the first seventy-eight clauses dealt with the reorganisation of central and local administration, particularly with the central court of justice, and the chancery; the last twenty-seven clauses took the form of petitions of the knights and good men of the towns, and dealt mainly with the maladministration of royal officials, financial exactions and oppression by the nobles.[8] On the other hand, at Alcalá, the ordinance and the collective petitions were conserved as separate legislative acts.[9] These collective petitions were at times petitions of the whole cortes, as in 1318,[10] but the majority of them emanated from one or other 'estate' or order. Thus, the bishops and abbots petitioned the crown in the Cortes of Burgos in 1315 and in the Cortes of Valladolid in 1325, and the abbots for themselves and the abbesses petitioned in

[5] *Part.* i, *tít.* i, *leyes* 17, 18, 19.
[6] *Ibid. tít.* ii.
[7] Gaibrois de Ballesteros, *Sancho IV*, iii, nos. 287, 295 (21 Jan.; 6 March 1290).
[8] *Cortes*, i, no. xxxv.
[9] *Ibid.* i, nos. lii, liii.
[10] *Ibid.* i, no. xlii (1318).

1322 at Valladolid.[11] By far the largest number of these petitions were, however, presented by the proctors of the cities and towns, either for the whole kingdom, as in 1307, 1317, 1325 and 1348,[12] or for the individual provinces, as in 1305 at Medina del Campo, when the towns of León, Castile and Extremadura presented separate petitions.[13] All these petitions were drawn up in a common form. Each clause began with the formula 'A lo que me pidieron [or 'dixieron']', or some such phrase, while the answer of the king or the regents, as the case might be, always began 'Tengo [or 'Tenemos'] por bien'.

The right to petition the king was an ancient right and one often exercised by corporate bodies in the twelfth and thirteenth centuries and with growing frequency by the towns. Petitions might be presented to the king when he visited a town or locality, and might be considered and answered on the spot or later, depending on the length and complexity of the petition and the pressure of other business on the king.[14] Petitions were sometimes presented when a town militia served in the army.[15] At other times, towns sent their representatives to the king with written or verbal petitions on various matters.[16]

Such petitions frequently dealt with town government. Alfonso X's reply to the petitions of the *concejo* of Sepúlveda in 1257 began with a short summary of the requests made to him when he had visited the town and then gave his answer to each request. These had dealt with such things as the office of *almotacén*, with the inspection of weights and measures and fines for possessing false weights, with fees due to the public notary of the town for contracts with Jews and with various regulations concerned with the repayment of debts to the Jews. An undated document addressed to the *concejo* of Medina del Campo has survived in the form of five additional laws to be added to the town *fueros* but it is, in fact, clearly the royal reply to a series of petitions made to the king by the proctors of the town ('por uestros procuradores'), which had concerned such subjects as the number and method of

---

[11] *Ibid.* I, nos. XL (1315), XLVI (1325), XLIV (1322).
[12] *Ibid.* I, nos. XXXIV (1307), XLI (1317), XLV (1325), LIII (1348).
[13] *Ibid.* I, nos. XXXI, XXXII, XXXIII.
[14] Ballesteros, *Itinerario*, 184 (16 Oct. 1257): 'viniemos a la villa de Sepuluega el conceio uinieron ante nos e dixieron'. The date of Alfonso's visit to Sepúlveda is not known.
[15] Ballesteros, *BRAH*, CIX, 381 (22 June 1265): 'Sepades que los caualleros e los omnes bonos del conceio [de Ciudad Rodrigo] que uenieron en mio seruicio a la Hueste de Granada me pidieron merced que...'
[16] E.g. *MHE*, I, no. XLVI (p. 101) (7 Aug. 1256); Ballesteros, *BRAH*, CVII, 59 (31 July 1262); CIX, 415 (12 April 1266), etc.

appointment of the *alcades* and the *alguacil* of the town, penalties for wounding and homicide, the times of meetings of the *concejo*, the holding of town pleas and the tolls to be paid for flocks passing through the lands of the town; the characteristic petition formula 'a lo que nos pidiestes...tenemos por bien.' is retained in the document in most cases.[17] This petition has survived only in the Escorial Library in a fourteenth-century mansucript, which seems at some time to have belonged to the *concejo* of Medina del Campo, since it includes a list of the *alguaciles* of Medina.[18] The rearrangement into *leyes* was probably made when the petitions and answers, taken from the original royal document, were transcribed into this manuscript, at which time the initial and final protocols of Alfonso's *carta* were suppressed. *Ley* 1 corresponds to the preamble, while *leyes* 2 and 5 each consist of two distinct petitions and answers. An important privilege of Alfonso X to Murcia, confirming earlier privileges and granting new ones, appears similarly to be based on a petition.[19]

The summoning of the representatives from the towns on royal demesne to the cortes gave those towns, of course, an additional opportunity to present petitions. In the fourteenth century petitions presented by, or granted to, individual towns, when the cortes were in session, generally referred specifically to this fact.[20] In the reign of Alfonso X such references were not included but at the end of Sancho IV's reign they appear in some answers to petitions from the *concejo* of León, presented in the Cortes of Valladolid in 1293; for example, 'Sepades quelos procuradores que uos embiastes a mi a estas cortes que yo agora fiz en Valladolit me mostraron'.[21] As we rarely know the exact dates for the assembling or dismissal of the cortes for Alfonso's reign, it is only when there is a clear correspondence in date of a petition with a document, such as a *cuaderno*, which we know was granted in cortes, that we can say definitely that such and such a petition was presented while the cortes were assembled. For example, we know that the cortes for the province of Extremadura were in session in April 1264, and that the *cuadernos* granted to Peñafiel and Cuéllar were

---

[17] Publ. Muedra Benedito, *AHDE*, v, 448–50.
[18] Zarco Cuevas, *Catálogo de los manuscritos castellanos en la Real Biblioteca de El Escorial*, III, 140, MS. Z, III, 2, items 3, 4.
[19] *CD Murcia*, I, no. XXXI (18 May 1267).
[20] *Memorias de Fernando IV*, II, nos. CCXI, CCLXXI, CCCXXX, CCCXXXI, etc.; BL, Add. Charter 12766 (4 Dec. 1307), answer to petition presented in the Cortes of Valladolid June 1307: 'Porque el Conçeio de Saluatierra de Alava nos embiaron mostrar por sus perssonersos a estas cortes que agora fiçiemos en Valladolit'.
[21] Gaibrois de Ballesteros, *Sancho IV*, III, nos. 471, 472; *BRAH*, LXXVI, 422, no. 3.

dated 15 and 29 April 1264. On 8 April Alfonso X granted a petition from the *concejo* of Escalona which dealt exclusively with the administration of that town.[22]

It cannot have taken long for the representatives to realise that some of the individual petitions and grievances were common to a number of, or to all, the towns, and that collective petitions, presented by all the towns of the kingdom, or of a province, stood a better chance of favourable consideration than one presented on behalf of a single town. Further, such a procedure facilitated the work of considering and answering petitions and was, therefore, acceptable to the king and his advisers. The towns soon realised, too, the advantage of collective petitions, drawn up in a positive form which the king could either grant or reject, over the mere statement of general grievances, such as complaints about a scarcity of consumer goods, which left remedies to be devised by the king and the *corte*.

How far had this pattern of collective petition developed before the death of Sancho IV? *Cuadernos* have survived for nine assemblies between 1250 and 1295: those for 1250, 1252/3, 1258, 1261, 1264, 1268, 1286, 1288 and 1293. Of these, the *cuaderno* granted to the towns of Extremadura in the Cortes of Seville of April 1264 and the separate *cuadernos* granted to the towns of León, Castile and Extremadura in the Cortes of Valladolid in 1293 are all in the form of collective petitions. The formulas used in them already approximate to those used in the fourteenth century. Thus, in 1264 the different clauses begin with such phrases as: 'De los que Nos mostraron', 'Otrossi de los que nos dixeron', 'Et de lo que nos pidieron merced', while the king's replies begin either 'Tenemos por bien', 'Mandamos', or 'Tenemos por bien e mandamos'.[23] The formulas used in similar situations in the *cuadernos* of the cortes of 1293 are more regular than those used in 1264; in most cases 'otrossi alo que nos pidieron...tenemos por bien que' is used.[24] The preambles of the three sets of petitions of 1293 are identical, and they throw light on the way in which such petitions were drawn up. They state that the king ordered the representatives to make known their grievances to him, and that they then consulted together and showed him all the matters in which they held themselves to be aggrieved. The form of the petitions from the towns of Castile differs considerably from those of León and Extremadura, although there are

---

[22] *MHE*, I, no. xcvi.
[23] BL, Add. MS. 9916, fols. 250–9; publ. Appendix, doc. vii, below.
[24] *Cortes*, I, nos. xix, xx; *DA Madrid, 1a series*, 139–55.

some clauses in common. Most of the petitions originating in León and Extremadura are identical, but here, too, there are a certain number of clauses which appear in one or other set of petitions only. During the minority of Fernando IV, from 1295 to 1301, only two of the numerous legislative enactments which survive are collective petitions presented by the towns – those of the towns of the kingdom of León, granted in the Cortes of Valladolid in 1299, in which the presentation of the petition is referred to in the preamble and in which each clause begins 'Otrossi me pidieron', and those granted to the towns of León in the Cortes of Zamora held in the summer of 1301, in which each clause begins 'Otrosí alo que me pedieron [or 'dizen']'.[25] In the decrees issued at the Cortes of Burgos held earlier in the same year, for the kingdom of Castile, this formula was also used in some clauses but most of them begin 'Otrosí mando', or 'Otrossi tengo por bien'; despite this they may, however, also have been based on a collective petition.[26] After 1302 this form was frequently used.[27] Thus, although the collective petition was used by the towns in the second half of the thirteenth century, it was not until the personal rule of Fernando IV that it became a frequent and normal form of legislation.

There is evidence that some of the other *cuadernos* of the thirteenth century, although not written in the forms associated with collective petitions, were nevertheless based, at least in part, on petitions from the towns. In the *cuadernos* of the Cortes of Valladolid of 1258, three clauses, for example, begin 'Otrossi piden merced al Rey'.[28] In the *cuaderno* of 1268 the first clause, which confirmed the *moneda de la guerra* for Alfonso X's lifetime, ends: 'E yo touelo por bien. Et otorgolo que sea asi.'[29] In 1288 two clauses, which laid down that *servicios* were not to be farmed out and that Jews were not to be tax collectors or tax farmers, stated that Sancho IV ordained this 'porque nos lo pidieron por merced'.[30]

The preambles of the various *cuadernos* also usually testify specifically to the part played in legislation by the representatives of the towns. That of 1250 shows clearly that the clauses in it confirming the *fueros* of the towns and restoring to them their alienated villages were

---

25 *Cortes*, I, nos. XXVI, XXVIII.
26 *Ibid.* I, no. XXVII.
27 *Ibid.* I, nos. XXIX (1302), XXXI (1305), XXXII (1305), XXXIII (1305), XXXIV (1307), XXXV, cls. 79–105 (1312), etc.
28 *Ibid.* I, no. XIII, cls. 12, 21, 28.
29 *Ibid.* I, no. XIV, cl. 1.
30 *Ibid.* I, no. XVIII, cls. 20, 21.

granted in response to a direct request: 'rogaron me e pidieron me merced por su villa que les touiesse a aquellos fueros e a aquella uida e a aquellos usos que ouieran en tiempo del rey don Alfonso mio auuelo e a su muerte'.[31] In the preambles of the *cuadernos* of 1252 and 1253 it is stated that the representatives had shown the king that certain enactments (*posturas*) of Alfonso VIII and Fernando III had not been kept as well as that the people were suffering from a scarcity of consumer goods accordingly. Alfonso, with the advice of those assembled, had granted the decrees contained in the *cuadernos* to remedy these grievances.[32] In 1258 the decrees themselves appear, perhaps, to have been drawn up by the assembly and then approved by the king: 'e lo que ellos pusieron otorgué yo de lo tener e de lo fazer tener e guardar por todos mis Regnos'.[33] These decrees also differ from those promulgated in other cortes in that, except in the preamble and the last clause, the king is elsewhere referred to in the third person. The clauses begin in different ways either with the plural 'Touieron [or 'Tienen'] por bien', or 'Manda el Rey', or simply 'Otrossí que'. Again, in 1268 it is clear from the preamble that the decrees were a reply to complaints from the towns about the continuing scarcity of consumer goods.[34] Sancho IV, at the Cortes of Palencia in December 1286, asked the representatives for a statement of their grievances and they consulted together before replying to him.[35] This was the same procedure as was followed at Valladolid in 1293, when the resulting legislation took the form of collective petitions. These collective petitions presented to the king in cortes can be compared to the commons' petitions of the English parliament. The Castilian petitions appeared rather earlier than the commons' petitions but they never developed into bills as they did in England.[36]

Of the nine codes promulgated in the cortes between 1250 and 1295, the earliest, that of Fernando III in 1250, stands somewhat apart from the rest, but some of its decrees were re-enacted or appeared in a slightly different form later. Four of Alfonso X's five codes – those of 1252/3, 1258, 1261 and 1268 – were predominantly economic in purpose and form a distinct group; the fifth, that of 1264, has little contact with the other legislation of the cortes during this period.

[31] *Fuero de Cuenca*, 859; also Appendix, doc. III, below.
[32] García Rámila, *Hispania*, v, 205; Appendix, doc. IV, preamble, below.
[33] *Cortes*, I, no. XIII.
[34] *Ibid.* I, no. XIV.
[35] *Ibid.* I, no. XVII.
[36] Gray, *The influence of the Commons on early legislation*, 201–26.

Of Sancho IV's three codes, that of 1288 was almost entirely financial, and those of 1286 and 1293 dealt mainly with administration. The decrees of 1264 can most appropriately be analysed first, separately from the rest, both because of the nature of the subject matter and also because modern historians have relied on the account of them given in the *Crónica de Alfonso X* which is both inaccurate and misleading, as will appear from a comparison of the *Crónica*'s narrative with the *cuaderno*.[37]

The *Crónica* has misdated the outbreak of the revolt of the Moors of Andalusia, placing it in 1261 instead of in 1264. For this reason, its author connected the ordinance of the latter year, which he ascribed to 1263, with the revolt of the Moors and the ensuing war with Granada, and so with Alfonso X's urgent need for troops.[38] In fact the cortes must have been dismissed a few weeks before the outbreak of the revolt, which took the king entirely by surprise. According to the *Crónica*, Alfonso issued his ordinances with the consent of those from the Extremaduras who were with him, and these were then sent to all the cities and towns of the province. At that time, it also asserts, the town militias served for up to three months on the frontier without payment, and the town knights had no share in the proceeds of the *fonsadera* paid by those who did not join the army. In this statement the *Crónica* is certainly wrong; there is evidence that in Alfonso X's reign, and probably earlier, the town knights did share in the *fonsadera*. The *Crónica de la población de Avila*, written shortly after 1255, implies that the knights of Avila shared in it,[39] and clause 12 of the *cuaderno* of 1264 itself implies the same generally for the towns of Extremadura. The main provisions of the ordinance of 1264, as given by the *Crónica*, were that all those who had horses and arms were to be exempted from the payment of *fonsadera* and *martiniega*, and that their dependants, such as millers, herdsmen and those of their immediate households, were also exempted. In return for these privileges they were to serve the king on the frontier whenever summoned to do so, without any other payment. However, in the case of at least some towns – for example, Peñafiel and Cuéllar – the exemptions

---

[37] E.g. Ballesteros, *BRAH*, cvii, 398; cviii, 24; *Alfonso X el Sabio*, 365–7, with the date corrected to 1264; Pescador, *CHE*, xxxiii–xxxiv, 189–90, under the incorrect date 1263.

[38] *Crónica Alfonso X*, cap. xii. On the correct date of the revolt, see Ballesteros, *BRAH*, cviii, 17–36, and *Alfonso X el Sabio*, 368–70.

[39] *Crónica de la población de Avila*, 47 cf. Sánchez-Albornoz, *Estudios*, 494, n. 28.

enumerated by the *Crónica* had certainly already been granted some years previously.[40]

The actual *cuadernos* of the meeting of the cortes in 1264 differ widely from the account given in the *Crónica*.[41] The preamble states that all the *concejos* of Extremadura presented their petitions to Queen Violante and that it was at her request that the king, with the advice of the archbishop of Seville, the bishops, masters of the military orders and nobles who were with him, granted them. The same procedure was followed in the case of the particular petition presented by the representatives of Escalona concerning the government of the town.

Six[42] of the thirteen clauses of the *cuadernos* granted certain privileges of knighthood to the knights of the towns of Extremadura, but these are not the same as those enumerated in the *Crónica*. According to these privileges the dependent sons, brothers and nephews of knights were excused from all *pechos* until they reached the age laid down by the *Fuero real*, after which they were to be excused only if they had a horse and arms of their own. Wives, widows and daughters of knights of the towns were now to receive, for any dishonour done them, the customary compensation due to the women-folk of *infanzones*. On the death of a knight, his horse and arms were to pass entire by inheritance to his eldest son. When they were with the army the knights were to have the customary number of *excusados*. A former privilege by which widows of knights were thenceforth excused *pecho* was extended to apply to those widowed before this privilege had been granted.[43] Finally, the king granted that those who had been knighted by him or his eldest son should hold town offices and enjoy the full privileges of knighthood, and that such privileges would be extended to those who had received knighthood from the other members of the royal house, or from *ricos hombres*, provided they presented themselves before the king and became his vassals. This clause was confirmed by Sancho IV at the Cortes of Valladolid in 1293 at the petition of the *concejos* of Extremadura.[44] It will be seen that these various privileges were privileges which traditionally were enjoyed by *caballeros de linaje* and were

---

[40] *MHE*, I, no. XLIII (19 July 1256). *CD Cuéllar*, no. 16 (21 July 1256). The list of those exempted (*excusados*) is almost identical with that given in the *Crónica*.

[41] Appendix, doc. VII, below.

[42] Cls. 5–9, 12.

[43] This privilege had been granted to Peñafiel and to Cuéllar in July 1256 at the time that the *Fuero real* was granted to these towns: *MHE*, I, no. XLIII; *CD Cuéllar*, no. 16.

[44] *DA Madrid*, 1a serie, I, 145–6.

in some cases extensions of privileges already granted to individual towns, generally in connection with the grant of the *Fuero real.*

Besides these clauses in the 1264 code which dealt with knighthood, there were seven other clauses which dealt with very different questions. Of them the *Crónica* makes no mention. The *concejos* had complained that they were not able to harvest their grain until the ecclesiastical authorities had collected the tithe and that this frequently meant loss to the townspeople; further, they complained that the collectors of that part of the *tercias* which belonged to the king did not collect it at the same time as the church took its part, and that, furthermore, the villagers themselves were required to transport the *tercias* from the villages to the town. To these complaints the king replied that they might harvest their grain and other produce when it seemed best to them; that the collectors of the *tercias reales* would be instructed to take these at the time that the church took its tithe and to collect them where they were grown (clauses 1, 2 and 3). Another clause directed that certain fines were to be used for the upkeep of the town walls and gates (clause 10). Three clauses dealt with judicial matters. One of these was concerned with the giving of sureties (clause 4); in another, the king granted that members of his household should not implead townsmen before the royal court until they had been impleaded before the town court according to the *fueros*, but that if the plaintiff held himself aggrieved at the decision of the court, appeal might be made to the king (clause 11). To a request that suits and petitions from the towns to the king should be dealt with expeditiously, the king replied that, if this were not already so, petitions should be handed to the *escribanos* appointed to receive them or, if there was still delay, to the queen (clause 13). Thus, the ordinance granted to the *concejos* of Extremadura was far from being the exclusively military code which some modern historians, relying on the *Crónica de Alfonso X*, have represented it as being.

The main purpose of Alfonso X's four economic codes (1252–3, 1258, 1261 and 1268) was to counter the rise in prices and the shortage of consumer goods which characterised the period. The means adopted were price fixing and stringent sumptuary laws aimed at the ostentation, extravagance and luxury of the wealthier classes of society.[45]

---

[45] The contents of the codes of 1252/3, 1258 and 1268 were analysed with copious quotations from, and some comparison between, the codes by Ballesteros, *Alfonso X el Sabio*, 71–4, 201–6, 435–45. Use is also made of the code of 1268

Of these four codes, that of 1261 is the least important, as most of its clauses repeat those of the codes of 1252/3 and 1258. It does, however, in some points anticipate that of 1268 and it serves as a link in the development of Alfonso's economic policy. Prices of livestock and some manufactured goods were fixed in 1252/3 and again in far greater number in 1268 and in the latter year wages in some occupations were also fixed. Sumptuary legislation was included in the three codes of 1252/3, 1258 and 1261 and, with some omissions, in 1268. The export of livestock and certain other commodities was forbidden in all four codes. Although the majority of their clauses dealt with economic policy, other subjects were also included, such as gambling, game law and the disabilities of Moors and Jews.

The *cuadernos* addressed to Burgos and Nájera in October 1252 and that addressed to Escalona in February 1253 are virtually identical.[46] There are some verbal differences, and some differences in the modern division into numbered clauses, so that the Burgos and Nájera *cuadernos* contain forty-five clauses, while that to Escalona contains forty-eight, but this results from the subdivision of two clauses and not from additional subject matter.[47] The number of prices fixed is sixty-one, of which no fewer than twenty-six are prices of various hawks and falcons, so making this document a valuable one for the history of hawking and falconry in thirteenth-century Spain. Livestock priced include horses, mules and asses, and cattle. Manufactured goods comprise shields, saddles and harness; furs and hides, and shoes. Thus, the range of goods priced was a restricted one. The prices of single items occasionally differ in one or other *cuaderno*, but such differences are few, and some may be due to mistranscription. By and large, the prices are the same in all three *cuadernos* and so presumably applied to the towns of Castile and Extremadura generally. The *cuaderno* addressed to the Tierra de Santiago consists of seventy-two clauses, but here the first twenty-four clauses are concerned with criminal law, and have nothing in common with the other *cuadernos*. On the other hand, the preamble and the last forty-eight clauses correspond to them, apart from verbal variations and some alterations dictated by historical

by Carlé, 'El precio de la vida en Castilla del Rey Sabio al Emplazado', *CHE*, xv, 132–56.
46 To Burgos, publ. García Rámila, *Hispania*, v, 204–22, from an original; to Nájera, publ. Ballesteros, *Cortes de 1252*, from a transcript; to Escalona, publ. Appendix, doc. IV, below.
47 Burgos and Nájera cl. 37 = Escalona cls. 37, 38; Burgos and Nájera cl. 45 = Escalona cls. 46–8. Clauses containing prices are 1–3, 7, 9–10, 17–18, 23–8.

necessity, such as the substitution of the reign of Alfonso X's grandfather, Alfonso IX of León, for that of his great grandfather, Alfonso
VIII of Castile, in time references.[48] The most important difference is
that the Santiago *cuaderno* distinguishes between the prices of livestock
'en tierra de León' and 'en tierra de Galicia'. For León the prices are
same as those given in the Burgos, Nájera and Escalona *cuadernos*, but
the prices given for Galicia are lower.[49] A similar distinction is not,
however, made in any of the other clauses fixing prices. In all four
cuadernos the normal penalty for exceeding the tariffs laid down
was that the vendor forfeited the purchase money and the buyer the
commodity purchased. Both, in addition, paid a fine, usually of 10
maravedíes.

Virtually no tariffs were included in the *cuadernos* of the Cortes of
1258 and 1261.[50] In the decrees issued at the Cortes of Jerez in 1268
much more comprehensive tariffs were imposed. Only one *cuaderno*,
that addressed to Seville, has survived, but in it prices are given for
different regions.[51] As a rule, these regions were three: (i) Andalusia,
(ii) the central region from the Sierra Morena northward, comprising
Extremadura, Castile and León, and (iii) the extreme northern and
north-western provinces of Asturias and Galicia. But this three-fold
division was not always observed: in some cases prices were given for
one or two, but not for all three regions; in others, the regions were
further subdivided. For livestock, as we have seen, only Asturias and
Galicia were distinguished from the rest of the country.[52] For clothes,
prices were fixed for Andalusia and the central region but not for the
north.[53] The commodities listed do not correspond for 1252/3 and
1268. Prices for shields, saddles, skins and furs, livestock, and hawks
and falcons were enumerated for both periods,[54] but the items were not
always the same, and in the case of livestock and skins and hides of
animals, the *cuaderno* of 1268 gave much longer and more comprehensive lists. Thus, while prices for horses, mules, pack asses, plough
oxen, cows, calves and bulls were fixed in both 1252/3 and 1268, the
cuaderno for the latter year added to these sheep, ewes, lambs, goats,

[48] Publ. López Ferreiro, *Fueros*, I, 347–72, from a *tumbo* (cartulary). Its editor
noted that the last forty-eight clauses were taken from the decrees of 1252.
[49] Cls. XLI, XLII.
[50] Publ. *Cortes*, I, no. XIII (1258); Rodríguez Díez, *Historia de Astorga*, 715–20
(1261).
[51] Publ. *Cortes*, I, no. XIV (1268).
[52] 1268, cls. 18, 19.
[53] *Ibid.* cls. 9, 10, 11.
[54] 1252/3, cls. 1–3, 9, 17–18, 23–8; 1268, cls. 11–13, 15–16, 18–19.

kids, pigs, boars, sucking pigs, ducks, chickens and small game such as hares, rabbits and partridges.[55] Again, the list of skins and furs priced in 1268 was much longer than in 1252.[56] On the other hand, the *cuadernos* of 1252 gave a much more detailed list of the various sorts of hawks and falcons and their value than did the *cuaderno* of 1268.[57] Besides these various items, the *cuaderno* of 1268 enumerated a number of commodities which did not appear in the *cuadernos* of the earlier period. These prices for 1 *quintal* (100 lb or 46 kg) of copper, tin, lead and iron; numerous articles of men's and women's clothing; and fish.[58]

The *cuaderno* of 1268 also included a comprehensive list of prices for various sorts of woollen cloth. This list shows that most fine cloth was imported from the cloth-producing towns of the Low Countries and France. Those named include Bruges, Ghent, Cambrai, Douai, Ypres and Lille; Blois, Rouen, Abbeville, Saint-Omer, Tournai and Montpellier. Cloth from England and from Navarre is also listed. The Castilian cloth-producing centres named are Zamora, Segovia and Avila.[59] It appears, therefore, that, although Castile at this time produced great quantities of wool, it was not, in the thirteenth century, a cloth-producing country on any large scale.

Wages for men and women servants, for labourers 'with spade and sickle', for carpenters, masons and other craftsmen employed in building and for women and boys employed in the vintage were also laid down in 1268 but not earlier.[60]

It is not possible on the basis of this material to make a full comparison between the cost of living, either in the two periods involved or in the different regions, but some generalisations can be made. Prices had risen between 1252/3 and 1268. This can be illustrated from those prices of livestock which appear for both these years. In 1252 it was laid down that the price of a war horse was to remain at 200 *maravedíes* up to, and for a year from, the next Martinmas; thereafter it was supposed to be reduced to 150 *maravedíes*; in 1268 the price was again fixed at 200 *maravedíes*. The price of a mare was 20 *maravedíes* in 1252 and 30 in 1268; that of a mule or palfrey rose from 50 to 70 *maravedíes*; that of a bullock from 5 to 10; that of a cow with calf from 4 to 6 and that of a bull from 4 to 7 *maravedíes*. A pack ass was valued

[55] 1252/3, cls. 17–18; 1268, cls. 18–19.
[56] 1252/3, cl. 9; 1268, cl. 11.
[57] 1252/3, cls. 23–8; 1268, cl. 16.
[58] 1268, cls. 2, 9, 20.
[59] *Ibid.* cls. 3, 4.
[60] *Ibid.* cls. 32, 33.

at 7 *maravedíes* in both years.[61] These were the prices in the central region of the kingdom, but the lower prices in Galicia and Asturias had also risen between the two dates.[62] In 1268 the cost of living, judged by this evidence, was highest in Andalusia and lowest in Galicia and Asturias , as appears both from the prices of cloth, clothes and livestock and from variations in the rate of wages.[63] The evidence of the *cuadernos* for 1252/3 and 1268 does nothing to support the assertion in the *Crónica de Alfonso X* that the fixing of prices, which it places in 1256, was a failure and that the king had to rescind these tariffs because the opposition of the merchants and traders led to a disappearance of commodities from the market and a worsening of the situation.[64] The *cuadernos* of 1252/3 prove that prices of some livestock and consumer goods were fixed in the first year of the reign and there is no evidence of any price fixing in 1256. The assertion of the chronicler is not to be explained as a simple case of an error in dating for there is equally no evidence for his statement that the tariffs were withdrawn; if they had been, it seems unlikely that Alfonso X would have attempted, after consultation with the merchants, to reimpose tariffs on a far wider range of goods in 1268. The evidence suggests rather that Alfonso's policy of imposing tariffs in 1252/3 was successful in check-ing the rise of prices, which remained reasonably steady for more than a decade. This period was ended by the revolt of the Moors of Andalusia in 1264 and the ensuing war with Granada which forced up prices, a process accelerated by the issue then of the depreciated *moneda de la guerra*, thus leading to the fixing of the new tariffs in 1268.

Sumptuary laws were prominent among the decrees of the economic codes of the second half of the thirteenth century. Laws intended to check the expenses of marriages and marriage feasts were included in Fernando III's decrees of 1250. No one was to give or receive a gift for the marriage of his kinswoman; whoever did so paid twice the value of the gift and a fine of 50 *maravedíes*. The maximum sum allowed for the purchase of wedding garments was laid down and a similar fine imposed for exceeding it. The number of guests at a wedding feast was limited to ten, five invited by the bridegroom and five by the bride, with a fine of 10 *maravedíes* for each additional guest![65] These restric-

---

[61] 1252/3, cl. 17; 1268, cl. 18.
[62] Santiago, 1253, cl. XLII; 1268, cl. 19.
[63] 1268, cls. 3–5, 9–10, 18–19.
[64] *Crónica Alfonso X, cap.* v.
[65] Ed. *Fuero de Cuenca*, 860; cf. Appendix, doc. III, below.

tions reappeared in all four of Alfonso X's economic codes, with certain modifications and additions, such as an increase in some of the fines and in the amount allowed for clothes. The number of guests allowed at the wedding feast was fixed at five men and five women, both for the bride and the bridegroom, exclusive of parents and godparents. The decrees of 1258 restricted the wedding festivities to two days, and those of 1268 added that the wedding feast might only take place in the house of the parents of the bride or groom.[66] Regulation of marriages and marriage feasts was not new in the second half of the thirteenth century, but it had hitherto been a local matter included in various town *fueros* – for example, in 1236 the *concejo* of Madrid limited to 50 *maravedíes* the permissible expenditure on clothes, food and wine, with a lesser sum where the bride was a widow or a village girl.[67]

Stringent regulations directed against extravagance in dress and food appeared in all four of Alfonso X's economic codes. In 1252 regulations were laid down for the making of saddles, harnesses and other trappings of horses, pennons and shields, so as to forbid the use of ornamentation and expensive materials. Similar prohibitions were included in 1258, and in 1261 the equipment allowed to the squire, the *rico hombre* and the knight were dealt with separaely.[68]

Laws concerned with clothes were very detailed and appeared in all four codes, although with considerable variations. In 1252 the use of striped cloth, gold thread and other forms of refined ornamentation was forbidden; the use of costly furs, such as ermine, was restricted; shoes were to be unornamented. In 1258 the number of new garments which might be purchased each year was limited to four; the use of ermine was now totally forbidden; outer cloaks made of scarlet cloth were reserved for the king alone and an even longer list of prohibited forms of ornamentation was included. Most of these restrictions were re-enacted in 1261 and in 1268.[69] Women's clothing was dealt with in 1252, when all forms of ornamentation by embroidery, jewels and gold and silver thread were prohibited but the use of ermine was allowed. In 1268 an upper limit on cost took the place of prohibition of ornamentation.[70]

Severe limitations were also placed on food. In 1252 it was laid down

---

[66] 1252/3, cl. 13; 1258, cl. 45; 1261, Rodríguez Díez, *Historia de Astorga*, 719; 1268, cl. 40.
[67] *DA Madrid*, 1a serie, I, 61.
[68] 1252/3, cl. 4; 1258; cl. 15; 1261, Rodríguez Díez, *Historia de Astorga*, 717.
[69] 1252/3, cl. 5; 1258, cls. 14, 15; 1261, Rodríguez Díez, *Historia de Astorga*, 715, 717; 1268, cl. 6.   [70] 1252/3, cl. 6; 1268, cl. 6.

that no meal was to consist of more than two kinds of meat – one of which might be dressed in two ways – and two kinds of fish. Meat and game obtained by hunting, and shell fish were excluded from these limitations. In 1258 three kinds of fish were permitted on fast days.[71] The *cuadernos* of 1261 and 1268 omitted all reference to food.

The decrees of 1258 differed from the others by including a sustained attack on the extravagance and ostentation of the royal court. It was specifically left to the king to have whatever food and clothing seemed good to him, but the expenses of the royal table were limited to 150 *maravedíes* a day, exclusive of the requirements of foreign guests. The king was to order the members of his household to eat more moderately and at less cost. The lesser functionaries and servants of the court such as scriveners, crossbowmen, falconers and porters were forbidden to wear the colours and materials generally reserved for *ricos hombres* such as white furs or *çendal* (a silk material), or to use saddles, spurs or shoes with gilt ornamentation or hats with gold or silver ornaments, a prohibition which, however, did not apply to the chief holder of each office. The clergy of the king's chapel were to have large tonsures, they were not to wear red, green or other coloured clothes and various other restrictions were placed on them, some relaxation being allowed, however, in favour of canons and other cathedral clergy. Finally, it was laid down that the king might give gifts to *joglares* (jongleurs) and *soldaderas* (strictly speaking, girl singers who performed with the jongleurs) once a year only and that only those of the latter who had the king's leave might remain at court.[72]

The *cuadernos* of Alfonso X's various cortes also contained certain provisions regulating commerce and trade in the interest of the consumer. In those of 1252 merchants and craftsmen were forbidden to combine to force up the prices of goods, but must sell their merchandise or products as best they could competitively, under pain of being at the king's mercy. Retailers (*regateros*) were not permitted to buy up freshwater or sea fish, nor to go outside the towns on to the highways to buy up kids, chickens or other meat. Those who did so were to forfeit their purchases and pay a fine of 10 *maravedíes* for each purchase so made. Craftsmen were not to buy wood for resale, but only as material for their own craft, under penalty of double the value of the wood and a fine of 10 *maravedíes*. The attempt to prohibit price-rings was re-

---

[71] 1252/3, cl. 12; 1258, cl. 13.
[72] 1258, cls. 1–6. On jongleurs and *soldaderas* at Alfonso X's court, see Menéndez Pidal, *Poesía juglaresca y juglares*, 212–37.

enacted in 1258, 1261 and 1268 and the prohibition of purchase for resale appeared in a different form in the *cuaderno* of 1268.[73]

Another matter which affected trade was, of course, the maintenance of standard weights and measures. In the *Fuero real* it was laid down that the same weights and measures were to be used both for the stranger and the townsman; officials of the town (*fieles*) were to inspect them in taverns and all houses; false weights were to be destroyed and those who used them to be fined and, on a third offence, both fined and expelled from the town.[74] These laws left the question of weights and measures a matter for individual towns, as it had been in the past; standard weights and measures, as elsewhere in Europe, differed in different towns, and regulations concerning them were included in many town *fueros*.[75] The earliest *cuaderno* in which this question was dealt with is that of 1261 and in it, for the first time, Alfonso X sought to enforce the use of uniform weights and measures for the whole kingdom.[76] *Cartas* on this matter, addressed to the *concejos* of Toledo and León and passed in the spring of 1261, have survived. In them it was laid down that for bread, the *cafis* of Toledo was to be used; for wine, the *moyo* of Valladolid; and for meat, the *arrelde* of Burgos. Standard weights and measures were despatched with the *cartas*.[77] The same provisions were incorporated in the *cuaderno* of 1268 (with the substitution of the *moyo* of Seville for that of Valladolid).[78]

We have already dealt (pp. (pp. 196–9) with the detailed regulations concerning imports and exports included in the *cuaderno* of 1268. Among internal financial exactions which affected trade and commerce, the most important were *montazgo* and *portazgo*. The former was, as we have seen, a toll imposed for the use of the *montes* (grazing lands), by flocks and herds on their way between their summer and winter pasturage. Originally the *montes* had been royal demesne but, by the thirteenth century, much of the *montes* had been granted to or

[73] 1252/3, cls. 11, 15, 16; 1258, cl. 38; 1261, Rodríguez Díez, *Historia de Astorga*, 718; 1268, cls. 27, 28.
[74] *Fuero real*, lib. III, *tít.* x, *ley* 1.
[75] G[arcía] de Valdeavellano, 'El mercado: apuntes para su estudio en León y Castilla durante la Edad Media', *AHDE*, VIII, 369.
[76] 1261, Rodríguez Díez, *Historia de Astorga*, 720; 'Et pusiemos otrossi que las medidas e los pesos de pan e de vino e de pannos e de otras cosas que sean todas unas por todo nuestro sennorio, assi como dizen en las nuestras cartas que nos enbiamos.'
[77] [Burriel,] *Informe sobre pesos y medidas*; Álvarez de la Braña, *BRAH*, XXXVIII, 134–7.   [78] 1268, cl. 26.

appropriated by monasteries, the military orders and the towns.[79] The *cuadernos* of 1252/3 sought to regulate the taking of this toll. *Montazgo* was to be taken once only within the lands of a military order, or religious body, or the territories of a town, but it could be imposed on the migrating flocks both going and returning. Such flocks and herds were usually composed of a thousand beasts, and the rate of the toll per thousand was exacted either in money or in kind. Thus, on a herd of a thousand cattle, the *montazgo* was either 2 beasts or 8 *maravedíes*; on a flock of a thousand sheep, 2 sheep or 1 *maravedí*, etc. It also laid down that the drovers' roads (*cañadas*) and the enclosed pastures (*deffesas*) should be as in the time of Alfonso VIII and that the tolls called *assaduras*, taken by lords for the passage of flocks and herds through their lands, should only be taken if the lord in question held a royal privilege.[80] Nearly all of this was included in the *cuadernos* of 1258, but not in those of 1261 or 1268.[81] *Portazgo*, a toll on transit for the use of roads and bridges, was taken from all travellers, with or or without merchandise. It, too, was also exacted from migratory flocks and herds. *Portazgo* was a royal tax and part of it was applied to the upkeep of the roads and bridges, but the right to collect it was frequently granted to corporate bodies and to individuals. In 1252 it was laid down that *portazgo* was to be taken only as it had been taken under Alfonso VIII or, in the case of the great towns which had been subsequently reconquered, as it had been taken by the Almohade rulers, except by royal privilege. This enactment reappeared in 1258 and 1261.[82]

Some attempt was made in the legislation in cortes to protect the inhabitants of towns and villages from oppression by the powerful – whether nobles or royal officials. One of the most abused rights was the taking of *conducho* (Latin: *conductum*), that is, provisions for a journey paid for at fair prices. This right was exercised by court officials on behalf of the king's household when on progress, by *merinos* in certain cases and by the nobles both over their tenants and in the *behetrías de linaje*. Such rights were minutely regulated by custom.

---

[79] Klein, *Mesta*, 163ff.
[80] 1252/3, cls. 32, 33. The *cuaderno* of 1253 to the Tierra de Santiago adds the places where the toll was to be taken by the military orders (López Ferreiro, *Fueros*, I, 365–6, cl. LVI). Klein thought this was a town privilege. See *MHE*, I, no. XXVIII (22 May 1255): *carta* to Toledo on *montazgo*.
[81] 1258, cls. 31, 32, 40.
[82] 1252/3, cl. 37; 1258, cl. 33; 1261, Rodríguez Díez, *Historia de Astorga*, 719.

The main abuses connected with *conducho* were the taking of it by force where it was not customary, or in excessive amounts, or without payment. Unlawful *conducho* was a crown plea, and in the *behetrías* royal *pesquisidores* held periodic inquiries into such misdemeanours. Attempts to prevent the abuse of *conducho* were included in most of the legislation of the cortes in the second half of the thirteenth century. In 1250 Fernando III forbade, in general terms, under pain of forfeiture, any official or powerful person to oppress the dwellers in towns or villages and, specifically, prohibited the exaction of *conducho* unlawfully or by force.[83] Legislation under Alfonso X and Sancho IV was more detailed. The decrees of 1258 forbade the taking of *conducho* in royal demesne and laid down that delinquents were to be treated as robbers. Further, no noble or knight was to lodge in a *behetría* for more than three days, nor take *conducho* unlawfully. In both cases the taking of *conducho* in lands belonging to religious orders or to other lords, except as was customary, was forbidden.[84] In 1293 the *concejos* of Castile petitioned that nobles, knights and *hidalgos* should not take *conducho* in royal demesne, and if they did so, *pesquisas* should be held, as in the *behetrías*.[85] The *concejos* of León, as well as those of Castile, also complained that royal officials abused their right to take food for the king's household. To guard against this, Sancho IV decreed that the necessary *conducho* should be collected by town officials and then handed over to royal officials, who might not themselves enter the houses of the town's inhabitants to take *conducho*.[86]

Another exaction which led to abuses was *yantar*, originally paid in kind but by the thirteenth century commuted for a money payment. It was taken by the king, the queen and in some cases by the heir to the throne, when personally present, in those places where it was owed, and customarily only once in any given year. It was also taken by certain royal officials acting as deputies for the king. It was occasionally, but comparatively rarely, granted to nobles and churches. Complaints about its abuse were frequent, and stricter definitions were included in the *cuadernos* of the cortes in the reign of Sancho IV. In 1286 it was decreed that *yantar* was to be taken only once in the year, as in the time of Alfonso VIII and Fernando III; that the king's *yantar* was to be 600 *maravedíes* and the queen's 200 *maravedíes*, calculated in

[83] 1250, *Fuero de Cuenca*, 859: 'nin les tomasse conducho a tuerto nin a fuerça'; see also Appendix, doc. III, below.
[84] 1258, cls. 19, 20; 1261, Rodríguez Díez, *Historia de Astorga*, 716.
[85] 1293, Castile, cl. 21.
[86] *Ibid.* Castile, cl. 8; León, cl. 13.

moneda de la guerra; and that it was to be demanded only when the king or queen was actually present. Similarly, the *merinos* were permitted to claim *yantar* only once a year and not until they had held office for a full twelve months.[87] Complaints of continued abuse were made by the *concejos* of Castile in 1293 when further definitions were laid down. The king and queen would take *yantar* only when personally present or during time of war, a siege, or the holding of the cortes, or during the queen's confinement. The Infante Don Fernando, the king's heir, was only to take the tribute, fixed in his case at 300 *maravedíes*, when doing justice on behalf of the king. The rates of *yantar* for the king and queen were confirmed at 600 and 200 *maravedíes* respectively. Only *merinos mayores*, not *merinos menores*, were now entitled to *yantar* – fixed for them at 150 *maravedíes* – once a year and when personally present.[88]

Complaints against malpractices by royal officials were frequent in Castile as, indeed, in any country in the Middle Ages, when control by the king over local affairs was intermittent and difficult to execute. From time to time attempts to rectify this were made by the cortes – increasingly so, as the practice of presenting general petitions developed. In 1286, at Palencia, it was decreed that the general *pesquisa*, an all-embracing inquiry into every sort of illegal action (to some extent the equivalent of the general eyre in England) and very unpopular because it was felt to be oppressive, should in future be held only on the direct authority of the king and not on orders from the *merinos* or *adelantados*. It was also laid down that copies of the *pesquisa* were to be given to those implicated and that they were to be judged by the relevant *fuero*.[89] In 1293, at the petition of the *concejos* of Castile, Sancho IV fixed the rate to be charged by tax collectors for quittances (*cartas de pagamiento*) given to the towns.

Attempts were also made to reform the central administration, particularly the chancery. In 1286 it was ordered that chancery fees for privileges and *cartas* were not to exceed those contained in Alfonso X's ordinance.[90] In 1293 at Valladolid the *concejos* of Castile, León and Extremadura all petitioned that *cartas desaforadas* which ran contrary to existing privileges, franchises, liberties and *fueros* were not to be passed, either by the chancery proper or under the secret seal (*sello de la poridad*).[91]

---

[87] 1286, cls. 4, 8.   [88] 1293, Castile, cls. 5, 6.
[89] 1286, cl. 7.   [90] 1286, cl. 9.
[91] 1292, Castile, cl. 17; León, cl. 16; *DA Madrid, 1a serie,* 149.

There is also some evidence of other ordinances and decrees of Alfonso X which have not survived. One of these was directed against the encroachments of ecclesiastical on secular jurisdiction, and on the use of excommunication and interdict by the bishops against secular judges who carried out the king's commands. Our only formal knowledge of this enactment is derived from the *cuaderno* of the Cortes of Zamora in 1301, when the same matter was raised and Alfonso's decree was confirmed.[92] In this *cuaderno* it is explicitly stated that Alfonso X had assembled the cortes and that the decree concerned was promulgated with their approval. Even though it is not contained in any known *cuaderno* of his reign, it may be noted that Alfonso X's prohibitions of excommunication and interdict were included among the grievances of the Castilian bishops in Pope Nicholas III's *memoriale secretum* of 1279.[93]

[92] *Cortes*, I, no. xxviii, cl. 11 (pp. 154–5).
[93] *Registres de Nicolas III*, no. 743.

I I

The *corte* (1230–1295)

With the adoption of the vernacular as the official language of the Castilian chancery, the term *corte* replaced the Latin *curia* and was used throughout the period now under review in the senses that *curia* had been in the preceding period – to describe the court in all its forms, whether acting as an advisory or legislative body, or as a judicial tribunal, and whether its members were few or many. Thus, Fernando III's sentence in 1250, confirming the bishop of Túy's lordship over the city, stated that Bishop Gil did homage to the king for the city, 'ante mi corte'.[1] In a suit between the bishop and *concejo* of Osma, which was begun before Fernando III and ended under his son, Alfonso X took counsel with the bishops and nobles 'que eran en mi corte' before giving sentence.[2] Laws concerned with usury and contracts between Jews and Christians were promulgated in 1260 'with the advice of many good men who were with us in our *corte*'.[3] A question concerning the law of mortmain 'fué yudgado por mi corte' in 1290.[4] It is not easy to distinguish between the small and the extraordinary or augmented *corte*, as so little information is given as to those present. In cases where the record merely states that a suit was judged in the court, or an action taken by the king after consultation with the court, it is imposible to determine with certainty whether the small or great *corte* was involved. In some cases, however, both when the word *corte* is used, and also when there is reference to consultation without the use of the word *corte* there is, nevertheless, some indication as to whether a specially summoned assembly was or was not involved. When phrases such as 'con los obispos e los ricos hombres que eran conmigo', or 'que eran hy a la sazón' are used, the reference is presumably to the

---

[1] *ES*, xxii, *ap.* xviii (4 July 1250).
[2] Loperráez Corvalán, *Descripción histórica del obispado de Osma*, iii, no. lix, The date is given as Seville, 6 Feb. 1256, but at that time Alfonso was at San Esteban de Gormaz; the year should probably be 1253.
[3] AHN, Clero, *carp.* 918/15 (April 1260); Appendix, doc. vi, below.
[4] Gaibrois de Ballesteros, *Sancho IV*, iii, no. 319 (6 Sept. 1290).

restricted *corte*.[5] Occasionally 'toda la corte' is used. Thus, in the *cuadernos* of 1250 Fernando III referred back to an occasion shortly after his accession as king of Castile, when he had sworn to observe the *fueros* of the towns 'ante toda mi corte', and the *Crónica Anónima II de Sahagún* stated that Fernando III's condemnation of the burgesses of Sahagún as traitors to their lord, Abbot Guillelmo III of Sahagún, took place before 'toda la corte'.[6] This use may indicate an extraordinary assembly, but as in the earlier period, there is not enough evidence for any definite conclusion. There are also instances when the king is said to have taken counsel with those 'que se acercaron y', or 'que eran y yuntados', phrases which seem to hint at a summons to attend. There is clear evidence of the summary of an extraordinary assembly in the account given in the *Crónica de Sancho IV* of the Corte of Toro in 1287, which is as follows: 'avia enviado por todos los ricos omes e prelados, e que alli avria su consejo con ellos; e ellos vinieron y luego todos, e des que fueron todos ayuntados con él, fablo con ellos'.[7] There can be no doubt here that this was a specially summoned meeting of the *corte* in its largest form.

The prelates and magnates who formed the *corte* in its largest form were also present in the cortes, and business proper to the *corte* might well be conducted during sessions of the cortes. We know that suits were often heard while the cortes were assembled. Prelates and magnates might also be summoned for a date earlier than that on which the representatives assembled. This may account for the use of the word *corte* in Archbishop Sancho's letter of December 1260 (see p. 130), indicating that the *corte* met at the end of 1260, while the cortes took place, as the *cuaderno* stated, 'in the month of January'. As the *cuaderno* was passed on 24 January 1261, the representatives to the cortes as such would presumably have been dismissed by the end of the month. There are, however, reasons to believe that the extraordinary *corte*, or at least an augmented corte, was still hearing suits in February and March. On 21 February 1261 Alfonso X pronounced a

[5] E.g. *DA Madrid, 2a serie*, I, no. 1 (24 Sept. 1248); López Ferreiro, *Fueros*, I, 216–19; 225–6 (6, 9 July 1250); *MHE*, I, no. LVI (5 Aug. 1257); ANTT, Extras, fol. 194 (11 March 1281): 'E auiendo nuestro acuerdo...con los otros omes buenos de nuestra corte que eran hy a la sazon'.

[6] Ed. Puyol, *BRAH*, LXXVII, 167–8. The revolt of the burgesses probably took place in 1245; see Puyol, *Abadengo de Sahagún*, 98–9. The death sentence against the leaders of the riot was not carried out.

[7] *Crónica Sancho IV*, cap. IV (p. 77). Gaibrois de Ballesteros, *Sancho IV*, I, 162, calls this assembly 'cortes de Toro' but there is no evidence of the presence of the representatives and she herself quotes a document which refers to a suit heard 'en corte del rey en Toro'.

long and important arbitral sentence on a variety of questions at issue between Archbishop Juan Arias and the *concejo* of Santiago de Compostela, after consultation with his brothers 'et con nuestros Ricos omes et con nuestros alcaldes et los otros omes buenos de nuestra corte, clerigos et legos que se acercaron y', and on 28 March he pronounced sentence in a suit between the Order of Calatrava and the *concejo* of Bolaños, 'auido conseio con mio hermano don Sancho, arzobispo de Toledo, y con los obispos y con los ricos omes y con otros omes buenos de nuestra corte que eran yuntados'.[8] The prelates and nobles may have remained in session for another two months after the dismissal of the representatives, or they may have been reconvened in February. Something of the same sort may have taken place in 1254. The cortes were in session early in March, but we do not know when they were dismissed. On 15 April, at Toledo, Alfonso X confirmed the *fueros* of Valle de Fenar 'per Rogo de nostros Ricos omnes et Arçobispos et obispos et de otros omnes bonos'. This appears to be an extraordinary meeting of the *corte*, but whether the cortes were still in session or not, we do not know.[9]

These references to consultation with members of the *corte* throw some light on its composition and show that, as well as members of the royal family, prelates and nobles, some of whom would be present at informal meetings and all of whom presumably would be summoned to extraordinary meetings, there were also others who did not fall within these categories. We have already seen (pp. 68–9, 91–2) that there were *iudices curie regis* in León, and *iudices* and *alcaldes curie regis* in Castile before the reunion of the kingdoms in 1230. After 1230 references to *alcaldes* were numerous in documents concerned with suits before the king's court.[10] There were also, as we know, persons described as 'learned in the law' – *sabidores de derecho* – experts in customary law and usages. They were consulted by the king in suits before his court,[11] and also in connection with legislation.[12] Occasionally refer-

[8] López Ferreiro, *Fueros*, I, 248 (21 Feb. 1261); AHN, Esc. Calatrava, IV, fol. 2 (28 March 1261).

[9] Díez Canseco, *AHDE*, I, 373.

[10] E.g. *DA Madrid*, 1a serie, I, 73–8 (20 June 1239), 79 (24 Aug. 1249); 2a serie, I, no. 1 (24 Sept. 1248); López Ferreiro, *Fueros*, I, 216–18, 225–6 (6, 9 July 1250); *RC Silos*, no. 152 (14 May 1254), etc.

[11] AHN, Calatrava, R. 108 (21 Oct. 1256): suit between the order and Don García Almoravid: 'auido consseio... con los otros omnes de mi corte sabidores de derecho'. *MHE*, I, no. LXXXIX: suit between Toledo and Talavera (11 Sept. 1262).

[12] *Fuero real*, prologue, 6. Caamaño, *AHDE*, XI, 509.

ences occur to knights of noble birth (*caballeros fijosdalgo*) who were presumably household knights, members of the king's *mesnada* (company at arms).[13] Besides all these, there are also references to persons described simply as 'otros omnes bonos'. This was not a new phenomenon; there had been *boni homines* in the curia of Alfonso IX of León, but more evidence is available about them in the second half of the thirteenth century. To begin with, we know who they were not. They were not bishops or nobles, *alcaldes* or *sabidores de derecho*, for they were mentioned together with these and were distinguished from them in various documents. Nor were they representatives of the towns. They were never called 'of the towns', and in the preamble to the *cuadernos* of the Cortes of Seville in 1252 both 'good men of the towns' and 'other good men' are mentioned: 'con conseio...de omnes buenos de las villas et de otros omnes buenos'. They were also definitely members of the *corte* and they were both clerks and laymen.[14]

Who were these other good men of the court? There is no certain answer, but the obvious place to look for them is among the greatly increased number of king's servants who staffed the organs of central government. Under Alfonso X a reorganisation of the chancery was carried out. The archbishops of Toledo and Santiago continued to hold the titular offices of chancellors in Castile and León respectively although the latter title soon fell into abeyance; the office of *chanceler del rey* which had lapsed after the death of Bishop Juan of Burgos in 1246 was not revived; instead a separate office of *notario mayor* was created by Alfonso X for each of the three provinces of León, Castile and Andalusia. Each was presumably responsible for the work of his province, but might also from time to time deal with that of the other regions. These three notaries were the effective heads of the chancery, although the three-fold division was not maintained throughout the reign and one or other office was vacant for long periods.[15] Under Sancho IV the archbishop of Santiago never held the title of chancellor of León and, indeed, the archbishopric was vacant for most of the reign. The office of *chanceler del rey* reappeared, but its holder, Bishop Juan Alfonso of Palencia, rarely authorised documents and the three *notarios*

---

[13] E.g. *Crónica Alfonso X*, cap. xxiv (p. 20); Gaibrois de Ballesteros, *Sancho IV*, III, no. 419 (20 April 1292); *Crónica Sancho IV*, cap. v (p. 78) (June 1288).

[14] AHN, Esc. Calatrava IV, fol. 2: 'auido conseio...con los obispos y con los ricos omes y con otros omes buenos de nuestra corte' (28 March 1261); López Ferreiro, *Fueros*, I, 248: '...otros omes buenos de nuestra corte, clerigos e legos' (21 Feb. 1261).

[15] Procter, 'The Castilian chancery during the reign of Alfonso X', *Oxford essays presented to H. E. Salter*, 104–21 (pp. 114–15).

mayores continued as effective heads of the chancery. In 1290 the archbishop of Toledo was entitled chancellor of León, Castile and Andalusia, Bishop Martín of Astorga became notary of all three provinces and the office of *chanceler del rey* again disappeared.[16] With the reign of Fernando IV the chancellor–archbishops, the *chanceler del rey* and the three notaries all reappeared and a fourth notary, that of the former kingdom of Toledo, was added.[17] The royal documents of the reigns of Alfonso X and Sancho IV also give evidence of the greatly increased number of clerks who staffed the chancery.

During the period of Alfonso X's candidature for the imperial crown, something approaching an imperial chancery, distinct from the royal chancery, can be discerned. It dealt with correspondence with the papacy about Alfonso's claims, and with his German and Italian supporters, and its periods of greatest activity were from 1257 to 1260 and from 1270 to 1275. It had its own seal – Alfonso's seal as king of the Romans – it prefixed the title *Rex Romanorum* to Alfonso's elaborate regal style, it used Latin not Castilian and it was staffed principally, but not entirely, with Italians under a *protonotarius sacri imperii*. Some of the Italians were commissioned to translate into Latin the Castilian versions of Arabic astrological works, and some remained in Alfonso's service after 1275, employed in the royal chancery drafting foreign correspondence in Latin, and on embassies to foreign rulers.[18]

The chancery, although the chief, was not the only writing office of the administration. Under Alfonso X a certain Sancho Pérez, treasurer of the cathedral of Jaén and later archdeacon of Baeza, was *escribano de la cámara del rey* from 1264 to 1272 and, from that year until 1277, notary of the chamber.[19] Under Sancho IV the office of notary of the chamber was of sufficient importance to be held by Bishop Gil of Badajoz from 1284 to 1288, and to be noted among the *confirmantes* of the *privilegios rodados*.[20] There is no reference to it for the rest of the reign, but the names of some *escribanos* of the chamber appear in the royal accounts of 1293–4 and in other documents.[21] Some sort of secre-

---

[16] Sánchez Belda, 'La cancillería castellana durante el reino de Sancho IV', *AHDE*, XXI–XXII, 175–90.

[17] See the *privilegios rodados* of Fernando IV, publ. *Memorias de Fernando IV*, II, and *Cortes*, I, no. XXV, cl. 13.

[18] Procter, 'The scientific works of the court of Alfonso X of Castille: the king and his collaborators', *Modern Language Review*, XL, 24–6, and *Alfonso X of Castile*, 127–30.

[19] As *escribano* from 9 Dec. 1264: Ballesteros, *Sevilla*, no. 138; as notary from 23 Dec. 1272, still acting 1 Sept. 1277: AHN, Clero, *carp.* 1355/5, 12.

[20] Gaibrois de Ballesteros, *Sancho IV*, III, nos. 39–211 (7 Jan. 1285–8 Aug. 1288).

[21] *Ibid.* I, xxxi, lxxxv, lxxxviii; III, nos. 363 (8 Aug. 1291), 416 (18 April 1292).

tariat was also attached to the *corte* in its judicial aspect and from the beginning of Alfonso's reign documents were at times authorised by *alcaldes* and written by other than chancery clerks.

During the same period a second seal of state, the *sello de la poridad*, which corresponded to the privy seal in England and to the secret seal in Aragon and France, made its appearance. It must have been in use throughout Alfonso X's reign, for in the *Setenario* confession is likened to the 'sseello de poridat que aguarda lo que es escripto en la carta de dentro por que ninguno non lo pueda ssaber', and the use of this seal may well date from the reign of Fernando III.[22] It was probably at first the personal seal of the king, which developed into a seal of state as written grants and orders increased in number, as was the case with the privy seal in England. There is little definite evidence of its use under Alfonso X, but Sancho IV had his secret seal, both as *infante* in the last years of his father's life and also as king, and, before the end of his reign, there was a chancellor of the secret seal with a staff of *escribanos* under him.[23]

The chancery, the chamber and the office of the secret seal provided the king with a number of literate and trained experts who could also serve him in spheres outside their official duties. Some of the *notarios mayores* were bishops when they were appointed to the chancery; others were elected while holding office, for the chancery was the surest avenue to ecclesiastical preferment.[24] Some officials of the chancery who did not reach the episcopate were also high in the confidence of the king, as is shown by the number of them who were sent on missions and embassies to foreign courts. To name but a few: García Martínez of Toledo, notary of Castile from 1256 to 1259, was Alfonso X's proctor 'ad tractandum de pace' with Henry III of England in 1254, and was again sent to England in the following year.[25] The one-time imperial protonotary, Master Peter of Reggio, and 'Bellus de Arculis, miles et portarius camere', were two of the three envoys sent to Charles of Salerno in 1280.[26] Juan Mate, chamberlain, and later admiral in the reign of Sancho IV, played an important part in the preparations for the campaign against Tarifa.[27] It is thus among the king's servants who

---

[22] *Setenario*, 208. A similar statement appears in BL, Add. MS. 20787, fol. 10r, tít. IV, *ley* 32 (*Primera partida*, ed. Arias Bonet, 38).
[23] Procter, 'Use and custody of the secret seal (*sello de la poridad*) in Castille', *EHR*, LV, 200–1, 210–11, 216–17.
[24] Procter, 'Castilian chancery', *Oxford essays*, 115, 120–1.
[25] *Foedera*, I, i, 297, 328, 340.   [26] Daumet, *Relations*, 167–9, no. XII.
[27] Gaibrois de Ballesteros, *Sancho IV*, II, 314–21, 327–9; and documents published in *BRAH*, lxxvii, 192–215.

staffed the expanding organs of central government that the *otros omnes buenos de la corte* are most probably to be found.

In spite of the development of the cortes as an additional organ of government and in spite of changes in the *corte* itself, the latter still carried on, to some extent, most of the functions which it had exercised in the earlier period. For our knowledge of its intervention in affairs of state, we have to rely mainly on the narrative sources. The chronicles of Alfonso X and Sancho IV both give instances of consultation with the *corte*, in either its small or extraordinary form, on questions of the succession, regency, home and foreign policy. Unfortunately, the errors of the *Crónica de Alfonso X* are so many that it is difficult to assess the amount of reliance which can be placed on it when it deals with these matters. Such considerations do not arise to the same extent with regard to the information given in the *Crónica de Sancho IV*.

Although the question of the recognition of the Infante Don Sancho as heir to throne was, as has already been explained (pp. 139–40), decided on in the Cortes of Burgos in 1276, the matter was first discussed in a *corte* at Toledo, of which the *Crónica* gives an account. According to its narrative Alfonso X, after hearing the representations of Don Lope Díaz de Haro, took the advice of his brother the Infante Don Manuel 'e otros de su consejo' – a phrase which denoted the restricted *corte*. In this discussion Don Manuel supported the claims of the Infante Don Sancho, on the ground that the son was nearer in blood to the king than was his grandson, and the account ends 'E en el escripto que se falla desde aquel tiempo, non dicen que en aquel consejo fuesen dichas mas palabras destas.'[28] How far can we accept this account? This *corte* at Toledo is not mentioned by Jofré de Loaisa, but this is not an insuperable difficulty, as Loaisa's chronicle is very concise and selective, and concentrates on a limited number of important events. Alfonso was certainly at Toledo in January 1276;[29] there tion is nothing inherently improbable in the *Crónica*'s account of the king's consultation with his intimate advisers. We have the author's assertion that he based his account on a written source, which he con-

---

[28] *Crónica Alfonso X*, cap. LXVII (p. 53). Bibliothèque Nationale, Paris, MS Espagnol 327, fol. 84, omits the reference to the contemporary *escripto*, but adds another sentence to Don Manuel's speech followed by a long speech from the king, which elaborates the claims of the second son to succeed. The MS. was written in 1458, at which date such a passage was unlikely to be interpolated. It was presumably interpolated in some earlier MS.

[29] Ballesteros, *Alfonso X el Sabio*, 782–3. On 21 Jan. 1276 the king was at Camarena near Toledo (AHN, Clero, *carp.* 1355/11).

sidered to be contemporary with the events which he described, and which must, at the very least, have been considerably earlier than the date of the chronicle itself. We can, therefore, accept that this consultation took place.

When he realised that he was dying, Sancho IV made provision for the government of the kingdom after his death, at Alcalá de Henares in 1295. These provisions were announced in the presence of Archbishop Gonzalo of Toledo, other bishops, his uncle the Infante Don Enrique and other *ricos hombres* and the masters of the military orders who were with him. There he appointed his wife Queen María both as guardian of his son the Infante Don Fernando, then aged nine, and as regent of the kingdom during the minority.[30] In this he was following the precedents set by Sancho III and Alfonso VIII, both of whom had made provision for the government of the kingdom when the heir was a minor.

There is, not unexpectedly, evidence that the *corte* in one form or another was consulted by the king on political questions. For example, immediately before and during the revolt of 1272–3, Alfonso X held frequent consultations with those who were with him. The majority of the nobles were disaffected, or in rebellion, but he took the advice of those bishops and nobles who were loyal to him and of others of his entourage of lesser rank.[31] Sancho IV also consulted his *corte* on matters of policy as, for example, on the demands of Lope Díaz de Haro that he should be given the title of count, the office of *mayordomo de la corte* and a promise that his lands should pass to his son on his death. On this occasion the king unwisely listened to the supporters of Don Lope, instead of to the queen, who opposed the concessions.[32]

The *corte* was also consulted, as it had been in the past, on questions of foreign policy, peace and war. After the surrender of Jaén, Fernando III asked the opinion of the nobles and masters of the orders who were with him about the next move to take against the Moors. He received varying advice; some were in favour of raids into the territory of Seville and others of attacks on some of the strongholds. Yet others, notably Pelay Correa, master of Sanitago, favoured a decision to besiege Seville itself. With this advice the king and all the others with him agreed in the end.[33] The *Crónica de Alfonso X* gives accounts of

[30] *Crónica Sancho IV*, cap. xii (p. 89); Gaibrois de Ballesteros, *Sancho IV*, ii, 363.
[31] *Crónica Alfonso X*, cap. xxi (p. 17), xxiv (p. 20), xliv (p. 34).
[32] *Crónica Sancho IV*, cap. iii (p. 74); Gaibrois de Ballesteros, *Sancho IV*, i, 136–8.
[33] *PCG*, ii, cap. 1071 (p. 747).

two other occasions when consultations were held, in both of which, as usual, there are errors of date and fact. One occasion concerned the embassy to Castile by the German princes who had elected Alfonso as Emperor. According to the chronicle the king consulted his brothers, his sons and all the *ricos hombres* who were with him and, after giving a favourable reply to the envoys, 'ovo consejo con los suyos de commo fuese al Imperio', that is, he first consulted with an assembly of the magnates on the question of acceptance and afterwards with a restricted number of his intimate advisers on the means to be taken.[34] As, however, the *Crónica* places this embassy in 1268, instead of in 1257, and states that it reached the king in Burgos, where the court was assembled for the marriage of the Infante Don Fernando to Blanche of France which took place in 1269, little reliance can be placed on its account. That Alfonso, in 1257, consulted his brothers, as well as the nobles and other magnates, is probable enough; but he can hardly have consulted his sons, the eldest of whom was only born in 1255. The chronicle's account has been fashioned to fit the erroneous date.

A fuller and more detailed description of a meeting of the *corte*, supposedly in 1269, is given by the *Crónica* in connection with relations between Castile and Portugal. According to this account, Alfonso's grandson Dom Dinis of Portugal – 'a boy of twelve or thirteen years of age' – was sent to Seville then to ask for knighthood from his grandfather, and also for the abrogation of the obligation of the kings of Portugal to provide general military assistance to the kings of León as well as a certain number of knights in wars against the Moors. The question of this 'tribute' was discussed in an assembly, to which all the *infantes* and nobles present at court were summoned. There the Portuguese request was put forward, on behalf of the young prince, by a knight who had accompanied him. The request was vehemently opposed by Don Nuño de Lara but the rest of those assembled, seeing Alfonso's anger at this opposition, declared themselves in favour of granting the request.[35] The whole account is very dramatic, with the arguments of the Portuguese knight and Don Nuño given in direct speech, but it contains many obvious inaccuracies. Dom Dinis was born in 1261 and was eight years old in 1269. The feudal dependence of Portugal on León had not been recognised for more than a century, and the tribute of knights appears to refer to a later obligation, incurred in 1264, when Alfonso X quitclaimed his usufruct of the Algarve to

---

[34] *Crónica Alfonso X, cap.* XVIII (p. 13).
[35] *Crónica Alfonso X, cap.* XIX (pp. 14–15).

Afonso III of Portugal and his heirs, in return for the service of fifty knights.[36] Nor can the date of this meeting of the *corte* be 1269, for by the Treaty of Badajoz in 1267, Alfonso X had already given up his claim to this Portuguese military tribute and the outstanding question of the frontier between the two kingdoms had been resolved.[37] There is, however, evidence that the young Dom Dinis *was* sent to his grandfather's court in Seville in 1266, when Afonso III of Portugal sent troops to aid his father-in-law against the Moors.[38] At some date, too, Dinis was indeed knighted by Alfonso X, but we do not know when.[39] The narrative of the *Crónica de Alfonso X* seems to be a confused combination of various events.

The reign of Sancho IV also provided numerous instances of consultation with the *corte* on foreign affairs and on questions of peace and war. Evidence of differences of opinion within the *corte* on such matters is also documented. Thus, in the autumn of 1285, after the Moroccan ruler Ibn Yuçef had raised the siege of Jerez, Sancho IV took counsel with all the nobles who were with him on the advisability of giving battle to the Moors, but the opposition of his brother the Infante Don Juan and of Lope Díaz de Haro forced him to abandon this plan and retire to Seville.[40] Shortly afterwards, when both Ibn Yuçef and Mahomet II of Granada made overtures for peace, Sancho IV again took counsel with the nobles, and on this occasion he took the advice of the majority to come to terms with Ibn Yuçef, contrary to that of Don Juan and Don Lope who favoured a separate peace with Granada.[41]

Early in 1288 Sancho IV held an extraordinary *corte* at Toro to which all the *ricos hombres* and prelates were summoned and there laid before it the alternatives of peace with Aragon or with France. Here, again, the same split between the Infante Don Juan and Don Lope Díaz on the one hand, and the queen and the majority of the nobles on the other, reappeared, and even the king's intimate advisers, whom the *Crónica* calls *privados del Rey*, were also divided between the two

[36] ANTT, *Liv. Afonso III*, III, fol. 14; publ. Brandão, *Monarchia lusitana*, parte IV, 434–5.
[37] ANTT, *Liv. Afonso III*, III, fols. 15, 16; publ. Brandão, *Monarchia lusitana*, parte IV, escs. XXXIV, XXXV.
[38] Partly publ. Brandão, *Monarchia lusitana*, parte V, 10.
[39] *Cronicón de Cardeña*, II, 379, includes Dom Dinis in a list of kings knighted by Alfonso X. It is improbable that he was knighted in 1266 as a child of five.
[40] *Crónica Sancho IV*, cap. II (p. 71). Cf. Jofré de Loaisa, *Crónica*, 25: 'Rex autem Sancius de consilio procerum suorum destitit ulterius persequi Abiucaf predictum.'
[41] *Cronica Sancho IV*, cap. II (p. 72); Gaibrois de Ballesteros, *Sancho IV*, I, 72–4.

parties.[42] The question of peace with France or Aragon was debated again, at Alfaro, in June 1288. On this occasion there was no general summons, but a large number of bishops and nobles – some of whom are named by the *Crónica* – and also *caballeros del rey* were present. It was this assembly which ended with the assassination of Don Lope Díaz de Haro.[43] During the war with Aragon in 1289 Sancho IV 'ovo su consejo con todos los ricos omes que eran con él' whether to invade Aragon, although, in fact, he appears to have made up his mind beforehand to do so. In June 1292 the king accepted the advice of the leaders of the army to besiege Tarifa instead of Algeciras.[44]

These instances suggest that during this period, and particularly during the reign of Sancho IV, the king often consulted the *corte* in some form or other on matters of war, peace and the making of treaties. They also suggest that consultation on such questions was more frequent with the *corte* than with the cortes. From the little we know of the occasions on which foreign policy was discussed in the cortes, these appear to have been mainly when the king required financial aid to carry out his projects. All this reinforces the conclusion that it was his *corte*, not the cortes, that Alfonso IX, in 1188 undertook to consult on questions of peace and war and the conclusion of treaties. The examples given also show that debates in which there were differences of opinion between those present were frequent; that individuals gave their views freely, even though they might risk the king's displeasure, but in the end it was the king's decision which was final.

The chronicles of Alfonso X and Sancho IV both at times use the word *consejo* to describe the institution which gave advice to the monarch, as well as the advice sought or given. Thus, in its account of the *corte* at Toledo in January 1276, the *Crónica de Alfonso X* states that the king consulted his brother the Infante Don Manuel 'e otros de su consejo'.[45] Again, in 1281, the king spoke 'con los de su consejo' about making known to Don Sancho his plans for compensating his grandson Don Alfonso by the creation of a kingdom of Jaén, subject to Castile.[46] The *Crónica de Sancho IV* enumerated as ambassadors sent to negotiate with the French at Bayonne

---

[42] *Crónica Sancho IV*, cap. IV (p. 77); Gaibrois de Ballesteros, *Sancho IV*, I, 181.
[43] *Crónica Sancho IV*, cap. V (pp. 78–9; Gaibrois de Ballesteros, *Sancho IV*, I, 188–93, who also used the account given in the fifteenth-century *Cuarta crónica general*. For the negotiations with France, see Daumet, *Relations*, 95–7.
[44] *Crónica Sancho IV*, caps. VI (p. 81), IX (p. 86).
[45] *Crónica Alfonso X*, cap. LXVII (p. 53).
[46] *Ibid.* cap. LXXV (p. 60).

in March 1286 Archbishop Gonzalo of Toledo, Bishop Alonso [*sic*] of Burgos, Bishop Martín of Calahorra 'e otros caballeros que eran del Consejo del Rey', as well as Abbot Gómez García of Valladolid.[47] The king also consulted 'los de su consejo' on the demands of Lope Díaz de Haro.[48] The account of the *corte* at Toledo given by the *Crónica de Alfonso X* was based on an earlier written source, but we do not know whether the word *consejo* was used in that. In the other instances the use of *consejo* in vernacular chronicles probably reflects the usage of the fourteenth century and cannot be taken as applicable to the thirteenth. There are, however, a few examples when documents of the thirteenth century apply the description *consejero* ('counsellor') to certain individuals. Thus, Sancho IV sent 'Magistrum Nicholaum, medicum et consiliarium nostrum' as one of his envoys to France in 1294.[49] Fernán Pérez was also described as 'conseylero del Rey de Castiella e cansellero de seelo suyo de la puridat'.[50] The use of this title may reflect the growing importance of the advisory functions of the restricted *corte* and foreshadow the substitution of *consejo* for *corte* in the fourteenth century.

Although much of the legislation of the second half of the thirteenth century was promulgated in cortes, and was based on the representations and petitions of the *concejos*, yet the *corte* still played an important part in legislation. Alfonso X's codes of law were drawn up by the legists of his court, and were approved by the *corte*, and promulgated in it, and not in the cortes. The prologue of the *Fuero real* stated that Alfonso took 'conseio con nuestra corte e con los omes sabidores de derecho',[51] and in the various *cartas* granting it to individual towns, it is described as 'aquel fuero que yo fiz con consejo de mi corte, escripto en libro e sellado con mio seello de plomo'.[52] The *Espéculo*, in its prologue, was referred to as

este libro que fiziemos con conseio e con acuerdo de los arzobispos e de los obispos de Dios e de los ricos omes e de los mas onrados sabidores de derecho que podiemos aver e fallar, e otrossi de otros que avie en nuestra corte e en nuestro regno.

[47] *Crónica Sancho IV*, cap. II (p. 73). The bishop of Burgos was Don Fray Fernando.
[48] *Ibid.* cap. III (p. 74).
[49] Daumet, *Relations*, nos. XXIII (p. 214), XXIV (p. 218).
[50] Giménez Soler, *La corona de Aragón y Granada*, 33; Gaibrois de Ballesteros, *Sancho IV*, III, nos. 522, 523, 572.
[51] *Fuero real*, 6.
[52] E.g. *MHE*, I, nos. XLIII, XLIV, XLV, LIX, LXXXIII, CII.

and the prologue ended with the statement that, if anything in the book needed amendment or rectification, 'que el rey lo pueda emendar e endereszar con conseio de su corte'.[53] The judicial *Ordenamiento de Zamora* of 1274 was, as we have seen, promulgated, not in the cortes, but in a *corte* at which *alcaldes*, *escribanos* and advocates gave expert advice to the king.[54]

The many town *fueros* granted by Alfonso X did not generally make any reference to advice or consent by the *corte* but occasionally such references were made in cases of revision and confirmation. In 1254 Alfonso X confirmed the *fueros* given to Valle de Fenar by Fernando I and also excused the inhabitants from all *pecho* and *pedido* except *moneda* at the request of his prelates, nobles and other good men.[55] Again, in 1256, in the vernacular version of the *fuero* of Palencia, it was stated that Alfonso X took counsel with his brothers, the bishops and nobles 'e con los otros sabidores de derecho de nuestra corte'.[56] Ordinances dealing with certain classes, or localities, and generally based on petitions, might also be the work of the *corte*. Early in his reign Sancho IV went on a royal progress through Galicia, a part of the kingdom rarely visited by kings, and responded to the petitions and grievances of the people against the wrongs done to them by prelates, nobles and knights by the issue of an ordinance prohibiting 'certain evil customs' in Galicia. Its text notes that the king had his accord with the bishop of Túy, the *pertiguero mayor* of Santiago, Don Esteban Fernández, Don Juan Fernández of Linea 'et con otros homes buenos que eran en Santiago conmigo'.[57]

Administrative ordinances were also considered by the *corte*. Thus, the ordinance farming the revenues to Abrahem el Barchilón in 1287 was promulgated with the advice of the Infante Don Juan, Don Lope Díaz, a small number of nobles and officials mentioned by name 'e de otros omnes buenos que eran y comigo'.[58] The *corte* also considered and advised on the interpretation of laws. Early in his reign Sancho IV had ordered that his *pesquisidores*, when inquiring into the unlawful passing of territories from *realengo* to *abadengo* status, should include in the scope of their inquiry lands or property held by individual clergy by

[53] *Espéculo*, 2.
[54] *Cortes*, I, no. XVI.
[55] Díez Canseco, *AHDE*, I, 373 (15 April 1254).
[56] Caamaño, *AHDE*, XI, 509 (18 July 1256).
[57] López Ferreiro, *Fueros*, I, 374–6 (9 Sept. 1286). Gaibrois de Ballesteros, *Sancho IV*, I, 121–2.
[58] Text published by Gaibrois de Ballesteros, *Sancho IV*, I, clxxxv–clxxxix (1 June 1287).

inheritance, gift or purchase. Subsequently the latter question was brought before the *corte* on two occasions, at Zamora, and at Toro, where it was judged that clerical possessions of this kind should not be included in these inquiries, as they did not belong to the church and were not *abadengo*, nor did the king lose his rights in them.[59]

A good illustration of the way in which both *corte* and cortes played a part in legislation is afforded by the various laws and regulations dealing with the question of usury. The problem was one of the main causes of friction between Christians and the Jewish and Moorish minorities, both because this lucrative means of making a livelihood was forbidden by the church to Christians (although some nevertheless practised it) and also because of the excessive rates of interest demanded by the money-lenders. It was a question which greatly exercised Alfonso X, and was dealt with not only in the *cuadernos* of the cortes but also in *cartas* to towns, in answers to petitions, in ordinances issued with the advice and approval of the *corte* and in the *Fuero real*, the *Espéculo* and the *Siete partidas*. The *cuadernos* of the cortes of 1252/3 merely decreed that the oaths and guarantees necessary in any dealings between Christians and Jews were to be as they had been in the time of Alfonso VIII.[60] In March 1253, however, the king despatched *cartas* to the *concejos* which laid down detailed regulations. Interest on loans was limited to 'tres por quatro', that is, an interest of 33⅓ per cent for a year, and bonds were not to be renewed until a year was complete. The maximum validity of bonds was to be limited in the future to four years, and existing bonds to four years from the date of this *postura*. These regulations were to apply to all Christians (as well as to Jews and Moors) who lent for usury – a clear indication that some Christians disregarded the prohibitions of the church. It was explained in the documents that these *cartas* were issued because 'cavalleros e omes de los pueblos' had complained to Fernando III, in his lifetime, and to Alfonso X, since his accession, of the grievances occasioned by the excessive usury taken by the Jews. For this reason the king had taken counsel with his uncle the Infante Don Alfonso de Molina, his brothers, his *ricos hombres*, the bishops and the masters of the military orders who were with him, on this matter. These statements imply a background of widespread petitions, some of which may have been presented

---

[59] Gaibrois de Ballesteros, *Sancho IV*, III, nos. 170, 319, 321 (15 Aug. 1287; 6, 30 Sept. 1290).
[60] *Cuadernos* to Burgos and Nájera, cl. 38; to Escalona, cl. 39; to Santiago, cl. LXXII.

at the Cortes of 1252/3, as well as consultation on the problem with an augmented *corte*. The use of the word *postura* also implies that the regulations were of general application.[61]

The rate of interest postulated in the *carta* of 1253 was included in the *Fuero real* where higher rates were declared invalid.[62] The actual contents of the *carta* of 1253 were incorporated, almost word for word, in the *cuadernos* of the Cortes of 1258.[63] Some years later, in the spring of 1260, Alfonso X, after consultation with the *corte* – 'con consseio de muchos omnes buenos que eran connusco en nuestra corte' – again confirmed the existing rate of interest and issued new detailed regulations to govern the making of contracts between Christians, Jews or Moors. These were contained in *cartas* sent to individual towns: bonds were to be entered into before one of the *alcaldes* of a *concejo* (or his deputy); the *escribano* appointed for this particular purpose and the necessary witnesses, who were to include Christians, Jews or Moors as appropriate. All such contracts were to be made on oath and were to be entered in a register kept by the *escribano*. Repayments or renewals of all or part of a debt were to be recorded in the same manner. The maximum validity of existing agreements was extended to twelve years and, in the case of those made in the future, to eight years from the date of the contract.[64] The formulas of the oaths to be taken were despatched separately.[65] They appear to have been taken from the *Espéculo*. The *cuaderno* of the cortes of 1261 laid down, succinctly, that the granting and repaying of loans from Jews and Moors were to be carried out as laid down in the royal *carta* of 1260.[66] A new rate of

---

[61] Amador de los Ríos, *Historia de los judíos de España y Portugal*, I, 320–1; II, 463–4; *Ap.* XXII: text from the *carta* sent to Cuenca.

[62] *Fuero real, liv.* IV, *tít*, ii, *ley* 6.

[63] *Cortes*, I, no. XIII, *cuaderno* of 1258, cls. 29, 30. The four years' validity was also included in Alfonso's answer to the petitions of Sepúlveda in 1257, publ. *CD Sepúlveda*, I, no. 7 (16 Oct. 1257).

[64] AHN, Clero, *carp.* 918/15; publ. Appendix, doc. VI, below. For another copy of this carta, see *Colección diplomática de Béjar*, 8. Ballesteros, *BRAH*, CVII, 29–31, cites *cartas* to Toro and Ubeda, and in *Alfonso X el Sabio*, 1081, nos. 457–8, to Alba de Tormes and León. An undated copy with a general address is prefixed to the *Leyes nuevas*, 181.

[65] Martínez Marina, *Ensayo sobre la antigua legislación*, 259, citing a *carta* of 3 May 1260 transcribed in the MS. 'Colección diplomática del P. Burriel', vol. DD 115. This collection is now conserved in the Biblioteca Nacional, but the volume in question has disappeared. For the oaths, see *Espéculo, lib.* V, *tít.* XI, *leyes* 15–17.

[66] 'Et pusiemos en razon de las usuras de los judios e de los moros que las den e las demanden en aquella guisa que nos mandamos por nuestra carta que fiziemos en era de mill e dozientos e noventa e ocho annos' (A.D. 1260): Rodríguez Diez, *Historia de Astorga*, 718.

interest of *cuatro por cinco*, 25 per cent, was introduced in the *cuaderno* of the Cortes of 1268, which otherwise repeated the regulations contained in the *carta* of 1260.[67] This new rate was subsequently rescinded: a privilege of Sancho IV, dated 24 March 1285, granted to Cuenca, containing reforms of the city's *fueros*, fixed the rate of interest at *tres por quatro*[68] and, at the cortes of 1293, the representatives complained to the king that Jews and Moors were not keeping the ordinance granted by Alfonso X, and confirmed by Sancho IV, that interest should not exceed 'tres por cuatro'.[69]

Except during the last decade of the reign of Alfonso X, when a professional judicial tribunal had come into existence, the *corte* was the central court of justice for the whole kingdom. After the political union of the kingdoms of León and Castile it heard cases arising in both kingdoms, administering the law appropriate to the locality in which the suit had originated – in León, the *Forum judicum* and in Castile, the body of customary law which formed the *Fuero viejo*, and the case law of the *fazañas*. As, however, Toledo, too, used the *Forum judicum*, and Fernando III had given this code, translated into the vernacular under the title of *Fuero juzgo*, to his Andalusian conquests, by the end of his reign the main distinction as far as legal codes were concerned, was between Old Castile and the Castilian Extremadura on the one hand, and the rest of his dominions on the other.

As we should expect, there were few suits in the king's court involving two ecclesiastical litigants, but there are instances in which Fernando III intervened in a case begun before papal judges-delegate. In 1239, in a suit between the Order of Alcántara and the abbot of San Isidoro of León about the possession of Pinos, begun before judges-delegate at Zamora, the abbot had recourse to the king's court on the grounds that the abbey had obtained possession of Pinos by exchange with Alfonso IX of León and could present that king's diploma. Both parties were summoned before the king and duly produced their title deeds; Fernando declared in favour of the abbey but granted the order in compensation an annual sum of 100 *maravedíes*, the equivalent of the rents from Pinos, secured on the royal rents from Ciudad Rodrigo. The papal judges-delegate formally approved this compromise.[70]

[67] *Cortes*, I, no. XIV, cls. 44–7.
[68] *Fuero de Cuenca*, p. 864.
[69] *Cortes*, I, no. XIX, cl. 23; no. XX, cl. 21.
[70] Lomax, 'Las milicias cistercienses en el reino de León', *Hispania*, XXIII, 36, and *aps*. 3, 4 (pp. 41–2).

In both León and Castile, but especially in the former, cases were also brought before the king's court in which *concejos* were involved with their ecclesiastical overlords. Such suits were either about services due to (or privileges won from) the overlord, or else because of riot and insurrection by the townsfolk in which damage had been done to ecclesiastical property. One of the earliest cases from León, which Fernando III heard after his accession to the throne of that kingdom, was a case of riot. The townsmen of Belver, a Leonese town subject to Sahagún, rose against the abbot, entered armed into the monastery of San Salvador of Belver, a priory of Sahagún, broke down houses and walls belonging to it, uprooted vines and cut down or uprooted trees in the vineyards and orchards belonging to the church. The abbot of Sahagún cited the *concejo* of Belver before Fernando III. Two separate questions were involved – the nature of the dues and services owed by the men of Belver to the abbey of Sahagún, and the compensation to be paid for the damage to church property. On the first, the king confirmed an agreement between the parties which had fixed the tribute to be paid by the *vecinos* to the abbot and accepted the right of the abbey to exact hospitality (*posada*) for its monks and servants when required; the *concejo* had also to hand over to the abbey the church of Santa María in Belver, with its rights and tithes. On the other hand, the abbey had to renounce certain of its claims against the townsmen and undertook not to proceed further against them in either civil or ecclesiastical courts. The question of compensation was placed in the king's hands. He ordered the men of Belver to rebuild, before the following Michaelmas, the houses and walls destroyed in the riot. The monastery's devastated vineyards and orchards were to be replanted by the town which, for the next ten years, was to hold them at a rent from the abbey and cultivate them at its own cost; at the end of the ten-year period they were to be handed back in a proper state of cultivation.[71]

A serious case of riot took place in Túy in 1249 when the citizens rose against the bishop, entered the cathedral, attacked the clergy, overthrew the lamps and committed other acts of sacrilege. The matter was brought before the king's court where the city was condemned to pay a fine of 1,000 *maravedíes* to the bishop and chapter, and three citizens, who had held office at the time of the insurrection, were sentenced to

---

[71] AHN, Clero, *carp.* 913/10, 11 (6 March 1231). For the text of the second document, see Appendix, doc. II, below, and Escalona, *Sahagún, ap.* III, *esc.* CCXXXIV.

do public penance before the High Altar of the cathedral. The bishop's lordship was confirmed.[72]

Other clashes between towns and their ecclesiastical overlords were less violent. In 1247 began a long series of suits between the archbishop and chapter of Santiago de Compostela and the *concejo* of the city. These disputes were to continue for nearly twenty years and to occasion many appearances before the courts of Fernando III and Alfonso X. The parties appeared before Fernando III in 1247 and 1250. One important question at issue was how far the privileges and immunities enjoyed by the citizens of the walled city ought to be extended to any possessions which they had acquired in the Tierra de Santiago; other issues were the form of the election of the city magistrates and their powers, the existence of a guild of shoemakers in the city of which the archbishop complained and the legality of the powers exercised by the archbishop's majordomo and other officials.[73] Suits also occurred between cathedral cities and their bishops when the former were royal cities not subject to ecclesiastical overlordships. For example, in 1241 there was a suit between the bishop and *concejo* of León about the rights which the *concejo* claimed to exercise over the vassals of the bishop who had acquired houses and lands in the city and its *alfoz*.[74] In Castile, also, suits arose between ecclesiastical overlords and their towns as, for example, the one in 1237 between the monastery of Oña and the *concejo* of Mijangos in which the later complained that the abbot sought to exact a higher rent than it had been accustomed to pay.[75] There were also suits between the military orders and royal towns – among them a land suit between the Order of Santiago and the town of Alcaraz in 1243 and a boundary suit between the Order of Calatrava and Jaén in 1251.[76] Suits between two *concejos* were a characteristic occurrence in Castile; of these the best known in our period was the long-drawn-out dispute between the *concejos* of Segovia and Madrid over the boundaries between the two towns and the use of the *montes*. This lasted well into the reign of Alfonso X. Under

[72] *ES*, xxii (Madrid 1767), *ap.* xviii, 293–4. Cf. Galindo, *Túy en la baja Edad Media*, 45–6; and Procter, *EHR*, lxxiv, 5–6.

[73] López Ferreiro, *Fueros*, i, 211–12, 216–34, 245–6, including documents of 6, 8, 9, 10 July 1250; cf. *Iglesia de Santiago*, v, 210–14, for a summary of the questions at issue.

[74] Muedra Benedito, *AHDE*, vi, no. vi (pp. 419–20).

[75] *CD Oña* ii, no. 480 (pp. 591–3) (3 Sept. 1237). Cf. Procter, 'The judicial use of *"pesquisa"* ', 6.

[76] AHN, Santiago, *caj*. 365/2 (18 Feb. 1243); Calatrava, R. 76 (26 April 1251), publ. Manuel Rodríguez, *Memorias*, 466–8, 525–7.

Fernando III the two *concejos* were impleaded in 1239, 1248 and 1249.[77]

Some traditional methods of proof had died out or were dying out in our period, while others were coming to be used with greater frequency. Proof by ordeal, except ordeal by battle in cases of *reto*, was no longer used. Proof by the method known as *pesquisa* may have been less used than in the earlier period but it was still frequently employed in all kinds of suits. Thus, it was used in a boundary suit between the abbot of Santo Domingo de Silos and the men of the parish of San Pedro within the town in 1233; in two suits between the bishop of Sigüenza and the men of La Riba and Atienza – one concerned with pasturage rights, the other with boundaries – in 1234; and in 1237 to determine the dues owed to the abbot of Oña by the men of Mijangos; other examples occurred throughout the reign.[78]

Documentary proof was used more frequently than hitherto, as written title-deeds became general. In 1243, in the land suit between the Order of Santiago and the *concejo* of Alcaraz, both parties produced documents in support of their claims and, after these had been examined, all but two of a large number of places in dispute were adjudged to the order. Again, in 1250, both the bishop and the *concejo* of Astorga produced documents in support of their claims to Cepada, to name but two examples.[79]

Professional judges now played an increasing part in the justice of the king's court, although nobles and bishops continued to judge cases with the king. In documents making reference to consultation between the king and the members of his court, the *alcaldes del rey* are often specifically included in such phrases as 'con conseio de mios Ricos Omnes e de Obispos e de Alcaldes e de otros omnes bonos que conmigo

---

[77] *DA Madrid*, *1a serie*, I, 73–8 (20 June 1239), 79–82 (24 Aug. 1249); *2a serie*, I, no. 1 (24 Sept. 1248).
[78] AHN, Clero, *carp.* 369/10 (29 Nov. 1233) deteriorated. The document is published in *Documentos lingüísticos*, no. 218, with missing words supplied from a confirmation of Alfonso X, and in *RC Silos*, no. 119; Minguella, *Historia de Sigüenza*, I, nos. CXCII, CXCIII (24 April 1234); *CD Oña*, II, no. 480 (3 Sept. 1237). Cf. also López Ferreiro, *Fueros*, I, 231–4 (9 July 1250).
[79] AHN, Santiago, *caj.* 365/2 (18 Feb. 1243), publ. Manuel Rodríguez, *Memorias*, 466–8, 512 (5 May 1250). See also Muedra Benedito, *AHDE*, VI, no. VI (pp. 419–20) (8 July 1241); López Ferreiro, *Fueros*, I, 245–6 (25 March 1247); AHN, Calatrava, R. 76 (26 April 1251), publ. Manuel Rodríguez, *Memorias*, 525–6: 'et el maestro et la orden de Calatrava mostraron me privilegios que les auia yo dado sobre aquellos terminos'.

eran'.[80] In spite of this growing professionalism, the part played by Fernando III personally is illustrated in many suits and in the reference made by the *Primera crónica general* to his tour of justice in 1242.[81]

The reign of Alfonso X brought notable innovations in the administration of justice which, however, because of the hostility which they evoked among all classes, failed to survive. The revolt of the nobles in 1272 was a turning point between two periods. From early in the reign, when the *Espéculo* was promulgated in the *corte*, this highly romanised code was the law administered in the king's court until Alfonso X was forced to rescind it during the revolt of the nobles. The hitherto rapid reception of Roman law was then checked until the *Partidas* were recognised in the *Ordenamiento de Alcalá* (1348). In 1274 Alfonso attempted to salvage something from the failure of his legal reforms by setting up a professional judicial tribunal within the *corte* under the *Ordenamiento de Zamora*, but this expert tribunal ceased to exist under his successor, Sancho IV, although some of the clauses of the ordinances dealing with procedure continued to be observed.

The *Espéculo* enumerated the various classes of judges appointed by the king, both in the king's court and in the provinces. Those connected with the *corte* were three: the *adelantados mayores de la corte del rey*, the *justicia de la casa* (or *corte*) *del rey* and the *alcaldes del rey*. The *adelantado* of the *corte* (who must be distinguished from the *adelantados mayores* ('governors') of the provinces) had to hear important pleas which the king was unable (or did not wish) to hear himself. Such pleas might include *reto*, suits between nobles, the military orders or the *concejos*. If women, widows, orphans, members of religious orders or lordless knights were involved in cases of *reto*, it was the duty of the *adelantado* to appoint an advocate to act for the defendant. The *adelantado* also heard appeals from the sentences of the *alcaldes del rey* or from those of the provincial *adelantados*.[82] The *adelantado de la corte* has left no trace in the documents of Alfonso X, but he appears to correspond to the *sobre juez* of the *Partidas*.[83] The *justicia de la corte* or *alguacil* was an administrative and executive officer, rather than a judicial one, although he had some judicial functions. It was his business to keep order in the court and to prevent brawls,

[80] *DA Madrid, 1a serie*, I, 79–82 (24 Aug. 1249); cf. López Ferreiro, *Fueros*, I, 216–18 (1 July 1250).
[81] *PCG*, II, *cap.* 1061 (p. 742).
[82] *Espéculo, lib.* IV, *tít.* II, prologue, and *leyes* 11, 13; *lib.* V, *tít.* XIV, *leyes* 12, 14.
[83] *Part.* III, *tít.* IV, *ley* I.

gaming and the taking of unlawful *conducho*. He also held preliminary hearings of pleas between members of the court and settled them, if possible, by agreement. If this failed, he then had to bring the suit before the *alcaldes del rey* and carry out their judgment. He had also to see that appeals were duly heard.[84] Although this office must have been in existence from the early years of Alfonso X's reign, there is no evidence of it in his documents until the period of the revolt of the Infante Don Sancho, when the then holder of the office, Don Tello Gutiérrez, a *rico hombre*, was one of those who remained loyal to the king and was with him at Seville; he witnessed the king's two wills and was referred to by Jofré de Loaisa.[85]

Alcaldes del rey had been attached to the king's court since early in the thirteenth century. They were appointed by the king to judge pleas daily in the court, and the *Espéculo* laid down minute regulations concerning the way in which they were to judge suits, their obligations to judge impartially, their bearing towards suitors, the hours at which they were to judge and the measures to be taken to shorten the length of suits.[86] References to them in Alfonso's documents were numerous. It was sometimes stated that the king had taken counsel with his *alcaldes* as well as with the bishops and nobles present at court.[87] From time to time *cartas* containing judicial sentences were authorised by the *alcaldes del rey*.[88] In some cases, where the king wished to spare the litigants avoidable trouble and expense, one of the *alcaldes* was sent to hear locally a suit which would otherwise have been heard by the king in person. Such a case occurred in 1266 in a dispute between the bishop and *concejo* of León as to whether the judge appointed by the bishop to keep the *Libro de León* should hear the pleas of the city jointly with the judges of the *concejo*. The *concejo* refused to appoint *personeros* because it said the suit ought to come before the king in person, although a number of good men of the city attended the hearing 'mas non por personeros'; the ancient testimony was in favour of

---

[84] *Espéculo*, lib. IV, tít. III, prologue, and *leyes* 1, 8, 14, 15.

[85] His name occurs in *privilegios rodados* of that period among those 'que con nusco touieron en verdad, e en lealtad': Ballesteros, *Sevilla*, nos. 232, 233. Daumet, *Bibliothèque de l'Ecole des Chartes*, LXVII; Jofré de Loaisa, *Crónica*, 24, 29.

[86] *Espéculo*, lib. IV, tít. II, prologue, and *leyes* 7, 15.

[87] E.g. *RC Silos*, no. 152 (p. 216) (14 May 1254); López Ferrero, *Fueros*, I, 248. (21 Feb. 1261).

[88] López Ferreiro, *Fueros*, I, 244 (8 Sept. 1253); *MHE*, I, no. XII (17 March 1254); *RC Silos*, no. 152 (14 May 1254); AC León, no. 1119, 'por mandado de Johan Bermúdez, alcalde del Rey' (24 June 1270); *CD Murcia*, I, no. LVI (pp. 81-2) (12 June 1272).

the church, and the *alcalde del rey*, Fernán Fernández, gave judgment for the bishop.[89] *Alcaldes del rey* were also appointed to view boundaries, as in a land suit in 1253 between the Order of Calatrava and the city of Toledo in which Alfonso X ordered Ruy López de Mendoza and Ruy Fernández *alcalde del Rey* to view the *términos*.[90] They acted as *pesquisidores*[91] or as arbiters between litigants, as in a land suit between the Order of Santiago and the *concejo* of Alcaraz in 1263, in which five arbiters were appointed, two by the order, two by the *concejo* and the fifth, 'Ferrand Perez de Cuenca nuestro alcalde', by the king.[92]

From the date of its promulgation until the revolt of the nobles, the *Espéculo*, as we have seen, was the law code in use in the king's court and the oath which it prescribed to be taken by the *alcaldes del rey* on appointment contained the specific undertaking to judge 'por estas leyes que son escriptas en este libro, e non por otras'.[93] The adoption of the *Espéculo* necessarily entailed changes in procedure, but ancient procedure was still followed in the royal court in some cases. Proof by *pesquisa* in civil cases was mentioned only incidentally in the *Espéculo*, in connection with land suits or other matters which did not impinge on royal rights.[94] Documentary proof of its continuance in suits between subjects is ample. To take one example: in 1264, in a suit between the Order of Calatrava and the *concejo* of Zorita in which the *concejo* complained that the order demanded higher dues and more services than had been customary under Fernando III, Alfonso X ordered a *pesquisa* to be held 'en omnes bonos e sin sospecha de las villas fazeras de Çorita e en omnes bonos de Çorita' to determine what had been customary in his father's reign and then gave judgment in accordance with the findings of the inquiry.[95] This use of *pesquisa* continued throughout the reigns of Alfonso X and Sancho IV.[96] It even lingered

89 Muedra Benedito, *AHDE*, vi, no. vii (pp. 421–4) (5 Jan. 1266).
90 BN, MS. 13094, fol. 132 (10 Nov. 1253).
91 López Ferreiro, *Fueros*, i, 279 (23 Feb. 1264).
92 AHN, Santiago, *caj.* 214/17 (22 March 1263).
93 *Espéculo*, lib. iv, tít. ii, ley 3; cf. also lib. iv, tít. ii, leys 10, 16.
94 *Ibid*. lib. iv, tít. xi, ley 14.
95 AHN, Calatrava, R. 143 (2 Jan. 1264). For other examples of the use of *pesquisa* in common pleas, cf. López Ferreiro, *Fueros*, i, 217, 278–80 (9 May 1263 and 30 Jan. 1264); Muedra Benedito, *AHDE*, vi, no. vi (p. 421) (5 Jan. 1266); *ES*, xxxv, *ap*. xii (2 June 1266).
96 E.g. *DA Madrid*, *1a serie*, i, 122–5 (26 Dec. 1275); *MHE*, i, no. cxlv (26 June 1278); *CD Oña*, ii, no. 698 (14 Feb. 1281); Gaibrois de Ballesteros, *Sancho IV*, iii, nos. 200, 268, 269, 299 (9 May 1288, 7, 22 Sept. 1289 and 20 March 1290), for *pesquisa* on lands of the nunnery of Fresnillo.

on into the first half of the fourteenth century, for in the *Ordenamiento de Alcalá* of 1348 Alfonso XI recognised that it was 'costumbre e uso' in his court that land suits and suits concerning pasturage rights might be settled by *pesquisa* and he confirmed this use.[97]

It is, however, clear from the text of the *Espéculo* that its compilers assumed that proof in civil cases between subjects would normally be by the production of documents, or else by witnesses (*testigos*) and each of these methods of proof was dealt with in detail.[98] The *Espéculo* laid down that certain documents were not valid. These included privileges and charters which were against the *fueros*, or against the common interest, or against the faith, or against the rights of the king, while privileges which had not been exercised for thirty years were obsolete and invalid.[99] Rules were also laid down by which a judge could determine whether a royal document had been falsified.[100] In cases in which the value of the land or goods sought was more than 10 *maravedíes*, the depositions were to be made in writing and not verbally, and so procedure became written and not oral.[101]

Records of suits before the king's court provide plenty of evidence of the use of documentary proof, which had by this time probably become the general form of proof in land suits. Two examples provided by suits in which the Order of Calatrava was involved will suffice. In 1256 the order was impleaded in a suit with Don García Almoravid. The order had granted to Alfonso X certain inheritances in Alfaro which the king had then given to Don García. The order claimed that Don García had taken possession of lands in Alfaro which had not been included in the transactions with the king. The *cartas de las donaciones* were produced and examined, after which Alfonso X, with the advice of the court, gave judgment for the order.[102] In a boundary suit between the order and Bishop Fernando of Córdoba in June 1262, the order contended that an agreement entered into on the boundaries had not been carried out, and Alfonso X ordered the bishop to send his proctor with the charter of partition to the court by St Martin's Day, when the king would judge the suit.[103]

---

[97] *Ordenamiento de Alcalá, tít.* xi, *ley única.* Cf. Procter, 'The judicial use of "*pesquisa*"', 18–19.
[98] *Espéculo, lib.* iv, *tít.* vi: 'De las querellas e de las cartes'; *tít.* vii: 'De los testigos'.
[99] *Ibid. lib.* iv, *tít.* vi, *leyes* 6–7, 14.
[100] *Ibid. lib.* iv, *tít.* xii, *ley* 50.   [101] *Ibid. lib.* iv, *tít.* iv, *ley* 1.
[102] AHN, Calatrava, R. 108 (21 Oct. 1256); for other suits where title-deeds were produced, see *MHE,* i, nos. lvi (15 Aug. 1257), lxxxix (11 Sept. 1262), xc (30 Dec. 1262).
[103] AHN, Esc. Calatrava, iv, fol. 11 (17 June 1262).

Such cases were commonplace occurrences. Of more general interest was a case heard in 1268 between the abbot of San Isidoro of León (a house of Augustinian canons) and the *concejo* of Mansilla concerning some messuages, which had belonged to two clerks of Mansilla, who, on entering San Isidoro, had bequeathed these inheritances to the abbey. The *concejo* took possession of them, and contended that they were royal demesne and could not pass to the church. The abbot's proctor produced privileges from former kings, whereby the abbey was able to purchase or inherit land belonging to royal demesne. The *personero* of the *concejo* contested the validity of these privileges, which had been granted before the law promulgated in 'las cortes que fizo en Benavente' which forbade the passing of *realengo* to *abadengo*. Alfonso X pronounced against the validity of the privileges because they were 'contra mio sennorio e danno de mi terra', a judgment in accord with the *Espéculo*. He reaffirmed the *postura* of 1202, but nevertheless allowed San Isidoro to inherit the messuages as a matter of grace.[104]

The *Espéculo* deals at length with witnesses, and begins by enumerating certain persons who could not be called as witnesses, such as slaves. Women could be witnesses in civil cases, but not in criminal cases in which the penalty was death, mutilation, forfeiture or exile – except when no man was available. No one less than fifteen years of age or, in criminal cases, less than twenty years, could be a witness. Other persons prohibited from thus acting against Christians were those 'de otra ley', that is, Jews, Moors and heretics; so, too, were the insane, criminals, others of ill fame as well as known perjurers. As a general rule, witnesses were heard after the plea had been begun and when the plaintiff and defendant had stated their cases.[105] All witnesses had to take an oath to speak the truth.[106] Witnesses were examined apart, and separately, and their evidence taken down in writing – if in the king's court, by the *escribanos de la corte*. The method of examination and the questions to be asked of witnesses were set out. Litigants might bring as many as twelve witnesses; there must be at least two, and their evidence must agree. Where a witness had to come from a great distance, he might be examined where he lived and his evidence taken down in writing.[107] Minute regulations for the taking of evidence and for deciding its reliability were included.

[104] Muedra Benedito, *AHDE*, VI, no. VIII (pp. 424–5) (6 April 1268).
[105] *Espéculo, lib.* IV, *tít.* VII, *leyes* 1–9.
[106] *Ibid. lib.* IV, *tít.* VII, *ley* 15.
[107] *Ibid. lib.* IV, *tít.* VII, *leyes* 17–20, 22.

The actual records of suits before the king's court are silent on the use of witnesses, although the *Leyes del estilo* refer to them.[108] It is possible that witnesses were called when documentary evidence was lacking. Suits between towns and their ecclesiastical or lay lords on questions of the services owed by the town to the lord were usually concerned with custom, for which there was no written evidence. But even in such suits there is no evidence that witnesses were examined – for example, in the suit between the Order of Calatrava and the town of Bolaños in 1261. There the king's sentence, given after consultation with the members of the *corte*, was prefaced by a summary of the contentions put forward by the *personeros* of the litigants, but without any reference to witnesses. It does not, however, follow that witnesses were not produced and examined during the course of the hearing.[109] It is possible that witnesses were called more often in crown than in common pleas.[110]

The most important change in procedure brought about by the *Espéculo* was the substitution of procedure by inquisition (*procedimiento inquisitivo*) for the Germanic procedure by accusation (*procedimiento acusativo*) in criminal cases. By this procedure suits were brought to court, not by the accusation of the injured party or, in the case of homicide, by the dead man's kin, but by the king or a royal official 'de su oficio' – that is, not by private accusation but by public prosecution or indictment. Indictment was followed by inquisition on oath, and on conviction the penalty was usually death, mutilation or confiscation of possessions. Although the word *pesquisa*, which had long been used for inquiries carried out in land and boundary suits, was also used for these criminal investigations, a distinction must be made between the two. Inquisitorial procedure might be general, held over all or only some of the inhabitants of a province, district, or town, either because of accusations of evil deeds whose perpetrators were unknown, or because of general accusations of ill fame, or because the king, on progress through the land, sought information. It might also be used in specific cases where the criminal was unknown or, in certain cases, such as unlawful *conducho*, where the criminal was known, or it might be used where the parties to a suit asked for it.[111] Not all of this was new. There are some traces of indictment in Alfonso IX's decrees of 1188 and in the unofficial thirteenth-century *Libro de los fueros de*

108 *Leyes* CLXXIX, CLXXX.
109 AHN, Esc. Calatrava, IV, fol. 2 (28 March 1261).
110 Guglielmi, *CHE*, XXIV, 186.
111 *Espéculo*, lib. IV, *tít.* XI. The substance of this title is also contained in *Part.* III, *tít.* XVII, but the order of the *leyes* is different.

Castilla. Permanent royal *pesquisidores* had been functioning since the last quarter of the twelfth century, and the general *pesquisa* was in use before the middle of the thirteenth. The use of the death penalty in criminal cases, instead of pecuniary penalties, can be found in a number of municipal *fueros*, and the *Fuero real* ordered the use of indictment *de oficio*, if there was no private accusation. The importance of the *Espéculo* lay in its fusion of these elements into a coherent procedure, which could be used in serious criminal cases as a normal method of bringing malefactors to justice.[112] Accusation could, however, still be used, even in cases where the death penalty was involved. With the rescinding of the *Espéculo*, the king's court reverted to the complex *status quo ante* which had obtained under Fernando III, with the addition, now, of the *Fuero real*, which continued to be used both as a municipal *fuero* by many towns and also in cases of appeal to the king's court from such towns.

The most important enactment of the last decade of Alfonso's reign was the *Ordenamiento de Zamora* of 1274. Its objects were defined as the prevention of delays in hearing suits and of miscarriages of justice, but it in fact concerned itself with much more and its most important provisions were those concerned with the establishment of a judicial tribunal within the *corte* to which a fixed number of professional judges were to be attached. These *alcaldes de la corte* were to number twenty-three – nine for Castile, eight for León and six for Extremadura. These were to divide the year between them, so that some from each region were always with the king. Two of the eight *alcaldes* of León were to be knights who knew the *Fuero juzgo* and the ancient custom of the kingdom. All these *alcaldes* were to be laymen.[113] There were also three judges of appeals (*alzadas*) – 'tres omes buenos entendidos e sabidores de los fueros que oyan las alzadas de toda la tierra'. If these three were unable to decide an appeal, they were to call in other judges and the final decision was to be by a majority. Final appeal came before the king in León, Extremadura, Toledo and Andalusia. For Castile the procedure was more complicated; there appeals from the local *alcaldes* went to the provincial *adelantados*, thence to the *alcaldes* of the king's court, thence to *the adelantado mayor* of Castile and finally to the king.[114] Minute regulations governed the conduct of the *alcaldes de la*

[112] See Procter, *The judicial use of 'pesquisa'*, 20–35; and Cerdú Ruiz-Funes, 'En torno a la pesquisa y procedimiento inquisitivo en el derecho castellano–leonés en la Edad Media', *AHD*, xxxii, 483–517.
[113] *Ordenamiento de Zamora*, cl. 17.
[114] *Ibid*. cls. 19–20.

corte, and were designed to prevent undue delay in justice as well as venality and partiality.[115] The king was to hear suits in person on Mondays, Wednesdays and Fridays, a re-enactment of one of the laws of 1258.[116] Crown pleas, which were always accustomed to be heard in the king's court, were enumerated as homicide, rape, breach of truce or safe-conduct, arson, *camino quebrantado* (violation of the peace which protected public roads), treason, *aleve* (treachery) and *reto*.[117]

Besides setting up this new tribunal within the *corte*, the ordinance also dealt with two classes of persons who played an important part in litigation – advocates and scriveners. It was laid down unequivocally that in Castile and Extremadura advocates might plead for litigants only in cases where the relevant *fueros* permitted it, but that in the kingdoms of León and Toledo, in Andalusia and in those towns which used the *Fuero real*, litigants might have their cases presented by advocates. As many of the towns of Castile and Extremadura in fact used the *Fuero real*, the prohibition of advocates in these provinces was less complete than might appear. In León all advocates were to be laymen, and the clergy might act there only in pleas touching themselves or their church. Advocates were not to appear in unimportant cases, except in those in which poor litigants were involved, and there were to be two salaried advocates attached to the court to plead for litigants who could not afford a fee. Advocates took an oath before the *alcaldes* that they would not plead maliciously, nor unduly spin out a suit, nor knowingly put forward a false plea; those who broke this oath were to be debarred from acting in future as advocates, witnesses or *alcaldes* and were also to be fined. Other regulations were designed to prevent corruption and the taking of exorbitant fees. The advocate was not to advise his client to appeal against a sentence which was manifestly just, nor to prevent litigants from reaching a settlement out of court, except in criminal cases (*pleitos criminales*) in which no compromise was permissible after the suit had been brought before the *alcaldes*.[118]

All *escribanos* attached to the royal court were to be laymen. It was their duty to take notes of the proceedings and at the completion of a case to draw up the document containing the sentence. As the court did not have its own seal, such documents were taken to the chancery to be sealed, and it was from the chancery that the scriveners obtained their

---

[115] *Ibid.* cls. 21–35.
[116] *Ibid.* cl. 42; cf. *Cortes*, I, no. XIII, cls. 8, 9.
[117] *Cortes*, I, no. XVI, cl. 46.
[118] *Ordenamiento de Zamora*, cls. 1–16.

supplies of parchment. Chancery fees were to be those laid down at Palencia in 1255.[119]

It is probable that much of the procedure laid down in this ordinance of 1274 was that customarily followed in the king's court, and some of it closely resembles that which had been laid down in the *Espéculo*. The provision for *alcaldes* from each of the provinces of León, Castile and Extremadura who knew the laws and customs of their own provinces met some of the demands made by the nobles during the revolt of 1272/3 and fulfilled some of the promises of concessions then made by the king. To that extent, then, the ordinance represented a victory for the party opposed to the romanisation and unification of the law throughout the whole kingdom. On the other hand, the professional character of the tribunal set up within the court, and the minute regulations of procedure laid down for it, helped to strengthen the king's control of justice, as did also the enumeration of the *casos de corte* – crown pleas – although these appear to have been those traditionally recognised as such. A further point to be noted is the lay character of judges and others connected with the new judicial tribunal.[120] Detailed rules for the bringing of appeals before the royal court were later included in the *Leyes del estilo*, a compilation probably put together about 1310 but based on the custom of the king's court during the reigns of Alfonso X and Sancho IV. These rules testify to the increasing importance of appeals.[121]

Under Sancho IV this tribunal ceased to exist. In consequence, justice was again administered by the *corte* itself, with or without the assistance of professional judges. Sancho IV also reverted to the practice of appointing ecclesiastics to hear cases. In 1285 'maestre fferrant mio Juyz, maestrescola de Córdoua' was thus deputed to hear a case to which the king could not at the time attend.[122] Again, when Sancho IV was engaged in the siege of Arronches, he left Don Lope Díaz de Haro, Bishop Martín of Astorga (notary in León) and Fernán Pérez (dean of Seville and notary in Castile) with the chancery 'porque librasen todos los pleitos en la su tierra', and the *Crónica de Sancho IV* goes on to describe Bishop Martín doing justice in Burgos, sitting in the

---

[119] *Ibid.* 36–41.
[120] On the *casos de corte* and their enumeration in various documents, see Iglesia Ferreiros, 'Las Cortes de Zamora de 1274 y los casos de corte', *AHDE*, XLI, esp. 945–6, 966–71.
[121] *Leyes del estilo*, leyes CXLIX–CLXIV.
[122] Gaibrois de Ballesteros, *Sancho IV*, III, no. 64 (10 April 1285). The *maestrescola* corresponded to the cathedral chancellor in France and England.

gate of the town house of the abbot of Oña, where he was lodging.[123] The *concejos* of Castile in the Cortes of 1293 petitioned that appeals from Castile should not be judged by an ecclesiastic. This the king granted 'en general' but reserved the right to appoint whom he would in cases in which the king was concerned.[124] The names of a number of expert lay judges who served Sancho IV have come down to us. These include Alfonso Pérez of Toledo and Durant Sánchez, *alcaldes del rey* who were ordered to hear appeals from Extremadura in 1291, Roy Sánchez de Vallodilid ('nuestro alcalde') and Paschal Martínez, a judge of the king's court who was sent on embassies to France in 1292 and 1294. The cleric 'Magister Johannes iudex curiae nostrae' was appointed in 1292 to settle with the king of England differences which had arisen between subjects of the Castilian crown and the men of Bayonne.[125] It is, however, clear from the *cuadernos* of the Cortes of 1286 and 1293 that, despite the abrogation of the *Ordenamiento de Zamora*, Sancho IV retained in the court *alcaldes* who could judge according to the *fueros* of the different provinces. The *cuaderno* of 1286 decreed that writs were not to be issued impleading anyone under the *sello de la poridad* or other seals, unless the writ had been authorised by the *alcalde* of the king's court who knew the particular *fuero* under which the suit would be judged.[126] In 1293 the *concejos* of Castile petitioned that the *alcaldes* of León and Extremadura should not judge suits from Castile, while those of León asked that the *alcaldes* for the kingdom of León in the king's court should judge according to the *Fuero juzgo*.[127] Both petitions were granted.

It is not possible to say how far the procedural rules laid down in the *Ordenamiento de Zamora* also continued to be observed. According to the *Leyes del estilo*, the various crown pleas enumerated in the ordinance, except *reto* (which was always heard before the king), were normally tried, not in the king's court, but in the municipal and local courts and according to the local *fueros*.[128] During the minority of Fernando IV an attempt was made in 1299 to revive the expert tribunal; it was agreed in the Cortes then that as many *alcaldes* as were

---

[123] *Crónica Sancho IV*, *cap.* iv (p. 76). Gaibrois de Ballesteros, *Sancho IV*, iii, no. 214 (6 Sept. 1288), is a confirmation by Sancho IV of a sentence pronounced by Bishop Martin. The siege of Arronches took place in 1287.
[124] *Cortes*, i, no. xix, cl. 20.
[125] Gaibrois de Ballesteros, *Sancho IV*, iii, nos. 383, 575; Jofré de Loaisa, *Crónica*, 31; Daumet, *Relations*, no. xxiii (pp. 213–17); *Foedera*, i, 790.
[126] *Cortes*, i, no. xvii, cl. 8.
[127] *Ibid*. i, no. xiv, cl. 14; no. xx, cl. 9.
[128] *Leyes del estilo, ley* xci.

necessary should be appointed in the royal household and that a judge to hear appeals in the king's court should also be appointed.[129] Nothing appears to have been done until, in 1312, the court first established by Alfonso X in 1274 was reconstituted with a full complement of *alcaldes* and judges of appeal.[130] It was not, however, until after the accession of the House of Trastámara to the throne (1369), that the court known as the *Chancillería* or *Audiencia*, completely independent of the king's court, was finally organised. But all that lies far beyond our period.

[129] *Cortes*, I, no. xxv, cl. 2; no. xxvi, cls. 8, 14.
[130] *Cortes*, I, no. xxxv, cls. 1–8, 23, 27–9, 78.

I2
Conclusion

In the foregoing chapters the composition and functions of the Castilian–Leonese curia, *corte* and, in greater detail, the cortes of the same kingdom during the period 1072 to 1295 have been described and analysed. General conclusions arising from each facet of our study have been pointed out at the end of each chapter and it would serve little purpose to repeat them here. Some readers may, however, wish for some information about the way in which similar institutions in the other Iberian kingdoms followed, or did not follow, the patterns of development in the central kingdoms. It seems, therefore, appropriate to end this work with some observations, necessarily of a somewhat summary character, on that question.

The beginnings of representative assemblies in the Peninsula as a whole can be traced, as we have seen, to the period when the municipalities were first summoned to send their representatives to court, not merely, as previously, to appear before the curia as suitors in cases in which individual towns were cited as plaintiffs or defendants but now to take part, as well, in some (though often not in all) of the other business to be transacted there. The first certain entry of the representatives of the towns for such purposes anywhere in the Peninsula relates to León and the date of this event was 1188, when Alfonso IX of León summoned citizens to the first great curia of his reign. The available evidence is not sufficiently precise to prove decisively, as has sometimes been suggested, that Alfonso VIII of Castile had summoned the *mayores* of the Castilian towns to his assemblies in 1187 and 1188. For Castile the first indisputable date of entry is 1214, when the towns did homage to Enrique I.

In the eastern Iberian kingdom, whose constituent parts formed the 'Crown of Aragon' (*Corona de Aragón*), the kingdom of Aragon proper and the county of Barcelona always both retained their separate great

254

curias, with or without the addition of townsmen, as a frequent occurrence, not as an occasional expedient. However, these two different
assemblies often met jointly. The earliest certain occasion on which
cities and towns were represented was at a joint assembly at Lérida in
1214, when representatives of Aragonese and Catalan towns did
homage to the child king, Jaime I.[1] The first separate assembly for
Catalonia at which townsmen were present was that at Villafranca in
1217; for Aragon, that at Zaragoza in 1220.[2] In Portugal, which, of
course, derived its institutions from the parent kingdom of León, there
is no certain evidence of the attendance of representatives of the towns
until 1253, at Lisbon, sixty-five years after their first appearance in
León.[3] In Navarre, some supposed instances before the mid-thirteenth
century must be treated as very dubious, but townsmen do seem to
have taken part in an assembly at Tudela in 1231 to take the oath to
observe the Adoption Treaty between Sancho VI of Navarre and
Jaime I of Aragon.[4] They may have been present in 1253 when
Teobaldo II swore to keep the *fueros* of Navarre and also on 1 March
1271, when Enrique I (1270–4) was proclaimed king.[5] During the
troubled months which followed Enrique's death on 22 July 1274,
leaving his infant daughter Juana to succeed him, and his French
widow Blanche of Artois as regent, the representatives of the towns
attended the *corte general* of Navarre on three occasions before the end
of the year: in August, probably at Pamplona; at the end of September
at Puente de la Reina; and in November at Olite.[6] Thus, except for
the Leonese instance in 1188, the earliest certain instances of the

---

[1] *Chronicle of James I, cap.* XI.
[2] *CD Jaime I,* I, no. IV; *Cartulaire général de l'ordre des Hospitaliers,* II, 268.
[3] *PMH: Leges,* I, 192: 'Et ego super hoc habui consilium cum riquis hominibus
sapientibus de curia mea et consilio meo et cum prelatis et militibus et mercatoribus et cum civibus et bonis hominibus de consiliis regni mei.' This appears to me
to be evidence of the attendance of representatives of the towns at a great
assembly, although the assembly at Leiria in the following year is usually
accepted as the first occasion.
[4] The Adoption Treaty of 1231 (*CDIACA,* VI, no. XVIII) makes provision for the
nobles and towns of both countries to swear to keep it. For Navarre the oath
was taken on 4 April 1231 at Tudela (*CD Jaime, I,* I, no. LXXXV). Cf. *Recull de
documents inedits del Rey En Jaume I,* no. CVIII, for a later reference to this
oath.
[5] Yanguas, *Diccionario,* I, 281–6; AGN, *caj.* 3/33 (1 March 1271), oath of
Enrique I to keep the *fueros* of Pamplona, inserted in a confirmation of 23 May
1272; cf. Yanguas, *Diccionario,* III, 516, with the document of 1271 wrongly
dated 1270.
[6] *Cartulario de Don Felipe III,* no. 157, place of issue not given, but Anelier,
Guerre de Navarre, l. 619, says 'las cortez foron mandadas...en Pampalona';
CDIACA, VI, nos. L, LII.

appearance of representatives of the towns in the general assemblies of the Iberian kingdoms were spread over the first three quarters of the thirteenth century.[7]

The significance of an early date of entry must not, however, be over-emphasised. In no case anywhere in the Peninsula was the first summons followed by regular attendances, and the appearance of the representatives was, generally speaking, infrequent. The great curia continued to meet without them. As we have already seen, the attendance of the townsmen in Castile and León took place at irregular intervals up to 1250, both before and after the union of the kingdoms. It was during the reign of Alfonso X of Castile that it became a normal occurrence. In the Crown of Aragon the cortes, whether joint, or for Aragon or Catalonia separately, met fairly frequently from 1214 to 1250, but rather less often for the rest of Jaime I's reign. Yet the General Privilege (promulgated at Zaragoza for Aragon proper in 1283), and the decrees promulgated at Barcelona for Catalonia in the same year, both conceded annual assemblies in which the towns were recognised as an integral part of the assembly – a concession not found elsewhere at that date.[8] In Navarre, under French rule after 1277, the cortes declined in importance and rarely met. They did meet, however, in 1283, on which occasion Pedro III of Aragon sent an embassy to Estella to protest about a projected Franco–Navarrese invasion of Aragon.[9] There seem also to have been meetings in 1298 and 1299.[10] It was not, however, until the fourteenth century that the Navarrese cortes revived, and that the towns had any share in legislation; their financial powers date from the accession to the throne of the House of Evreux (1329).[11] In Portugal, also, the cortes met only infrequently during the long reign of Afonso III (1248–79).[12]

---

[7] For early instances in Italy, see Post, *Studies in medieval legal thought*, 85–8; and in Languedoc, Bisson, *Assemblies and representation in Languedoc*, 79–80, 150–63, 193–8. Continental historians are inclined to date the beginning of the English Parliament from the attendance of the burgesses in 1265 and to overlook the earlier attendances of the knights of the shire in 1226, 1254 and 1258: Stubbs, *Charters*, 353, 365–6.

[8] *Fueros y observancias* I, fol. 8. *Cortes de Cataluña*, I, i, no. XXII, cl. XVIII. The annual summons was not observed. In 1301 in Catalonia it was changed to once in three years, and in 1307 in Aragon, to once in two years.

[9] ACA, Perg. Pere II, 369 (27 July 1283). The document refers to the presence of the 'omes de las villas e de los logares de Navarra'.

[10] AGN, *caj.* 4/114 (23 Aug. 1298) and 120 (31 Aug. 1299) seem to refer to assemblies of some sort. Cf. Yanguas, *Diccionario*, I, 290–5.

[11] Merriman, 'The cortes of the Spanish kingdoms', *AHR*, XVI, 494.

[12] At Lisbon in 1253, at Leiria in 1254, at Coimbra in 1261 and at Santarém in 1273: *PMH*: *Leyes*, I, 192, 193–6, 210–12, 229–31.

Another important moment in the evolution of such assemblies is the date at which the representatives were instructed to bring with them mandates from their constituent communities. This change from the older, looser form of representation to the stricter, proctorial type, based on Roman law, took place as a result of the revived study of Roman law in the later twelfth century, and its spread throughout Western Europe, through law schools such as that of Bologna and through canon law. It is, therefore, not surprising that the earliest example of the use of the second type should have occurred in the papal states in 1200.[13] In other countries we should expect the change to take place somewhat later, but the fact that few writs of summons, or mandates, have survived anywhere for the thirteenth century makes it difficult to determine when the change to mandates took place. There is a possible early example in the Crown of Aragon. The *Chronicle of James I* states that at Lérida in 1214, when the oath of allegiance was taken to the child king, ten men from each city were present 'furnished with powers from the rest to approve that which might be done by all'. The chronicle was written several decades later; it is certainly incorrect in stating that each city sent ten men in 1214, so that it is not wholly reliable evidence about events there. It should, however, be remembered that Cardinal Peter of Benevente, papal legate in Languedoc, presided over the Cortes of Lérida and may have insisted that the town representatives should bring mandates. He was also probably responsible for introducing the practice of the taking of the oath to the king, a practice hitherto unknown in Aragon.[14] Fourteen years later, on 6 February 1228, in a general court at Daroca, *probi homines* from thirty cities and towns of Aragon did homage and swore fealty to Jaime's infant son Alfonso. The deputations varied in number from two to fourteen and swore 'pro se et pro tota vniuersitate de...' in the case of Lérida, Zaragoza, Huesca, Jaca, Tarazona and Daroca, and 'pro toto concilio de...' in the case of the other towns. There is no evidence what mandates, if any, they brought with them.[15] At the Cortes of Monzón in 1236 the text confirming the coinage of Jaca included the names of representatives from ten cities and towns, and

13 Post, *Studies in medieval legal thought*, 95–8, 108–10.
14 *Chronicle of James I, cap.* XI (p. 9). The original Catalan is 'e de cada ciutat x homens ab auctoritat dels altres de ço que els farien que fos feyts': *Llibre del feyts, cap.* XI; cf. Zurita, *Anales,* lib. II, *cap.* LXVI. Miret i Sans, *Itinerari de Jaume I,* 19, n. 1, publishes a list of those who took the oath to the king. This shows that the deputations varied in number and in most cases were five or fewer.
15 Bisson, 'A general court of Aragon (Daroca, February 1228)', *EHR,* XCII, 107–24.

the preface to the *Fueros de Aragón*, promulgated in the Aragonese Cortes of Huesca in 1247, refers to citizens of cities and towns 'pro suis conciliis destinatos'.[16] In 1270 we have the specific use of the term 'proctor'. The *concejo* of Teruel, having been summoned to attend cortes to be held at Zaragoza, appointed 'procuradores nuestros sindicos et actores' to appear before the king, though there is no evidence that these cortes actually met.[17] *Procuratores* of eight Aragonese towns were certainly present at the Cortes of Zaragoza in 1283.[18] The representatives of the Catalan towns were also described as 'procuratores' in 1292. From the beginning of the fourteenth century writs of summons were transcribed into chancery registers, and those then addressed to towns of Catalonia regularly required their proctors to bring with them full powers to bind their constituents.[19] When the earliest summons to the Peninsular towns to attend the curia were issued about the middle of the thirteenth century or somewhat later, it is probable that their representatives were then instructed to bring with them mandates since, by that time, the towns were already accustomed to give mandatory powers to those who appeared on their behalf in law suits before the *curia regis*. According to the *Chronicle of James I*, the Navarrese citizens and townsmen who took the oath to the Aragonese king under the Adoption Treaty at Tudela in 1231 had authority to bind their constituents, but again, for the reasons already stated, this is not conclusive evidence.[20] It is not until after the death of Enrique I (1274) that we have much information about the Cortes of Navarre. The contract by which the towns of Navarre formed a league to defend their *fueros*, at the Cortes of August 1274, was sealed by the representatives of the towns 'por nos et por conceillo de . . .' in each case.[21]

Broadly speaking, the main functions of these thirteenth-century assemblies fall under four headings: the doing of homage and taking of oaths of allegiance, which might at times include some element of consultation; a duty to give counsel and advice to the king in political

16 *CD Jaime I*, i, no. CLIII; *Fori et observantia Aragonum*, fol. ii.
17 Miret i Sans, *Itinerari de Jaume I*, 442.
18 *Fueros y observancias*, I, fol. 6.
19 *Cortes de Cataluña*, I, i, nos. XXII, XXV, XXVIII, XXIX, XXX, etc.
20 *Chronicle of James I, cap.* CXLIII.
21 *Cartulario de Don Felipe III*, no. 157. For variations in the wording of the writs of summons to the English shires and boroughs from 1254 to 1295, see Edwards, 'The *Plena potestas* of English parliamentary representatives', *Oxford essays presented to H. E. Salter*, 141–3. For the Agennais, Quercy and other fiefs of Languedoc, see Bisson, *Assemblies and representation in Languedoc*, 97, 274, 293–4.

matters, should he require it; the granting of extraordinary taxes to the king; and the promulgation of legislation. As we have seen, the doing of homage was the chief, if not the only purpose for which representatives of the towns were summoned to the Castilian cortes before the union of Castile and León. In Aragon oaths of allegiance were sworn to the king in cortes, as in 1214 to Jaime I, and also to the heir to the throne, as in 1228 at Daroca to Jaime's eldest son Alfonso, as heir to the kingdom of Aragon, and in 1276 at Zaragoza, on the occasion of the coronation of Pedro III, to his son Alfonso, as his heir.[22] In Navarre, in 1274, the Queen Regent, Blanche of Artois, appointed Pedro Sánchez, lord of Cascante, as governor of the kingdom, 'de voluntat' of the nobles, knights and good men of the towns assembled in cortes, and oaths of allegiance were then sworn to him.[23]

It is difficult to estimate the part played by the representatives outside León–Castile in questions of general policy when these were discussed during meetings of the cortes. Jaime I of Aragon (1213–76) summoned the cortes of Catalonia to meet in Barcelona before his expedition against Majorca in 1228, although his reason for doing so appeared to be to ascertain what military, naval and financial aid the prelates, nobles and towns would provide, rather than to take advice about whether the conquest should be attempted. He had already made up his mind that it would.[24] The joint Cortes of Monzón in 1232 and in 1236 were, however, concerned with the war against Moorish Valencia.[25] It was the failure of Jaime's successor, Pedro III, to consult the Aragonese cortes before his invasion of Sicily in 1282, which led to the clause in the General Privilege (*Privilegio general*) of 1283 laying down that in war, and in matters which concerned the kingdom generally, the king must always take counsel with nobles, knights, citizens and men of the towns, as his father had been accustomed to do.[26] In Navarre the inconclusive negotiations with the king of Aragon, who claimed the throne of Navarre, and which took place between August and November 1274, were carried out, under the governorship of Pedro Sánchez, through the Navarrese cortes.[27] The Cortes of Estella which met in

[22] Zurita, *Anales*, lib. II, cap. LXVI; lib. IV, cap. II; Bisson, *EHR*, XCII, 107–22.
[23] *Cartulario de Don Felipe III*, no. 157; Anelier, *Guerre de Navarre*, ll. 614–29.
[24] *CD Jaime I*, I, no. LXIII; *Chronicle of James I*, caps. XLVIII–LV.
[25] Zurita, *Anales*, lib. III, cap. XV; *CD Jaime I*, I, nos. CLIII, CLIV.
[26] *Fueros y observancias*, I, fol. 7v, cl. 5. Bisson, 'The military origins of medieval representation', *AHR*, LXXI, 1149–1218, discusses the possible connection between military assemblies and national assemblies such as parliament, the cortes, etc. This appears to be more applicable to Aragon than to Castile–León.
[27] *CDIACA*, VI, nos. L, LI, LII. Cf. Soldevila, *Pere el Gran, primera part.* II, 269–86.

1283 were summoned in connection with preparations for a Franco-Navarrese invasion of Aragon.[28]

The financial necessities of the crown and the need for extraordinary taxation were important factors in the development of representative assemblies in the thirteenth century in the various Spanish kingdoms, as elsewhere in Western Europe. *Moneda* as a tribute due to the crown is found not only in León and Castile but also in Portugal and, under the name of *monedatge*, in Aragon and Valencia.[29] Its early history is obscure, but there is more evidence about it for Aragon and Portugal than for León and Castile. In Aragon it appears to have been first collected in 1205 by Pedro II,[30] but it is possible that he had made an earlier, unsuccessful attempt to impose it, some time before 1199.[31] During the minority of Jaime I his father's coinage from the mints at Jaca circulated in the kingdom of Aragon and also in the Catalan cities of Lérida and Tortosa and in the counties of Urgel and Pallars, while the rest of Catalonia used the coinage of Barcelona. The coinage of Jaca was confirmed for ten years at the joint curia held at Lérida in September 1218, and it was again confirmed for seven years in the Aragonese curia which met at Huesca in April 1222.[32] Soon afterwards Jaime I issued a new coinage with his own image and superscription, but at Daroca in 1224 he was forced to withdraw it and to reinstate his father's coinage, because of his earlier oath to maintain the latter unchanged for ten years. On this occasion he imposed a *monedatge* for what the sources explain was the third time – presumably the two earlier ones had been taken in 1218 and 1222. There is no certain evidence that the towns were represented in either 1218 or 1222, but at Daroca in 1224 the assent and advice of the citizens of Zaragoza, Lérida and Huesca, and the good men of the principal towns of Aragon, specially summoned for the purpose, were referred to in the confirmation of the coinage.[33] The matter came up again in the joint Aragonese and Catalan Cortes of Monzón in October 1236. Besides bishops and nobles from Aragon proper and from Catalonia, the representatives of Lérida and Tortosa and those of eight Aragonese

---

[28] ACA, Perg. Pere II, 369.
[29] The *corts* of Valencia were set up by Jaime I and were an artificial creation.
[30] Zuritas, *Anales*, lib. ii, cap. lii.
[31] Bridrey, *La Théorie de la monnaie*, 317–22.
[32] *CD Jaime I*, i, no. x; Botet i Sisó, *Les monedes catalanes*, iii, no. v. Zurita, *Anales*, lib. ii, cap. lxxvi, places the assembly at Huesca in 1221.
[33] *CD Jaime I*, i, no. xxxiii. The town representatives appear to have been summoned for this purpose only.

cities were present. It was decreed at Monzón that the coinage of Jaca was to be retained, unchanged in value and weight, by the king and all his successors; in return, every owner of a house or property worth 10 *áureos* or more was to pay a *monedatge* of 1 *maravedí* every seven years.[34] This bargain appears to have been kept in the main. In 1254 the tax was taken from Lérida, and possibly from other towns, but Jaime I admitted that the payment was not due for another three years.[35] The agreement of 1236 was also confirmed in 1260, when Jaime I issued a special, limited coinage for a projected crusade in the Holy Land which did not take place.[36] There is evidence that the tax was being levied in 1264 and in 1284; in the first half of the fourteenth century it was taken in 1300, 1307, 1328 and 1342, dates which suggest a fairly regular septenniel collection.[37] In Valencia it was first levied in 1266. *Monedatge* does not appear to have been levied in Catalonia, except on those towns and districts which used the coinage of Jaca. Thus, in 1258, when Jaime I issued a new coinage of Barcelona for circulation in Catalonia, he undertook never to seek or exact *monetaticum* by reason of the coinage.[38] The promise made by Pedro III in 1283 to the Catalans not to take *monetaticum* from clergy, nobles, knights or citizens, except as it had been taken in the time of his father, presumably safeguarded the king's right to take it in those districts which used the Aragonese coinage.[39]

In Portugal the earliest instance of the sale of the coinage and the grant of *moneda* in the cortes occurred in the Cortes of Leiria in 1254.[40] This was certainly not, however, the first time that the tax had been taken for, in 1250, at Guimarães, Afonso III replied to petitions presented by the bishops of the Portuguese sees; included among the grievances then put forward by the bishop of Oporto was the complaint that the clergy had been obliged to 'buy the coinage', a practice described as unheard of in the kingdom.[41] Later the preamble of some decrees fixing prices, promulgated at the end of 1253, stated that the rise in prices was caused by the fear that the king would 'break the

[34] *Ibid.* I, no. CLIII.
[35] Miret i Sans, *Itinerari de Jaume I*, 242–3.
[36] Botet i Sisó, *Les monedes catalones*, III, no. VI; Miret i Sans, *Itinerari de Jaume I*, 303–4.
[37] Forey, *The Templars in the 'Corona de Aragón'*, no. XXIII, 394–5. Russell, 'The medieval *monedatge* of Aragon and Valencia', *Proceedings of the American Philosophical Society*, 106, 484–5.
[38] Botet i Sisó, *Les monedes catalanes*, III, no. IV.
[39] *Cortes de Cataluña* I, i, no. XXII, cl. VI.
[40] *PMH: Leges*, I, 193.
[41] *Ibid.* I, 188.

coinage' because the time for this was approaching.[42] It has been suggested that the earlier sale of the coinage took place in 1247.[43] This may be so, but there is no definite evidence of such a transaction, nor of a meeting of the cortes or even of the great curia at which such an greement might have been reached.

In 1255 Afonso III attempted to impose *moneda* again, but was forced to back down because of the opposition of the higher clergy and the nobles.[44] When in 1261 the seven-year agreement ended, Afonso duly issued a new coinage but this again aroused opposition and after taking counsel at Coimbra with the cortes (at which the 'communitates regni' were represented) the whole question was finally resolved: both old and new coinage were to be allowed to circulate and their relative value was laid down; no more of Afonso's new coinage was to be minted for four years; the coinage was not to be 'broken' during the rest of his reign; and succeeding kings were to issue new coinage once only in each reign. In return for these royal promises a septenniel *moneda* was imposed. This took the form of a graduated tax on those who owned moveables and land of more than a certain value. It fell most heavily on the poorer classes; many exemptions favouring the better off were also allowed. The exempt included bishops, heads of military orders, members of religious orders, cathedral clergy, sword-bearing knights and, in most cases, some of their dependants. Afonso III also acknowledged that the right to 'break the coinage' was granted by the cortes.[45]

The history of *moneda* during the thirteenth century in León, Castile, Aragon and Portugal thus has marked similarities. In no case have we certain knowledge of when the initial imposition took place but in all these kingdoms, except Castile, there is evidence of its imposition in the cortes. In all four cases, too, it soon became a levy taken by right every seven years, without further reference to the cortes. In Aragon and Portugal, this was part of a bargain agreed between the king and the cortes, and rested on the royal undertaking not to depreciate the coinage arbitraily. In León and Castile there is no

---

[42] *Ibid.* I, 192.
[43] Gama Barros, *História da administracão pública em Portugal*, III, 136; Sánchez-Albornoz, *Curia regia portuguesa*, 156–7.
[44] *PMH: Leges*, I, 196–7.
[45] *Ibid.* I, 210–12; cf. Herculano, *História de Portugal*, III, 67–71; Gama Barros, *Historia da administração pública em Portugal*, III, 138–40; Livermore, *History of Portugal*, 141–2. In the Agennais and in Quercy there was a similar connection between the coinage and *fouage* (hearth tax); see Bisson, *Assemblies and representation in Languedoc*, 95–7, 127–8.

evidence of such a bargain. The rebel nobles in 1272–3 demanded that *moneda* should be taken as it had been by former kings, but there was no reference to any specific agreement.

Legislation formed an important function of the cortes in León under Alfonso IX, but not in Castile until after the union of the two kingdoms. From 1250 onwards legislation promulgated in the cortes was frequent except during the eighteen years between 1268 and 1286. Legislation was also an important function of the Portuguese, Catalan and Aragonese cortes. There is a strong resemblance between some laws promulgated in Lisbon in 1253 and the economic codes of Alfonso X of Castile. These Portuguese laws were drawn up after Afonso III had consulted with prelates, nobles, knights and 'cum mercatoribus et cum ciuibus et bonis hominibus de consiliis regni mei', as Alfonso X was to take counsel in 1268 with the merchants and good men of Castile, León, Extramadura and Andalusia, as well as with prelates and nobles. The Portuguese code of 1253 fixed prices of commodities for sale and purchase, as did the Castilian codes of 1252 and 1268, but the Portuguese decrees covered a wider range of goods than the Castilian decrees of 1252 and approached more nearly those of 1268. Thus, they fixed the value of the coinage and the prices of metals, the prices of cattle, sheep, goats and pigs, as well as of skins and hides, saddles and harness, and a long list of foreign cloths very similar to that included in the latter Castilian code. The Portuguese, however, was more limited than its counterparts in Castile in that it did not include any decrees concerning justice, law and order or the Jews.[46] The Portuguese household ordinances of 1258 and 1261, however, were drawn up by the officials of the royal household, on the orders of the king, without the intervention of either the curia or the cortes.[47]

In Catalonia the main form of legislation, under Jaime I, was the land peace. Land peaces for Catalonia were promulgated in the joint Cortes of Lérida in 1214 and those of Villafranca in 1218, and in the Catalan *Corts* of Tortosa in 1225 and of Barcelona in 1228. The last named land peace was frequently confirmed.[48] The land peace of 1214 had set out a long list of persons and things under peace. These included churches and clergy, religious and military orders; widows, wards, orphans and 'omnes miserabiles persone' and their possessions;

[46] *PMH: Leges*, I, 192–6.
[47] *Ibid*. I, 198–201.
[48] *Cortes de Cataluña*, I, i, nos. XIV, XV, XVI, XVII.

citizens, burghers and inhabitants of royal and ecclesiastical towns; merchants and pilgrims using the king's highway; persons going to and from the royal court; plough oxen, dovecots, olive orchards, etc. The document also laid down regulations for the enforcement of the peace. In every city two citizens, one 'de majoribus' and the other 'de populo', were to be elected, who, with the royal vicar, were to enforce the peace. They possessed powers to distrain the goods of those breaking it and punishments for the contumacious included excommunication by the bishop of the diocese. All nobles, knights, citizens and every town-dweller of fourteen years old and upward were to take an oath to keep the peace. These provisions were re-enacted in later land peaces with some variations and additions. Such land peaces were, of course, ulti-mately derived from the ecclesiastical *Pax Dei* and *Treuga Dei* pro-claimed in the late tenth and early eleventh centuries by provincial synods in Southern France and the Spanish March. In the twelfth century the civil power was called in to co-operate with the church in its operation. In 1131 'Constitutions of Peace and Truce' were issued by the bishops in the presence of Ramón Berenguer III, count of Barcelona, and his magnates; in 1173 and 1188 they were proclaimed by Alfonso II of Aragon, with the advice of the bishops and mag-nates; under Pedro II, in 1198 and 1202 they were proclaimed 'in curia'.[49]

The presence and consent of the representatives of the Catalan towns was not necessary to legislation under Jaime I. Thus, two important pieces of legislation were enacted in the winter of 1235 at Tarragona. On 7 February the first of these was promulgated after consultation with the bishops, abbots and other ecclesiastical dignitaries. It dealt mainly with ecclesiastical matters, such as the extirpation of heresy, but it also confirmed the land peace of 1228 and limited usury, payable to the Jews, to 20 per cent.[50] About five weeks later, in a great curia consisting of prelates and nobles, another set of decrees of a miscel-laneous nature was promulgated. The most interesting of these were some sumptuary laws which regulated food, and forbade the use of expensive furs and gold and silver ornamentation in dress – laws similar to, but less far-reaching than the sumptuary laws contained in Alfonso X's codes. Other clauses dealt with the sale of grain – a matter which affected the grain-exporting towns of the Catalan sea-board, who,

---

[49] See Procter, 'Development of the Catalan *corts*', *Homenatge a Rubió i Lluch*, III, 534–5, and references given there.
[50] *Cortes de Cataluña*, I, i, no. XVIII.

however, were not consulted.[51] A detailed edict on the Jews and usury, issued in 1241, appears to be a royal edict or pragmatic, issued by Jaime I, without reference to any assembly.[52] However, some forty years later, the essential role of the town representatives was formally recognised. In December 1283, at Barcelona, Pedro III accepted and agreed to a long list of petitions presented by the magnates, prelates, citizens and men of the towns of Catalonia 'nomine sui et tocius universitatis Catalonie'. The Catalan *corts* thus now definitely claimed to speak for the whole country. The concessions were of wide application, but two of them were of particular importance in the evolution of the institution. For the future they were to be summoned at least once a year, within the boundaries of Catalonia, and at these meetings prelates, barons and men of the towns were to treat with the king 'de bono statu et reformacione terre'. Further, Pedro III undertook not to promulgate any general statute or constitution except 'de approbacione et concensu prelatorum baronum militum et civium Catalonie vel ipsis vocatis maioris et sanioris partis eorumden'.[53] For the future, therefore, any legislation of general application required the consent of the *corts*, which were seen as speaking for the whole community and of which, institutionally, the representatives of the towns were an integral part. These are significant facts, for in this respect the Catalan *corts* were in advance of other representative assemblies elsewhere in Western Europe.

The cortes of Aragon proper also played a part in legislation. Decrees *De confirmatione pacis* were proclaimed in cortes at Almudévar in 1227 and at Zaragoza in 1235.[54] The two most important legislative acts promulgated in cortes in this period were the *Fueros de Aragón* and the *Privilegio general*. The former, compiled by Vidal de Canellas, Bishop of Huesca, at the order of Jaime I, were issued at the Cortes of Huesca in 1247, at which the cities and towns were represented. The code was intended for use in the king's court and combined customary and Roman law.[55] Thus, in some respects, it corresponded to Alfonso X's *Espéculo*, but the Aragonese code was promulgated in cortes, not in the *corte*. Nor was it later rescinded, as was the *Espéculo*.

---

[51] *Ibid.* I, i, no. XIX: sumptuary laws, cl. V–VII; sale of grain, cls. XVI, XVIII–XIX. In the *Sénéchaussées* of Beaucaire and Carcassonne the towns were consulted on the price and export of grain. Bisson, *Assemblies and representation in Languedoc*, 188–98, 211–18.

[52] *Cortes de Cataluña*, I, i, no. XX.

[53] *Ibid.* I, i, *no.* XXII, preamble, and cls. IX, XVIII.

[54] *Fori et observantae Aragonum*, fols. xxvii, xxviii.

[55] Vernacular version ed. Gunnar Tilander, *Fueros de Aragón*.

It therefore contributed to the gradual reception of Roman law in Aragon. The so-called General Privilege of 1283 primarily represented Pedro III's concessions to a baronage in revolt, but it was nevertheless based on petitions presented in the Cortes of Zaragoza, and the proctors of the towns joined with the nobles in putting forward the demands concerned. There is no evidence that town representatives had been present at Ejea in 1264, when Jaime I had made earlier concessions to the nobles. It should be noted, however, that no cortes were held in 1287, when Alfonso III, driven still further along the path of submission to the nobles, was forced to grant them the notorious Privilege of Union.

During the thirteenth century, the various representative assemblies which we have studied developed alongside each other but not inter-dependently in the kingdoms of the Spanish Peninsula. Although citizens were summoned to the Leonese curia as early as 1188, it is probable that the Romano-canonical form of representation did not supersede the earlier, less formal type in either León or Castile until about the time of the union of the kingdoms, and in this respect Aragon may have been in advance of the central kingdoms. Though *monedatge* appeared in Aragon at much the same time as *moneda* appeared in León, it was not imposed in Portugal until about fifty years later. Although the Leonese Cortes took part in legislation in 1188, 1202 and 1208, it was not until the second half of the thirteenth century that legislation became frequent in the cortes of the united kingdoms of León–Castile, and it was in Catalonia, with its strong tradition of the ecclesiastical 'Peace and Truce of God', that, before the end of the century, consent to general legislation as a right was first claimed by the *corts* and admitted by the ruler. In no case did the towns first demand representation; the initiative came from the sovereigns.

Much stress has been laid on the importance of the cortes as a tax-granting body. From the king's point of view the need for additional revenue, and the necessity to obtain the consent of those who paid taxes, may well have been the strongest single inducement to summon the cortes, but it is possible to over-emphasise the importance of the role of finance. There were clearly other factors at work, as is shown by the number of meetings of the cortes – including early assemblies – at which no taxation was asked for or voted. In León–Castile the gap between the time when *moneda* became a customary payment, and the first imposition of a general *servicio* in 1269, was nevertheless a period of legislative activity in the cortes and saw the promulgation of Alfonso X's four economic codes there. Broadly speaking, it may even be said that the development of representative assemblies in the Peninsula in the thirteenth century was largely due to administrative convenience; it was easier to exact oaths of allegiance in an assembly than on progresses through the country; it was quicker to obtain consent to taxation from an assembly than by local negotiations. Petitions presented in the cortes, whether by individual towns or collectively, enabled the king to obtain information about local administration and to deal expeditiously with genuine grievances, while the promulgation of legislation in the cortes helped to publicise new or amended laws throughout the country.

By the end of the thirteenth century, then, these representative assemblies played a distinctive part in the machinery of central government in all the kingdoms of the Peninsula. Their functions were then still often ill-defined, especially in the political sphere, but with one exception – Navarre, where French domination retarded development for half a century – they all exercised some control over the grant of extraordinary taxation and they all played an important part in legislation.

Appendix of documents

I

11 June 1220, Burgos

Fernando III of Castile confirms the sentence pronounced by Gonzalvo Rodríguez, *mayordomo de la corte*, and García Ferrández, *mayordomo* of the queen-mother, Berenguela, in the king's court, in a suit brought by Abbot Esteban and the monastery of La Vid against Don Lope Díaz.

Archivo Histórico Nacional, sección 1, Clero, *carp.* 379, no. 19. Original.

[Chrismon]. Ut facta regum ac pricipum memoriam qua digna sunt assequantur scripture sunt beneficio solidanda. Ea propter modernis ac posteris presentibus innotescat quod ego Ferrandus Dei Gratia Rex Castelle et Toleti una cum uxore mea domina Beatrice regina et cum fratre meo Infante domino Alfonso ex assensu ac beneplacito domine Berengarie regine genitricis mei facio cartam concessionis confirmationis et stabilitatis Deo et monasterio beate marie de la Vid et domino Stephano eiusdem instanti Abbati suisque successionibus necnon et toti canonicorum conuentu ibidem Deo seruientium presenti et futuro perpetuo ualituram. Concedo itaque et confirmo sentenciam diffinitiuam que super intemptatione qua dominus Lupus Didaci dictum Abbatem et canonicos de la Vid super Alcolia eiusdemque aldeis et suis terminis intemptabat per dominum Gonçaluum Roderici dilectum maiordomum meum et dominum Garsiam Ferrandi maiordomum serenissime matris mee in conspectu meo plena curia mea nuper cognitis hinc inde allegationibus lata fuit: uidelicet quod idem dominus Lupus Didaci ab eadem intemptatione desisteret et in eadem causa supersederet eodem recipiente et non contradicente nec appallante sentencian suprascriptam, coram multis baronibus et nobilibus meis, scilicet domino Mauritio Burgensis episcopo, Roderico Gonçalui, domino Murellio, Petro Roderici, Roderico Guterii, Ordono Garsie, Roderico Garsie, Aprili Garsie, Vda Garcie, domino Johanne cancellario aule regalis, et domino Petro Semenii alcaldo meo. Hanc autem sentenciam concedo roboro et confirmo, ne aliquis super hiis dictum monasterium uel abbatem siue canonicos eiusdem ulterius audeat intemptare, siue indebite molestare. Siquis uero hanc cartam infringere seu diminuere in aliquo presumpserit iram Dei omnipotentis plenarie incurrat et cum Juda Domini

268

proditore penas sustineat infernales et regie parti mile aureos in cauto persoluat, et dampnum eis super hoc illatum restituat dupplicatum. Facta carta apud Burgis XI die Junii Era M^a CC^a L^a octaua. Anno regni mei tercio, eo uidelicet anno quo ego prefatus Rex F. in monasterio Sancte Marie Regalis de Burgis manu propria cingulo milicie me accinxi et tercia die post dominam B. Reginam Philippi quondam Regis Romanorum filiam duxi sollempniter in uxorem. Et ego Sepedictus Rex F. regnans in Castella et Toleto hanc cartam quam fieri iussi manu propria roboro et confirmo.

[Rueda] Signum Ferrandi Regis Castelle
Lupus Didaci de Faro alferiz domini Regis confirmat
Gonçaluus Roderici maiordomus curie Regis confirmat
Rodericus Toletane sedis archiepiscopus hyspaniarum primas confirmat.

[1st column]
Mauricius Burgensis episcopus conf.
Tellius Palentinus episcopus conf.
Geraldus Secobiensis episcopus conf.
Rodericus Segontinus episcopus conf.
Garsias Conchensis episcopus conf.
Melendus Oxomensis episcopus conf.
Dominicus Abulensis episcopus conf.
Dominicus Placentinus episcopus conf.

[2nd column]
Rodericus Didaci conf.
Aluarus Didaci conf.
Aluarus Petri conf.
Alfonsus Tellii conf.
Rodericus Roderici conf.
Johannes Gonçalui conf.
Suerius Tellii conf.
Garsias Ferrandi maiordomus Regine domine Berengarie conf.
Gonzaluus Petri maior merinus in Castella conf.
Johannes domini Regis cancellarius, abbas Vallisoleti conf.
Egidius iussu iamdicti cancellarii scripsit.

II

6 March 1231, Alba de Tormes

Fernando III of Castile and León fixes the compensation and reparations to be made by the *concejo* of Belver to the abbot and monastery of Sahagún for damages done to property of the priory of San Salvador de Belver during a riot.

Archivo Histórico Nacional, sección I, Clero, *carp*, 913, no. 11. Original. Publ. Escalona, *Sahagún, ap.* III *esc.* ccxxxiv (pp. 585–6); Manuel Rodríguez, *Memorias*, 383ff.

Ferrandus Dei Gratia Rex Castelle, et Toleti. Legionis et Gallecie. Concilio et alcaldibus de Belueer salutem. Por el pleito que el abbat e el conuento de sant ffagund uos demandauan ante mi del danno e delos tuertos que les fiziestes en sus casas que les echastes e robastes e de su vinna que les descepastes e delos arbores que les cortastes e arrancastes e de los otros tuertos que les fiziestes sobre que embiastes a mi uuestros bonos ommes con uuestra carta de procuracion abierta et seellada. Sepades que plaziendo al abbat e al procurador del conuento e alos uuestros procuradores pidiendo me todos mercet recibi el pleito en mi mano e yo con plazer e consentimiento de todos mando esto, que uos el concejo fagades las casas e las paredes que derribastes del abbat en uuestra villa tan buenas o meiores como eran antes e sean fechas al mas tardar fata el dia de sant miguel primero que sera enel mes de setyembre. E la uendimia et el mueble que de su casa e de fuera de casa leuastes sea luego dado segund el prior dixiere e el prior sea creido de quanto dixiere. Et mando que la vinna que descepastes quela pongades luego de tan buenas uides como ante o de meiores e que la labredes e criedes a uuestra despensa fata diez annos, e el fructo della sea uuestro. E depues delos x annos torne la vinna al monasterio libremientre e uos quitos dela lauor e dela renta. E otrosi mando de todos los arbores que fueron cortados e arrancados, que los pongades e los criedes tan buenos o meiores como los otros eran. E que labredes las huertas daqui a diez annos e sea el fructo uuestro. E delos diez annos adelante finquen las huertas libres e quitas al monasterio de sant Saluador e uos dent adelante quitos de la lauor e dela renta. El mando que dedes el fructo de la uinna e delas huertas daqui alos diez annos al abbat o aqui el mandare quanto podien ualer en saluo ante que cortas fuessen seyendo bien labradas. Et todas estas cosas que sobredichas son delas casas fazer e las paredas de las huertas e del labrar de la vinna e de las huertas e de quanta renta cadanno den al abbat fata los diez annos por la vinna e por las huertas, sea en aluedrio de don Pariente canonigo de Zamora e de don Diego de Castronueuo e de Pedro moro frayre de Morerola que tyene la obra e assi como estos tres o los dos dellos aluedriaren e mandaren assi lo complir todo el concejo e el abbat e el prior assi sean pagados, fueros el mueble que finca en el dicho del prior e si uos complir non quisieredes esto todo que sobredicho es assi como yo he mandado, mando a este mio portero que esta carta lieua que uos pendre e uos constringa firmemientre e uos lo faga todo complir. E ruego e mando a estos tres arbitros que en esta carta son nombrados que luego uengan facer esto que en esta carta dize, entre uos e el abbat e sepades que quanto en esta mi carta dize, que todo plogo al abbat e al procurador del conuento e alos uuestros procuradores que aca embiastes e si alguno pennas emparasse al portero pecherie ami cien morabetinos en coto. Ffacta carta apud Aluam de Tormes, rege exprimente, vi die marcii Era Mª CCª LX nona anno Regni mei quartodecimo.

III

25 November 1251, Seville

Fernando III grants to the city of Alcaraz the privileges granted to the towns of Extremadura at the Cortes of Seville, 1250.

Archivo Municipal de Alcaraz, *leg.* 1, no. 22. Original.

Sepan todos los que esta carta vieren como yo don Ferrando por la gracia de Dios rey de Castiella e de Toledo, de Leon e de Gallizia, de Sevilla, de Cordova, de Murcia e de Jahen enbie mis cartas a los conceios e a los bonos omnes de la Extremadura de Castiella que enbiassen sos omnes bonos de cada conceio ante mi por cosas que havia de veer e de fablar con ellos por buen paramiento de Estremadura, e vos el conceio de Alcaraz enbiastes ante mi uuestros omnes bonos, e yo fable con ellos aquellas cosas que entendi que eran buen paramiento de la tierra e ellos sallieronme bien e recudieronme bien a todas las cosas que les yo dix de guisa que les yo fuy su [*sic*] pagado. Et esto passado rogaronme e pidieronme merced por vos que vos toviesse a aquellos fueros e a aquella vida e a aquellos usos que oviestes en tiempo del rey don Alfonso mio auuelo e a su muerte assi como vos los yo prometí e vos los otorgue quando vuy rey de Castiella que vos lor ternia e vos los guardaria, ante mi madre e ante mios ricos omnes e antel, arçobispo e ante los obispos e ante caveros de Castiella e de Estremadura e ante toda mi corte. Et yo bien conosco e es verdat que quando era mas ninno que aparte las aldeas de las villas en algunos logares e a la sazon que esto fiz era me mas ninno e non pare hy tanto mientes. Et porque tenia que era cosa que devia a emendar ove mio conseio con don Alfonso mio fiio e con don Alfonso mio hermano e con don Diago Lopez e con don Nunno Gonzalez e con don Rodrigo Alfonso e con el obispo de Palencia e con el obispo de Segovia e con el maestro de Calatrava e con el maestro de Hucles e con el maestro del Temple e con el gran comendador del Ospital e con otros ricos omnes e con caveros e con otros omnes bonos de Castiella e de Leon e tove por derecho e por razon de tornar las aldeas a las villas assi como eran en dias del rey don Alfonso mio auuelo e a so muerte e que esse fuero e esse derecho e essa vida oviessen los de las aldeas conbusco e vos con los de las aldeas que oviestes en dias del rey don Alfonso mio auuelo e a so muerte. Et pues que esta gracia e este amor vos fiz e tove por derecho de tornar las aldeas a la villa mando otrossi a vos los de la villa e deffiendo vos so pena de mio amor e de mi gracia e de los cuerpos e de quanto havedes que nenguno tan bien jurado como alcalde como otro cavero de la villa poderoso o otro qualquiere que mala cuenta ni mal despechamiento nin mala premia nin mala terreria nin mal fuero fiziesse al pueblo tan bien de la villa como de las aldeas nin les tomasse conducho a fuerça nin a tuerto que yo que me tornasse a los que lo fiziessen a fazerles justicia en los cuerpos e en los haveres e en quanto han como en omnes que tal yerro e tal tuerto e tal atrevimiento fazen a sennor. Et maguer yo entiendo que todo esto devo vedar por mio debdo e por mio

derecho como sennor plogo a ellos e otorgaronmelo e tovieron que era
derecho que yo que diesse aquella pena sobredicha en los cuerpos e en los
averes a aquellos que me errassen e tuerto me fiziessen a mios pueblos assi
como sobredicho es en esta carta. Et mando a tengo por bien que quando
yo enbiare por omnes bonos de uuestro conceio que vengan a mi por cosas
que ouiere de fablar con ellos o quando vos quisieredes a mi enbiar uuestros
omnes bonos por pro de uuestro conceio que vos catedes caveros de uuestro
conceio a tales quales touuieredes por guisados de embiar a mi e aquellos
caveros que en esta guisa tomaredes pora enbiar a mi que les dedes
despesa en esta guisa, que quando vinieren fata Toledo que dedes a
cada cavero medio maravedi cadadia e non mas, et de Toledo aca contra
la ffrontera que dedes a cada cavero un maravedi cadadia e non mas. Et
mando e defiendo que estos que a mi enbiaredes que non sean mas de tres
fata quatro sinon si enbiasse yo por mas. Et otrossi mando e tengo por bien
que quando yo enbiare por estos caveros assi como es dicho o vos los
enbiaredes a mi por pro de uuestro conceio que traya cada cavero tres tres
[sic] bestias e non mas e estas bestias que gelas apprecien dos jurados e dos
alcaldes quales el conceio escogieredes pora esto e apprecien cada una que
vale quando fizieren la muebda del logar que si por aventura muriere
alguna daquellas bestias que sepades el conceio que havedes a dar por ella
e que dedes tanto por ella por quanto fuere apreciada daquellos dos
jurados e dos alcaldes assi como sobredicho es.

Otrossi mando que los menestrales non echen suerte en el judgado por
seer juez. Ca el juez deve tener la senna e tengo que si a affruenta viniesse
o a logar de periglo e omne vil o rafez toviesse la senna que podrie caer el
conceio en grand verguenza e en grand onta por ende tengo por bien e
mando que el que la senna oviere a tener que sea cavallero e omne bono e
de verguenza.

Otrossi se que entre vos que se fazen unas coffradrias e unos ayuntamientos malos a mengua de mio poder e de mio sennorio e a danno del
conceio e del pueblo o se fazen muchas malas encubiertas e malos paramientos e mando so pena de los cuerpos e de quanto havedes que estas
coffradrias que las desfagades e que daqui adelante non fagades otras
fuera en tal manera pora soterrar muertos e pora luminarias e pora dar a
pobres e pora coffuerços, mas non pongades alcaldes entre vos nin coto
malo e pues que vos yo do carrera por o fagades bien e almosna e merced
con derecho si algunos a mas quisiessen passar a otros cotos o a otros
paramientos o a poner alcaldes en coffradrias a los cuerpos e a quanto
oviessen me tornaria por ello. Et mando que nenguno non sea osado de
dar nin de tomar calças por casar su parienta ca el que las tomasse
pecharlasye duppladas al que gelas diesse e pecharie en coto cinquaenta
maravedis, los veynt a mi e los diez a los jurados e los diez a los alcaldes e
los diez al que los descubriesse con verdat.

Et mando que todo omne que casare con mançeba en cabello que nol de
mas de sessaenta maravedis pora pannos pora sos bodas e qui casare con
biuda que nol de mas de quarenta maravedis pora pannos pora sos bodas
e qui mas diesse desto que yo mando pecharie cinquaenta maravedis, los

veynt a mi e los diez a los jurados e los diez a los alcaldes e los diez al que lo descubriesse con verdat. Et otrossi mando que non coman a las bodas mas de diez omnes cinco de la parte del novio e cinco de la parte de la novia quales el novio e la novia quisieren e quantos demas hy comiessen pecharie cada uno diez maravedis, los siete a mi e los tres al que lo descubriesse con verdat e esto sea a buena fe e sin escatima e sin cobdicia nenguna. Et mando que las otras cartas que yo di tan bien a los de las villas como a los de las aldeas que las aldeas fuessen apartadas de las villas e las villas de las aldeas, que non valan. Et mando e deffiendo firmemientre que nenguno non sea osado de venir contra esta mi carta nin de quebrantarla nin de menguarla en nenguna cosa. Ca aquel que lo fiziesse aurie la yra de Dios e la mia e pecharmie en coto mill' maravedis.

Ffacta carta apud Sibillam rege exprimente XXV^a die Novembris, Michael Petri scripsit, era M^a CC^a LXXX^a nona.

[The seal has been lost; but the red and yellow wool strands which once held it still remain.]

Copy made by D. W. Lomax.

IV

27 February 1253, Seville

Economic decrees promulgated in the Cortes of Seville, 1252/3.

British Library, Add. MS. 9916, fols. 172–88. Transcript XVIIIc.

[fol. 172r] El Ordenamiento sobre comestibles y artefactos publicado en Sevilla, año de 1256 [sic].[1] Sacose del Archivo de la villa de Escalona donde esta original.

Don Alfonso por la gracia de Dios Rey de Castilla, de Toledo, de Leon, de Galicia, de Sevilla, de Cordoba, de Murcia, e de Jaen: Al concejo de Escalona de Villa, e de Aldeas, Salut e gracia: Sepades que vi posturas que ficieron el Rey Don Alfonso mio Visabuelo, e el Rey Don Fernando mio Padre a pro de ellos e de sos pueblos e de toda su tierra: et por que habie sazon que non fueron tenudos por guerras et por grandes priesas que les acaescieron: agora quando Dios quiso que la tierra que el Rey mio Padre, que Dios perdone, conquisto con la mercet de Dios, e con la ayuda et el servicio que vos le fecistes e vos que me mostrastes los daños que recibiedes por que las pos (fol. 172v) turas nonse tenien asi como fueron dadas: et otrosi por que me mostrastes muchas veces los daños que recibiedes enlas sobeianias que se facien, e enlas carestias grandes de las cosas que se vendien, ademas tobe por bien e por guisado de aquellas posturas que ellos ficieron, e delo que nos agora acordamos por pro de mi e de todos vos

---

[1] The year should be 1253. Alfonso X was not in Seville in February 1256, but in Castile, and the decrees correspond to those in *cuadernos* granted to other towns in October 1252 and February 1253: see above, p. 126 n. 30. Ballesteros, *Itinerario*, 21–2, cites a *cuaderno* addressed to Escalona, dated 27 February 1253.

que sea todo tenudo: et las posturas fizlas con conseio e con acuerdo de
mio tio Don Alfonso de Molina, e de mios hermanos Don Fernando [sic,
for Fadrique] e Don Felipe e Don Manuel, e de los obispos e delos Ricosomes, e delos Cavalleros, e de las Ordenes, e de omes buenos dellas Villas,
e de los otros omes buenos que se acercaron con migo=et esto fago yo por
grant sabor que he de vos guardar de daño, e de sobeiania, que se vos
torne en daño, e de meiorar vos en todas vuestras cosas por que seades mas
ricos e mas abondados, e hayades mas e valedes mas e podades a mi facer
mas servicio, et las posturas son estas:

1. De quanto valan los Brisones
Mando que los meiores Brisones, e de mas caras colores que non valan
mas de siete maravedis los [fol. 173] meiores Escudos, e siella e en esta
cuenta que entre el pintar de capiello: et el que por mas los vendiere, o
non los quisiere dar por este coto, que peche diez maravedis, e el que por
mas los comprare que peche diez maravedis e pierda los Brisones.

2. De quanto vala Escudo e Siella de Caballo e de Rocin
Et mando que las armas, escudos, e Siella de Cavallo, e pintar el capiello
las meiores, e de mas caras colores, e guarnidas que non valan mas de
veinte maravedis e con siella de Rocin de señal la meior con freno, e peital
colgado, e dorado que non vala mas por todo de treinta e cinco maravedis,
e si el vendedor por mas vendiere, o el comprador por mas comprare, que
pierda el vendedor los maravedis e el comprador las armas e peche cada
uno de ellos tanto quanto fuere la compra.

3. De quanto vala siella de Barda
Otrosi mando que siella de Barda de señal la meior, que non vala mas de
quince maravedis la meior con estriveras doradas e granadas e freno e
peital colgado e dorado, e el que por mas lo [fol. 173v] vendiere, o por mas
lo comprare, que el comprador pierda la siella, e el vendedor los maravedis,
e peche cada uno de ellos de mas en coto quince maravedis por cada siella
tambien el comprador como el vendedor.

4. Que ninguno non traya siellas con oropel nin con argenpel
Mando que non trayades siellas ferpadas nin con oropel nin con argentpel
sinon de tres dedos por la orla entallado sobre los cueros e sobre los cueros
de tres dedos, e carancol del, e los orle de tres dedos so el cuero, e so el
paño entallado, e de suso de otros tres dedos: et mando que non guarne-
scades nin las cubrades las siellas de nengun paño, et mando que trayades
argentpel et orpel cintas en coberturas e en perpuntes e en sobreseñal, e en
cofias e en pendones: et que non pongades nengunas.......fundas de los
Escudos nin en fondas, nin en corasas delas siellas, e en linjauera e en
sombrero que trayades orpel et argentpel, e que non trayades cascabeles
en ninguna cosa, si non en sonajes, o en coberturas para bofordar: e que
non fagades señales en las coberturas con cascabeles, et que non pongades
en escudo nen [fol. 174r] guno bocla sinnon de cobre dorado, o argentado
o pintado: et el Rico ome o el cavallero, o otro qualquiere que esto pasare,
que yo que gelo viede asi como qui pasa mandamiento de Rey e de señor,
et el armero o qual menestral quiere que lo ficiere, quel corten el polgar, e
si non le pudieren haber que el peche cient maravedis en coto, et que non

se escuse por que diga que las facie para ome de otro Regno, et si despues
le pudieren haber que el corten el polgar, e las armas que son fechas que
las trayan fasta esta Pasqua mayor primera que verna.

5. Que nenguno non bastone paños
Otrosi mando que nenguno non bastone paños, nin los entalle, nin los
ferpe, nin ponga orfres nin cintas, nin sirgos en nengun paño, e que
fagades vuestros paños planos e si quisieredes a meatad, e que los pongades
cuerdas si quisieredes cabeadas con oro que sean de una mano en luengo,
e nengunas cuerdas que pusieredes que non sean mas luengas desto, e si
quisieredes poner coneio o Nutria que lo pongades perfilado, e en el manto
el trascol, e non mas, e que non trayades [fol. 174v] ninguna camisa a
cuerda, e que trayades zapatos dorados, que non sea ferpados, et si lo
ficiere Ricoome o Cavallero o otro ome qualquiere nenguna cosa destas,
vedargelo he yo, asi como qui pasa mandamiento de Rey o de señor e el
Alfaiate e la Alfaiata que lo ficiere que corten el polgar de la mano diestra,
e si fugiere que peche treinta maravedis e quandol pudieren haber quel
corten el polgar et el zapatero que ferpare el zapato haya esta pecha
sobredicha del Alfaiate.

6. Que nenguna Muger non traya orfres nin cintas ni alioffares
Otrosi mando que nenguna muger non traya orfres, nin cintas nin aliofares
nin margome camisa con oro, nin con plata, nin con sirgo nin cinta, nin
margome paños nengunos, nin traya tocas orelladas con oro, nin con
argent, nin con otra cosa nenguna si non blancas, mas mando que trayan
armiño e nutria como quisieren. Et si alguna [half a line left blank] [175r]
como sobre dicho es, si non como yo mando que peche veinte maravedis
en coto por quantos dias los vistiere, e mando que las que quisieren tener
bocas de mangas que las trayan.

7. De quanto valan las tocas de seda
Otrosi mando que las tocas de seda la meior non vala mas que de tres
maravedis, e que sean tan grandes como son agora, e el que por mas la
vendiere, nin por mas la comprare, que el vendedor pierda los maravedis e
el comprador la toca.

8. De como anden los paños
Otrosi mando que los paños anden como andan agora.

9. De quanto valan las peñas
Et mando que la peña la meior que non vala mas de ocho maravedis e
que las trayan tan buenas e tan complidas como solien: e la peña deslo-
mada que non vala mas de siete maravedis la meior, e que las fagan tan
buenas e tan complidas como solien, et la peña apuntada de seis tiras que
non vala mas de quatro maravedis la meior, e que sea de sason, et la peña
de cinco tiras, que non vala mas de dos maravedis e medio la meior, e que
sea de sazon: et la peña vera la meior [fol. 175v] que no vala mas que de
veinte e cinco maravedis: et peña armiña, et peña grisa que non vala mas
de treinta a cinco maravedis la meior; et peña de corderos que non vala
mas de quatro maravedis la meior, et peña de lirones que non vala mas de
maravedi e tertia la meior: et peña blanquicoxa que non vala mas de
quatro maravedis la meior et peña blanca de liebres que non vala mas de

maravedi e medio la meior: e peña de esquiroles que non vala mas de diez maravedis la meior; et piel de corderos tres maravedis la meior et non mas, e el que por mas vendiere la peña nin la piel o la comprare, que el vendedor pierda los maravedis e el comprador la peña, e peche demas cada uno dellos diez maravedis e cada peña que vendieren por mas del coto.

10. De quanto valan Zapatos dorados
Otrosi mando que zapatos dorados valan seis pares un maravedi de los meiores, et qui mas quisiere dar, que mas de, et delos zapatos de mugier dorados, seis pares por un maravedi de los meiores: et zapatos prietos de cabrito entallados de a [fol. 176r] cuerda, cinco pares por un maravedi de los meiores: et de cordoban e entallados e de acuerda seis pares por un maravedi delos meiores: et de los cueros tres pares por un maravedi de los meiores: et el zapatero que por mas los vendiere e el que por mas los comprare que peche cada uno dellos diez maravedis.

11. Que nenguno menestral nin mercadero non se coteen sobre los pueblos
Otrosi mando que nenguno mercadero nin menestral de qualquier menester que fuere que non se coteen sobre los pueblos mas que venda cada uno so menester, segunt como sobre dicho es, et como meior pudiere a qualesquiere quelo ficieren al cuerpo e a quanto oviere me tornarie por ello.

12. Que nenguno non coma mas de dos carnes e de dos pescados
Otrosi mando que ninguno de mio Regno, que non coma mas de dos carnes de qualesquiere e la una dellas adobada em dos guisas: et si oviere caza de monte, o de ribera quel den o que caze, e que non sea de compra que la coma como [fol. 176v] quisiere. Otrosi mando que nemguno non coma mas de dos pescados, de este guisa e que coma...e que non sea contado por pescado et Rico Ome o Cavallero o otro home que quiere que este mio mandamiento pasare, sepa quel faré yo, asi como quien pasa mandamiento de Rey e de Señor.

13. E razon de las bodas que nenguno non sea osado de dar nin de tomar calzas
Otrosi mando en razon de las bodas, que nenguno non sea osado de dar nin de tomar calzas pora casamiento de su parienta, e el que las tomare, quelas torne dobladas alque gelas dio e peche cient maravedis en coto, tambien el que las dio como el que las tomo; et el que casare si quiere con Manceba en Cabello o si quiere con Viuda, quel non de mas de sesenta maravedis pora paños pora sus bodas, et el que mas diere de esto que yo mando, peche en coto cinquenta maravedis, los veinte a mi, e los diez alos Jurados, los diez a los Alcaldes, e los diez alque los descubriere con verdat, et mando que non coman a las bodas mas de cinco barones e cinco mugieres de parte del Novio et otros tantos de par [fol. 177r] te de la Novia, sin compaña de su casa, e estos sean sin el Padrino e la Madrina e el Padre e la Madre de los Novios, e que non duren las bodas mas de dos dias; e si el Padre o la Madre de los novios, o el Novio o la Novia, o el facedor de la boda mas convidare de quantos yo mando que peche pora cada ome diez maravedis de quantos i fueren comer sin convidados que pechen diez maravedis cada ome. E si alguno criare pariente o parienta o otro criada

e non oviere Padre o Madre que aquel quel crio que vaya en logar de Padre, e mando que el dia de la boda a un mes quel novio nin otro por el non embie presente, nin combide mas de quantos manda el coto sobredicho.

14. Que non fagan cofradias nin iuntas malas

Otrosi mando que non fagan cofradias nin iuntas malas, nin ningunos malos ayuntamientos que sean a daño dela tierra, e a mengua de mio sennorio, si non pora dar a comer a pobres o para soterrar muertos o para enfuercos e que se coman en casa de los muertos e non para otros paramientos malos e que non haya i otros alcaldes [fol. 177v] nengunos para jazgar en las cofradias, sinon los que fueren puestos por mi en las villas o por el fuero e a los que lo ficieren a los cuerpos e a quantos ovieren me tornare por ello, e el alcalde que recibiere esta alcaldia sepa que perdera quanto oviere e será el cuerpo a mi mercet, et mando que las cofradias que son fechas en esta razon que se desfagan luengo si non sepan que yarán en esta pena sobredicha.

15. Que nengun Regatero non compre pescado fresco

Otrosi mando que nengun Regatero nin Regatera non compre nengun pescado fresco de Rio, nim de Mar para revender, nin trucha nenguna, nin fresca nin otra, e que nengun Regatero non compre pescado fresco en razon de Ricohome, nin de otro home nenguno, e que non salga fuera dela Villa a los caminos para comprar cabritos nin Gallinas nin vianda ninguna, e el que lo comprare que lo pierda e peche demas en coto diez maravedis por cada cosa, e por cada vegada que lo ficiere, e el que non oviere de que peche el coto sepa que yara en mi prision quanto yo quisiere.

16. De los Ragateros que non compren madera

Otrosi mando que ningun Regatero nin home nenguno non compre madera ninguna para vender si non fuere maestro para labrarselo el de su menester sin engaño e que la non pueda vender si non labrada cada uno segund so menester de obra acabada [a line has been omitted here] e que me peche en coto diez maravedis.

17. De quanto vala Cavallo e Yegua e Mula e Palafren

Otrosi mando que el Cavallo que vala de aqui fasta Santo Martin, e de este Sant Martin primero que viene a un año doscientos maravedis el meior e dent adelante que vala ciento e cinquenta maravedis el meior, et la yegua veinte maravedis la meior de luengo, e el Mulo o la Mula, o Palafren que vala de luego cinquenta maravedis el meior e non mas. Et el asno de yeguas el meior quince maravedis et el asno de carga siete maravedis el meior e la asna seis maravedis la meior, et qualquiere que sacare a mercado o a fe [fol. 178v] ria caballo o Yegua o Mulo o Mula o Palafren o Asno o Asna e lo dierre a corredor para vender e alguno i oviere que quiera dar por ello el precio sobredicho, que lo tome por el. E el que por mas lo vendiere de quanto manda este coto que pierda los maravedis e el comprador las bestias e esto que sea mio: et quien este faciere por poridad que quando quiere que sea probada, o averiguado que peche las bestias, e cient maravedis a mi tambien el comprador como el vendedor, et si los maravedis non ovieren que les tomen quanto les fallaren, et esta prueba et este averiguamiento sea de vecino a vecino segunt so fuero, e a los estaños segunt el fuero de alli, o fuere la vendida fecha: et si alguno acusare a otro en esta razon e non gelo pudierre probar segunt so fuero, como dicho es que se pase a la pena que debie haber el acusado.

18. De quanto valan los Bueyes e los Novellos

Otrosi mando en razon de los Bueyes que el meior Buey domado que saliere a feria o a [fol. 179r] mercado o a quiere quel vendan quiere de carro quiere de arada, que non vala mas de cinco maravedis el meior e la vaca con su fijo becerral que non vala mas de quatro maravedis la meior. Et la vaca sin fijo que non vala mas tres maravedis la mejor et el toro quatro maravedis el meior et el Noviello por domar quatro maravedis el meior. Et quien por mas le vendiere o por mas le comprare, que pierda el vendedor los maravedis, e el comprador el ganado, et peche cada uno dellos diez maravedis en coto por cada cabesa.

19. Que non saquen de mios Regnos Cavallos, nin yeguas nin Rocines, nin Mula nin Mulo, chicos nin grandes, si non fuere mula de carga que vaya cargada de mercadura o que lieve el Mercadero con su trofa, nin peñas nin corambre de conejos nin corambre por labrar, nin grana, nin sirgo, nin argent vivo nin nengunas cosas de quantas [fol. 179v] fueron vedada por mandado del Rey Don Alfonso mio Visabuelo, o por mandado del Rey Don Fernando mio Padre, et el que lo sacare peche quanto sacare doblado e peche en coto de mas mil maravedis. E si los maravedis non pudiese haber que yaga en mi prision quanto fuese mi mercet.

20. Que non saquen de mios Regnos Carneros nin Vacas nin Puercos nin nengun ganado

Otrosi mando que non saquen carneros, nin vacas, nin Puercos, nin cabras, nin nengun ganado de mios Regnos, e de esta guisa entiendo que habrá abondo de ganados en todos mios Regnos, et el que lo sacare que peche el ganado doblado, e peche de mas en coto mil maravedis, et si non oviere los maravedis que yaga en mi prision quanto fuere mi mercet.

21. Que non tomen los huebos a los Azores

Otrosi mando en razon de los Azores que no tomen los huebos a los Azores nin a los Gavilanes, nin alos Falcones, et que non tomen nin saquen Azor, nin Gavilan del nido fasta sea de dos [fol. 180r] negras, et los Falcones que los non tomen fasta de mediado el mes de Abril, et que nenguno non sea osado de sacar Azor nin Gavilan nin Falcon de mios Regnos si non fuere con mi mandado. Et el que sacare qual Ave quiere de estas de los Regnos, que peche la Ave doblada e demas en coto por cada Ave cient maravedis. E el que tomare Azor o Falcon, o Gavilan o huebos contra este mio coto sobredicho, quel corten la mano diestra, e si otra vegada gelo fallaren, que le enforquen, e si non oviere el coto sobredicho que yaga en mi prision quanto fuere mi mercet.

22. Que non tomen al Azor, nin al Falcon, nin al Gavilan yaciendo

Otrosi mando quel al Azor, nin al Falcon, nin al Gavilan, quel non tomen yaciendo sobre los huevos nin faciendo son nido, nin mientre que tobiere fijos o huevos. Et Azor mudado nin Gavilan, nin Falcon Borni nin Bahari quel non tomen de una muda en adelante e los Falcones Neblis que los tomen mudados, e como mejor pudieres, et qualquiere [fol. 180v] que nenguna cosa de estas ficiere quel corten la mano, et si otra vegada lo ficiere quel enforquen por ello.

23. De quanto valan los Azores

Otrosi mando que Azor mudado Garcero que non vala mas de treinta maravedis el meior, et el Azor anadero o perdiguero el meior que non vala mas de viente maravedis, et el Azor torzuelo que cazare el meior que non vala mas de seis maravedis et el Azor pollo prima que non cazare seis maravedis el meior e el Azor torzuelo que non prenda dos maravedis el mejor, et el mas fermosa.

24. De quanto vala Falcon Borni

Otrosi mando que Falcon Borni prima e mudado, e lebrero que non vala mas de doce maravedis el mejor e el Falcon Borni prima e pollo que mate que non vala mas de diez maravedis el mejor. E el Falcon Borni torzuelo mudado e lebrero seis ma [fol. 181r] ravedis el mejor, et el Falcon Borni pollo e torzuelo e lebrero quatro maravedis el mejor. Et Falcon Borni prima que non caze el mas fermosa e el mejor tres maravedis e el Falcon Torzuelo Borni que non caze quatro maravedis el mejor.

25. De quanto vala Falcon Bahari

E el Falcon Bahari prima que cazare el mejor que non vala mas de ocho maravedis. E el Falcon Bahari Torzuelo que cazare el mejor un maravedi et el Falcon Bahari prima que non cazare el mas fermoso que non vala mas de dos maravedis et Falcon Bahari Torzuelo que non caze un maravedi el mejor.

26. De quanto vala Falcon Nebli

El Falcon Nebli prima que caze, que non vala mas de doce maravedis el mejor e Falcon Nebli Torzuelo que caze quatro maravedis el mejor, e Falcon prima que non caze, que non vala mas de cinco maravedis el mejor: E Falcon Nebli Torzuelo que non caze, que non vala mas de un maravedi el mejor [fol. 181v].

27. De quanto vala Falcon sacre

Otrosi mando que Falcon prima sacre que cazare que non vala mas de veinte maravedis el mejor, e Falcon Torzuelo sacre que non vala mas de ocho maravedis, et Falcon prima sacre que non caze que non vala mas de seis maravedis el mejor, e Falcon Torzuelo sacre que non caze que non vala mas de tres maravedis el mejor.

28. De quanto valan los Gavilanes

Otrosi mando que gavilan prima que non caze, que non vala mas de medio maravedi el mejor, e el mas fermoso e el guado, et el Gavilan prima cercetero que non vala mas de quatro maravedis el mejor, e el Gavilan prima guadorniguero que non vala mas de dos maravedis el mejor, et qualquier que nenguna Ave de estas sobredichas por mas la vendiere nin por mas la comprare de quanto yo mando, quel vendedor pierda los maravedis e el comprador pierda el ave e peche en coto cada uno de ellos tan [fol. 182r] tos maravedis doblados quantos costare el ave por cada Ave.

29. De la caza de las perdices e de las Liebres e de los conejos

Otrosi mando en razon de la caza de las Perdices e de los conejos e de las liebres mando que non tomen los huevos alas Perdices nin tomen la Perdiz yaciendo sobre los huevos nin tomen los Perdigones fasta que non sean eguados, et los conejos e las Liebres e las Perdices que lo non cazen con nief a tal que non pueda foir la caza. Otrosi mando que non cazen con tuso en nengun logar nin con alar, et mando que nenguno non caze desde las carnestolliendas fasta Sant Miguel, si non fuere con Ave. Et qualquiere que a nenguna cosa de estos cotos pasare de la caza que por cada vegada que cazare veinte maravedis, e pierda la caza, et el que non oviere de que pechar esta caloña que yaga en mi prision quanto yo toviere por bien. Et si en algunos logares han mayores cotos sobre la caza que les vala.

30. Que non pongan fuego a los montes

Otrosi mando que nenguno non ponga fuego para quemar los montes e el que gelo fallaren faciendo quel echen dentro et si non le pudieren haber quel tomen quanto oviere.

31. Que non echen yervas en las aguas para matar el pescado

Otrosi mando que nenguno non eche yervas, nin cal nin otra cosa ninguna en las agnas con que muera el pescado, e mando que en la tierra o son los salmones, que non tomen los pequeños que han nome gorgones. Et qualquiere que nenguna cosa destas ficiere que peche en coto cient maravedis, e pierda el pescado, e si non oviere de que pechar el coto que yaga en mi prision quanto que toviere por bien.

32. De los montazgos

Otrosi mando en razon de los montazgos, que todos los ganados que vinieren a estremos, que non tomen montazgo mas de en un logar en todo el termino de qual Villa quiera et en toda la Orden de Cala [fol. 183r] trava, o de Vcles, o de Alcantara, e del Temple o de Hospital, o de todas las otras Ordenes que non tomen montazgo mas de en un logar por toda la Orden, e que lo tomen dela parte que saliere o de la parte que entrare el ganado, e que lo tomen de esta guisa: De mil Cabezas de Vacas dos vacas e que vala cada vaca quatro maravedis e si los maravedis quisieren dar, que non les tomen las vacas. Et de mil obejas dos carneros, que vala cada carnero medio maravedi, et si los dineros quisieren dar que non les tomen los carneros: otrosi de mil puercos dos, e que vala cada puerco diez solidos de los pepiones, e si los dineros quisieren dar, que non les tomen los Puercos. Et de mil cabezas de yuso que tomen a esta razon: Otrosi mando que en nengun logar non tomen asaduras, et en estas cosas sobre dichas de los montazgos, salvos los Privilegios que dieron los Reyes que con derecho debieren valer. Et quien pasare esto que yo mando que peche cient mara [fol. 183v] vedis en coto e todo el ganado doblado que tomare.

Otrosi mando que las cañadas que sean asi como fueron en tiempo del Rey don Alfonso mio Visabuelo, e que den las aguas a los ganados assi como entonces. Et las aguas e las cañadas que tornen a aquel estado que estaban en tiempo del Rey Don Alfonso, e quien esto pasare que peche cient maravedis, e el daño doblado.

33. De las Defesas

Otrosi mando que las dehesas que erran en aquello que fiz conquisto en tiempo del Rey Don Alfonso que sean ansi como eran en tonce e en lo que fue conquistó despues de la muerte del Rey Don Alfonso a aca que las defesas non fagan aguisadas. Et en aquellos logares ó las han por privilegios que non tomen mas de quanto mandan los Privilegios, e el que esto pasare que peche en coto mil maravedis e el daño doblado.

34. Que non pendren de Villa a Villa
Otrosi mando que de Villa a Villa que non fagan prenda ninguna, e si alguno ficiere [fol. 184r] prenda e sabidol fuere quien prendó, que la torne doblada a aquel que la tomó, e demas que peche en coto treinta maravedis, los diez a mi e los diez a los Alcaldes, e los diez a los Jurados, e demas todo el daño al querelloso, et si aquel que la prenda ficiere negare alguna cosa della, que el pedidoso que juré por su cabeza por quantol prendaren, e que gelo peche aquel que gelo prendró doblado asi como sobredicho es. Et si Portero fuere a Vocero alguna vegada que el derecho dela Porteria que lo peche aquel que fizo la prenda.

35. De como fagan los Jurados e los Alcaldes derecho a todo querelloso
Otrosi mando a los Jurados, e a los Alcaldes de cada logar que fagan facer derecho a todo querelloso segunt manda su fuero, e sus hermandades, e si por culpa de Jurado o de Jurados o de Alcalde o de Alcaldes fincare que non fagan derecho asi como fuero manda, o sus hermandades, que aquel querelloso faga testigos de homes de Orden e de otros homes buenos los mejores que [fol. 184v] haber pudiere, e sobre venga se querellar a mi daquel o daquellos quel non quisieren facer derecho, et entonce darle yo mi Carta con mio Portero quel entregue en casa daquel, o daquellos que non le quisieren facer derecho por el duplo e por las carreras et las carreras seran tales: al cavallero quatro sueldos de Pepiones cada dia e al Peon dos sueldos, et estos dos dias sean tantos quantos jornadas hubiere del logar dond morare el querelloso fasta o yo fuere de ida e de venida. Et mando que los derechos de la Porteria que los peche aquel o aquellos por quien menguo el derecho. Et delas villas de las Ordenes que así como de Villa en Villa. Et dela pendra de los Ricosomnes e de los Cavalleros que sea asi como solie ser en tiempo del Rey Don Alfonso mio Visabuelo fasta que yo salga alla a la tierra.

36. Que non pendren Bueyes de arada
Otrosi mando que las pendras qui ha de facer de villa a ville que sean asi como puesto es, et las otras pendras o entregas que han de facer por mio mandado, o de Merino o de Alcaldes, o de Jurados o de Prestamero o de mayordomo o de qui [fol. 185r] quiere que lo haya de facer con derecho que fallando otra prenda de mueble que non pendren Bueyes de Arada e el que la ficiere peche en coto treinta maravedis por cada pendra que ficiere e todo el daño doblado.

37. Que non tomen Portazgo si non fue en tiempo del Rey Don Alfonso
Otrosi mando en razon de los Portazgos que non tomen Portazgo en otro lugar si non en aquellos logares o lo solien tomar en tiempo del Rey Don Alfonso mio Visabuelo o en las Villas grandes que son conquistas ó lo solien tomar en tiempo de Miramomelin, salvos los privilegios que dieron los Reyes. E quien esto pasaré peche en coto cient maravedis que cada querelloso a quien lo tomare e el daño doblado.

38. Otrosi mando que nengun Vocero non faga pleito con aquel cuya fuere la voz que non adobe su pleito quando quisiere: Et que nengun home que pleito oviere, que non traya mas de un vocero a su pleito ante los Alcaldes, o ante aquellos los ovieren de juzgar, e que otro nenguno non venga por atravesador por de estorvar a nenguna de las partes, et si el vocero, o el dueño del pleito qui [fol. 185v] siere haber mas consejo que lo haya a parte, e los que dieren el consejo que non atraviesen en el pleito, et el vocero que pleito pusiere, que non adobe el dueño del pleito con su contendor quando quisiere que me peche cient maravedis en coto, ela demanda doblada a aquel a quien puso el pleito, et el que mas adustiere de un vocero que me peche cient maravedis en coto, e a la otra parte toda la demanda doblada, e cada uno de los atravesadores que me peche cient maravedis en coto, e el que los maravedis non oviere que yaga en mi prision quanto fuere mi mercet.

39. De las Juras e las salvas que se han de facer de Judio a Cristiano
Otrosi mando que las juras e las salvas e las firmas que se han de facer de Christianos a Judios e de Judio a Christiano que se fagan segunt facien en tiempo del Rey Don Alfonso, et si en algunos logares andaba seello en tiempo de Rey Don Alfonso que ande agora ansi como entonces.

40. Que nenguno non corte arbol ageno
Otrosi mando que nenguno non sea osado de cor [fol. 186r] tar arbol ageno, nin de arrancarle, e si algunol cortare per pie ol arrancare en los lugares ó a fuero que peche segunt so fuero manda et en los logares, ó non a fuero que peche por el Arbol diez maravedis al que perdio el Arbol, et esto sea en los Arboles que sea fuera de las Villas, et en los Arboles que son dentro en las Villas, e que el Arbol quiere que sea que peche veinte maravedis al que perdio el Arbol et qui acachare rama o cortare por que el arbol haya daño que peche por la primera rama cinco sueldos de la moneda de la tierra e por la segunda diez sueldos e de dos ramas arriba que mas cortare por mal facer que peche todo el coto del Arbol assi como sobredicho es.

41. De como anden vestidos los moros
Otrosi mando que los moros que moren en las Villas que son pobladas de Cristianos que anden cercenados a derredor o el cabello partido sin topet e que trayan barbas asi como manda su ley e que non trayan cendal en nengun paño nin peña blanca nin paño bermejo nin verde nin sanguino nin Zapatos blancos nin dora [fol. 186v] dos et qualquiere que ficiere nenguna cosa de este coto, que peche por cada vez que lo ficiere treinta maravedis, e que non oviere el coto, que yaga en mi prision quanto fuere mi merced.

42. Que non crie Cristiana fijo de Judio nin de Moro
Otrosi mando que nenguna Cristiana non crie fijo nin fija de Judio nin de Moro nin Judia non crie cristiano nenguno, e la que esto pasare que peche en coto diez maravedis quantos dias de tobiere. Otrosi mando que nengun home non saque nin escuse a nenguno de los mios moros de peche, ca el que lo ficiere a el me tornare por ello.

43. Que los mozos coronados que pechen segunt el tiempo del Rey Don Alfonso

Otrosi mando en razon de los mozos coronados, e de los otros que andan
segunt clerigos e son casados, que pechen asi como solien pechar en tiempo
del Rey Don Alfonso mio Visabuelo.

44. Que non den mas de un diezmo de los ganados
Otrosi mando que de todos los ganados que non [fol. 187r] den mas de un
diezmo, e que lo den alli ó lo solien dar en tiempo del Rey don Alfonso
mio Bisabuelo, et qualquiere que en otro logar lo tomare, si non en aquellos logares o lo solien tomar en tiempo de dicho mio Bisabuelo, que peche
cient maravedis en coto, los cinquenta maravedis a mi e los cinquenta al
querelloso, e quel torne todo lo que le tomo doblado.

45. De las tercias
Otrosi mando que las tercias que sean asi como fueron en tiempo del Rey
Don Alfonso mio Bisabuelo, fasta que yo salga alla a la tierra.

46. Otrosi mando que todo ome tenga Cavallo e armas e este guisado
segunt manda su fuero.

47. Otrosi mando que nengun moro, nin nenguna mora non sea osados de
tornar Judio nin Judia, moro nin mora, nin seer en fecho nin en conseio
de tornarlos, et los que lo ficieren, o fuesen en conseio de lo facer mando
que me peche cada uno cient maravedis, e si non oviese de que me los
pechare que esté en mi prision fata que me los de. Et si los que lo ficiesen
tornar o fue [fol. 187v] sen en el conseio algo oviesen de aquel que se
tornase moro o mora o fuese en sacarlos, que se me pare a la pena como
de furto. Et si Judio o Judia se tornase Moro o Mora por si o por otri que
sea mio cativo, et me peche cient maravedis en coto et todo lo al que
oviese que finque a sus fijos e si fijos non oviese que finque todo a mi e sea
mio. Et otrosi mando que nengun Moro, nin nenguna Mora non sea osado
de se tornar Judio o Judia nin nenguno Judio nin nenguna Judia non sea
en conseio de lo tornar et aquel Judio o aquella Judia que fuesen en
conseio de lo tornar Moro o Mora o lo tornasen que me pechen cient
maravedis fuera si fuesen sus cativos, e en sus cativos que sea asi como
solia seer, et si non oviese de que me peche aquelos cient maravedis, que
este en mi prision fata que me los dé, et si losque lo ficiesen tornar, o
fuesen en el conseio a los oviesen daquel que se tornase Moro o Mora si
fuese en sacarlo, que se me pase a la pena como de furto. Et el Moro o la
Mora que se tornase Judio o Judia e non oviese otro señor que [fol. 188r]
sea mi cativo e me peche cient maravedis en coto, e lo al que oviese que
finque a sus fijos e si fijos non oviese que sea todo mio et si el Moro o la
Mora que se tornase Judio o Judia e oviese otro señor que sea suyo el
cuerpo e peche a mi los cient maravedis et si non oviese de que me de los
maravedis que esté en mi prision fata que me los de.

48. Otrosi mando que todas estas cosas sobredichas que se ovieren a probar
o averiguar que se prueben e averiguen de Vecino a Vecino segunt manda
el fuero de su Villa, et los extraños segunt manda el fuero dalli o fuere la
cosa fecha. Et mando que todas estas cosas sobredichas que sean tenudas e
que dure esta postura tanto quanto yo tobiere por bien. Et mando a los
Jurados delas Aldeas que son e seran adelante que fagades guardar e tener
e complir esto que yo mando. Et el que en estas penas sobredichas cayere

que lo afrontedes, e que lo recabdedes para mi assi como sobredicho es; et mando que estas caloñas sobredichas que se partan de esta guisa: que tome [fol. 188v] yo la metad, e la otra metad que tomen la meatad la Justicia, e la otra meatad el mostrador.

Dada en Sevilla el Rey lo mando veinte et siete dias de Febrero: Gonzalbo Martin lo escribio en era de mil doscientos noveinta e quatro años.

V

1 January 1256, Vitoria

Alfonso X of Castile grants the towns of San Sebastián and Fuenterrabía to Teobaldo II of Navarre for life.

Archivo General de Navarra, *caj.* 3, no. 3. Original.

In Dei nomine. Conesçuda cosa sea a todos quantos esta carta uieren e hoyeren. Como yo Don Alfonso por la gracia de Dios Rey de Castilla de Toledo de Leon de Gallizia de Sauilla de Cordoua de Murcia e de Jahen. Do en amor a mi amado pariente e amigo Don Tibalt por essa misma gracia Rey de Nauarra de champanna e de Bria Conde Palazin Las dos villas de Sant Sebastian e de ffuenterrabia con todas sus rendas de mar e de terra e esto se do yo que tenga de mi en amor en toda su uida. Et otorgo e prometo que de vn anno adelante que meta este dono de susso dicho assi como dicho es de susso en la carta de las conuenençias que son entre mi e el Rey de Nauarra juradas e seellada de mio seello. Et en testimonio e en confirmamiento desto do esta mi carta abierta al sobredicho Rey de Nauarra seellada con mio seello colgado. Ffecha la carta en Bitoria el Rey la mando primer dia de Enero. Era de mill cc e nouaenta e quatro annos. P. Martinez la fiço por mandado de Don G. Perez Notario del Rey.

Wax seal of Alfonso X, broken.

VI

29 April 1260, Ucles

Regulations concerning usury promulgated by Alfonso X with the advice of the *corte*.

Archivo Histórico Nacional, sección 1, Clero, *carp.* 918, no. 15. Original.

Don Alffonso por la gracia de dios Rey de Castiella, de Toledo, de Leon, de Galliçia, de Seuilla, de Cordoua, de Murçia e de Jahen, Al conceio de Sant ffagund, salut e gracia. Ffaçemos uos saber que auiendo nos muy grand sabor de poner en buen estado fecho de nuestros Regnos e de nuestro sennorio. Catando con consseio de muchos omnes buenos que eran connusco en nuestra corte, aquellas cosas que serien mas a pro de nuestra tierra e por toller muchas cosas que son agrauiamiento de uos todos. Tenemos por bien e mandamos e conffirmamos la postura que pusiemos primeramiente por nuestro privilegio, que los judios non den a vsuras mas de a tres por quatro e esto mismo mandamos alos moros que den a vsuras, ca tenemos que los cristianos non deuren dar a vsuras por ley nin por derecho. Et por que en este fecho non se pueda façer encubierta mala nenguna, mandamos que quando el cristiano ouiere de sacar alguna debda de judio o de moro, o de renouar carta o de sacar dineros sobre pennos o de façer algun pleyto con alguno dellos en otra manera qual quiere que en esta razon tanga, que non la pueda façer a menor de seer delante alguno delos alcaldes en qual se abinyeren el cristiano e el judio o el moro, o otro omne bueno que de aquel alcalde mismo e el escriuano de conceio de aquellos que son dados para façer estas cartas, e que sea ante cristianos e judios. Et si el pleyto fuere entre cristianos e judios, que se faga ante cristianos e judios e si fuere entre cristianos e moros, otrossi que se faga ante cristianos e moros, que sean y por testimonio, e que yure el cristiano que non sse façe aquella carta mas de a tres por quatro nin ha de pagar mas por ella nin de dar pan nin dineros, nin otra cosa nenguna, el nin otri por el por razon de aquella debda. Et otrossi que yure el judio o el moro, que diere aquella debda, que non da mas de a tres por quatro, nin recibe nin recibia mas de a tres por quatro, nin pan, nin dinero ni otra cosa ninguna en razon de aquello que da el nin otri por el. Et si alguno quisiere echar pennos que valan fata dos maravedis e non mas pueda los echar sin prueua nenguna mas denda arriba non pueda sin estas prueuas que auemos dichas de suso e yurando todauia que si acaesciere contienda sobre aquel penno, que el judio o el moro non dio mas de a tres por quatro e otrossi el cristiano que non lo recibio a mas. Et el judio o el moro que recibiere pennos, en qual quisa quiere ante testigos assi como sobredicho es, e despues gelo demandaren por razon de furto o de fuerça, sea escusado dela penna del furto o dela fuerça, mas non se pueda deffender de façer derecho, al que la cosa demandare por suya, segund el fuero del logar. Et el judio o el moro que tomo pennos aquella cosa tornesse por la debda que auie sobrello, a aquel de quien tomo los pennos. Et estas yuras uos enbiamos escriptas de como se deuen façer. Et mandamos que las reciba el alcalde o el omne bueno que diere en su logar con el Escriuano ante las testimonyas. Et si el debdor quisiere pagar toda la debda o parte della pague la ante el alcalde o ante aquel omne, e ante el escriuano, e ante las testimonyas como sobredichos es. Et el escriuano desfaga la nota luego de so libro e rompa la carta si la pagare toda, e si pagare ende alguna cosa faça carta nueua de aquello que finca e meta la en su libro, e remate la otra carta que fue fecha primeramiente e aquello que pagare que sea descontado del cabdal que saco, e delas usuras que crescieron fata aquel dia. Et delo que fincare por pagar del cabdal, cresca la usura segund la quantia que finca, assi como sobredicho es. Et si alguno quisiere façer su paga de toda la debda, e traxiere los dineros por dar los a aquel que los deue, e non le pudiere auer, o non lo quisiere recebir la paga, faça testigos que uiene para pagar e meta los dineros en mano delos alcaldes o de otro omne bueno en que sea seguro, e de gelos ante testigos para dar los a aquel que los auie de dar e dally adelante non logre. Et otrossi mandamos que las cartas que fueron fechas ante desto que nos agora mandamos, que non ualan mas del dia e del Era que fueron fechas fata doçe annos, e estas que las puedan demandar fata esta Navidat primera que uiene. Et las que fueren fechas daqui adelante que non las puedan demander nin ualan mas de fata ocho annos della Era de la carta enque fuere fecha la debda. Et esto non se entiende por los Ricos omnes, nin por aquellos que tienen tierra de nos. Et los porteros e los otros omnes que ouieren de façer las entregas delos judios e delos moros, mandamos que non las fagan menos de Alcaldes, e de yurados, o de otros omnes buenos. Et aquel que fuere fallado que contra alguna cosa deste nuestro mandamiento passare, quier cristiano o judio o moro, por qual manera quiere que en otra guisa lo fiçiere, mandamos alos alcaldes e alos merinos e alos nuestros omnes que estudieren en las villas, o a qual quiere dellos quel recabdan el cuerpo, e toda quanto que ouiere para ante nos. Et mandamos nos que non dedes por esta carta, a aquellos que nos la leuaren dela nuestra Chanceleria por amor nin por furto nenguna cosa. Dada en Vcles el Rey la mando, yueues xxvIIII dias de abril, Alffonso martinez la fiço. Era de mill e docientos e Nouaenta e ocho annos.

[A strip of parchment to which the seal and ties were appended has been torn off the bottom of the *carta*.]

VII

15 April 1264, Seville

Replies to the petitions of the towns of Extremadura presented in the Cortes of Seville, April 1264.

British Library, Add. MS. 9916, fols. 250–9. Transcript XVIIIC.

[fol. 250] D. Alonso X. Peticiones de los pueblos de Estremadura respondidas en las Cortes de Sevilla de 1264. Sevilla 15 de Abril, Era 1302 Año de Cristo 1264. Sacadas del Original que esta en el Archivo de la villa de Peñafiel.

[fol. 251 blank]

[fol. 252r] Ordenamiento de Don Alonso X hecho en las Cortes de Sevilla en el año de 1264. Dirigido a la Extremadura.

Porque entre todas las cosas, que los Reyes deben a facer sennaladamiente estas dos les convienen mucho, la una de dar gualardon a los que bien e lealmiente los servieron, la otra, que maguer los omnes sean abdebdados con ellos por naturaleza, et por sennorio de les facer servicio han de darles aun mas faciendo les bien et mercet por que cabo adelante hayan mayor voluntad de los servir, et de los amar. Por ende, Nos Don Alfonso por la gracia de Dios, Rey de Castilla, de Toledo, de Leon, de Galicia, de Sevilla, de Cordova, de Murcia, de Jaen, et del Algarve, Cuemo todos concejos de Extremadura embiasen Cavalleros, et omes buenos de los pueblos, con quien embiaron pedir mercet a la Reyna Donna Violant, mi muger, que nos rogase por ellos que les tolliesemos algunos agraviamientos que dicen que habian, et que los ficiemos bien et honrar, por galardonarlos el servicio que ficieron aquellos, onde ellos vienen, alos de nuestro linage et ellos otrosi a Nos. Et porque de aqui adelante oviesen ma [fol. 252v] yor voluntad de nos servir, et lo pudiesen mayor facer, Nos por ruegos de la Reyna, et con consejo de el Arzobispo de Sevilla et de los obispos, et de los Ricos omes, et de los maestres, et de los otros omes de orden, que con nusco eran, facemos estas mercedes et estas honras que son escritas en este privilegio a vos los cavalleros, et al Concejo de Pennafiel.

1. De los que Nos mostraron vuestros cavalleros en razon de los diezmos, que non osabades coger vuestros panes en las eras, nin encerrar los fasta que tanien la campana, et por este causa, que perdiedes muchos dellos, et los era grande danno: tenemos por bien, et mandamos que cojades vuestros panes cada quando que quisierdes, et que vos non fagan, y otra premia, nin otro agraviamiento ninguno, et vos dat vuestros Diezmos bien, et derechamiente, et sin escatima asi cuemo debedes et los clerigos recivanlos. Et si algunos omes y ovieren que non quisieren dar los Diezmos asi cuemo deben, el Obispo, y los Clerigos que los han de haber, muestren lo a la justicia, et el faga gelos dar, si el obispo, o los clerigos los quisieren haben por el.

2. Et otrosi delos que nos dixeron que vos agrabiabades [fol. 253r] que los arrendadores, e los que recabdaban aquella parte que á Nos dán delas tercias, que vos facen muchas escatimas en ellas, e que vos non quieren tomar el pan, et el vino, et los corderos, et las otras cosas, quando el Obispo et los Clerigos tomaban su parte. Et que los demandaban, quando ellos se quisieren, et si alguna cosa menguaba, o se perdié, o se podrié, que la facien pechar a los terceros en manera que se vos tornaba en grande danno. Nos por facer vos bien et merced, tenemos por bien, e mandamos que los nuestros arrendadores, e los que ovieren a recabdar aquella nuestra parte delas tercias, que dan a nos, que paguen en cada uno de los logares, quien lo recabde et lo tome por ellos a la sazon quel obispo, et los clerigos tomaren su parte. Et si non lo ficieren asi, que les non recudan por los dineros que acaecieron por culpa delos arrendadores, ó delos que lo ovieren a recabdar, et si los terceros quisieren guardar su pan y su vino, é los otros derechos, que los arrendadores debieron haber, que les dén las cuesstas, et las misiones que y ficieren segunt fuere razon et guisado, et mandamos que los nuestros arrendadores, o los que ovieren a recabdar esta parte delas tercias que a [fol. 253v] Nos dan que non tomen ninguna cosa de la tercia que finca en las Iglesias, et que fique su parte quita á la Iglesia. Et si cuestras, et mesiones ficieren los terceros por guardar, ó allegar las tercias, que esto que salga todo del alfoli comunalmiente ante que ninguna cosa se parta ende.

3. Et delos que Nos dixieron que vos facien traher el pan por fuerza de las villas* aldeas a la villa et de unos logares á otros; Atendamos que los que recabdaren la nuestra parte delas tercias, que tomen el pan et el vino, et las otras cosas en aquellos logares ó fuere, et los cayere, et que non les fagan otro graviamiento nin otra fuerza por traerlos.

4. Et por que Nos mostraron que vos era agraviamiento en razon de la tregua del ome que no habie valia de cient maravedís, que diese fiador rayado por la tregua de quantia de cient maravedis. A esto tenemos por bien que dé fiador en quanto que ha e si non oviere nada o fuere sospechoso, et mal infamado, que los Alcalles, et la Justicia quel echen de la villa, et del termino, et quel dén plazo á que pueda salir de la Villa^b tierra. Et si despues [fol. 254r] del plazo le fallaren quel recabdor,^c et que nos lo enbien decir. Et si el ome fuere atal que non sea sospechoso, maguer non haya nada, este sobrela su tregua.

5. Et de lo que Nos pidieron mercet que los Cavalleros oviesedes paniaguados, asi cuemo fijos, et hermanos, et sobrinos que fuesen escusados: Nos por vos facer bien et mercet mandamos que sean escusados fasta el tiempo de la edad, que manda el libro del fuero, a que puedan demandar sus bienes. Et dende adelante si non ovieren cavallos, et armas que non sean escusados.

6. Otrosi delo que Nos dixeron, que vos agraviades, por que las mugeres, vibdas et las doncellas, que non habien calona ninguna en el fuero por el denosteo, et por otra deshonra, que los ficiesen, et que las casadas habien trescientos sueldos, et Nos pidieron mercet, que oviesen alguna calona las vibdas, e las doncellas. Tenemos lo por bien et mandamos, que la muger casada haya los tres cientos sueldos, asi cuemo el fuero dice, et la vibda doscientos et la doncella en cavello cient sueldos.

7. [fol. 254v] De lo alque Nos pidieron mercet que quando el Cavallero embiddase que el Cavallo, et las armas que oviese, que fincasen al Cavallero et los fijos, nin los parientes dela muger que non partiesen ende ninguna cosa. Et otrosi quando el Cavallero finase, que ficase el Cavallo et las armas al hijo mayor: Tenemos lo por bien, et mandamos que quando Cavallero finase, que finguen el Cavallo et las armas en el hijo mayor, et que non entren en particion dela muger, nin delos otros fijos, mas que finguen al fijo mayor. Et si este oviere armas de suyo, que finguen a otro fijo que oviere çerca del mayor. Et si mas armas oviere el Padre sacado ende armas cumplidas de Cavallero, las otras que las metan en particion et esto mesmo sea, quando finare la muger del Cavallero, que finguen las armas cumplidas al marido, et non partan en ellas los parientos della, nin los fijos mas que finguen en el, et despues en el fijo asi cuemo sobredicho es. Et si mas armas oviere de cumplimiento para Cavallero entren en particion, et sinon oviere fijo que finguen al pariente mas propinquo que las non oviere.

8. [fol. 255r] Otrosi delo que Nos pidieron en razon delos escusados que solien haber, quando iban en hueste Nos por facerles bien et merced, mandamos que los hayan asi cuemo los solien haber.

9. Et delo que Nos mostraron que en el privilegio que Nos diemos alas Vibdas, que fuesen escusadas, que non dice que las Vibdas que embibdaron antes que les nos ficiesemos esta franqueza, et nos pidieron mercet que fuesen aquellas Vibdas escusadas asi cuemo eran las otras. Nos por facer bien et mercet, mandamos que las Vibdas que eran ante, que uos diesemos el previlegio alas que embibdaron despues, que las que fueron mugeres de

Cavalleros, que tienen Cavallos et armas et eran escusados sus maridos ala sazon que finaron, que sean escusadas, asi las de ante, como las de despues, et que hayan aquella franqueza que dice nuestro previlegio que Nos diemos sobre esta razon.

10. Et por que Nos pidieron mercet que las calonnas que facen los que entran los exidos del Concejo, que vos las diciemos para pro de vuestro Concejo. Nos por facervos bien et mercet catando que los muros de [fol. 255v] la Villa, et otrosi las puentes que habiades mucho mester, son á pro et a guarda de vos, e que son cosas de que vos habedes mucho á servir, et que non podedes escusar; tenemos por bien que las calonnas que den por razon delos exitos, que sean para estas cosas sobredichas. E que dedes dos omes buenos, que lo recabden, et estos que lo metan en labrer los muros et las puentes, et que den cuenta cada ome^d a la justicia et al Escrivano de Concejo que Nos pusieremos por que sepan en que entra, et nos den recabdo quando gelo mandaremos.

11. Et de loque Nos dixeron é mostraron que Vos agraviabades, que los omes de nuestra casa aplazavan algunos de vos por querellas que habien que les viniesedes responder ante Nos non vos demandando antes por el fuero. Esto non queremos que sea, y tenemos por bien et mandamos, que si el nuestro ome quisiere querellar de alguno de vos, o vos de el, si el oviere casas ó heredamiento, o otra cosa et fuere vecino en el logar ó fuere el demandado, que responda ante el fuero, el ó el que tuviere lo suyo por el. Et que del juicio se agraviare, alzese [fol. 256r] a Nos asi cuemo debe.

12. Et sobre todas estas cosas sobredichas que los cavalleros Nos pidieron, et les ficimos por ruego de la Reyna, aun por facerles mas honra, et bien, et mercet tenemos por bien que el Cavallero que Nos ficieremos, ó nuestro fijo heredero que haya quinientos sueldos, et esto por razon dela Caballeria que tomare de Nos, ó de nuestro fijo que oviere á regnar despues de Nos, et mandamos que estos Cavalleros puedan haber Alcaldia, et justicia, et hayan todos sus escusados, asi cuemo el previlegio dice, que los diemos sobre esta razon, et los otros escusados por razon de la hueste, et parten en la fonsadera, et que hayan las partes delas calonnas de sus paniaguados, que han en los Alcaldes et todas las otras franquezas, que les diemos por nuestro previlegio, o algunos de los otros que tengan cartas de nuestro otorgamiento. Et que haya su muger quinientos sueldos et quando la muger embibdare et mantoviere vibdidat haya los quinientos sueldos.^e

Otrosi por facerles mayor mercet, otorgamos que los otros cavalleros que fueron fechos fa [fol. 256v] ta el dia del era de este privilegio delos Infantes ó delos Ricosomes que quisieren venir a Nos, et que Nos dieremos nuestras cartas de otorgamiento cuemo son nuestros vasallos que hayan aquesta honra de los quinientos sueldos. Et todas estas franquezas et las otras que han por nuestro previlegio. Elo que de esta guisa non vinieren, et Nos non les dieremos nuestra carta, et fueren vasallos delos Infantes ó delo ricos omes que non hayan los quinientos sueldos, nin nungun portiello en la villa, nin ninguna de estas franquezas que en este previlegio dice nin de las otras, que antes les habemos dadas.

Otrosi por facer honra et mercet á los Cavalleros, que Nos ficieremos, o nuestro fijo heredero á los que dieremos en esta razon nuestras cartas que son nuestros vasallos, si alguno ficiere alguna cosa por que meresciese en el Cuerpo Justicia de muerte ó de esterramiento: tenemos por bien et mandamos que sinon mataré, seyendo en tregua ó sobre salvo, e non ficiere traicion ó aleve, o mataré en otra guisa o ficiere cosa por que debia morir ó haber otra justicia en el cuer [fol. 257r] po quel.ᶠ Et Nos embiarle hemos mandado aquello que tuvieremos por bien e por derecho. Pero si acaesciese cosa por que Nos fuesemos fuera de nuestros Regnos: mandamos que lo cumpla aquel que Nos dexaremos en nuestro logar.

E por facer a los Cavalleros mas bien et mas mercet por que en el nuestro previlegio que les diemos en razon de cuemo hubiesen sus excusados, non dicie, que oviesen mayordomos: Damosles é otorgamosles que hayan los Cavalleros sendos mayordomos, et que los excusen dela quantia, que han los otros escusados segunt dice en el nuestro previlegio que les diemos.

Otrosi por facer bien et mercet alos Cavalleros que el fueroᵍ de suso dixiemos, damosles que hayan de estos paniaguados la parte de las calonnas que habian los Alcaldes.

Et por facer les mas bien et mas mercet otorgamos les los nuestros previlegios, et el libro de el fuero que les diemos.

13. Et delo que Nos dixieron, que quando viniedes a Nos, que non vos librasemos tan ayna cuemo [fol. 257v] oviedes mester: tenemos por bien que si Nos non vos libraremos tan aina, que dedes las peticiones alos escrivanos, que Nos pusieremos que las reciviesen, et si ellos non vos las librasen luego, que lo mostrarles a la Reyna, et ella mostrarlos á Nos.

E mandamos et defendemos que ninguno non sea osado de ir contra este previlegio para crementarlo, nin para menguarlo en ninguna cosa: E qualquier que lo ficiere avrie nuestra ira, et pecharnos y en coto mil maravedis et alos que el tuerto reciviesen, todo el danno doblado. Et por que esto sea firme, et estable, mandamos siellar este previlegio con nuestro siello de plomo. Fecho el previlegio en Sevilla por nuestro mandado, martes quince dias andados del mes de Abril, en era de mill et trescientos, et dos annos. Et Nos el sobredicho Rey Don Alonso regnante en uno con la Reyna Donna Yolant mi muger, et con nuestros fijos el Infante Don Fernando primero, et heredero, et con el Infante Don Sancho, et con el Infante Don Pedro, et con el Infan [fol. 258r] te Don Johan en Castiella, en Toledo, en Leon, en Gallicia, en Sevilla, en Cordova, en Murcia, en Jahen, en Baeza, en Badalloz, et en el Algarve otorgamos este previlegio, et confirmamoslo.

La Iglesia de Toledo, vaga. Don Ramon Arzobispo de Sevilla, Don Alfonso de Molina, Don Felipp. Don Yugo de Bergonna vasallo del Rey. Don Gui Conde de Flandes, vasallo del Rey, Don Enrri de lo Regne, vasallo del Rey; Don Alfonso fijo del Rey Johan [Dacre Emperador] de Constantinople, et de la Emperadriz Donna Berenguela, Conde do vasallo del Rey; Don Loys, fijo del Emperador e de la Emperadriz sobredichos, Conde de Velmont, vassallo del Rey: Don Joan fijo de el Emperador e de

la Emperadriz sobredichos, Conde de Montfort, vasallo del Rey: Don
Gaston, Vizconde de Beart, vasallo del Rey; Don Gui Vizconde de
Limoges vasallo del Rey: Don Joan Arzobispo de Santiago chanceller del
Rey, Don Lois, Don Aboabdille Abenazar Rey de Granada vasallo del
Rey: Don Martin obispo de Burgos. Don Fernando obispo de Palencia;
Don Fr. Martin obispo de St [fol. 258v] govia; Don Andres obispo de
Siguenza; Don Agostin obispo de Osma: Don Pedro Obispo de Cuenca,
Don Fr. Domingo obispo de Avila; Don Vivian electo de Calahorra. Don
Fernando obispo de Cordova, Don Adan Obispo de Plasencia, Don
Pasqual obispo de Jaen. Don Fr. Pedro obispo de Cartagena. Don Pedro
Yvannes maestre de la Orden de Calatrava. Don Pedro Guzman Adel-
antado mayor de Castilla. Don Nunno Gonzalez. Don Alfonzo Lopez. Don
Alfonso Thellez. Don Joan Alfonso. Don Fernando Royz de Castro. Don
Joan Garcia. Don Dia Sanchez. Don Gomez Roiz. Don Rodrigo Rodriguez.
Don Suer Tellez Portero mayor del Rey. Don Enrique Perez Repostero
mayor del Rey. Don Martin obispo de Leon. Don Pedro Obispo de
Oviedo. Don Suero obispo de Zamora. Don Pedro obispo de Salamanca.
Don Pedro obispo de Astorga. Don Domingo obispo de Orens. Don Gil
obispo de Tuy. Don Munno obispo de Mondonnedo. Don Fernando
obispo de Coria. Don Garcia obispo de Silves. Don Fr. Pedro obispo de
Badalloz. Don Pelay Perez maestre de la Orden de Santiago. Don Garci
Fer [fol. 259r] rando maestre de la Orden de Alcantara. Don Martin
Nunnez maestre de la Orden del Temple. Don Gutierrez Suarez adelantado
mayor de Leon. Don Andres adelantado mayor de Galicia. Don Alfonso
Ferrandez fijo del Rey. Don Rodrigo Alfonso, Don Martin Alfonso. Don
Rodrigo Frolaz, Don Joan Perez, Don Ferrand Ibanez. Don Ramir Diaz.
Don Ramir Rodriguez. Don Alvar Diaz=En la Rueda=El Infante Don
Manuel hermano del Rey e su Alferez mayor Confirma. El Infante Don
Ferrando fijo mayor del Rey et su mayordomo Confirma=yo Johan Perez
de Burgos lo escrivi por mandado de Millan Perez de Aellon, en el anno
doceno que el Rey don Alfonso regnó. [fol. 259v.] Variantes que resultan
de cotejo que se ha hecho de este exemplar con el de Don Jph. Ruiz de
Celada sacado del original que esta en la Villa de Peñafiel.

a. En el de Celada falta Villas
b. tambien falta en el mismo, Villa
c. recabden
d. cada año
e. En el de Celada se añade 'et non los haya', y al margen se pone la
siguiente Nota: Esta diminuta esta clausula y lo que falta es la privacion
en caso de pasar a segunda nupcias.
f. En el de Celada se añade 'quel recabden, et que Nos lo embien decia et
Nos embiarlos hemos mandar'.
g. En el de Celada falta 'el fuero'.

VIII

28 April 1282, Valladolid

The Infante Don Sancho confirms the privileges of the Abbey of Sahagún, during the Cortes of Valladolid.

Archivo Histórico Nacional, sección 1, Clero, *carp.* 919, no. 24. Original. Publ. Escalona, *Sahagún, ap.* III, *esc.* CCLXV.

Sepan quantos este Privilegio vieren. Como yo Inffante Don Sancho fijo mayor et heredero del muy Noble Don Alfonso por la gracia de Dios Rey de Castiella de Toleda de León de Galliçia de Seuilla de Cordoua de Murcia de Jahen e del Algarbe. Por façer bien e merced a uos Don Martin por essa misma gracia abad de Sant ffagund do e otorgo e confirmo a uos Abad para siempre jamas e al uuestro conuento e a todos uuestros vassalos e del monesterio de Sant ffagund todos uuestros fueros e uuestros buenos vsos e bonas costumbres e libertades e ffranguesas e Privilegios e cartas, asi como lo meior ouiestes en el tiempo del Rey Don Alffonso mio visauuelo e del Rey Don fferando mio auuelo e de todos los otros Reyes que ffueron dante en Espanna e del emperador. E otrosi del Rey Don Alffonso mio padre aquellos de que uos pagaredes a todos en uno e a cada uno de uos por si. E. juro a Dios e a Santa Maria sobre la cruz e sobre santos evangelios enque meti mis manos quando esto jure. E demas fago uos Pleyto e omenage que nunca uos passe contra estas cosas sobredichas nin contra nenguna dellas nin consinta a ninguno que uos passe contra ellas. E que me pare con busco e que uos ayude con el cuerpo e con todo mio poder asi contra el Rey commo contra todos los ommes del mundo, que uos quisieren passar en qual manera quier contra uuestros fueros e vsos e costumbres e libertades e ffranquesas e Privilegios e cartas asi como sobredicho es. Et si pora ventura yo Inffante Don Sancho non guardasse todo esto o uos ffuesse contra ello o uos non ayudasse contra quien quier que estas cosas sobredichas o cada vna dellas quisiesse passar o menguar en alguna manera uos diçiendo melo o enbiando melo deçir, por Corte o en otro lugar qualquier que yo sea e non uos lo emendare quanto en aquella cosa en que uos menguare. Mando uos que uos amparedes e uos deffendades tan bien del Rey como demi como de todos los otros que despues demi vinieren, a tener e a guardar uuestros fueros e vsos e costumbres e libertades e ffranqueças e Privilegios e cartas segunt sobredicho es e que non ualades por ello menos vos nin aquellos que despues de uos vinieron. Otrosi tengo por bien e mando que si pora ventura alguna carta desafforada saliere demi casa quela vean aquellos que estudieren por jueçes o por alcaldes en uestros lugares e si fallaren que es contra fuero que pongan en recabdo todo aquello quela carta mandare segund uuestro fuero en guisa que quando me fuere mostrado que se pueda complir la Justiçia en aquello que ffuere con fuero e con derecho. Et desto do uos este Privilegio seellado con mio seello de plomo. Ffecho en Valladolit veynte e ocho dias de abril. Era de mill e treçientos e veynte annos. Yo Pero Sanchez lo fiç escreuir por mandado del Infante.

[Green silk ties, seal of lead. Obverse: Don Sancho armed and mounted. Legend+*Sigillum infantis: Sancii.* Reverse: Arms of Castile and León. Legend (partly erased) *Veritas Domini* [*Manet in eternum*].]

IX

8 May 1291, Burgos, and (inserted) 1 December 1290, Madrid.

Carta of Sancho IV to the *concejo* of Pamplona, inserting a carta to the town of Fuenterrabía granting safe-conduct and certain rights to trade in Castile to foreign merchants passing through the port of Fuenterrabía on their way to and from Navarre, and, further, granting to the merchants of Pamplona, in time of war between Castile and Navarre, security for forty days during which Navarrese merchants in Castile might leave the kingdom.

Archivo Municipal de Pamplona, *caj.* A, no. 17. Original.

Sepan quantos esta carta vieren. Commo Nos Don Sancho por la gracia de Dios Rey de Castiella de Toledo de Leon de Gallizia de Seuilla de Cordoua de Murcia de Jahen e del Algarbe. Por façer bien e merçed al concejo de Pamplona e atodos los otros logares del Reyno de Nauarra e por que la nuestra villa Ffuenterrabia sse pueble meior. Mandamos dar nuestra carta allos de Ffuenterrabia fecha en esta guisa. Sepan quantos esta carta vieren. Commo Nos Don Sancho por la gracia de Dios Rey de Castiella de Toledo de Leon de Gallizia de Seuilla de Cordoua de Murcia de Jahen e del Algarbe. Por façer bien e merçed al concejo de Ffuenterrabia por rrazon que non an camino e por que esse logar se pueble meior. Tenemos por bien que todos los mercaderes que vinieren al puerto de Ffuenterrabia de fuera de nuestros rreynos que quissieren passar por este puerto con sus mercaduras contra Nauarra o de Nauarra en fuera por esse mismo puerto de Ffuenterrabia contra otra parte qualquier que uayan e uengan saluos e seguros pagando ellos sus derechos, asi commo los pagauan en el tiempo del Rey Don Ffernando nuestro auuelo. Saluo ende que si ellos quisieren comprar algunas mercaduras de nuestros Reynos de las que non son uedadas e las ssacaren del Reyno o si metieren mercaduras de fuera del Reyno e las uendieren en nuestros Reynos que paguen el diezmo asi commo derecho es. Et defendemos firmemiente que ninguno non sea osado delos peyndrar ni de los enbargar nin de los passar contra esta merced que los nos façemos por ninguna manera si non fuere por su debda conoscuda o por fiadura manifiesta que por si ayan fecha. Ca qual quier que lo fiçiesse pechar nos ye en pena mill marauedis de la moneda nueua. E alos mercaderes o aqui su boç touiesse todo el danno doblado. Et demas al cuerpo e a quanto ouiese nos tornariemos por ello. Et desto las mandamos dar esta carta seellada con nuestro seello de çera colgado. Dada en Madrit primo dia de Deziembre. Era de mill trezientos e ueynte e ocho annos. Yo ferrand Martinez la fiz escriuir por mandado del Rey. Garci Perez. Martin Falconero. Johan Martinez. Agora los de Ffuenterrabia

fiçieron nos entender que los de Pamplona que querien una tal nuestra
carta commo es esta nuestra sobredicha. E mas de merçed que ouiese en
ella que si por auentura acahesçiesse lo que Dios non quiera que entre los
nuestros reynos e el Reyno de Nauarra ouiesse algun desacuerdo que todos
los mercaderes que fueren de Pamplona o del Reyno de Navarra sobredicho e estudieren en nuestros Reynos que fasta quarenta dias pueden
sacar asi e todas las sus cosas saluas e seguras e nos touiemos lo por bien.
E desto mandamos dar allos de Pamplona sobredichos esta nuestra carta
seellada con nuestro seello de çera colgado. Dada en Burgos ocho dias de
mayo. Era de mill e treçientos e ueynt e nueue annos. Yo Alfonso
Rodriguez chantre de Cibdat la fiz escriuir por mandado del Rey.

[Pendant wax seal of Sancho IV, broken.]

Bibliography

I Manuscript sources

Archivo de la Catedral de León
Documentos reales
Archivo de la Catedral de Pamplona
Arca BB, no. 54
Archivo de la Corona de Aragón, Barcelona
Pergamino Pere II (of Catalonia; Pedro III of Aragon), 369
Registro de la Cancillería, no. 47
Archivo General de Navarra, Pamplona
Sección de Comptos. Documents from *cajones* 3, 4, 5
Archivo Histórico Nacional, Madrid
Sección 1. Clero secular y regular
Documents from the following *carpetas* (folders) are cited in the text:
nos. 230, 369, 379, 380, 528, 904, 913, 916, 918, 919, 1355
Sección 2. Ordenes militares
Orden de Santiago. Documents from the following *cajones* (boxes)
are cited: 90, 99, 100, 102, 214, 222, 260, 326, 365, 372
Orden de Calatrava. Documentos reales; Escrituras de Calatrava, IV
Archivo Municipal de Alcaraz
Legajo (bundle) 1, no. 22
Archivo Municipal de Pamplona
Documents from *cajones* A and B
Arquivo Nacional da Torre do Tombo, Lisbon
Livros da Chancellaria de Afonso III, nos. I, III
Livro das Extras
Gaveta (drawer) 14, *Maç.* I, no. 11
Biblioteca Nacional, Madrid
Sección de Manuscritos. MSS. 13075, 13077, 13094
British Library (formerly British Museum)
Department of Manuscripts
Add. MSS. 9915, 9916 (vols. 1 and 2 of a 'Colección de cortes' formed
*c.*1775 by Don Ignacio Jordán de Asso y del Río and Don Miguel de
Manuel Rodríguez)
Add. MS. 21448, 'Cortes de España' (collection formed at the end of
the eighteenth century by Don Ignacio Miguel de Espinosa)

Add. MS. 20787, 'Fuero de las leyes', late thirteenth century (an early version of the *Primera partida*)
Add. Charter 12766

II Printed Primary Sources

A Chronicles and other literary sources
Alfonso X (Afonso X, o Sábio), *Cantigas de Santa Maria*, ed. Walter Mettmann, 4 vols. (Coimbra 1959–72)
  see also Primera crónica general
Anales toledanos, III (VIII), ed. E. Flórez, *ES*, XXIII, 410–23
Anelier de Toulouse, Guillaume, *Histoire de la guerre civile de Navarre*, ed. Francisque Michel (Paris 1856)
Annales compostellani, ed. E. Flórez, *ES*, XXIII, 318–25
Chronica Adefonsi Imperatoris, ed. L. Sánchez Belda (Madrid 1950)
Chronicle of James I of Aragon, translated by John Forster, 2 vols. (London 1883); *see Llibre dels feyts*
Corónica de España (*Las quatro partes enteras de la*), ed. Florián de Ocampo (Zamora 1541)
Crónica de Alfonso X, ed. D. Cayetano Rosell, BAE, LXVI (Madrid 1875) 1–66
Crónica de Fernando IV, ed. D. Cayetano Rosell, BAE, LXVI (Madrid 1875), 93–170
Crónica de la población de Avila, ed. Amparo Hernández Segura, Textos Medievales, 20 (Valencia 1966)
Crónica de Sancho el Bravo (Sancho IV), ed. D. Cayetano Rosell, BAE, LXVI (Madrid 1875), 69–90
Crónica geral de 1344, ed. L. F. Lindley Cintra, I (Lisbon 1951)
Crónica latina de los reyes de Castilla, ed. M. Desamparados Cabanes Pecourt (Valencia 1964)
'Crónicas anónimas de Sahagún (Las)' (II), ed. Julio Puyol y Alonso, *BRAH*, LXXVII (1920), 51–9, 151–91
Cronicón de Cardeña, I, II, ed. E. Flórez, *ES*, XXIII, 370–81.
Gesta regis Henrici secundi, ed. W. Stubbs, Rolls Series (London 1867)
Gil de Zamora, 'De preconiis civitatis Numantiae', ed. Fidel Fita, *BRAH*, V (1884), 131–200
Historia compostelana, ed. E. Flórez, *ES*, XX (Madrid 1765; repr. 1965)
Historia silense, ed. Francisco Santos Coco (Madrid 1921)
Jofré de Loaisa, 'Chronique des rois de Castille', ed. A. Morel-Fatio, *Bibliothèque de l'Ecole des Chartes*, LIX (1898), 325–78; new edn, Antonio Ubieto Arteta, *Crónica de Jofré de Loaisa* (Valencia 1971)
Llibre dels feyts esdevenguts en la vida del molt alt senyor Rey, En Jacme lo Conqueridor, ed. M. Aguiló y Fuster (Barcelona 1873)
Lucas of Túy, *Chronicon mundi*, ed. A. Schott, *Hispaniae illustratae*, IV, 1–116 (Frankfurt 1608)
Pelayo of Oviedo, *Crónica del obispo Don Pelayo*, ed. B. Sánchez Alonso (Madrid 1924)

Primera crónica general de España, ed. Ramón Menéndez Pidal, 2 vols. (Madrid 1955)
Rodrigo of Toledo (Rodrigo Jiménez de Rada), *De rebus Hispaniae*, ed. F. de Lorenzana, *Opera patrum toletanorum*, III (Madrid 1793)

B Catalogues, collections of Documents, registers, editions of fueros and legal treatises
Alfonso X: see *Espéculo, Fuero real, Primera partida, Setenario, Siete partidas*
Ballesteros y Beretta, Antonio, *Las Cortes de 1252* (Madrid 1911)
Barrau-Dihigo, L., 'Chartes royales léonaises', *Revue Hispanique*, X (1903), 349–454
Bullarium de Calatrava, ed. I. J. de Ortega y Cotes, J. F. Alvarez de Basquedano and P. de Ortega Zúñiga y Aranda (Madrid 1761)
Calendar of Close Rolls of Henry III, 1256–1259 (London 1932)
Cartulaire général de l'ordre des Hospitaliers de S. Jean de Jerusalem, 1100–1310, 4 vols., ed. J. Delaville le Roulx (Paris 1894–1906)
Cartulario de Don Felipe III, ed. M. Arigita (Madrid 1913)
Cartulario del monasterio de Eslonza, ed. V. Vignau (Madrid 1885)
Cartulario del monasterio de San Vicente de Oviedo, ed. L. Serrano (Madrid 1929)
Cartulario del monasterio de Vega, ed. L. Serrano (Madrid 1927)
Cartulario de San Millán de la Cogolla, ed. L. Serrano (Madrid 1930)
Cartulario de San Pedro de Arlanza, ed. L. Serrano (Madrid 1925)
Castro, José Ramón, *Catálogo del Archivo General de Navarra, Sección de Comptos*, I: *Años 842–1331* (Pamplona 1952)
Chancelarias medievais portuguesas, I: *Documentos da chancelaria de Afonso Henriques*, ed. A. E. Reuter (Coimbra 1938)
Colección de documentos de la catedral de Oviedo, ed. S. García Larragueta (Oviedo 1962)
Colección de documentos inéditos del Archivo de la Corona de Aragón, VI, ed. P. de Bofarull y Mascaró (Barcelona 1847)
Colección de documentos para la historia del reino de Murcia; I: *Documentos de Alfonso X el Sabio*, ed. Juan Torres Fontes (Murcia 1963); II: *Documentos del siglo XIII*, ed. Juan Torres Fontes (Murcia 1969)
Colección de privilegios a varios pueblos de la corona de Castilla (vols V, VI of *Colección de cédulas y otros documentos concernientes a las provincias vascongadas*) (Madrid 1830, 1833)
Colección diplomática de Cuéllar, ed. Antonio Ubieto Arteta (Segovia 1961)
Colección diplomática de Jaime I, el Conquistador, ed. A. Huici, 3 vols. (Valencia 1916–22)
Colección diplomática de San Salvador de Oña, ed. Juan del Alamo, 2 vols. (Madrid 1950)
Colección diplomática de Sepúlveda, I, ed. Emilio Sáez (Segovia 1956)
Colección diplomática municipal de la ciudad de Béjar, ed. A. Martín Lázaro (Madrid 1921)

Cortes de los antiguos reinos de Aragón y de Valencia y principado de Cataluña publicados por la Real Academia de la Historia (Cortes de Cataluña), I (Madrid 1896)

Cortes de los antiguos reinos de León y de Castilla, I, II (Madrid 1861, 1863)

Documentación pontificia hasta Inocencio III (La), ed. D. Mansilla Reoyo, Monumenta Hispaniae Vaticana: Registros, I (Rome 1955)

Documentos del Archivo General de la Villa de Madrid, 1a serie, I, ed. T. D. Palacio (Madrid 1888)

2a serie, ed. A. Millares Carlo and E. Varela Hervías (Madrid 1932)

Documentos lingüísticos de España. Reino de Castilla, ed. R. Menéndez Pidal (Madrid 1919)

Documentos para la historia de las instituciones de León y de Castilla, ed. E. de Hinojosa (Madrid 1919)

Espéculo (El), in *Opúsculos legales del Rey Don Alfonso el Sabio*, I, 1–474 (Madrid 1863)

Foedera, conventiones, litterae et acta publica, I, Record Commission edn (London 1816)

Fori et observantiae Aragonum (Zaragoza 1542)

Fuentes para la historia de Castilla, ed. L. Serrano, 3 vols. (Valladolid 1906–10)

Fuero de Cuenca, ed. R. de Ureña y Smenjaud (Madrid 1935)

Fuero de Ledesma, ed. A. Castro and F. de Onís, in *Fueros leoneses de Zamora, Salamanca, Ledesma y Alba de Tormes* (Madrid 1916)

Fuero de León, ed. L. Vázquez de Parga (Madrid 1944)

Fuero de Miranda de Ebro, ed. Francisco Cantera (Madrid 1945)

Fuero de Salamanca, ed. A. Castro and F. de Onís, in *Fueros leoneses de Zamora, Salamanca, Ledesma y Alba de Tormes* (Madrid 1916)

Fuero de Salamanca, ed. J. Sánchez Ruano (Salamanca 1870)

Fuero real (El), in *Opúsculos legales del Rey Don Alfonso el Sabio*, II, 1–169 (Madrid 1836)

'Fuero romanceado de Palencia (El)', ed. Carmen Caamaño, *AHDE*, XI (1934), 503–22

Fueros de Aragón según el manuscrito 458 de la Biblioteca Nacional de Madrid, ed. Gunnar Tilander (Lund 1937)

Fueros de Sepúlveda, ed. E. Sáez, R. Gibert, M. Alvar and A. G. Ruiz-Zorrilla (Segovia 1953)

Fueros leoneses de Zamora, Salamanca, Ledesma y Alba de Tormes, ed. Américo Castro and Federico de Onís (Madrid 1916)

Fueros y observancias del reyno de Aragón, I (Zaragoza 1667)

Fuero viejo, ed. M. Martínez Alcubilla, in *Códigos antiguos de España* (Madrid 1885)

García Gallo, A., 'Textos de derecho territorial castellano', *AHDE*, XIII (1936–41), 308–96

García Larragueta, S., *Catálogo de los pergaminos de la catedral de Oviedo* (Oviedo 1957)

García Rámila, Ismael, '"Ordenamientos de posturas y otros capítulos

generales" otorgados a la ciudad de Burgos por el rey Alfonso X',
Hispania, v (Madrid 1945), 179–235, 385–439, 605–50

García Villada, Z., *Catálogo de los códices y documentos de la catedral de
León* (Madrid 1919)

Gayangos, Pascual de, *Catalogue of the manuscripts in the Spanish
language in the British Museum*, 4 vols. (London 1875–93)

Guallart, J., and María del Pilar Laguzzi, 'Algunos documentos reales
leoneses', *CHE*, i–ii (1944), 363–81

Gutiérrez del Arroyo, Consuelo, *Privilegios reales de la Orden de Santiago
en la Edad Media* (Madrid n.d.)

Jacobo de las Leyes, *Obras de maestro Jacobo de las Leyes*, ed. R. de
Ureña y Smenjaud and A. Bonilla y San Martín (Madrid 1924)

Leyes del estilo (Las), in *Opúsculos legales del Rey Don Alfonso el Sabio*, ii,
235–52 (Madrid 1836)

Leyes nuevas (Las), in *Opúsculos legales del Rey Don Alfonso el Sabio*, ii,
179–209 (Madrid 1836)

Liber feudorum maior, ed. F. Miguel Rosell, 2 vols. (Barcelona 1945–7)

Marcos Rodríguez, F., *Catálogo de documentos del archivo catedralicio
de Salamanca* (Salamanca 1962)

Memorial histórico español, i, ii (Madrid 1851)

Memorias de Don Fernando IV de Castilla, ed. Antonio Benavides, 2 vols.
(Madrid 1860)

Muedra Benedito, Concha de, 'Adiciones al Fuero de Medina del Campo',
AHDE, v (1928), 448–50

'Textos para el estudio de la curia regia leonesa', *AHDE*, vi (1929),
412–28

Opúsculos legales del Rey Don Alfonso el Sabio, 2 vols. (Madrid 1836)

Ordenamiento de Alcalá, in *Cortes*, i, 402–593

Ordenamiento de Zamora, in *Cortes*, i, 87–94

Portugaliae monumenta historica: Leges et consuetudines, i (Lisbon 1856)

Primera partida (La) (manuscrito Add. 20787 del British Museum), ed.
J. A. Arias Bonet (Valladolid 1975)

Recueil des chartes de l'Abbaye de Cluny, iv, v, ed. A. Bruel (Paris 1894)

Recueil des chartes de l'Abbaye de Silos, ed. M. Férotin (Paris 1897)

Recull de documents inedits del Rey En Jaume I, ed. E. González
Hurtebise (*Congreso de historia de la Corona de Aragón*, i, part ii)
(Barcelona 1913)

Registres d'Alexandre IV (Les), iii, ed. C. Bourel de la Roncière, etc.
(Paris 1902)

Registres de Clément IV (Les), ed. E. Jordan (Paris 1893)

Registres de Grégoire IX, ii, ed. L. Auvray (Paris 1890)

Registres de Grégoire X (Les), ii, ed. J. Guiraud (Paris 1892)

Registres d'Innocent IV (Les), i, ed. E. Berger (Paris 1881)

Registres de Martin IV (Les), ed. par les membres de l'Ecole Française de
Rome (Paris 1901)

Registres de Nicolas III (Les), ed. J. Gay (Paris 1898)

Repartimiento de Sevilla, ed. Julio González, 2 vols. (Madrid 1951)

Setenario (El), ed. Kenneth H. Vanderford (Buenos Aires 1945)

Siete partidas (*Las*), 3 vols. (Madrid 1807)

Stubbs, W., *Select charters and other illustrations of English constitutional history*, 9th edn revised by H. W. C. Davis (Oxford 1913)

Uhagón, F. R. de, 'Indice de los documentos de la Orden Militar de Calatrava', *BRAH*, xxxv (1899), 1–167

Vázquez de Parga, L., 'Decretos de Alfonso IX de león para Galicia publicados en 1204', *AHDE*, xiii (1936–41), 265–8

Zarco Cuevas, E. J., *Catálogo de los manuscritos castellanos en la Real Biblioteca de El Escorial*, 3 vols. (San Lorenzo de El Escorial 1924–9)

III Books used mainly for the documents printed in them

Ballesteros y Beretta, Antonio, *Sevilla en el siglo XIII* (Madrid 1913)

Brandão, A., *Monarquia lusitana*, partes iv, v, vi (Lisbon 1725, 1751, 1752)

Colmenares, Diego de, *Historia de la insigne ciudad de Segovia* (Madrid 1637); Nueva edición anotada, 2 vols. (Segovia 1969)

Escalona, R., *Historia del real monasterio de Sahagún* (Madrid 1782)

España sagrada, ed. E. Flórez, M. Risco *et alii*, 51 vols. (Madrid 1747–1879)

Gaibrois de Ballesteros, Mercedes, *Historia de Sancho IV de Castilla*, 3 vols. (Madrid 1922–8) (iii: *Colección diplomática*)

González, Julio, *Alfonso IX*, 2 vols. (Madrid 1944) (ii: *Colección diplomática*)

El reino de Castilla en la época de Alfonso VIII, 3 vols. (Madrid 1960) (ii, iii: *Colección diplomática*)

Regesta de Fernando II (Madrid 1943)

Loperráez Corvalán, J., *Descripción histórica del obispado de Osma*, 3 vols. (Madrid 1788) (iii: *Colección diplomática*)

López Ferreiro, Antonio, *Fueros municipales de Santiago y de su tierra*, 2 vols. (Santiago 1895)

Historia de la santa iglesia de Santiago de Compostela, iii, iv, v (Santiago 1900–2)

Manuel Rodríguez, Miguel de, *Memorias para la vida del Santo Rey Don Fernando III* (Madrid 1800)

Rassow, Peter, 'Die Urkunden Kaisers Alfons VII, von Spanien', *AFUF*, x (1928), 327–468; xi (1930), 66–137

Serrano, Luciano, *Obispado de Burgos y Castilla primitiva desde el siglo V al XIII* (*El*), 3 vols. (Madrid 1935) (iii: *Cartulario de la catedral de Burgos*)

Yanguas y Miranda, José, *Diccionario de antigüedades del reino de Navarra*, 3 vols. (Pamplona 1840)

IV Secondary sources: printed books and articles

Alvarez de la Braña, R., 'Igualación de pesos y medidas por Don Alfonso el Sabio', *BRAH*, xxxviii (1901), 134–44

Amador de los Ríos, José, *Historia social, política y religiosa de los judíos de España y Portugal*, new edn, 2 vols. (Buenos Aires 1943)

Ariz, Luis, *Historia de la grandezas de la ciudad de Ávila, 3a parte* (Alcalá de Henares 1607)

Ballesteros y Beretta, Antonio, *Alfonso X el Sabio* (Barcelona 1963)

Alfonso X, Emperador (Electo) de Alemania (Madrid 1918)

'Burgos y la rebelión del Infante Don Sancho', *BRAH*, CXIX (1946), 93–194

El itinerario de Alfonso el Sabio: 1: *1252–1259* (Madrid 1935); continued as 'El itinerario de Alfonso X, rey de Castila, 1260–1267', *BRAH*, CVII (1935), 21–76, 381–418; CVIII (1936), 15–42; CIX (1936), 377–460

Historia de España, III (Barcelona 1922)

Bermejo Cabreno, José Luis, 'En torno a la aplicación de las *Partidas*, fragmentos del *Espéculo* en una sentencia real de 1261', *Hispania*, XXX (Madrid 1970), 169–77

Biggs, Anselm Gordon, *Diego Gelmírez, first archbishop of Compostela* (Washington 1949)

Bisson, Thomas N., 'A general court of Aragon (Daroca, February 1228)', *EHR*, XCII (1977), 107–24

Assemblies and representation in Languedoc in the thirteenth century (Princeton 1964)

'The military origins of medieval representation', *AHR*, LXXI (1966), 1149–1218

Bó, Adriana, and María del Carmen Carlé, 'Cuando empieza a reservarse a los caballeros el gobierno de las ciudades castellanas', *CHE*, IV (1946), 114–24

Botet i Sisó, J., *Les monedes catalanes*, 3 vols. (Barcelona 1908–11)

Bridrey, E., *La Théorie de la monnaie au XIVe siècle* (Paris 1906)

[Burriel, A. M.] *Informe de la imperial ciudad de Toledo sobre pesos y medidas* (Madrid 1758)

Caamaño, Carmen, 'El fuero romanceado de Palencia', *AHDE*, XI (1934), 503–22

Carlé, María del Carmen, 'Boni homines y hombres buenos', *CHE* XXXIX–XL (1964), 133–68

Del concejo medieval castellano–leonés (Buenos Aires 1968)

'El precio de la vida en Castilla del Rey Sabio al Emplazado', *CHE*, XV (1951), 132–56

Carramolino, Juan Martín, *Historia de Ávila*, 3 vols. (Madrid 1872)

Cerdá Ruiz-Funes, J., 'En torno a la pesquisa y procedimiento inquisitivo en el derecho castellano–leonés en la Edad Media', *AHDE*, XXXII (1962), 483–517

Cirot, Georges, 'Appendices à la "Chronique latine des rois de Castille"', *Bulletin Hispanique*, XIX (1917), 2–101; XX (1918), 27–39, 149–84; XXI (1919), 173–92

'Recherches sur la "Chronique latine"', *Bulletin Hispanique*, XXI (1919), 193–217, 276–80; XXV (1923), 97–107

Colmeiro, Manuel, *Cortes de los antiguos reinos de León y de Castilla. Introducción*, 2 vols. (Madrid 1883)

Daumet, Georges, 'Les testaments d'Alphonse X', *Bibliothèque de l'Ecole des Chartes*, LXVII (1906), 70–99
Mémoire sur les relations de la France et de la Castille (Paris 1913)

David, Pierre, *Etudes historiques sur la Galice et le Portugal du VIe au XIIe siècle* (Lisbon 1947)

Defourneaux, Marcelin, *Les Français en Espagne aux XIe et XIIe siècles* (Paris 1949)

Díez Canseco, L., 'Sobre los fueros del Valle de Fenar, Castrocallón y Pajares: notas para el estudio del Fuero de León', *AHDE*, I (1924), 337–81

Edwards, J. G., 'The *Plena potestas* of English parliamentary representatives', in *Oxford essays in medieval history presented to H. E. Salter*, 141–54 (Oxford 1934)

Fernández del Pulgar, P., *Historia secular y eclesiástica de Palencia*, 3 vols. (Madrid 1679–80)

Fernández Rodríguez, Manuel, 'La entrada de los representantes de la burguesía en la curia regia leonesa', *AHDE*, XXVI (1956), 757–66

Fita, Fidel, 'Bernardo de Perigord', *BRAH*, XIV (1889), 456–61
'Cortes de Toro en 1216', *BRAH*, XXXIX (1901), 524–30

Fletcher, Richard, 'Diplomatic and the Cid revisited: the seals and mandates of Alfonso VII', *Journal of Medieval History*, II (1976), 305–38

Forey, A. J., *The Templars in the 'Corona de Aragón'* (Oxford 1973)

Gaibrois de Ballesteros, Mercedes, 'Tarifa, y la política de Sancho IV de Castilla', *BRAH*, LXXIV (1919), 418–36, 521–9; LXXV (1919), 349–5; LXXVI (1920), 53–77, 123–60, 420–48; LXXVII (1920), 192–215

Galindo Romeo, Pascual, *La diplomática en la 'Historia compostelana'* (Madrid 1945)
Túy en la baja Edad Media, siglos XIII–XV (Madrid 1923)

Gama Barros, Henrique da, *História da administração pública em Portugal nos séculos XII a XV*, 2nd edn by T. de Sousa Soares, I, II (Lisbon 1945), III (Lisbon 1946)

García de Valdeavellano, Luis, *Curso de historia de las instituciones españolas* (Madrid 1968)
'El mercado: apuntes para su estudio en León y Castilla durante la Edad Media', *AHDE*, VIII (1931), 201–405
Historia de España, I (Madrid 1952)
Sobre los burgos y los burgueses de la España medieval (Madrid 1960)

García Gallo, Alfonso, 'Aportación al estudio de los fueros', *AHDE*, XXVI (1956), 387–446
'El "Libro de las leyes" de Alfonso el Sabio', *AHDE*, XXI–XXII (1951–2), 345–528

García Larragueta, Santos, 'La Orden de San Juan en la crisis del imperio hispánico del siglo XII', *Hispania*, XII (Madrid 1952), 483–524

García Rámila, Ismael, 'Cortes de Castilla', *RABM*, *3a época*, XLIX (1925), 84–99, 262–78

García Villada, Zacarías, *Paleografía española*, 2 vols. (Madrid 1923)

García y García, Antonio, 'Un nuevo códice de la *Primera partida*', *AHDE*, XXXIII (1963), 267–343

Gibert, Rafael, *El concejo de Madrid y su organización en los siglos XII al XV* (Madrid 1949)

'El derecho municipal de León y Castilla', *AHDE*, XXXI (1961), 695–753

Giménez Soler, Andrés, *La corona de Aragón y Granada* (Barcelona 1908)

González, Julio, 'Aportación de fueros castellano–leoneses', *AHDE*, XVI (1945), 625–54

'Aportación de fueros leoneses', *AHDE*, XIV (1942–3), 560–72

'Sellos concejiles de España en la Edad Media', *Hispania*, V (Madrid 1943), 339–84

Gorosterratzu, J., *Don Rodrigo Jiménez de Rada* (Pamplona 1925)

Grassotti, Hilda, 'Para la historia del botín y de las parias en León y Castilla', *CHE*, XXXIX–XL (1964), 43–132

'Un empréstito para la conquista de Sevilla', *CHE*, XLV–XLVI (1967), 191–247

Gray, H. L., *The influence of the Commons on early legislation* (Cambridge, Mass. 1932)

Guglielmi, Nilda, 'La curia regia en León y Castilla', *CHE*, XXIII–XXIV (1955), 116–267; XXVIII (1958), 43–101

'Posada y yantar', *Hispania*, XXVI (Madrid 1966), 5–40, 165–219

Herculano, Alexandre, *História de Portugal desde o começo da monarchia até a fim do reinado de Affonso III*, 2nd edn, 4 vols. (Lisbon 1853)

Herriott, J. Homer, 'A thirteenth-century manuscript of the *Primera partida*', *Speculum*, XIII (1938), 278–94

Ibáñez de Segovia Peralta y Mendoza, Gaspar, Marqués de Mondéjar. *Memorias de Alonso el Noble, octavo del nombre* (Madrid 1783) *Memorias de Alonso el Sabio* (Madrid 1777)

Iglesia Ferreiros, A., 'Las Cortes de Zamora de 1274 y los casos de corte', *AHDE*, XLI (1971), 945–73

Kleffens, E. N. van, *Hispanic law until the end of the Middle Ages* (Edinburgh 1968)

Klein, Julius, *The mesta* (Cambridge, Mass. 1920)

Lévi-Provençal, E., *Islam d'occident* (Paris 1948)

Linehan, P., *The Spanish church and the papacy in the thirteenth century* (Cambridge 1971)

Livermore, H. V., *A history of Portugal* (Cambridge 1947)

Llorente, Juan Antonio, *Noticias históricas de las tres provincias vascongadas*, 4 vols. (Madrid 1805–8)

Lomax, Derek W., *La Orden de Santiago, 1170–1275* (Madrid 1965)

'Las milicias cistercienses en el reino de León', *Hispania*, XXIII (Madrid 1963), 29–42

'The authorship of the "Chronique latine des rois de Castille" ', *Bulletin of Hispanic Studies*, XL (1963), 205–11

'The Order of Santiago and the kings of Léon', *Hispania*, XVIII (Madrid 1958), 1–37

López Ortiz, J., 'La colección conocida con el título "Leyes nuevas" ', *AHDE*, XVI (1945), 5–70

Macdonald, Robert A., 'Alfonso the Learned and the succession', *Speculum*, XL (1965), 647–53

Maldonado y Fernández del Torco, José, 'Las relaciones entre el derecho canónico y el derecho secular en los concilios españoles del siglo XI', *AHDE*, XIV (1942–3), 227–385

Mansilla Reoyo, Demetrio, *Iglesia castellano–leonesa y curia romana en los tiempos del Rey San Fernando* (Madrid 1945)

Marín, Tomás, 'Confirmación real en documentos castellano–leoneses', in *Estudios dedicados a Menéndez Pidal*, II, 583–93 (Madrid 1951)

Martínez Marina, Francisco, *Ensayo histórico–crítico sobre la legislación de los Reinos de León y Castilla, especialmente sobre el Código de las Siete partidas de Don Alonso el Sabio* (Madrid 1808)

Teoría de las cortes o grandes juntas nacionales de los reinos de León y Castilla, 3 vols. (Madrid 1820)

Mateu y Llopis, Felipe, *La moneda española* (Barcelona 1946)

Menéndez Pidal, Ramón, *La España del Cid*; 4th edn, revised, 2 vols. (Madrid 1947)

Poesía juglaresca y juglares (Madrid 1924)

Merriman, R. B., 'The cortes of the Spanish kingdoms', *AHR*, XVI (1911), 476–95

The rise of the Spanish Empire in the Old World and the New, 4 vols. (I, New York 1918)

Millares Carlo, Augustín, 'La cancillería real en León y Castilla hasta fines del reinado de Fernando III', *AHDE*, III (1926), 227–306

Paleografía española, 2nd edn (Madrid 1932)

Minguella y Arnedo, Toribio, *Historia de la diócesis de Sigüenza y de sus obispos*, 3 vols. (Madrid 1910–13)

Miret i Sans, J., *Itinerari de Jaume I* (Barcelona 1918)

O'Callaghan, Joseph F., 'The beginnings of the cortes of León–Castile', *AHR*, LXXIV (1969), 1503–37

'The cortes and royal taxation during the reign of Alfonso X', *Traditio*, XXVII (1971), 379–98

Ortiz de Zúñiga, Diego, *Anales eclesiásticos y seculares de la ciudad de Sevilla* (Madrid 1677)

Palomeque, Antonio, 'Contribución al estudio del ejército en los estados de la reconquista', *AHDE*, XV (1944), 205–351

Pescador, Carmela, 'La caballería popular en León y Castilla', *CHE*, XXXIII–XXXIV (1961), 101–238; XXXV–XXXVI (1962), 56–201; XXXVII–XXXVIII (1963), 88–198; XXXIX–XL (1964), 169–262

Piskorski, Wladimiro, *Las cortes de Castilla en el período de tránsito de la Edad Media a la Moderna, 1188–1520*, trans. C. Sánchez-Albornoz

(Barcelona 1930); reissued 'con un estudio sobre las cortes medievales castellano–leonesas en la historiografía reciente por Julio Valdeón Baruque' (Barcelona, 1977)

Portilla y Esquivel, Miguel, *Historia de la ciudad de Compluto*, I (Alcalá 1725)

Post, Gaines, *Studies in medieval legal thought* (Princeton 1964)

Procter, E. S., *Alfonso X of Castile. Patron of literature and learning* (Oxford 1951)

'Materials for the reign of Alfonso X of Castile', *Transactions of the Royal Historical Society*, 4th series, XIV (1931), 39–63

'The Castilian chancery during the reign of Alfonso X', in *Oxford Essays in medieval history presented to H. E. Salter*, 103–21 (Oxford 1934)

'The development of the Catalan *corts* in the thirteenth century', in *Homenatge a Antoni Rubió i Lluch*, III, 525–46 (Barcelona 1936)

'The interpretation of clause 3 of the decrees of León (1188)', *EHR*, LXXXV (1970), 45–53

'The judicial use of "*pesquisa*" in León and Castille, 1157–1369', *EHR*, supplement 2 (London 1966)

'The scientific works of the court of Alfonso X of Castille: the king and his collaborators', *Modern Language Review*, XL (1945), 12–29.

'The towns of León and Castille as suitors before the king's court in the thirteenth century', *EHR*, LXXIV (1959), 1–22

'Use and custody of the secret seal (*sello de la poridad*) in Castille from 1252 to 1369', *EHR*, LV (1940), 194–221

Puyol y Alonso, Julio, *El abadengo de Sahagún* (Madrid 1915)

El presunto cronista Fernán Sánchez de Valladolid (Madrid 1920)

Ramos y Loscertales, José María, 'La sucesión del rey Alfonso VI', *AHDE*, XIII (1936–41), 36–99

Rassow, Peter, *Der Prinzgemahl, ein Pactum matrimoniale aus dem Jahre 1188* (Weimar 1950)

Reilly, B. F., 'The *Historia compostelana*: the genesis and composition of a twelfth-century Spanish *gesta*', *Speculum*, XLIV (1969), 78–85.

Rivera Recio, J. F., 'Personajes hispanos asistentes en 1215 al IV Concilio de Letrán', *Hispania Sacra*, IV (1951), 335–58.

Rivero, Casto María del, *Indice de las personas, lugares y cosas notables que se mencionan en las tres crónicas* (Madrid 1942)

Rodríguez Díez, Matías, *Historia de la ciudad de Astorga*, 2nd edn (Astorga 1909)

Russell, J. C., 'The medieval *monedatge* of Aragon and Valencia', *Proceedings of the American Philosophic Society*, 106 (1962), 483–504

Sáez, Emilio, 'El monasterio de Santa María de Ribeira', *Hispania*, IV (Madrid 1944), 3–27, 163–210

Sánchez, Galo, 'Para la historia de la redacción del antiguo derecho territorial castellano', *AHDE*, VI (1929), 260–328

Sánchez-Albornoz, C., '¿Burgueses en la curia regia de Fernando II de León?', *Revista Portuguesa de História*, XII (1969), 1–35
'Dudas sobre el Ordenamiento de Nájera', *CHE*, XXXV–XXXVI (1962), 315–36
España: un enigma histórico, 2 vols. (Buenos Aires 1957)
Estudios sobre las instituciones medievales españolas (Mexico 1965)
La curia regia portuguesa (Madrid 1920)
'Señoríos y ciudades', *AHDE*, VI (1929), 454–62
Sánchez Alonso, B., *Historia de la historiografía española*, I, 2nd edn, revised (Madrid 1947)
Sánchez Belda, L., 'La cancillería castellana durante el reinado de Doña Urraca', in *Estudios dedicados a Menéndez Pidal*, IV, 587–99 (Madrid 1953)
'La cancillería castellana durante el reinado de Sancho IV, 1284–95', *AHDE*, XXI–XXII (1951–2), 171–223
'Notas de diplomática', *RABM*, LIX (1953), 85–116
Serrano, Luciano, 'El canciller de Fernando III de Castilla', *Hispania*, I: v (Madrid 1941), 3–40
Silva Lopes, J. B. da, *Memórias para a história ecclesiástica do bispado do Algarve* (Lisbon 1848)
Soldevila, F., *Pere el Gran i l'infante*, 3 vols. (Barcelona 1950–6)
Tormo, Elías, 'El estrecho cerco de Madrid de la Edad Media por la admirable colonización segoviana', *BRAH*, CXVIII (1946), 46–205
Zurita, Jerónimo, *Anales de la Corona de Aragón*, I (Zaragoza 1610)
Indices rerum ab Aragoniae regibus gestarum (Zaragoza 1578)

Subject Index

adelantado de la corte, 243
adelantados mayores, 243; de Castilla,
249; de la frontera, 136, 137
advocates (assertores), 37, 66, 88–9, 144,
250, 282 cl. 38
alcaldes: de la corte, 249–50, 251; del
rey, 86, 91–2, 137–8, 236, 242, 243–
5; hijosdalgo, 180; of the towns, 66,
89, 92, 100, 206, 238
alférez, 11, 47, 71
alfoz, 30, 88, 95; see also término
alguacil, 243–4
Almorávides, 9, 19, 27–8
Almohades, 78, 79
Anales toledanos, III, 121, 139 n.
appeals to royal court, 67–8, 92
assemblies at Valladolid and Salamanca
(1279), 145–6, 151, 163, 169–70
ayuntamiento de Almagro (1273), 134–
5, 151, 153, 158, 180, 191, 198
ayuntamiento de Avila (1273), 134, 135,
151, 161, 185

bishoprics: under Alfonso VI and
Alfonso VII, 13; in Castile, 72; in
León, 47; under Fernando III and
Alfonso X, 156
boni homines (good men): members of
the curia, 51–2; representatives of
towns in suits, 67, 86; witnesses in
suits or in pesquisas, 90; see also
hombres buenos

caballeros de las villas, 2, 97, 98, 166–7,
210–11; privileges granted to those
of Extremadura (in 1264), 211–12,
288–90 cls. 5–9, 12
caballeros hidalgos (or de linaje), 96,
134, 160, 167, 180, 188
cartas abiertas (letters patent), 47, 127,
284
cartas de personería (or de procuración):
in suits before the curia, 118, 160,

164–6, 270; in the cortes, 163–4,
166
cartas desaforadas, 144, 222
cartas rodadas, 46–7, 71–2, 268–9; see
also privilegios rodados and rueda
chancellor, 11, 12–13, 47, 71–2, 227
chancery, 11, 13, 222, 227–8, 229,
250–1
Chronica Adefonsi Imperatoris, 8, 9,
11, 15, 20–1
Chronicle of James I of Aragon, 257,
258
Chronicon mundi (Lucas of Túy), 44,
68
cofradías (trade guilds), 98, 272, 277 cl.
14
coinage, 26–7, 54–6, 83, 147, 200; of
Barcelona, 260, 261; of Jaca, 257,
260–1; dineros prietos, 141–2;
moneda de la guerra, 195, 198, 208,
216, 221–2; see also moneda (1)
collective petitions, 150, 204–5, 207–9,
286–91
concejos (town councils), 99–100; representation of in the cortes, 161–2,
166–7; suitors before the curia, 36,
64–5, 67, 88–9; suits between
concejos and their ecclesiastical overlords, 240–2
conducho, 220–1, 271
Confederation of Lerma, 133
confirmantes, 10–17, 40–9, 71–3, 155–6,
269, 290–1
Convention of Vitoria (1276), 140–1,
142–3
Corónica de España, 78, 108–9
corte, 172, 173, 225–6, 238; composition of, 226–30; functions of: in
affairs of state, 230–1, in foreign
policy, 185, 231–3, 233–4, in legislation, 235–7, 284–6; judicial functions
of: appeals, 249, changes in methods
of proof and in procedure: in civil

307

Mozárabes, 30, 95
Mudéjares, 95, 98, 99

notaries of the royal chancery, 12–13;
 notarios mayores of León, Castile,
 Andalusia and Toledo, 227–8

Ordenamiento de Alcalá (1348), 34, 85,
 122, 204–5, 243, 246
Ordenamiento de Cuéllar (1282), 162
Ordenamiento de la Mesta (1278), 145
Ordenamiento de Valladolid (1312),
 204, 253
Ordenamiento de Zamora (1274), 137–
 8, 236, 243, 249–51

Pere Marín, *Los miráculos romanzados*,
 127, 153
personeros, representatives of the towns:
 in suits before the king's court, 66–7,
 165; in the cortes, 162–3; see also
 procuradores
pertiguero mayor de Santiago, 61–2,
 236
pesquisa (inquest): proof by, in civil
 suits, 40–1, 63, 64, 67, 90, 245–6;
 use in criminal procedure, 248–9
pesquisadores, 40–1, 63, 123, 236
petitio, petitum, 29, 53–4, 82, 91, 199
placita, 30, 31, 59–60
portazgo, 220, 281 cl. 37
price-fixing, 127–8, 160; clothes, 215;
 furs, hides, silks and shoes, 213, 215,
 275–6 cls. 7–10; hawks and falcons,
 213, 279 cls. 23–8; imported woollen
 cloth, 215; livestock, 213–15, 277–8
 cls. 17–18; shields and horse trappings, 213, 214, 274 cls. 1–3; in Portugal, 263
Primera crónica general, 73, 113, 115
privilegios rodados, 127, 130, 137, 141,
 155; see also *cartas rodadas*
procuratores (proctors): in suits before
 the king's court, 67, 164–5, 269–70;
 in the cortes, 162, 163, 205, 258
revolt of the nobles (1272–3), 119–20,
 134–5
ricos hombres (nobles), 94, 154, 159,
 180, 217
Roman law, influence and study of, 67,
 69, 91, 203, 257
rueda, 46, 71

sabidores del derecho, 203, 226, 235–6
seals: royal, 13, 16; imperial seal of
 Alfonso X, 228; secret seal (*sello de la
 poridad*), 222, 239; town seals, 101, 103
servicios (subsidies), 132, 134, 135–6,
 150, 190–5

servicios (or *diezmos*) *de los ganados*,
 132, 195–6, 199, 200, 283 cl. 44
Setenario, el, 121, 229
Siete partidas, las, 121–5, 159, 237;
 Primera partida, two versions of, 123;
 and *el Espéculo*, 123, 203; *Segunda
 partida*, 123, 179; *Tercera partida*,
 123, 165
signifer, 47; see also *alférez*
spoliation of the church: under Urraca
 and Alfonso VII, 28–9; under Alfonso
 X and Sancho IV, 201–6
succession to the throne, 18–19, 20, 49–
 50, 74, 76, 77, 139–41, 142–3, 178–9,
 231
sumptuary laws: clothes, 217, 275 cls.
 5–6; food, 217–18, 276 cl. 12; marriage feasts, 216–17, 272–3, 276–7
 cl. 13; royal household, 218; shields,
 217, 274 cl. 4; in Catalonia, 264

tax farming, 199–200
tenencias and *tenentes*, 15, 48, 72
tercias (ecclesiastical), 71, 80, 201, 212,
 283, cl. 45, 287 cl. 2
tercias reales, 146, 199, 201–2, 212, 287
 cl. 2
término, 95–6, 98, 99, 103; see also
 alfoz
towns, 2, 30, 94–104 *passim*; characteristics of, 94–5; fairs and markets of,
 98–9; *fueros* of, 101–2; government
 of, 99–100, 103–4; military service
 owed by, 102–3; officials of, 100–1;
 political importance of, 102–3; social
 classes in, 96–8; see also *concejos*
Treaties: Badajoz (1267), 156, 233;
 Benavente (1230), 113; Cabreros
 (1206), 90; Campillo (1281), 184;
 Carrión (1141), 21; Cuenca (1177),
 79; Fresno-Lavandera (1183); 51;
 Guadalajara (1207), 90; Guadalajara
 (1217), 103; Sahagún (1158), 51;
 Sahagún (1170), 79; Seligenstadt
 (1188), 75, 109; Tamara (1127), 21;
 Toro (1216), 103; Tudela (1231 Adoption Treaty), 255, 258

usury, laws on, 122–3, 237–9, 282 cl. 39;
 284–6

voceros, see advocates

weights and measures, 100, 172, 205,
 219
writs of summons, 118, 139–40, 148,
 168–9

yantar, 221–2

Index of Proper Names